HOUSEHOLD POLITICS:
MONTREAL FAMILIES AND POSTWAR RECONSTRUCTION

The reconstruction of Canadian society in the wake of the Second World War had an enormous impact on all aspects of public and private life. For families in Montreal, reconstruction plans included a stable home life hinged on social and economic security, female suffrage, welfare-state measures, and a reasonable cost of living. Because differences of class, gender, language, religion, and region naturally produced differing perspectives, in *Household Politics* Magda Fahrni examines postwar reconstruction from a variety of angles in order to fully convey its significance.

Reconstruction was not simply a matter of official policy. Although the government set many of the parameters for public debate, federal projects did not inspire a postwar consensus, and families alternatively embraced, negotiated, or opposed government plans. Through in-depth research from a wide variety of sources, Fahrni brings together family history, social history, and political history to look at a wide variety of Montreal families – French-speaking and English-speaking; Catholic, Protestant, and Jewish – making *Household Politics* a particularly unique and erudite study.

MAGDA FAHRNI is an assistant professor in the Department of History at l'Université du Québec à Montréal.

STUDIES IN GENDER AND HISTORY

General Editors: Franca Iacovetta and Karen Dubinsky

HOUSEHOLD POLITICS

Montreal Families and Postwar Reconstruction

DISCARD

Magda Fahrni

UNIVERSITY OF TORONTO PRESS
Toronto Buffalo London

© University of Toronto Press Incorporated 2005
Toronto Buffalo London
Printed in Canada

ISBN 0-8020-3849-2 (cloth)
ISBN 0-8020-4888-9 (paper)

Library and Archives Canada Cataloguing in Publication

Fahrni, Magdalena, 1970–
   Household politics : Montreal families and postwar reconstruction /
   Magda Fahrni.

   (Studies in gender and history)
   Includes bibliographical references and index.
   ISBN 0-8020-3849-2 (bound). – ISBN 0-8020-4888-9 (pbk.)

   1. Family – Quebec (Province) – Montreal – History – 20th century.
   2. Households – Quebec (Province) – Montreal – History – 20th century.
   3. Montreal (Quebec) – Social conditions – 20th century.   4. Canada –
   Social policy.   5. Canada – Social conditions – 1945–1971.   I. Title.   II. Series.

   HN110.M6F32 2005   306.85'09714'2809044   C2005-902576-X

University of Toronto Press acknowledges the financial assistance to
its publishing program of the Canada Council for the Arts and the
Ontario Arts Council.

University of Toronto Press acknowledges the financial support for
its publishing activities of the Government of Canada through the
Book Publishing Industry Development Program (BPIDP).

This book has been published with the help of a grant from the Canadian
Federation for the Humanities and Social Sciences, through the Aid to
Scholarly Publications Programme, using funds provided by the Social
Sciences and Humanities Research Council of Canada.

In memory of Margaret Morton Fahrni

Contents

Illustrations follow page 84.

Acknowledgments

First books are long in the making, and it is a pleasure to acknowledge the many debts that I have incurred along the way. I first came to both the study of history and the city of Montreal as an undergraduate at McGill University. At that institution I was fortunate to encounter such fine teachers and committed scholars as Craig Heron, Andrée Lévesque, and Shirley Tillotson. Bryan Palmer took me on as a novice graduate student at Queen's University in Kingston and encouraged me to continue. The origins of this book lie in a doctoral dissertation undertaken at York University in Toronto. Bettina Bradbury was a rigorous and generous supervisor, and I continue to look to her work as a model of meticulous and compassionate scholarship. For their comments on that dissertation, I would also like to thank Stephen Brooke, Craig Heron, Susan Houston, and James Struthers. Members of the York Women's History Group, especially Bettina Bradbury, Lisa Chilton, Kathryn McPherson, Liz Millward, and Camille Soucie, provided valuable feedback on the thesis as it took form, as did the members of the Toronto Labour Studies Group.

More recently, my colleagues in the Department of History at the Université du Québec à Montréal have provided an extremely stimulating environment in which to teach, write, and learn Quebec history. I would also like to thank my students, both graduate and undergraduate, for their good humour and their enthusiasm. Marc Ouimet, in particular, supplied much-appreciated eleventh-hour assistance with the newspaper research for Chapter 6, while Yasmine Mazani devoted several days to going over the notes and bibliography. Amélie Bourbeau helped me with the index, with her customary intelligent efficiency. Some of my most enjoyable moments over the last few years have been spent in the company of fellow members of the Groupe de recherche sur l'histoire de Montréal, based at UQAM, and the Montreal History Group, based at McGill. Special thanks go to Suzanne Morton for her wise counsel and good company.

Much of the research in these pages was facilitated by doctoral fellowships from the Social Sciences and Humanities Research Council of Canada. At the University of Toronto Press, Len Husband, Karen Dubinsky, Franca Iacovetta, Barbara Tessman, and Pamela Erlichman skilfully guided the book through the various stages of the publication process. Carolyn Podruchny generously shared thoughts and advice on writing and rewriting as we worked our way through our respective manuscripts.

Parts of Chapter 3 appeared previously in 'The Romance of Reunion: Montreal War Veterans Return to Family Life, 1944–1949,' *Journal of the Canadian Historical Association*, n.s., 9 (1998): 187–208, while an earlier version of Chapter 5 was published as 'Counting the Costs of Living: Gender, Citizenship, and a Politics of Prices in 1940s Montreal,' *Canadian Historical Review* 83, 4 (December 2002): 483–504.

I would also like to acknowledge the support of family and friends. Three friends in particular – Julie Perreault, David Tortell, and David Kimmel – have listened to me talk about this project for years. Each now regularly reminds me, over bottles of red wine, that Montreal present is as enjoyable as Montreal past. Finally, Jake Estok, more than anyone, deserves heartfelt thanks. That I am emerging from this process relatively sound of mind and body owes much to his constant encouragement and his progressive household politics.

Abbreviations

ACC	Action catholique canadienne
ACJC	Association catholique de la jeunesse canadienne-française
APCM	Alliance des professeurs catholiques de Montréal
BASF	Bureau d'assistance sociale aux familles
BNA	British North America
CAC	Canadian Association of Consumers
CASW	Canadian Association of Social Workers
CCF	Co-operative Commonwealth Federation
CECM	Commission des écoles catholiques de Montréal
CTCC	Confédération des travailleurs catholiques du Canada
CWC	Canadian Welfare Council
CYC	Canadian Youth Commission
DAB	Dependents' Allowance Board
DBT	Dependents' Board of Trustees
DND	Department of National Defence
DPNH	Department of Pensions and National Health
DVA	Department of Veterans' Affairs
FNSJB	Fédération nationale Saint-Jean-Baptiste
FOCCF	Fédération des œuvres de charité canadiennes-françaises
FPTQ	Fédération provinciale du travail du Québec
JCPC	Judicial Committee of the Privy Council
JCWB	Jewish Child Welfare Bureau
JFWD	Jewish Family Welfare Department
JOC	Jeunesse Ouvrière Catholique
JOCF	Jeunesse Ouvrière Catholique Féminine
LCW	Local Council of Women

LOC   Ligue Ouvrière Catholique
LOCF   Ligue Ouvrière Catholique Féminine
MCSA   Montreal Council of Social Agencies
MPAP   Montreal Parks and Playgrounds Association
MSWL   Montreal Soldiers' Wives League
NDG   Notre-Dame-de-Grâce
QPCA   Quebec Public Charities Act
RCMP   Royal Canadian Mounted Police
SAPE   Société d'adoption et de protection de l'enfance
SPWC   Society for the Protection of Women and Children
SSVP   Société de Saint-Vincent de Paul
UCC   Union catholique des cultivateurs
WPTB   Wartime Prices and Trade Board
YWCA   Young Women's Christian Association

HOUSEHOLD POLITICS

Introduction

Everything our men overseas hold dear is bound up in the bundle of life, represented by their wives and children back home.

Mrs T.G. Hodge,
Royal Canadian Army Service Corps Women's Auxiliary, 21 July 1941[1]

As politics today have to do with the home and family[,] politics should be our business.

Montreal Council of Women Minutes, 8 December 1948[2]

We want security for Canadians, all of them, everywhere.

Brief by Kathleen M. Jackson to the Royal Commission on Prices, 1948[3]

No one could have accused Montreal Liberals of failing to grasp the end-of-war *Zeitgeist*. On 1 June 1945 an advertisement appeared in the city's mass-circulation daily, *La Presse*, urging readers to vote Liberal in the upcoming federal election. Sponsored by Montreal's Comité Central Libéral, the advertisement featured a photograph of Prime Minister Mackenzie King and was headlined 'King, ET LA FAMILLE CANADIENNE.' This astute piece of electoral propaganda captured both the self-fashioning of King and the federal Liberal Party, and the ways in which visions of family were central to reconstruction and the postwar public realm.

The advertisement positioned the bachelor prime minister as the father of 'la FAMILLE de son pays.' It emphasized the progressive social legislation that King had enacted for his 'family,' and reminded readers that, like a good father, 'KING EST VOTRE SÉCURITÉ.' King's 'Belle Famille Canadienne' was a harmonious entity that transcended the bitter divisions of politics, ethnicity, and class that had fractured the country in wartime. Not only did the advertisement conceive of Canada's citizens as a family, it explicitly spelled out postwar roles for individual members of Canadian families. Fathers were to be breadwinners, mothers the 'queens of the home,' children 'the hope of tomorrow.' Liberal policy-makers assumed, quite rightly, that the Montrealers who went to the polls on June 11th would be voting with their families, and social security, in mind.[4]

At the same time that Mackenzie King and his 'Ottawa men'[5] were making policy for postwar Canadians, Montreal's families were experiencing the end of the war and planning for the peace in their own ways. David and Norma Klein, for instance, came to the attention of Montreal's Jewish Family Welfare Department (JFWD) in May 1944. David and Norma, each of whom had been born in Montreal twenty-two years earlier, lived on the Plateau Mont-Royal. They had three children, aged three, two, and one; a fourth child would be born in May 1945. The couple had married a week after the birth of their first baby (a boy), their hand 'forced' by David's mother. In their first years of married life, they lived with each set of in-laws in turn. David initially worked as a dress salesman, but the couple required assistance from their families in order to make ends meet. In July 1943 David enlisted in the Canadian Army. He was discharged six months later with health problems: a 'nervous stomach' and ulcers. Within a month, the Veterans' Welfare Bureau had placed him in the parts shop of Noorduyn Aircraft; his hours and earnings were irregular, however, because of his poor health. According to the agency worker assigned to the family, David was 'very ashamed of the fact that he is not able to adequately provide for his family. As a result, at times he becomes depressed.' The couple owed money to their neighbourhood grocer, to their landlord, and to the city's Water Tax Department. Their grocer had 'threatened to bring the family to court'; their landlord had repeatedly threatened them with eviction, until the JFWD intervened and provided five months' worth of rent money. On other occasions, the agency supplied furniture, appliances, clothing, and money for food; David's relatives also chipped in with food, coal, clothing, furniture, and cash.

Norma did not work outside the home; her days were no doubt fully occupied with the care of the couple's three young children. The family lived in what the agency worker described as 'a dilapidated four room house, where the plaster is falling in the kitchen, and the walls are covered with roaches.' The caseworker recognized that the poor condition of the house made it difficult to keep clean, but nonetheless labelled Norma a 'poor housekeeper.' Norma's mother-in-law also claimed that she was slovenly and that the children were not properly cared for. When examined by the JFWD in October 1944, two of the three children had enlarged tonsils, skin conditions such as rashes and boils, and 'signs of having rickets when younger.' A cousin had complained to the Jewish Child Welfare Bureau that Norma was neglecting the children; a public health nurse had likewise reported Norma to the Juvenile Court for leaving the children alone in the house. Despite the family's financial troubles, and despite strained relations with in-laws, the JFWD recorded affectionate relationships among members of the immediate family. David, in particular, was described as having become 'quite attached to his family during the past four months' and as having recently begun to help with household chores and childcare.[6]

Albert Toupin and Rita Boucher grew up two blocks away from one another in Saint-Henri, the Montreal neighbourhood made famous in 1945 by Gabrielle Roy's novel *Bonheur d'occasion*.[7] Both were involved with the Jeunesse Ouvrière Catholique as young adults. When they married in 1939, Albert (the son of an electrician) was a twenty-two-year-old day labourer; Rita (the daughter of an unemployed painter) was twenty-one years old and employed at housework. Their first home as a married couple was a rented four-room flat in Saint-Henri, only a few blocks away from the homes of their parents. Their first child, Lucien, was born less than ten months after their wedding, at the Hôpital Sainte-Jeanne d'Arc. Denis was born ten months later, and Gérard two and a half years after Denis.

Albert, who had been exempted from military service because of his essential war job, worked as an operator for the Montreal Tramways Company. A year after their marriage, his wife described his salary as simply 'passable,' but by 1944 he was working seven days a week, including evenings. The couple rarely had time for evening activities because of Albert's busy work schedule and a lack of babysitters. By 1947, the Toupins found life to be somewhat calmer. After an accident with his streetcar, Albert had been transferred to the garage, where he no longer had to work Sundays or evenings. He now had time to participate in the Ligue Ouvrière Catholique (LOC) activities of his parish. Rita did not work outside the home but found her days to be full, especially as she did her own sewing. She described herself as 'très grasse' and not particularly healthy, suffering from rheumatism and high blood pressure and, after her third Caesarian delivery, unable to have any more children.

Her sons, she informed the LOC, were a source of great comfort. 'Des vrais [*sic*] perfections' who ate well, slept well, and were never ill, they constituted her 'belle petite famille, dont je suis très fier [*sic*] bien qu'elle se compose que de 3 petits garçons. J'aurais aimé une petite fille. A la volonté de Dieu il n'y a plus d'espérance. Le magasin est fermé par malheur.'[8]

These two brief sketches illuminate some of the larger themes of this book. They suggest, first, the variety of ways in which the war affected Montreal families. To some, like the Toupins, it brought financial stability. David Klein's ulcers, however, underscore the toll that war took on enlisted men. Both stories show us, in these years of supposed prosperity, poor neighbourhoods and crowded housing. The two accounts suggest that at the dawn of the nuclear age, extended family continued to be important for many young couples. The Toupins, for instance, set up house just around the corner from their parents. Family, however, was double-edged: in the Klein case we see family members offering monetary and other kinds of assistance, but we also see extended family reporting Norma to the Jewish Child Welfare Bureau and in-laws slighting her to agency workers. The Kleins' story illustrates that men's inability to provide for their wives and children could be a potent source of shame. In both families, we see births spaced very close together and mothers tied closely to their homes and domestic responsibilities. The total of three children in the Toupin family and the four children (by May 1945) in the Klein family are not, however, the huge families that many English Canadians assumed populated Quebec in this period. Moreover, at a time when some Canadians and Quebecers[9] worried about increasing state intervention into private lives, we see a great deal of 'private' interference in these families by in-laws, extended family, the Jewish Child Welfare Bureau, and the Jewish Family Welfare Department. In the case of the Kleins, we glimpse relations between clients and caseworkers. Clearly, the coal, ice-box, stove, bed, mattress, rent, and food money provided by the JFWD helped the Kleins to make do through the mid-1940s. But it came accompanied by labelling ('slovenly,' 'poor housekeeper,' 'dull') and by attempts to re-educate them in housekeeping, budgeting, and proper family relations. Finally, these stories suggest the diversity of 'family' in postwar Montreal. The city's families differed along religious and linguistic lines, by the kinds of resources available to them, and by the ways in which they weathered the war and its aftermath.

This book explores the meanings of postwar reconstruction for Montreal families. It argues that reconstruction plans, for these families, included a stable home life scaffolded on social and economic security. These plans also involved expanded definitions of citizenship that included not only female suffrage (secured, in Quebec, in 1940), but also welfare-state measures and a reasonable cost-of-living. Although Mackenzie King and the federal Liberals set some of the parameters for public debates around reconstruction, *Household Politics* insists that we cannot assume a postwar consensus centred on these federal projects. Reconstruction was more than a matter of federal policy and must be examined from a variety of angles in order for its significance in the 1940s to be fully understood. Differences of class, gender, language, religion, and region produced differing perspectives on what postwar reconstruction ought to entail.

A case study – in this instance, the city of Montreal – allows us to explore the meanings of reconstruction for postwar families. It enables us to see the ways in which they embraced, negotiated, or opposed the reconstruction plans of federal Liberals. Taken collectively, I argue that the reconstruction projects of Montreal families might be seen as 'household politics.' These were politics that involved both the renegotiation of roles within the household in the wake of the war, and, more particularly, the placing of household issues in the public sphere and on the formal political agenda. The 1940s, I propose, were a sustained moment in which the public and political spheres were particularly receptive to questions of household and family. Montrealers' 'household politics' in fact served to expand the scope of what was considered to be public and political.

Montrealers' expectations of the postwar period drew, not surprisingly, on their recent experiences of depression and war. These expectations were shaped, in part, by broader currents: the reconstruction plans of Canadian Liberals, most notably federal welfare state measures; international plans for social security, such as the New Deal assembled by American president Franklin D. Roosevelt during the 1930s; the ideas of British economist John Maynard Keynes; the 'four freedoms' proclaimed by Roosevelt and incorporated into the 1941 Atlantic Charter; and England's Beveridge Report of 1942, which promised social security 'from cradle to grave.' They were also shaped, however, by the social and political context of Quebec: the reforms such as female suffrage, compulsory schooling, and child-labour legislation implemented by Liberal premier Adélard Godbout in the early 1940s, and the desire for provincial autonomy defended by Union Nationale premier Maurice Duplessis after 1944. Moreover, although the state was increasingly important in the 1940s, it was not everything. Montrealers' postwar expectations of family, and of social and economic security, were also structured by private welfare providers, voluntary associations, and religious institutions – notably, but not exclusively, the Catholic Church. Throughout this book, my focus is the local – the ways in which the politics rooted and played out in households and in neighbourhoods reflected and shaped Montreal families' visions of postwar reconstruction. At the same time, I pay attention to the ways in which such local politics were both inspired, and sometimes limited, by provincial, federal, and international currents. The specificity of Montreal needs to be acknowledged here. Canada's highly industrialized metropolis had much in common with other large postwar cities (Toronto, Boston, New York). And yet important national and linguistic differences, along with the social, political, and institutional importance of the Catholic Church, mean that its history cannot simply be assimilated to that of other North American cities. Conversely, Montreal's religious diversity, along with the demographic, economic, and social importance of its English-speaking minority, meant that it was in many ways unlike other towns and cities in Quebec.

Structure

Household Politics begins with a snapshot of the city's social geography and labour market in 1945. The first chapter suggests the diversity of families in postwar Montreal: this was a city of various communities (French-Catholic, English-Catholic, English-Protestant, and Jewish), where the meanings of family varied by religious affiliation, language, and class. I argue that the particular kinds of household politics explored in subsequent chapters were shaped not only by federal proposals for reconstruction, but also by the local social context presented in this chapter. Chapter 2 then considers the policies that federal, provincial, and municipal governments established to provide for postwar families, and notes the many instances in which private agencies, voluntary associations, and the Catholic Church remained essential in providing for needy postwar citizens. I argue that the new public measures implemented by the federal government in the 1940s did not sweep away older private measures before them. Rather, the private and the public coexisted throughout the 1940s.

Chapter 3 turns to the particular problems faced by soldiers, veterans, and their families during and after the war. Although the family was viewed as an agent of postwar healing, it was apparent to many that postwar families were themselves in need of rebuilding. This was a source of considerable concern to the government agencies charged with supervising soldiers and their relatives, such as the Dependents' Allowance Board (DAB) and the Dependents' Board of Trustees (DBT). Marital infidelity and wives' 'illegitimate children,' for instance, threatened the morale of soldiers on the battlefront but were also seen to pose a problem for the emotional health of families in the postwar period. Evidence of women's sexual autonomy, 'discovered' by government bureaucrats and private social workers but also clear to family, friends, and neighbours, suggested that postwar conjugal domesticity might not be easily achieved. The complexity of 'family' revealed in the process of applying for dependents' allowances – for instance, young male soldiers with dependent parents and siblings – belied an idealized version of family that consisted simply of breadwinning husbands and dependent wives and children. The workings of the DAB and the DBT provide insight, moreover, into women's relationship to the emerging welfare state and the nature of female citizenship in wartime.[10] Under the dependents' allowance system, women's social citizenship rested upon their dependent status – that is, their familial relationships with men enlisted in the service of their country. Yet the wives and mothers of servicemen felt entitled to their allowances, complaining when they did not receive their cheques and demanding that allowance rates be indexed to the rising cost-of-living. This was a rehearsal, in a way, for subsequent forms of social welfare and more expansive visions of citizenship. At the same time that they called for improved public provisions, however, servicemen's wives resented the scrutiny and moral censure that often accompanied their cheques, and demanded privacy with regard to family matters. This chapter argues, then, that the wartime experiences of soldiers and their families created a sense of entitlement both as citizens and as family members. These experiences also made them critical of federal measures and ready to contest them or demand modifications or improvements. The postwar conceptions of citizenship espoused by soldiers, veterans, and their families grew in part out of their negotiations of the gendered assumptions built into dependents' allowances and the Veterans Charter.

Chapter 4 takes as a focus the Cent-Mariés: 105 Catholic, working-class couples who participated in a mass marriage in Montreal's east-end Delorimier Stadium on Sunday, 23 July 1939 under the auspices of the Jeunesse Ouvrière Catholique (JOC). Conceived as a response to the material and spiritual dearth of the Depression, the JOC flourished in the wake of the war and spawned the Ligue Ouvrière Catholique (LOC) for married Catholic workers. After the wedding, the Cent-Mariés moved from the supervision of the JOC to that of the LOC, who traced the paths of these couples as they embarked on married life. This study begins with the couples' fifth wedding anniversary, in 1944, and ends with their tenth anniversary in 1949. An examination of these couples, and of the public discussion of their marriages well into the postwar period, sheds light on the family life of a particular group of francophone Quebecers. It provides insight into the place and relative importance of the Action catholique in postwar Montreal, and it highlights the existence of a '*mouvement familial*' in Montreal in this period. In educating its constituents for family life, and in making demands on behalf of Quebec's working-class families, the Ligue Ouvrière Catholique competed with the assorted secular experts of the day. The chapter illustrates, moreover, the ways in which religion blurred the boundaries of private and public. Scholars generally characterize church welfare services as private, and certainly one of the church's major functions was to provide the forms for private worship. Yet we see, in the Cent-Mariés episode, the Action catholique assuming a very public role – attempting to maintain a place, in fact, in the postwar public. In sum, Chapter 4 argues that the JOC and the LOC offered an alternative vision of reconstruction to the one proposed by the federal state. The Action catholique's vision insisted upon the specificity of French-Canadian families and the importance of recognizing differences of religion and social class.

Chapters 5 and 6 take apart couples to examine, first, the demands of married women, and second, the claims of fathers. Chapter 5 explores the ways in which Montrealers, and Montreal women in particular, adopted consumer activism as a form of protest, a means of claiming citizenship rights, and a method of inserting the family into the public sphere in the postwar period. Consumer activism often straddled lines of class, language, and ethnicity, bringing people of disparate socioeconomic backgrounds together to wage common cause as shoppers, as citizens of an economic democracy and, sometimes, as wives and mothers. Such activism demonstrates that while consumers welcomed some forms of government intervention in private life (such as price ceilings and rent controls), they opposed others (such as the prohibition of margarine). This chapter is also a response to a significant body of literature (much of it American) that proposes and celebrates a 'high consumption' era after the war. The characterization of the postwar period as one of Fordist mass production, high wages, and high consumption has much value for many times and places. In this chapter, however, I insist upon the cautious consumption of necessities (food, clothing, household goods) to which most Montrealers were forced to limit themselves in the years immediately following the war.

If Ottawa and the Wartime Prices and Trade Board saw it as their job to teach people how to save, reuse, and salvage during the war, spokespersons for working-class Montrealers, such as unions, the JOC, and the LOC, also thought it essential that working families learn how to consume wisely. Labour newspapers such as *Le Front Ouvrier* and *Le Monde Ouvrier* took it upon themselves to teach workers how to buy, and when not to buy. A lack of money – which at one point might have been something to be ashamed of – was now turned into a political statement in the face of high prices and a rising cost-of-living. Thus working families turned to consumer boycotts alongside protests at the point of production. They lobbied their governments, moreover, for cheaper consumer alternatives such as margarine. Chapter 5 argues that a reasonable cost-of-living and economic citizenship were essential aspects of Montreal families' visions of postwar reconstruction. Moreover, consumer activism, as 'household politics,' was one way that both women and gender configured the political and the public in this period.

Chapter 6 explores the claims of fathers (and, to a lesser extent, of children) in the context of the postwar housing crisis and new compulsory schooling legislation. The Squatters' Movement of 1946–7 illustrates the importance, for Montreal fathers, of being able to provide decent housing for their families. It also suggests ways in which fatherhood and veteran status could be used to claim consideration as deserving citizens in the 1940s. The 1949 strike by Catholic schoolteachers provided opportunities for citizens to articulate claims, in public, as parents (and particularly as fathers) concerned about their children's education. As the state stepped in to regulate family and private life, fathers worried about losing authority and influence. Household politics in Montreal thus bore the imprint of fathers' activism. Their vision of reconstruction, and of social citizenship, included the right to decent housing for their family, children's right to education, and the right to a voice in their children's education.

Household Politics concludes by considering the specificities of Montreal as a case study. Did reconstruction, or family, acquire different meanings in Montreal than elsewhere in postwar Quebec or Canada? Was postwar Montreal truly shrouded in the *grande noirceur* of 'Duplessisme'? Were there hints, in the late 1940s, of the social and political transformations that would become manifest in the 1960s? And if the Quiet Revolution did begin earlier than has traditionally been thought, what role did 1940s Montreal families play in laying its foundation?

Historiographical Contributions

Although centred on the households and neighbourhoods of 1940s Montreal, this book, I argue, contributes to the broader historiography in at least five ways. To begin with, *Household Politics* engages with the literature on postwar reconstruction. It argues that reconstruction was a process that took place as much down on the ground as in the various departments that made up the federal state. The historiography on reconstruction has generally remained at the federal level and has tended to focus on policy (for employment, for social welfare, for veterans, for married women) and on the Dominion-Provincial Conference on Re-construction.[11] The failure of this conference, from Ottawa's point of view, should alert us to the challenges posed to the federal Liberals' reconstruction plans in the postwar years. Ottawa was important, and perhaps seldom as important in Canadian history as in the 1940s, but it was not the only locus of reconstruction. Provincial planners and politicians drew up blueprints for the provinces in the postwar world. Local governments, as Kevin Brushett has argued, were also concerned with reconstruction.[12] Unions and other social movements, ranging from consumer groups to Quebec's Action catholique, organized in the hope that the postwar period could be different from what had preceded it. Recently, historian Len Kuffert has identified a 'culture of reconstruction' in English Canada, a culture that valued postwar planning, democracy, and citizens' participation in public life.[13]

A focus on reconstruction suggests the need to rethink the periodization of postwar Canada. This book explores the final months of the Second World War and the years immediately following the war. As Gail Cuthbert Brandt and other scholars have noted, reconstruction plans were underway well before the end of the war.[14] Indeed, in Quebec, 1944 might be considered a turning point as important as 1945. The year 1944 saw Maurice Duplessis's return to power as Quebec's premier; the provincial election of 1944 was also the first in which Quebec women voted. The book ends in 1949, a convenient chronological marker, but also a point by which reconstruction no longer seemed a pressing concern. The 1940s, I suggest, were unlike the 1950s, in that they were a sustained moment when a variety of possibilities for postwar Canada were vigorously and publicly debated.[15] Would the federal government maintain its activist role, or would it allow the provinces to reassert their autonomy? Would Canada remain a relatively 'planned' society, or would free-market forces have their way? Would married women remain in paid employment, or would they seek satisfaction in home and family? The avenues that Canadians eventually took into the 1950s were not inevitable; nor, from the vantage point of V-E Day, were they even very obvious. As a recent edited collection suggests, not only does the immediate postwar period need to be considered separately from the later postwar years, but the assumption of a postwar consensus needs to be critically interrogated.[16]

The second contribution of this book is to the abundant historical literature on the family. Feminist scholars of war note that reconstruction typically involves attempts to restore some idealized version of 'normal' gender roles and family relations.[17] In 1940s Canada, the debate over the effects of the war on gender roles was vigorous.[18] But most Canadians had no desire to recreate the 'normal' relations of the Depression years; new meanings, it is clear, were invested in family in the wake of the war. Family was thus at the centre of both the official reconstruction plans of federal Liberals and the various forms of 'household politics' played out in the streets of postwar Montreal.

The considerable attention paid to family after the Second World War and to a house-bound wife as the linchpin of that family has inspired an international historiography on the effects of the war on women. Did war 'liberate' women? Did it sow the seeds of 'second-wave' feminism? Or was this liberation only for the duration? How liberating could women's war experiences have possibly been if they retreated in such large numbers to their newly furnished homes after their men returned? Did they go willingly?[19] In part, the importance of this scholarly debate lies in its implications for a second debate: women's roles in the postwar era. This latter debate is particularly evident in the American literature. On the one hand, Elaine Tyler May depicts a nation of conservative and home-centred women, focused on their children and the comforts of the bungalows and split-levels that dotted the suburban landscape. Expanded visions of women's work and public activity, she claims, were never intended to endure beyond the war.[20] In response, a number of American historians, including Joanne Meyerowitz and, most recently, Sylvie Murray, insist that postwar women were 'Not June Cleaver,' and point to the diversity of women's experiences in 1950s America. They argue that the 1950s were not the nadir of a trough separating two waves of feminism, and demonstrate the ways in which women continued to organize politically and to challenge gendered constraints in the postwar period.[21]

In Canada, the lines of debate have not been as clearly drawn. The central work on Canadian women's wartime experiences, *'They're Still Women After All'* by Ruth Pierson, suggests that (whether willingly or under coercion) women returned home after the war, and that 'Fluffy Clothes Replaced the Uniform.'[22] But a growing literature on women ensconced in postwar domesticity, by historians such as Veronica Strong-Boag, Doug Owram, Mary Louise Adams, Mona Gleason, and Valerie Korinek, draws a more complex portrait of domestic and suburban life than the received wisdom would have it.[23] Gleason and Adams attempt to dissect the various discourses and forces that made heterosexuality, domesticity and conformity 'compulsory' in postwar English Canada. Strong-Boag's work on Canadian suburbs and Korinek's study of *Chatelaine* readers point to a range of experiences among suburban women and varying degrees of attachment to domestic ideals. Historians of working-class women, for their part, point to the resonance of the breadwinner/homemaker ideal among working-class families but note the difficulty that many of these families had in achieving this ideal. Few of these studies overturn the conventional portrait of a postwar period steeped in domesticity; most, however, acknowledge the ways in which wartime experiences altered women's sense of the possible.[24]

With a few notable exceptions, little of this work deals with Quebec.[25] The debate about women, war, and social change, which has flourished in scholarly circles in Britain, the United States, Australia, and New Zealand, has received little attention from historians of Quebec, and historians of postwar Canada have largely excluded Quebec from the scope of their analyses. *Household Politics* is, in part, an attempt to address this absence. Like the authors collected in *Not June Cleaver*, I critique the stereotype of postwar women as domesticated and apolitical, lulled into complacency by prosperity, an abundance of consumer goods, and the joys of safe and clean suburbs. Such a portrait accurately describes the lives of only some Canadian women, and even these women lived more politically active lives than historians have acknowledged. This book, then, expands conventional definitions of politics to examine the ways in which women did mobilize in the postwar years.[26] It asks, as does Nancy Hewitt in another context, 'Did Women Have a Reconstruction?'[27] It explores women's community efforts and their relationship to the state in order to understand the ways in which the political and the public were gendered. For the fact that most of Montreal's married women did not work outside the home in the late 1940s does not mean that they had no interests beyond the walls of their households. Married women engaged in a variety of public activities and made claims to public provisions both during and after the war. In Chapter 3, for instance, we see soldiers' wives demanding increases in their dependents' allowances, and soldiers' mothers arguing that they deserve allowances as substantial as those of wives. In Chapter 5, we see married women, both working-class and middle-class, organizing in consumers' groups, union auxiliaries, and the Ligue Ouvrière Catholique to demand affordable household necessities such as groceries. And in Chapter 6, we see mothers involved with the École des parents and the Catholic Parents' League intervening to bring about an end to the 1949 Montreal teachers' strike.[28]

Furthermore, this study finds a variety of families in postwar Montreal. It is clear that, despite what the popular wisdom might suggest, not all postwar North American families were nuclear, or prosperous, or suburban. Montreal housed families with numerous children, working children, and young male soldiers supporting siblings and parents. We see, in this book, unfaithful, separated and divorced spouses; families headed by widows or widowers; and families living (sometimes uncomfortably and unhappily) with in-laws. We see families on the margins of consumption – at a time, we are told, when North American families embraced consumer durables. And we see families crowded into walk-up apartments and brick triplexes, often without what would soon become such basics as refrigerators, at a time when, we hear, North Americans moved en masse to private bungalows with large backyards in the suburbs. The families discussed in this book were not, by and large, families who participated in the continental race for automobiles and soon, television sets – or at least, not for a while. Canadian historians might do well to consider the British 'austerity' model of the early postwar years along with the American 'prosperity' model.[29] Montreal families were, moreover, heterogeneous in terms of religion, language, and ethnicity – and this long before the great waves of post–Second World War immigration.

In studying postwar families, this book attempts to interrogate rather than assume the postwar model of a breadwinning husband and dependent wife and children. Chapter 6 is about recreating fathers – in the wake of a war in which married women and, especially, children, had worked for pay, but also in the wake of a decade-long Depression that had taxed men's abilities to provide for their families. Working-class men in Montreal had a long history of earning wages insufficient to support their families without waged and unwaged assistance from other family members.[30] Many hoped that the improved economy, increased wages, and newfound union security of the war years would provide, at last, an opportunity for men to be breadwinners. The importance of fathers' 'provider' role was both acknowledged and reinforced in the 1946–7 Squatters' Movement, explored in Chapter 6. And yet, some wondered whether an increasingly interventionist federal state would in fact replace fathers; this distinct impression of a diminishing public voice for fathers is glimpsed in the discussion of the 1949 teachers' strike, also in Chapter 6.

Historians have noted the increased influence of 'experts' on family life over the course of the twentieth century: while experts were not new in the postwar period, a wider cross-section of society proclaimed the need for their services in the wake of depression and war.[31] Chapter 4, for instance, on the Cent-Mariés and the Ligue Ouvrière Catholique, is a chapter about creating and celebrating proper husbands, wives, and married couples. Like many non-religious organizations across North America during the war and the immediate postwar years, the LOC argued that family life had been seriously undermined by the material and emotional deprivations of the Depression and the war, and that people needed to be taught how to become good spouses and good parents. Commemorating and tracking the married lives of the 105 Catholic, French-Canadian, working-class couples who had been married in a mass wedding in Montreal in 1939 was one way of educating Quebecers about marriage and family. Yet many of the experts that we see in this book – priests, advice columnists, labour journalists, parents' groups – are not the experts typically discussed in histories of postwar North America.[32] Some of them, such as the LOC, were particular to Quebec. Some, like the LOC and the journalists who wrote for *Le Monde Ouvrier*, could be characterized as grassroots experts. This complicates the criticism typically made of twentieth-century experts, which is that their prescriptions were top-down and frequently irrelevant to working-class audiences.

The third body of literature addressed by this book is that on citizenship. In the context of the Canadian Citizenship Act of 1946, discussions of political citizenship were topical.[33] Public debate about the gendered dimensions of political citizenship was also current in Quebec, as women had obtained the provincial vote in 1940 and had exercised it in the election of August 1944.[34] Furthermore, contemporary definitions of citizenship were expanding to include social citizenship and economic citizenship: the right to, respectively, social welfare measures and full participation in democratic capitalism.[35] These redefinitions of citizenship were taking place in the aftermath of a war effort that had relied upon federal coercion and controls and the sacrifice of self-interest to public interest. They were redefinitions shaped, in part, by the efforts of postwar governments to inculcate a sense of democracy in the context of military victory, the building of a federal welfare state, and the early Cold War. But this was also a movement from below, as people accustomed to wartime obligations and constraints and the duties of citizenship (ranging from military service to higher taxes to purchasing Victory Bonds to accepting wage controls and rationing to participating in recycling drives) now demanded the rights of citizenship and claimed a place in the public arena. In illustrating the ways in which Montrealers worked out the meanings of various kinds of citizenship, *Household Politics* explores the significance of a relatively abstract concept for real people.

The emergence of a federal welfare state was one reason for the debates around citizenship that took place in the 1940s. In most Canadian provinces, early state-welfare measures, such as means-tested mothers' allowances and old age pensions, had been implemented in the wake of the First World War, in part because of the new visibility of war widows and elderly mothers bereft of the support of their sons.[36] The core of the federal welfare state, however, was delivered during and after the Second World War. The war itself inspired measures such as federal dependents' allowances and provisions for veterans, the latter consolidated under the rubric of 'the Veterans Charter.'[37] These measures, directed specifically at enlisted men and women and their families, joined new social provisions such as unemployment insurance, legislated in 1940, and universal family allowances, adopted in 1944. 'By 1943,' Canadian social scientist Leonard Marsh recalled some years later, 'social security was in the air as never before.'[38] The pervasiveness of 'welfare-state thinking' in the later years of war and the early years of peace drew in part on international currents.[39] But the development of a federal welfare state was also shaped by indigenous experiences of depression and war. Domestic factors such as the intricacies of federalism, regional economic disparities, provincial opposition, and, not least, an allegiance to liberalism and free-market thinking on the part of some powerful federal Liberals, all dictated the particular structure of the emerging Canadian welfare state.

Historians agree that a variety of actors pushed for a federally directed welfare state. Federal civil servants seduced by the promise of Keynesianism and state intervention were key, as were Liberal politicians feeling the heat of CCF pressure on the left and cognizant of the electorate's increasingly vocal desire for measures of social security. In fact, as Harry Cassidy noted in 1945, 'Spokesmen for all three of the leading political parties, Liberals, Conservatives, and the Co-operative Commonwealth Federation, reiterated and amplified earlier statements in favour of broad measures of social security after the war. In principle there was agreement on the political front, however differently the various parties might propose to implement the principle.'[40] Moreover, as historians have begun to demonstrate, the creation of a Canadian welfare state, and of a sense of social citizenship, was not simply a top-down process. Ordinary citizens pushed for social welfare, through writing to their political leaders,[41] through attending unemployment rallies in the 1930s and cost-of-living rallies in the late 1940s, and through their unions. Wartime exigencies provided an additional spur: family allowances, for instance, were seen by the federal government as a way of satisfying workers' demands for wage increases without having to lift wartime wage controls.[42] The fear of another postwar depression sparked the desire to maintain the purchasing power of ordinary Canadians: unemployment insurance, family allowances, and veterans' benefits were intended to encourage workers to spend, rather than hoard, in the wake of the war.

Despite the fact that the push for social security measures sometimes came from those other than workers, working-class citizens soon came to view the welfare state as their own, and as something to which they were entitled. Over the course of the late 1940s and the 1950s, for instance, unions lobbied for family allowances to be indexed to the increased cost-of-living.[43] The welfare state was thus shaped at least in part by its beneficiaries. These beneficiaries complained, moreover, when their allowances were insufficient, or when they thought that eligibility rules were too strict or inappropriate.[44] There were, to be sure, limits to what ordinary citizens were able to accomplish through their letters to government, their public protests, and their unions. 'Executive federalism' meant that powerful cabinet ministers worried about costs, or convinced of the value of a market unfettered by government intervention, exercised a great deal of influence over federal policy in the 1940s.[45] The constitutional division of powers posed obstacles – occasionally real, often convenient – to the implementation of social programs. Montrealers dealt not only with Ottawa Liberals, but also with Duplessis and the

Union Nationale. Like Ontario's George Drew and Nova Scotia's Angus L. Macdonald, Duplessis did little to accelerate or expand the delivery of social welfare in these years. As a result, much of the welfare state imagined during the war – health and hospital insurance are two obvious examples – would not be realized until the late 1950s and 1960s. The loud and persistent demands by Quebecers for affordable housing that we see in Chapter 6 were also inadequately addressed. A broad spectrum of citizens – working-class and middle-class, veterans and civilians, conservatives, liberals, social democrats, and Communists – called for state intervention in the form of continued rent controls and the construction of government-subsidized, affordable housing. And yet, in the end, a market model of housing favouring single-family home ownership won out, despite the wartime promises of the federal Liberals and the recommendations of the Curtis Report on housing.[46]

The political, social, and economic citizenships encouraged, to a certain extent, by the state and demanded by the populace were gendered, and were frequently framed in the language of familial roles and responsibilities. Women's social citizenship often depended on their roles as wives and mothers, as we see with the wartime dependents' allowances and the universal family allowances discussed in this book. The 'economic citizenship' explored in Chapter 5 – the conviction that in a victorious, postwar, capitalist democracy, citizens were entitled to participate in democratic capitalism on reasonable terms – was often the expression of organized women's groups or, less obviously, individual women who made private choices about what and what not to buy for their families and households. Women claimed this right of citizenship as wives, as mothers, and as consumers, using what Susan Porter Benson has called the 'trope of the good manager.'[47] They claimed it also as something that was only fair, as their part of the bargain they had struck with the state during the war, when they had cultivated their awareness of prices and the cost-of-living and adhered to wartime directives and controls.

In Chapter 6, we see that working-class men also made prices their business when they organized as 'squatters' to protest the lifting of rent controls and the lack of affordable housing in postwar Montreal. These men claimed the perquisites of social and economic citizenship as breadwinners and heads of families. Moreover, standing up to a state that had disappointed them (through not addressing the woes of the Depression) or coerced them (through conscription and wartime controls), and demanding a role in shaping the state, was manly. Citizenship, then, both rewarded and further entrenched notions of appropriate gender roles and responsibilities.

Despite the new purchase of state welfare in the 1940s, the measures adopted in the wake of the war had their limits. Canada's welfare state was implemented by a Liberal, not a Labour, government; most prominent federal policy-makers in the 1940s were liberals, not social democrats.[48] Older ideas of 'less eligibility,' of distinctions between the deserving and the undeserving poor, persisted amid new senses of entitlement and democracy. Distinctions along the lines of gender and familial roles were instrumental in shaping the structure and delivery of welfare-state measures; questions of morality and respectability continued to determine who would be eligible for dependents' allowances, for instance. In many ways, the construction of a federal welfare state in the wake of the Second World War was an exercise in nation building as much as it was an attempt to alleviate real need. Moreover, there was no rapid, straightforward, or wholesale move from private charity to a full-blown welfare state in the 1940s. Private and public welfare coexisted in these years across the country but perhaps especially in Quebec.[49] State welfare programs depended on the resources and labour of private social agencies – one example of what Jane Lewis has called 'a mixed economy of welfare' and what Mariana Valverde has referred to as a 'mixed social economy.'[50] Private social agencies were themselves attempting to modernize and professionalize in this period, so as to distinguish themselves from old-fashioned charity.[51]

Moreover, the federal government's appearance on the social welfare scene did not go unchallenged. Provincial governments and, in Quebec, the Catholic Church, defended their role in the realm of welfare. They faced a difficult task, however, in a context where the federal government was intent on maintaining the preeminent role it had established during the war. Historians Vernon Fowke and Michael Behiels have delineated Ottawa's attempts to craft a 'new national policy' or, more broadly, a 'new federalism,' from the late 1930s on.[52] Unlike the period of reconstruction after the First World War, and in response to the labour revolt and economic recession that had followed that conflict, the federal government intended to act boldly and to plan for this postwar period. Its plans for 'high and stable employment' and for the building of a welfare state (its 'revanche administrative,' to use Dominique Marshall's apt phrase)[53] had significant implications for federal-provincial relations and, in particular, for relations between Ottawa and Quebec City. Already resentful of federal wartime incursions into territory declared provincial by the British North America Act, Quebec's Duplessis, like Ontario's George Drew, was wary of further attempts by Ottawa to expand its sphere of influence.[54]

The importance of family to postwar reconstruction efforts, and of reconstruction to postwar families, reinforces the argument that boundaries between the public and private spheres in the past were 'ragged' at best and frequently permeable.[55] The idea of the public – the fourth body of literature addressed by this book – is at the heart of a number of scholarly literatures. Women's history, for instance, has since its inception been concerned with matters of public and private and the boundaries between them. Michelle Rosaldo's early influential article about women's historic lack of access to the public sphere was followed by scholarly studies of 'separate spheres,' which examined the assocation of women with a private domestic sphere and of men with a public sphere of political power and commerce.[56] Studies of separate spheres were succeeded by explorations of 'women in public,' which demonstrated women's frequent occupation of public space and which suggested that the borders between the spheres were in fact blurred and mutable.[57]

Debates about public and private were reinvigorated with the translation into English of Jürgen Habermas's *The Structural Transformation of the Public Sphere* in 1989. Habermas conceives of the liberal, bourgeois public sphere as an arena of discourse and discussion, separate from the state, where citizens participate and claim a stake in the polity. The public, in this view, acts as a check on the state. The 'process of making proceedings public (*Publizität*) was intended,' Habermas claims, 'to subject persons or affairs to public reason, and to make political decisions subject to appeal before the court of public opinion.'[58] Habermas's work inspired numerous historians of women to debate the nature and possibilities of the public sphere.[59] Yet many feminist historians had already illuminated the construction of another nineteenth-century sphere: a feminized 'social' that constituted, in Denise Riley's words, 'a blurred ground between the old public and private.'[60] Neither Parliament nor domestic hearth, 'the social' included female-led benevolent societies, institutions of social welfare, and practices such as poor-visiting. Preceding and then coexisting alongside state-welfare provisions, private welfare enabled by middle-class female labour produced a 'mixed social economy' of welfare in Canada and elsewhere.[61] A more recent literature interrogates the nature of a specifically twentieth-century public: in particular, the construction of a welfare state and changing meanings of citizenship. Works by historians such as James Struthers, Dominique

Marshall, and Shirley Tillotson examine relationships among welfare, the state, the public, the private, liberalism and democracy in mid-twentieth-century Canada and Quebec.[62]

An international literature, then, demonstrates that boundaries between the private and the public in the past were both fluid and permeable.[63] *Household Politics* goes beyond an illustration of the continual interaction of the private and public spheres to suggest that, in the mid-twentieth century, the spheres themselves were undergoing a transformation. In the 1940s, the public was expanding under pressure from various groups of citizens who, in demanding measures of social and economic security, made private matters public for political purposes. If, as British sociologist T.H. Marshall declared in 1949, the meaning of social citizenship included not only 'the right to a modicum of economic welfare and security' but also 'the right to share to the full in the social heritage and to live the life of a civilized being,' then it included, as Nancy Fraser and Linda Gordon argue, 'a common set of institutions and services designed for *all* citizens, the use of which constitutes the *practice* of social citizenship: for example, public schools, public parks, universal social insurance, public health services.'[64] More expansive visions of citizenship demanded a larger, more accessible public sphere. The fact that some Montreal residents exposed family needs to public view and called for state-funded solutions to private troubles bears out the argument that the private and the public have historically been linked in innumerable ways. In the 1940s, we see an expanding public: a public that, for a sustained moment, appeared to be encompassing many aspects of life hitherto thought 'private.'[65] The family not only became absorbed into the public, but also fashioned the public. In this book, we see, for instance, that conceptions of family shaped the administration of war and of government – two pillars of a public typically thought masculine. Under reconstruction, then, the family and the public became increasingly intertwined.

The 'public' discussed in this book is centred on the formal apparatus of the state, but includes the institutions of civil society important to Habermas's public arena, such as the press, voluntary organizations, and sometimes, the Catholic Church. It encompasses, moreover, the public institutions central to T.H. Marshall's model of social citizenship, such as public schools, hospitals, and playgrounds.[66] *Household Politics* asks, among other questions: Who shaped the public? Who had access to the public? And what could be said in public? It looks at families not simply as the object of public discussion, but as agents: the ways in which they inserted themselves and their claims into 'the public.' They did so by voicing family needs in public spaces such as newspapers, supermarkets, and picket lines, and by demanding that household matters be addressed in government (public) legislation. Finally, this book suggests that in the wake of the war, the public was an ideal as much as a place, and was twinned with ideas of full (or fuller) citizenship.

Yet alongside, and within, the postwar expansion of the public, calls for privacy, and for the private regulation of family matters, endured. We see, in this study, important moments of resistance to an expanding state. Such resistance was sometimes rooted in liberal convictions about the importance of privacy or in liberal preferences for a small, noninterventionist state. In Chapter 3, for instance, the example of private social agencies complaining that the state was using 'Gestapo' methods and creating public scandals over infidelity and marital breakdown suggests that 'the private' remained integral to this postwar liberal democracy. Calls for universal welfare measures were also a claim to privacy within families, in that they meant freedom from intrusive social workers and humiliating means tests. At other moments, resistance to Ottawa's expansionist projects had its origins in the conviction that the Quebec government, the Catholic Church, or local, private associations were best positioned to understand and respond to the welfare needs of Quebecers. Such moments of opposition to, or ambivalence about, state intrusions into private life help to explain why the expansion of the federal 'public' slowed dramatically in the later 1940s. It was not just that conservative voices among the federal Liberals won out over the advocates of reform, or that provincial premiers opposed Ottawa's activism on the grounds of provincial autonomy and the provisions of the British North America Act. As we see in the case of Montreal, ordinary citizens also demonstrated mixed feelings about an interventionist federal state. Thus in Chapter 3, we see women articulating a sense of entitlement to their dependents' allowances – but protesting the monitoring of their behaviour and the moral censure that frequently accompanied them. In Chapter 4, we see the Ligue Ouvrière Catholique calling for measures that would ensure the social and economic security of Catholic, working-class households – but arguing that Ottawa's version of such measures was not always appropriate for, or acceptable to, Quebec families. In Chapter 5, we see citizens of various political stripes demanding continued price controls. We also see, however, consumer organizations, unions, and middle-class women's groups using the language of liberalism, democracy, and the free market to call for an end to government prohibition of margarine and for the consumer's right to choose. And in Chapter 6, we see men demanding state intervention in order that they might house their families. We see approval of compulsory schooling legislation, but we also see concern about parents' inability to make their voices heard to the state that increasingly controlled their children's education.

The fifth and final body of literature addressed in *Household Politics* is that on postwar Quebec. For too long portrayed as a Great Darkness in which Duplessis and the Catholic bishops reigned unchallenged, post-war Quebec is increasingly turning out to be, in historians' accounts, raucous and contested. Duplessis defended provincial autonomy through a conservative nationalism that made the church a kind of junior partner in the governing of the province.[67] Most of Quebec's educational, health, and welfare services, for instance, were provided by the Catholic Church well into the twentieth century.[68] Yet while paying lip service to a vision of Quebec that highlighted its rural and Catholic dimensions, the pre-mier also encouraged the rapid postwar industrialization of the province at the hands of English-Canadian and American capital. Such an incon-sistency ought to alert us to the possibility of other complexities in postwar Quebec. Labour historians have long noted the militant strikes of the 1950s, such as those at Louiseville, Dupuis Frères, Murdochville, and Radio-Canada.[69] Cultural historians have long pointed to the *Refus global* of 1948 as a cry in the Duplessiste wilderness.[70] Recently, scholars have demonstrated that challenges to Duplessis's conservative politics and policies came not simply from isolated 'points of light' such as the liberal publication *Cité libre*, but from larger groundswells of opposition such as the student movement and the various branches of the Action catholique.[71]

One reason that private, denominational assistance persisted in post-war Montreal was that the Union Nationale confined its social welfare initiatives to limited and means-tested measures. Content to let the Catholic Church (and to a much lesser extent, Protestant and Jewish associations) act as a 'junior state,' Duplessis largely abdicated responsi-bility for innovations in social welfare at a time when the church could no longer adequately supply this assistance.[72] Yet while Duplessis's laissez-faire vision of the state was out of step with the increasingly popular Keynesian thinking of the 1930s and 1940s elsewhere (among certain planners and politicians in Britain, Canada, and the United States), it differed very little from that of his contemporary, Ontario Premier George Drew. Debates about the role of the state, the relative importance of the federal and provincial arms of the state, and the roles of private charitable workers and trained social workers were taking place across Canada in the wake of the Second World War. Furthermore, not only was the Catholic Church not a monolithic institution, but many of its component parts were initiating and accelerating social change and even secularization in the years following the war.[73] This study joins a number of recent works in attempting to examine the ways in which the Catholic Church adapted to the changes taking place in Quebec in the mid-twentieth century. In its examination of the Cent-Mariés phenomenon and the Ligue Ouvrière Catholique, *Household Politics* concludes, with other recent works in Quebec history, that some religious bodies were caught up in the democratic spirit of the 1940s and were attempting to ensure that Catholicism remained relevant to the lives of parishioners.[74]

This book, then, supports the now substantial body of work that argues that the Quiet Revolution was a much longer 'evolution' that began well before 1960.[75] Quebec was not a province mired in a *grande noirceur*, fettered by conservatism and clericalism until liberated by former federal cabinet minister Jean Lesage and his Liberal *équipe de tonnerre* in 1960. Historians have pointed to the existence of ideological diversity and debate, and to the centrality of liberalism in Quebec, long before the 1960s.[76] As Fernande Roy argues, the fact that the Catholic Church was a significant presence in Quebec 'n'est cependant pas une raison pour lui laisser toute la place dans le paysage idéologique.'[77] The modernization of Quebec society was hastened by the economic and industrial activity of the Second World War, and by the 'revanche administrative' undertaken by the federal government in the 1940s. As Dominique Marshall has persuasively argued, postwar federal measures paved the way for Quebecers' acceptance of the provincial Liberals' state-centred, neonationalist reforms in the 1960s.[78] Ottawa's aggressive occupation of constitutional realms that properly belonged to the provinces, moreover, provoked some Quebecers into demanding that subsequent reforms be undertaken by the provincial arm of the state.[79]

Sources

This book draws on a wide range of sources, including government records, the papers of private social welfare agencies and of women's voluntary associations, the records of Catholic institutions, including the Société de Saint-Vincent de Paul and organizations affiliated with the Action catholique, union records, school board files, and newspapers representing Montreal's mass-circulation, nationalist, labour, and religious press. These sources reveal various experiences of family in 1940s Montreal. They also help us to understand the ways in which family matters were made central to public discussions of postwar reconstruction. The records of the federal Dependents' Allowance Board and the Dependents' Board of Trustees, for instance, bring to light intimate family secrets – situations that were no longer secret once exposed to the gaze of civil servants, but that were nonetheless discussed behind closed doors. Yet these family details became public, in a way, when the DAB or the DBT communicated with private welfare agencies or municipal bodies, or when civil servants' exposure to such secrets influenced the shaping of public policy. Private social agencies, while committed (to varying degrees) to client confidentiality, used such family confidences (made them public, so to speak) as justification for their demands for more state support, less state intervention, or changes in state policy. Associations such as the Société de Saint-Vincent de Paul learned the private details of family through home visiting. Participants in the specialized movements of the Action catholique knew first-hand many of the trials of working families; they deliberately made them public in order to secure certain gains from the state and from the community. When members of service clubs or labour unions adopted resolutions, circulated petitions, or went on strike, they, too, made the private needs of their constituents public. Finally, newspapers played an important role in making personal lives public, and in educating readers about familial needs. Photographs reproduced in the press helped to shape public opinion; poll results and electoral campaigns, reported in daily newspapers, gave readers insight into what other members of the 'public' supposedly considered their priorities.

The fact that historians can unearth family needs and wants in these sources does not necessarily mean that families intended to leave their mark there for posterity. The most detailed sources of information on these 1940s families are the records of private social agencies and of federal departments dealing with the families of enlisted men. These are accounts of families in need – by and large, working-class families. Sometimes men and women sought assistance or advice from these organizations, implicitly agreeing to expose their private lives to examination. Occasionally, they criticized official policy. At other times, families appear in the sources as the objects of scrutiny, having unwillingly come to official attention – as when, for instance, wives were reported to the Dependents' Allowance Board for having failed to act in a manner appropriate to women in receipt of state funds. The Klein family, whom we saw in the first few pages of this chapter, is made visible to historians through the files of private social service agencies active in Montreal in the 1940s. These files allow us glimpses of intimate details that we might not find in other kinds of sources. The files exist, however, because this was a family in trouble: the Kleins first came to the attention of these private agencies because a cousin had reported what he or she believed to be the neglect of the Klein children. The families that historians come to know well, whether through case files, government records, or court proceedings, are generally families like this one, and we meet them at complicated moments in their lives.[80] The records created by the Ligue Ouvrière Catholique about the 105 married couples that participated in the mass wedding of 1939, into which we peer in Chapter 4, are rather different. These men and women were voluntary participants in this public event – and the letters and survey responses that exist are from those couples who chose to maintain their relationship with LOC organizers. And clearly, couples decided what and how much to tell the LOC about their private trials and triumphs. The celebratory element of the Cent-Mariés phenomenon, and the fact that these files include letters written by the Cent-Mariés themselves, mean that we can find happiness in these records. They depict contented marriages, joy at births, relief at finding work – alongside more tragic events such as illness and death.[81]

Attempting to piece together elements of families' lived experiences in 1940s Montreal is a hazardous undertaking. Archival evidence is fragmentary and partial, and we read it across six decades of historical change. Moreover, as poststructuralist scholars have convincingly argued, the search for some kind of 'pure' experience in the past is at best complicated and perhaps even futile. Experience, we know, is mediated, or understood, through culturally constructed sets of meanings ('discourses') specific to their time and place.[82] This study of Montreal families and postwar reconstruction is not, however, simply or even primarily a study of discourses. I am interested, rather, in the ways in which discourses interacted with – that is, both reflected and structured – lived experiences. In engaging in household politics, Montreal families were attempting to send messages, make claims, persuade politicians, and secure tangible gains. They drew on rhetoric, vocabulary, and cultural references that they thought would be effective. Understanding the systems of meaning in place in the 1940s is important. But to focus exclusively on the rhetoric – on the calculated bids for sympathy or support – is to lose sight of the sincerity and the necessity of these public appeals, of the people behind the appeals, and of the conditions that engendered the appeals.

chapter one

Summer 1945

On Tuesday, 8 May 1945, Montreal residents awoke to a city that was, if not yet at peace, nonetheless triumphant. Victory in Europe had been declared the preceding morning, and Montreal streets had teemed with revellers the entire day. Beginning at around ten o'clock on Monday morning, people congregated along Sainte-Catherine Street, celebrating with friends and strangers alike at every intersection. Streetcars ground to a halt behind crowds of celebrants and cars overflowing with teenagers. Civilians applauded men in uniform. Shopkeepers locked their doors and joined the crowds. Now, on a cloudy Tuesday morning, municipal workers had already begun to clean up the piles of confetti and debris that had been tossed from office windows onto the streets below. Celebrations would continue but would be a tad more sedate: that day, close to five thousand Montrealers gathered in the rain for a memorial service at Dominion Square.[1]

Three months later, Montrealers celebrated again – this time, in tribute to Victory in Japan and a definitive end to six years of war. Sainte-Catherine Street filled with late summer revellers, who danced, sang, and paraded as the sounds of car horns mingled with those of the ships in the harbour. Residents of the city's Chinatown, in particular, celebrated Japan's defeat.[2] What kind of city was Montreal in August 1945, as Canada and the world around it emerged from the Second World War? Did it truly embody Hugh MacLennan's 'two solitudes'? Was it an essentially Catholic city, dotted with churches and *collèges classiques*? Or was it a city of jazz and burlesque on rue Saint-Antoine and the Main? Was this the commercial metropolis of St James Street, Anglo-Canadian capital, and the headquarters of all major Canadian banks? Or Canada's industrial workshop, producing tanks and airplanes in Rosemont and

Ville Saint-Laurent, locomotive parts in Pointe Saint-Charles, and women's coats and children's shoes in the sweatshops that lined Saint-Laurent Boulevard? Was it Gabrielle Roy's Saint-Henri: shabby and grey? Or the green slopes of Mount Royal and the carefully tended gardens of Westmount? Or was this the city of Mordecai Richler's Duddy Kravitz: narrow neighbourhoods of cramped flats and synagogues?[3]

If not all things to all people, Montreal was certainly many things to many people in the late 1940s. As in Christine Stansell's industrializing New York, there were numerous cities within this postwar city.[4] This chapter maps the social geography of postwar Montreal from a familial perspective. It draws attention, moreover, to the city's economic, linguistic, and religious diversity. I argue that in conjunction with the federal Liberals' reconstruction plans, the social context presented here – high rates of family formation, a healthy employment market, albeit one segregated by age and gender, a severe housing shortage, a high cost of living, widespread adolescent labour and thus early school-leaving – helps to explain the particular kinds of household politics that we see in the chapters to come.

People

In the 1940s, Montreal was Canada's metropolis, with over a million people calling it home at the beginning of the decade.[5] It was largely a French-Canadian city: 62.6 per cent of the residents of metropolitan Montreal cited French origins in the 1941 Census. Yet the 24.7 per cent of the population that traced its ethnic origins to the British Isles, and the 5.6 per cent who were European Jews, shaped the city to an extent disproportionate to their numbers, and left indelible imprints on the city's cultural landscape. Another 2.2 per cent of the city's residents were of Italian descent; 4.9 per cent listed 'other' ethnic origins.[6]

In the early nineteenth century, immigrants from Scotland, England, Ireland, and the United States outnumbered francophones in Montreal. Waves of French-Canadian migration from the surrounding countryside beginning in the 1830s, and the massive influx of Irish famine migrants in the 1840s and 1850s, meant that by the end of the century the city had become more francophone and more Catholic.[7] By the dawn of the twentieth century, Montreal was also home to a rapidly growing Jewish community. A small number of British Jews had settled in Lower Canada in the late eighteenth century. Most were relatively well integrated with the rest of Montreal's English-speaking population; many were soon financially comfortable. The huge number of Eastern European Jews who arrived in the city in the first two decades of the twentieth century had an entirely different history and demographic profile. Many of those who arrived before 1917 came from various parts of the Russian empire – Lithuania, Romania, the Ukraine, and Belarus – and were thus in themselves a diverse group. Generally poor and Yiddish-speaking, they came from rural areas and small towns, and found work in garment factories and provisioning the community as grocers, butchers, pedlars, and shopkeepers.[8] A small number of Italians had migrated to Montreal in the 1860s and 1870s, but it was not until the very end of the nineteenth century and the first decade of the twentieth that a significant Italian community formed in the city. This community was to some degree integrated with the French-Canadian population, owing to a shared religion, common workplaces in the case of men and unmarried women, and initially, shared neighbourhoods.[9] During and immediately after the Second World War, war brides from Britain and the Netherlands landed in the city, many with children in tow. And in the very late 1940s and 1950s, new immigrants and refugees – Poles, Italians, Romanians, Hungarians, and Jews of various European nations – would arrive, often as families, from the war-torn cities and displaced persons camps of Europe.[10] In the postwar years, religion remained a key marker of identity. Francophone Quebecers were almost without exception Catholic; 86.8 per cent of Quebec residents were Catholic in 1941.[11] Some anglophone Quebecers were also Catholic; others attended Anglican, Presbyterian, and United Churches. In the city of Montreal proper in 1951, 78.6 per cent of residents were Catholic; 6.5 per cent Jewish; 5.7 per cent Anglican; 3.9 per cent United Church; and 2.3 per cent Presbyterian.[12]

Montreal, like most large cities, had more than its share of transients and of single people. War production, in particular, had attracted young, single, French-Canadian men and women from the surrounding countryside anxious to secure paid work in the city's booming factories. Armed services personnel – both Canadians and overseas members of the British Commonwealth Air Training Plan – were stationed in Montreal throughout the war, adding to the city's young, transient, and male population. But this was also a city of families, and in the wake of the war, this was increasingly the case, as rates of family formation rapidly increased. According to the Census, 197,840 'families' lived in the city of Montreal proper in 1941; by 1951, the number of families in the city had grown to 246,389.[13] Marriage rates, which had begun to climb soon after war was declared, continued apace in the first days of peace.[14] From 1945 through 1948, in fact, marriage rates in Montreal were higher than the rates for both Quebec and Canada as a whole. All three sets of marriage rates peaked in 1946.[15] Historically, a greater proportion of women in Quebec than of women elsewhere in Canada had remained unmarried; when they did marry, they tended to do so later than women in the English-speaking provinces.[16] In January 1945, however, the Association catholique de la jeunesse canadienne-française (ACJC) claimed that it was not unusual to see young people marrying at age nineteen or twenty; a survey conducted by the Jeunesse Ouvrière Catholique (JOC) two years later found that the average 'jeune travailleur' married at age twenty-two or twenty-three.[17] Canada-wide, the average age of marriage at the end of the war was twenty-four for men and twenty-one for women.[18]

Notwithstanding both francophone clerico-nationalist and English-Canadian rhetoric that had long insisted upon Quebec's large families, the postwar baby boom had less demographic impact in Quebec than in the anglophone provinces.[19] Moreover, contemporaries knew then, and historians have noted since, that even at the height of the boom, it was not that women were having more children; rather, more women were having children.[20] The boom was fuelled, as Angus and Arlene McLaren observe, by 'some women "catching up" and having babies postponed by the war, and by other women marrying earlier and having their children sooner and closer together.'[21] Thus while the number of families in Canada increased in the postwar period, the number of children per family did not. Hervé Gauthier has found that Quebec women born in 1922–3 (and thus likely to have had their children in the late 1940s) had, on average, 3.6 children each.[22] A fertility survey conducted by the Université de Montréal in 1971 also found that the generation of Quebec women born between 1921 and 1925 had an average of 3.6 children each.[23] Yet Montreal – Canada's highly urbanized and industrialized metropolis – was a slightly different story. Despite its higher marriage rates, the city's birth rates from 1945 through 1948 were lower than those of both Quebec and Canada.[24]

Places

Montreal's class and ethnic divisions were reflected in the geography and topography of the city. Saint-Laurent Boulevard (the Main) divided the city between east and west. The western half of the city tended to be more English-speaking and more affluent than the east side, although this tendency was not absolute. Westmount, nestled into Mount Royal, was the bastion of English-Canadian wealth: here lived industrialists, bankers, financiers. As novelist Morley Callaghan noted bluntly in 1951, 'Nearly all the rich families in Montreal lived on the mountain.'[25] Notre-Dame-de-Grâce (NDG), just west of Westmount, was mixed: to the north of the CPR tracks, it housed lower middle-class, white-collar workers and salaried employees, largely English-speaking and described in 1948 as 'community-minded.' Below the tracks, the neighbourhood was less affluent.[26] By the mid-1950s, the northern and western reaches of NDG were filled with newly constructed apartment blocks 'housing a large number of young married couples with small children.'[27] Housing for munitions workers and war veterans had also been built in NDG, as it had been in Cartierville, Park Extension, Montreal-North, and the new suburb of Ville Saint-Laurent, on the northern edge of Montreal and near the Canadair factory and the Noorduyn Aircraft plant.[28]

Below Westmount lay the neighbourhoods that nineteenth-century industrialist Herbert B. Ames had termed 'The City Below the Hill': the industrial districts of Pointe Saint-Charles, Griffintown, Saint-Henri, Sainte-Cunégonde, and Saint-Joseph. These ethnically mixed neighbourhoods provided the labour force for Montreal's factories and transportation sector, as much in the 1940s as when Ames had described them in the 1890s. The residents of Pointe Saint-Charles, south of the Lachine Canal and north of the St Lawrence River, were largely working-class and English-speaking Protestants; many of the neighbourhood's adult men worked in the local Canadian National Railway yards. Griffintown, on the other side of the Lachine Canal, was home to both Irish-Canadian and French-Canadian Catholics; social workers and wealthier Montrealers considered the district 'a crowded slum area.'[29] The residents of Saint-Henri, Sainte-Cunégonde, and Saint-Joseph were largely, but not exclusively, French-speaking. They were, however, almost uniformly poor; many of the men in the area worked as unskilled labourers and on a seasonal basis. Novelist Gabrielle Roy described the crowds who congregated in Place Saint-Henri each evening as

Masons covered with lime, carpenters with their toolboxes, workmen carrying lunch pails, spinners, girls from the cigarette factory, puddlers, steelworkers, watchmen, foremen, salespeople, shopkeepers; the six o'clock crowd included not only employees from the neighborhood but also workers from Ville-Saint-Pierre, Lachine, Saint-Joseph, Saint-Cunégonde and as far away as Hochelaga, some of whom lived on the other side of town and traveled vast distances in the streetcar before reaching home.[30]

Saint-Antoine Street was the commercial heart of Montreal's small Black community. Close to the headquarters of the Canadian Pacific Railway, which employed African-Canadian men as sleeping-car porters, the street was home to nightclubs and cabarets where some Black Montrealers worked as musicians and performers.[31] Montrealers who could count on steadier employment and higher wages than residents of the Pointe or Saint-Henri chose to live in Verdun: a 'respectable' working-class suburb, to the south of the Lachine and Aqueduct Canals and bordering the St Lawrence River, that housed both French-speaking Catholics and Anglo-Protestants.[32]

The east side of Montreal was largely francophone. The francophone elite – in this period, professionals such as doctors, lawyers, and notaries, and some industrialists and financiers – lived in Outremont, over the mountain from Westmount. French-Canadian workers lived in the neighbourhoods that stretched east of Saint-Laurent Boulevard: the Plateau Mont-Royal, Rosemont, and east as far as Hochelaga and Maisonneuve. Rosemont was a linguistically mixed, working-class neighbourhood to the north of the Angus Shops (the CPR's locomotive repair shops), which employed many neighbourhood men. Described by one social worker as poor but 'self-respecting' working people, Rosemont residents were active participants in the creation of community gardens and children's playgrounds.[33] Some wartime housing was built in the northern section of Rosemont.[34] In the late 1940s and 1950s, some French-Canadian families faced with Montreal's housing crisis and high rents began moving to Ville Jacques-Cartier, on the South Shore. Across the bridge from Montreal's east end, this was an impoverished district initially without running water, electricity, or welfare services, where families built their own homes out of tarpaper, heavy cardboard, and sheet metal. Future Front de libération du Québec (FLQ) member Pierre Vallières, who grew up there, described Ville Jacques-Cartier in the early 1950s as 'a totally new town made up of shacks and exiles.'[35]

Saint-Laurent Boulevard, or the Main, had been the heart of Montreal's Jewish community since the early twentieth century. Here were synagogues and Yiddish newspaper offices, smoked meat shops and kosher butchers. Here also were garment factories and sweatshops, where Jews were both owners and workers. Many Jewish families lived just off Saint-Laurent on Saint-Urbain, Bagg, Saint-Dominique, and Villeneuve: residential streets of brick triplexes. The wealthiest of Montreal Jews lived in Outremont, alongside French-Canadian neighbours, a proximity that was sometimes a source of ethnic tension.[36] By the late 1940s, more affluent Jewish families were also moving to new suburbs to the north and the west: Snowdon, Hampstead, and Côte Saint-Luc. One popular historian of Montreal has found that Jewish families migrating westward would leave their flats near the Main, including their furnishings, to the new waves of Jews arriving from Europe in the late 1940s.[37] Further north on Saint-Laurent Boulevard, near Jean-Talon, were the shops, markets, and cafés that constituted the commercial core of Montreal's Italian neighbourhood.[38]

Montreal was a port town, a commercial hub, and an industrial city. Shipping activity took place along the St Lawrence River and the Lachine Canal, and most financial and commercial transactions occurred in the downtown core. Montreal's industry had historically been concentrated along the river and the canal, although by the 1940s some plants, including war industries, had moved north of established residential areas in search of greater expanses of space.[39] Mount Royal (landscaped by Frederick Law Olmsted in the late nineteenth century as part of the City Beautiful movement) provided an oasis of greenery in the middle of the city, as did Île Sainte-Hélène, in the harbour, and Parc Lafontaine, on the city's east side.[40] Larger homes in Westmount and Outremont often had gardens, but most residents of the city had scant green space of their own, availing themselves instead of the small parks, playgrounds, and community gardens that had begun to spring up around the metropolis in the early twentieth century.[41] Yet even such innocuous projects as community gardens and children's playgrounds embodied the ethnic divisions embedded in the city. Anglophones and francophones tended their vegetables under the auspices of the Community Garden League and the Service de jardins ouvriers respectively;[42] the Œuvre des terrains de jeux de Montréal and the Montreal Parks and Playgrounds Association generally worked in parallel rather than together.[43]

Postwar Montreal faced a severe housing crisis. This was a city of flats and 'plexes': in 1951, 92 per cent of the city's total occupied dwellings were apartments or flats, while 97 per cent of rented dwellings were apartments or flats.[44] Montrealers were, by and large, tenants: nearly 83 per cent of the city's 'occupied dwellings' were rented, rather than owned, by their inhabitants in 1951. The housing crisis had multiple dimensions. First, there was not enough housing for a population that had grown considerably over the course of the war, due to in-migration for munitions production, the influx of air force personnel associated with the British Commonwealth Air Training Plan, the immigration of British brides and their children, and the high rate of family formation involving new marriages and births.[45] Second, the housing that did exist was often in poor condition. The poverty of the Depression and the rationing and material shortages of the war had done nothing to improve the state of Montreal's residences. Finally, postwar housing in the metropolis was overpriced. The high cost-of-living offset the improved wages of Montreal citizens; this, combined with the poor supply and increased demand for housing, raised rents beyond the reach of many.

Those families unable to find private dwellings lodged in rooms, which contributed to the overcrowding of those who did have their own housing. The 1951 Census found that 21 per cent of Montreal households were 'crowded' (defined as more than one person per room) and that 22.58 per cent of tenant households were crowded.[46] Such aggregate numbers, however, disguised the class and ethnic dimensions of overcrowding. The Ligue Ouvrière Catholique (LOC) declared in 1947 that 64 per cent of Montreal's working-class homes were overcrowded, and that 94 per cent of working-class homes on the (largely francophone) east side of the city were overcrowded. 41.4 per cent of the homes surveyed by the LOC used the living room as a bedroom, and 39 per cent of the homes had no bath.[47] That same year, the Montreal branch of the Canadian Association of Social Workers conducted its own survey of the housing conditions of 298 families known to the city's Family Welfare Association (who would have been largely Protestant). It declared: 'Four and five children were found sleeping in one bed, parents and children sleeping in the same room.'[48] Those families with the least money or luck squatted in public buildings, abandoned military barracks, sheds, garages, and stores.[49]

The housing crisis had a serious impact on family life. Observers and activists ranging from the Jeunesse Ouvrière Catholique to J.O. Asselin, chairman of the executive committee of Montreal's city council, claimed that thousands of young Montrealers were postponing their marriages because they could not find adequate housing.[50] One young man, a resident of Lachine, wrote to the Ligue Ouvrière Catholique–affiliated Commission nationale de l'habitation in January 1948 for help in finding an apartment in Lachine or Ville Lasalle. He had decided to marry in May if he could find housing; otherwise, the wedding would have to wait until June, July, or August. He did not want to start married life lodging in rooms, he and his fiancée could not live with his parents because his family was too large, and his fiancée did not want to begin married life in her own parents' home. This letter from 'un jeune ouvrier' ended with a heartfelt plea: 'Mon Dieu, Logez-nous.'[51]

The Commission nationale de l'habitation representative who responded to this call for help agreed that it was 'most desirable' for a newlywed couple to have private living quarters in order to adapt to married life.[52] The common wartime practice of soldiers' wives and children living with their parents or in-laws while their husbands and fathers were away had demonstrated that overcrowded housing and a lack of privacy placed serious strains on familial relationships.[53] Surely new unions, celebrated in peacetime, should not have to begin in such circumstances. Yet some young couples decided to proceed with their weddings even if it meant spending the first months of their marriage lodging with strangers or crowded into their parents' homes.[54] Conflicts between young wives and mothers-in-law became the stuff of everyday conversation: what Colette, *La Presse*'s widely read advice columnist, called 'L'éternelle histoire de la belle-mère et de la bru qui habitent sous le même toit et refusent d'admettre que les affaires de l'une ne sont pas nécessairement celles de l'autre.'[55]

Poor housing conditions meant more work for both parents, but especially wives, in terms of cleaning, upkeep, and repairs. This increased burden strained couples' relationships.[56] Families with numerous children had difficulty securing adequate dwellings: partly because of the shortage of large apartments, but also because landlords could afford to be choosier in a time of scarce supply.[57] Some landlords had no qualms about being deliberately difficult in order to force tenants out, particularly in the context of rent controls.[58] Landlords took advantage of the housing shortage to charge outrageous rents to new tenants, to demand six months' rent at a time, or to insist that would-be tenants purchase used furniture at sky-high prices. Keeping children out of landlords' way was more often the job of mothers than of fathers.[59] In the most severe cases, families were split up as parents unable to find proper accommodation boarded their children with relatives or strangers or placed them in institutions such as crèches and orphanages. Montreal's children's homes themselves became overcrowded in the 1940s, reflecting the city's general housing shortage. The Protestant Children's Aid Society attributed its increased intake in 1948 to the housing crisis; the Catholic crèches and orphanages affiliated with the Conseil des Œuvres registered similar complaints of congestion, for the same reason, in 1946 and 1947.[60] Sometimes these placements were permanent; more often, they were until parents could find a suitable home. The Montreal Ladies' Benevolent Society, for instance, reported in September 1945 that two girls and their brother had left the LBS Home for children because their mother had found a place to live.[61]

Those children who stayed with their parents nonetheless felt the impact of the housing shortage because they were without adequate space in which to play, do their homework, or entertain their friends. As the Montreal branch of the Canadian Association of Social Workers warned, 'Older children were ashamed to bring their friends home and instead met them on street corners and spent their recreation time at downtown amusement centres.'[62]

Gender, Age, and the Labour Market

Since the early days of European settlement in North America, Montreal had been central to the colony's economic development, whether through the fur trade, shipping, railways, light and heavy industry, finance, or commerce. The city's geographic setting – near the junction of the St Lawrence and Ottawa Rivers – was partially responsible for this economic preeminence. The Northwest fur trade was directed in large part from Montreal; the city became home to such early-nineteenth-century Scots- and English-Canadian commercial barons as the McGills, the Molsons, and the McTavishes. Montreal was a major hub for the Grand Trunk Railway and later the CPR; by the end of the nineteenth century, it was unquestionably Canada's foremost industrial city. The prominent Canadian banks (such as the Bank of Montreal and the Royal Bank) that established their headquarters on St James Street, and the presence in the city of successful entrepreneurs, ensured that it remained the repository for much of the nation's money.[63] By the end of the Second World War, the city's position as metropolis of Quebec and Canada meant that it was at the hub of a network of economic relationships that spanned the continent and crossed the Atlantic. The war had fuelled the city's industry, adding tanks, airplanes, and munitions to prewar manufacturing staples such as clothing, tobacco, and food. By 1951, 38 per cent of Montreal's male labour force was employed in manufacturing; service, trade, transportation, and construction were the other major industries employing the city's men.[64]

The experience of war continued to shape the nature of men's work in late-1940s Montreal. The spectre of postwar unemployment had haunted the city's workers even as they reaped the benefits of wartime labour shortages, long working hours, and improved wages. Policy-makers, employers, and industrial workers alike suspected that this war, like the previous one, would be followed by an economic recession. Yet social welfare payments, contributions to the reconstruction of Europe, greater integration with the booming American economy and, later, Cold War spending, ensured that the Canadian economy remained relatively healthy through the late 1940s and certainly through the 1950s.[65] Of course, aggregate statistics that paint a rosy picture of the postwar Canadian economy need to be taken apart to look at the impact of economic transition on particular cities, neighbourhoods, and families. Montreal did experience some transitional unemployment and minor shocks as the city, a significant centre of wartime munitions production, shifted to peacetime industry and services.[66]

Despite the cancellation of war contracts, the city's industrial base persisted. Production for war gave way to the manufacturing of consumer goods for peacetime. Thus a large proportion of the city's male workers continued to benefit from the wartime gains made in the manufacturing sector: the industrial legality of PC 1003, the provincial Loi des relations ouvrières, and the Rand Formula; significant rates of unionization; and relatively high wages. Postwar Fordism, premised on state regulation, management-labour accommodation, and wages that permitted high levels of consumption, maintained high levels of production.[67] In 1951, 22 per cent of Montreal's 314,682 male workers over the age of fourteen worked in jobs considered 'Manufacturing and Mechanical.' They were followed by clerical workers (10 per cent), transportation workers (10 per cent), labourers (10 per cent), construction workers (9 per cent), service workers (8 per cent), those employed in commercial occupations (7 per cent), and professionals (7 per cent).[68] The city's male job market was thus diverse. Moreover, it had not yet been radically transformed by the rapid increase in white-collar, clerical, and sales jobs and the corresponding decrease in blue-collar, manual work described by Desmond Morton as a Canada-wide phenomenon in the 1950s.[69] Factory workers continued to predominate in the male labour pool,[70] and the postwar building boom, within the city and especially in its suburbs, improved the job opportunities for construction workers and manual labourers.[71]

The attempt to return newlywed and long-married women to the home at the close of the war has been well documented by North American historians.[72] Canadian women's labour-force participation did plummet immediately after the end of the war, and the wartime high in their participation rate would not be equalled until the 1960s. But this reduced female labour force increased steadily, especially after 1951. And within this reduced but growing female workforce, the paid work of married women became progressively more important.[73] Canada-wide, the decade between 1941 and 1951 saw the number of married women in the labour force increase by approximately three and a half times.[74] One analyst of the 1951 Census, writing in 1954, thought it possible, and even likely, 'that the wartime phenomenon of working wives will become an established and normal development of our Canadian society,' rather than 'a temporary phenomenon.'[75]

Observers of postwar Montreal, in particular, described a 'Fuite vers le travail payé de la mère de famille,' claiming that married women 'often' left their homes to work in factories and to supplement husbands' inadequate salaries.[76] In 1951, 30 per cent of Canada's female labour force was married. In Quebec, 17.3 per cent of the female labour force was married, and in Montreal, 20.9 per cent.[77] Examined from another angle, only 11.8 per cent of Montreal's married women were considered to be part of the labour force that year.[78] If the war had marked the beginning of wives' permanent entry into the paid labour force, it was a trend that was clearly still in its infancy in Montreal through the 1940s. An examination of Census data comparing male and female labour-force participation by age groups reveals that Montreal men and women worked for pay in roughly similar numbers from age fourteen through age nineteen. Considerably fewer women aged twenty to twenty-four worked than their male counterparts, and the drop-off in female labour-force participation was marked among women aged twenty-five to thirty-four.[79] The less than 12 per cent of wives who worked for pay contrasts with the 19.3 per cent of Montreal widows and the 68.4 per cent of Montreal divorcées who were included in the city's labour force in 1951.[80] It also appears a surprisingly small group compared to the 19.8 per cent of wives who worked in (for instance) Hamilton, Ontario, that same year.[81] Moreover, the almost 10 percent gap in 1951 between the 30 per cent of the Canadian female labour force that was married and the 21 per cent of Montreal's female labour force that was married is considerable. These percentages appear particularly low given the metropolis's abundance of jobs in the manufacturing, clerical, and service sectors: supply and demand are clearly inadequate to explain this discrepancy.

According to the Clio Collective, the increase in married women's labour-force participation that did take place in Quebec between 1941 and 1951 was particularly marked in the manufacturing sector.[82] The National Selective Service had certainly targeted married women for factory work during the war.[83] Yet Montreal's Local Council of Women (LCW) claimed in October 1945 that 'most factories want young, unmarried girls under 25 years of age' and that older and married women found it much more difficult to secure factory employment, with the possible exception of work in the sewing trades.[84] Francine Barry argues that Quebec women's paid work became more varied after 1941. Sectors of paid employment such as office work, for instance, expanded over the course of the 1940s.[85] Yet in clerical work, too, married women faced obstacles, as the end-of-the-war campaign to remove wives from the federal civil service suggests.[86] In 1950, the LCW's delegate to the Unemployment Insurance Commission claimed that many firms were 'becoming more selective in their choice of workers.' There was increasingly a trend, she argued, against the hiring of married women, and younger women were replacing older female employees. As early as October 1945, a survey of women's employment in Verdun found that employers were reluctant to hire married women and older women, and that in most fields, the demand was for 'young, pretty women workers.'[87] The LCW's Trades, Business and Professions Committee conducted a study of 'the problem of the older woman worker' in 1949–50 and discovered that six of the sixteen Montreal firms surveyed hired women only between the ages of twenty-five and thirty-five.[88] The 1951 Census counted 13,872 Montreal women as 'professional' workers, but it is unclear how many of these were married.[89] In 1947, the LCW decried the 'alarming' decline in the number of social workers, teachers, and nurses, and called for the amendment of income tax regulations so that married women and their husbands would not be penalized when wives continued to work for pay.[90]

No doubt many means of earning a dollar were ignored by the federal Census. *La Presse*'s Colette, for instance, suggested in 1947 that married women in need of extra income might consider undertaking paid work at home.[91] Paid work in someone else's home remained an option, as the demand for domestic help always exceeded the supply of women willing to undertake this work. Service as a live-in institution was dealt a serious blow by the growth of other work opportunities for women during the war; the LCW's chronic complaints about the shortage of domestic servants were even louder than usual in the wake of the war.[92] Increasingly, domestic service became an occupation filled by recent immigrants and women of colour.[93] In any case, live-in domestics had almost always been single. But service persisted as a day job, and some married women hired themselves out as cleaning women.[94] In the more 'public' service sector, we see Steinberg's supermarket advertising in 1947 for women to work as cashiers: young and single women were specifically requested.[95]

The paid work of married women in postwar Montreal was generally characterized by low wages.[96] It was, moreover, irregular and usually contingent on husbands' earnings and employment. The mothers of the children who attended Griffintown's Garderie Sainte-Anne, mostly Irish-Canadian labouring women ('femmes de peine') and office workers, often took part-time and seasonal work: more children attended the nursery, for instance, around Christmas.[97] Mothers without spouses sought ways to support themselves and their children, as did women whose husbands were ill, unemployed, or earned inadequate wages. Social agencies found, for instance, that a mother might go out to work if her husband 'drank to excess and lost jobs,' or if he was 'blind and unemployable.'[98] In the immediate postwar years, moreover, the high cost-of-living was frequently cited as a reason why 'housewives find it necessary to seek full or part time employment to supplement the family income.'[99]

Like working wives, working children suggested that the breadwinner ideal was far from attainable for many of the city's families. Despite a much-vaunted 'postwar prosperity,' children continued to contribute to family economies. Indeed, for many working-class families in Montreal, the wages of children were essential to postwar financial security.[100] The child-labour problem that continued to plague postwar social workers and administrators of the emerging Canadian welfare state was largely a matter of youth or teen labour.[101] For their families, this 'problem' was actually a 'strategy' designed to cope with an increased cost-of-living[102] and adult male wages that remained insufficient despite a local labour market vastly improved since the days of the Great Depression. Class and ethnic differences produced differing perspectives on whether the work of adolescents was considered to be a problem or a strategy.[103] Generational differences also determined attitudes toward this work. For teenagers, their parents' financial strategies, which involved their own paid labour, might constitute a problem inasmuch as they prevented them from participating in the youth cultures of their peers.[104]

The Second World War had significantly expanded the employment of children and teens across the nation.[105] Like women, they were hired to fill the jobs vacated by men departed for the front. The large number of adolescents employed in munitions factories during the war was the most visible sector of youth employment; highly concentrated in specific locales, they attracted a disproportionate amount of attention. But adolescents worked in a wide variety of occupations: girls in the garment industry, the textile and food trades, and as domestic servants; boys as industrial workers, messengers, delivery boys, newsboys, and apprentices in a trade. Many of these were occupations defined specifically as children's jobs.[106] Quebec was perceived to have the worst child-labour 'problem' in the country.[107] This may have been, in part, a judgment by anglophone social workers and federal civil servants, related to perceptions of large French-Canadian families and inadequate provincial public welfare services. Yet francophone observers also decried Quebec's 'worst possible situation' in regard to child labour.[108] Moreover, the 1951 Census showed that Quebec had the largest percentage of children aged fifteen to twenty-four in the labour force in the country (almost 60 per cent), as well as the largest increase in this percentage over the decade 1941–51.[109] Contemporaries argued that children's earnings were essential for many Quebec families because of the inadequacy of both adult male wages and social services in the province.[110] Historian Dominique Marshall suggests that Quebec children's employment may have increased during the war in part because the work of wives was so actively discouraged by provincial commentators. Marshall's study of postwar Quebec demonstrates that children continued to work for wages even after compulsory schooling was implemented in 1943, and even after family allowances softened the edges of many parents' poverty.[111] The Canadian Youth Commission heard from Quebecers that among those who benefited most from wartime improvements in the economy were 'families with working sons and daughters.' Some adolescents, in fact, told the commission that 'they were already the principal means of financial support for their parents.'[112] Thérèse Hamel attributes the chronic high rates of children's employment in twentieth-century Quebec, and corresponding low rates of school attendance, to the importance of light industry (which required neither extensive education nor much physical strength) in Montreal, and to the persistence of the self-sufficient family farm outside the metropolis.[113]

The LOC and the JOC claimed that children as young as thirteen, fourteen, and fifteen were kept out of school and sent to work because of their parents' poverty.[114] In fact, the JOC argued in 1948, 44 per cent of young people began working for pay at or before age fifteen, and 69 per cent at or before age sixteen.[115] Montreal's Société de Saint-Vincent de Paul commented in 1944 on the widespread problem of children leaving school for work at the age of fourteen, while the Montreal Council of Social Agencies (the city's umbrella organization for Protestant agencies) remarked that same year on the large number of children under sixteen and even under fourteen working full- and part-time.[116] One family that came to the attention of the Jewish Child Welfare Bureau in 1947 had two daughters, aged sixteen and seventeen, who lived out and worked as domestics. At least one of the daughters had been working irregularly since the age of thirteen, in a clothing factory and elsewhere.[117] Classifieds in *La Presse* in 1944 advertised light work in a cigar factory for girls under the age of sixteen and noted that the perquisites of the job included annual paid vacations, group insurance, and free milk. Applicants, the posting noted, had to provide certificates of age and of studies. Meanwhile, boys under the age of sixteen who desired a 'métier d'après-guerre' and a chance of advancement were encouraged in 1944 to apply for jobs as messengers and apprentice jewellers.[118]

Clearly, daughters as well as sons went out to work. Only slightly fewer girls aged fourteen to seventeen worked for pay than boys of the same age in 1951, and more eighteen- and nineteen-year-old girls worked than eighteen- and nineteen-year-old boys in Montreal that year.[119] This differs from late-nineteenth-century Montreal, when, Bettina Bradbury argues, daughters were considerably less likely than sons to work outside the home, in large part because their families required their unpaid domestic labour.[120] Yet Dominique Marshall points out that in the postwar period, many of the children kept out of school were girls whose labour was needed at home. The unpaid work of farmers' sons and working-class daughters, she argues, remained officially tolerated lacunae in the administration of children's 'new universal rights.'[121] Many of the 13,128 Montreal children aged fourteen to twenty-four who are listed in the 1951 Census as neither working for pay nor attending school were likely girls undertaking unpaid domestic work at home.[122]

Postwar Montreal, then, offered an abundance of jobs to men, particularly in the city's manufacturing districts and in the construction trades that were increasingly important to the expanding suburbs. Teenage boys delivered messages between downtown office buildings, sold newspapers on street corners, and transported parcels and groceries from shops to homes. Girls and young women rode the streetcar to their industrial jobs, staffed the counters at downtown department stores, and cooked and cleaned in the city's larger houses in Westmount, Outremont, and the Golden Square Mile. And slowly but steadily, married women, too, were beginning to leave their homes on a daily basis in order to help make ends meet in the postwar metropolis. Although the wages earned by these women, men, boys, and girls were essential to the survival of their households, we shall see in the following chapter that they were not always enough.

chapter two

A Web of Welfare: The Mixed Social Economy of Postwar Montreal

The wages earned by members of Montreal households were not always reliable or sufficient. Many of the city's families counted, at least on occasion, on additional kinds of support in the immediate postwar years. This was certainly the case for many working-class families, who had long had intermittent recourse to charity and to public welfare measures. As the federal state began to adopt more universal provisions in the 1940s, however, social welfare increasingly became part of the world of middle-class families as well.

In Montreal, as in other Canadian cities, social welfare had historically been largely a private matter, looked after by kin, friends, neighbours, and religious and charitable organizations. The Catholic Church had traditionally assumed the major responsibility for poor and needy French Canadians. By the 1940s, French-Catholic charities tended to be affiliated with the Fédération des œuvres de charité canadiennes-françaises (FOCCF), under lay control, and with the diocesan Conseil des Œuvres. The city's Protestants, Jews, and English-speaking Catholics turned to their own charitable organizations, such as those affiliated with the Montreal Welfare Federation, the Federation of Jewish Philanthropies and the Federation of Catholic Charities. After 1921, private bodies benefited from some state assistance through the Quebec Public Charities Act,[1] which provided small subsidies to indigent citizens under the care of private welfare institutions. The costs of maintaining these clients were split three ways: among the province, the municipality, and the private institution in question.[2] Provincial needy mothers' allowances, established in 1937, also provided small sums of money to widowed and deserted wives, although the eligibility criteria were strict and the selection process somewhat arbitrary.[3] Ottawa had established cost-shared, means-tested, old age pensions in 1927; Quebec began participating in this program in 1936.[4]

By the mid-1940s, the federal government had made significant inroads into the realm of social welfare, legislating unemployment insurance in 1940 and family allowances in 1944 alongside wartime measures such as dependents' allowances and veterans' provisions. The state was thus assuming some of the functions that, in an earlier period, had been assigned to that in-between realm known as 'the social.'[5] But only some: in Montreal, I argue, federal and provincial public welfare measures coexisted with, rather than supplanted, older private forms of social welfare. Those citizens who found the new public provisions inadequate continued to turn to private charity. Private agencies, meanwhile, increasingly found themselves without the material resources to deal with the demands of their clients, and some looked to the state to step in. This was, without question, the 'mixed social economy' that Mariana Valverde has identified as being characteristic of English Canada over the past two centuries.[6] The existence of such a mixed economy highlights the many links between private and public, and underlines the necessity of avoiding a whiggish narrative of the 'rise of the welfare state.' Under Premier Maurice Duplessis, moreover, the provincial arm of the state was notoriously reluctant to increase its responsibility for the poor and the needy.[7] Thus, the executive director of the Montreal Welfare Federation noted in 1945 the 'indispensable role of private charity or welfare work in [this] City and Province giving to [our] Federation a measure of urgency which Chests and Federations do not always have in other communities.'[8] The firm opposition to federal intrusions into social welfare by premiers such as Ontario's George Drew, however, suggests that Quebec was not unique in this regard, and that private agencies would continue to play a role in delivering welfare measures across the country.[9] Charlotte Whitton, executive director of the Canadian Welfare Council, for one, argued at the dawn of the 1940s, 'This whole question of division of responsibility by sound principles between voluntary and public liability is just about the most urgent one that we have to face.'[10]

Private Provisions

Father André-M. Guillemette, o.p., director of the Conseil des Œuvres, observed that Montreal in the early 1940s 'comptait tout près de 200 œuvres ou agences sociales catholiques d'expression française, toutes et chacune nées d'une initiative privée au fur et à mesure qu'un groupe de personnes généreuses découvraient des besoins auxquels aucun service existant ne pouvait répondre, de sorte que la ville était couverte d'œuvres grandes et petites, agences ou organisations, chacune travaillant à sa guise selon l'esprit et quelquefois l'arbitraire des personnes qui s'en étaient constituées responsables.'[11]

Many of these private social agencies were affiliated with the FOCCF, a federation established in 1932 by francophone businessmen and the Montreal archbishopric. In 1935, the FOCCF created the Conseil des Œuvres to coordinate the work of Catholic charities (both religious and lay); in 1943, Montreal Archbishop Joseph Charbonneau designated the Conseil the official diocesan umbrella organization for the city's Catholic, French-language charities.[12] The Société de Saint-Vincent de Paul (SSVP), which had addressed the material needs of the Catholic poor in Montreal since the mid-nineteenth century, was among the Conseil's most important members. Run by Catholic laymen, the SSVP was organized at the parish level and emphasized the importance of conducting home visits. Participants in Montreal's ninety-two SSVP councils, who included such respectable citizens as judges and notaries, met regularly to determine which of their parishioners' needs were legitimate and worthy.[13] The presidents of at least some of these councils were periodically accused of not being particularly sympathetic to those poor families who came to them for assistance; the president of the central council, J.A. Julien, felt compelled to remind them in 1945 'qu'on doit traiter le pauvre avec beaucoup d'égards et de courtoisie.'[14] A women's branch of the SSVP, known as the Services Bénévoles Féminins, existed to train bourgeois women in voluntary work and home visiting.[15] Other organizations affiliated with the Conseil des Œuvres included the Gouttes de lait (well-baby clinics that offered mothers advice and medical assistance); l'Assistance maternelle, which provided new and needy Catholic mothers with a layette, bedding, and medical services; l'Aide aux Vieux Couples; the Action catholique-affiliated Ligue Ouvrière Catholique (LOC); and the LOC's l'Entr'Aide Familiale.[16] Various Catholic orders, including the Sisters of Charity (also known as the Grey Nuns), the Sisters of Providence, and the Sisters of the Miséricorde, operated crèches, orphanages, industrial schools, homes for the elderly, and homes for unwed mothers.[17] By the 1940s, the staff of the Miséricorde maternity home included both religious sisters and lay social workers.[18]

Chief among the FOCCF's social agencies was the Bureau d'assistance sociale aux familles (BASF), formed in 1938: the first family welfare agency, strictly speaking, for the city's francophone population.[19] The BASF's unique position in French-speaking Montreal as a casework agency with lay social workers meant that it was soon seriously overworked and short of funds. Its minimal resources were taxed by the fallout from the Depression and war. During the war, for instance, many of the BASF's scarce resources were devoted to administering and supervising federal dependents' allowances and supplementary aid provided by the federal Dependents' Board of Trustees.[20] The fact that the agency's staff were primarily laypersons complicated its dealings with some of the city's religious social services. One Bureau worker was quoted in 1945 as saying that 'a lot of difficulties in relationship [sic] with other agencies and communities and the Archbishop's Palace would be lessened or would not exist if the head of the agency were a priest. The Bureau was really imposed upon the community and it really has never been accepted as part of it.'[21] Conflict existed, for instance, between the BASF and the Société de Saint-Vincent de Paul. On numerous occasions, the BASF accused the latter of refusing to help poor families or of giving only parsimoniously.[22]

Although clerical and lay social services were said to be roughly equal in number in Montreal by the late 1940s, the Conseil des Œuvres declared that 'les œuvres religieuses accomplissent toutefois la plus grande partie du travail.'[23] Lay social services and social workers depended a great deal upon the cooperation of existing charitable organizations and religious orders.[24] Yet disagreements occasionally arose between religious and lay personnel, between social workers and charity workers, between agency workers and the state, and between the federal and provincial arms of the state.[25] Father Guillemette, Director of the Conseil des Œuvres, was quoted in 1944 as claiming, with regard to long-term cases of need, that 'people in the French Canadian section of the community prefer the Q.P.C.A. [Quebec Public Charities Act] set-up under which a private agency handles the case, thinking of the private agency as more individual and human in its operations.' Father Guillemette felt it necessary to insist to the Board of the Conseil des Œuvres 'that the private agencies in the French community simply could not cope with existing need and ... that there must be a Public Welfare programme to deal with it.'[26] The Conseil des Œuvres criticized the Quebec Public Charities Act (QPCA) in 1946–7 as 'inadéquate' and occasionally 'malfaisante,' and called for more and better-funded family welfare agencies.[27] Despite the fact that they were responsible for the bulk of the city's population, Catholic agencies had few financial resources.[28] The English-language *Gazette* suggested in 1944 that the expenditures of the agencies affiliated with the FOCCF were low 'partly because the French Federation's activities have been less elaborately and comprehensively developed, partly because such a large proportion of the work of member agencies is maintained by voluntary [lay and religious] personnel.'[29]

Organizations devoted to the needs of English-speaking Catholics were affiliated with the city's Federation of Catholic Charities. The Catholic Welfare Bureau was the most prominent of these agencies; it was organized at the parish level and cooperated closely with the SSVP.[30] A Child Welfare Bureau, a Boys' Bureau, and a Family Welfare Association, the latter run by a priest, also existed for the city's Anglo-Catholics.[31] The city's English-speaking Protestants were well served by private social agencies; indeed, the affluence of an important sector of this community meant that they were relatively better provided for than their French-Canadian neighbours.[32] The Montreal Council of Social Agencies (MCSA) was the umbrella organization for approximately sixty non-Catholic organizations, including the Family Welfare Association, the Ladies Benevolent Society, the Society for the Protection of Women and Children, the Old Brewery Mission, and the Protestant Foster Home Centre.[33] The MCSA, and the Montreal Welfare Federation more broadly, were sharply critical of the lack of adequate public welfare in Quebec, at both municipal and provincial levels. As the MCSA noted in 1946, 'The voluntarily financed social agencies in Montreal still bear the burden of maintenance costs for dependent families and children to a far greater degree than in other cities of the Dominion.'[34] The need for social agencies to be 'an ambulance service' prevented them, the MCSA argued, from undertaking 'positive preventive programmes' or 'true remedial treatment,' and from becoming 'a major educational force in social living.'[35] The MCSA saw 'no reason why the City of Montreal should be the one City on the Continent singled out as being unable to operate an adequate Social Welfare Department.'[36] It was ironic, the MCSA observed in 1950, that 'in this Province of Quebec where we hold family life particularly sacred that we are so very reluctant to strengthen and bolster it, right where it needs it, in the heart of the home.'[37] Protestant agencies' criticism of the provincial government was rooted not only in the inadequacy of public welfare in Quebec, but also in their suspicion that Duplessis looked more favourably on the requests of Catholic welfare institutions than on those of social agencies catering to English-speaking Montrealers.[38]

Jewish families in need of assistance looked to organizations affiliated with Montreal's Federation of Jewish Philanthropies, in particular the Jewish Family Services of the Baron de Hirsch Institute (the Jewish Family Welfare Department and the Jewish Child Welfare Bureau). The Baron de Hirsch Institute's Family Welfare Department and Legal Aid Department was, in the 1940s, 'the largest private Jewish family welfare agency in Canada.'[39] Needy families in the community also turned to the Jewish Immigrant Aid Society and the United Jewish Relief Committee. Many Jewish agencies were affiliated with the largely Protestant Montreal Council of Social Agencies.[40] The Jewish Family Welfare Department was frustrated by the lack of a 'public welfare set-up in Montreal,' because this lack meant that most of the agency's time and resources went to 'the providing of financial help to those families who through ill health or death of the breadwinner, are unable to look after their own basic needs.'[41] Likewise, in a discussion of what the city's Protestant and Catholic agencies were doing for the 'employable unemployed' in 1946, the Jewish Family Welfare Department's Case Committee 'felt very definitely that such financial assistance should come from Government funds, and that pressure must be brought on the Government to provide this help.'[42]

In 1949, a Canadian Welfare Council worker reported back to Ottawa on her visit to Montreal's Société d'adoption et de protection de l'enfance (SAPE). The Société's executive director, Father Paul Contant, 'asked *specifically*,' she noted, that the CWC 'make it their job of intepreting [*sic*] to English speaking Canada the child welfare situation in Quebec: its institutional set-up which has grown up of the past tradition, its Catholic set-up, its recent efforts to modernize gradually its methods of work. Comparisons with other provinces should be avoided because they are unfair to every one concerned, he said, and really, because there is no possible basis for comparison.'[43] The perception that Catholic social welfare services were unprofessional – anachronistic, even – was widely shared among Anglo-Protestant observers. Canadian Welfare Council staff, Protestant and Jewish agency workers, and some francophone welfare workers argued that French-Canadian charitable institutions were slow to adopt 'modern' methods of organized social work. They charged that those who undertook good works were untrained, and that the poor, sick and needy were too often institutionalized rather than treated in their homes or communities.[44] Even the city of Montreal, itself frequently criticized for its lack of initiative in social welfare, accused the SSVP of poor administrative practices.[45] Yet, as Father Contant insisted,

Catholic welfare agencies were attempting 'to modernize gradually' their 'methods of work' in these years. His own agency, the SAPE, employed lay social workers.[46] A School of Social Work affiliated with the Université de Montréal opened in 1939; even before then, a number of francophone women had trained at the Montreal School of Social Work, affiliated with McGill.[47] Moreover, many female members of religious orders and male members of the clergy were seeking training in social work. Sister Saint-Jean Vianney, the former director of the Miséricorde's social service, for instance, was sent to Laval University's School of Social Work for training in 1952.[48]

Conversely, nonfrancophone and non-Catholic agencies in the city of Montreal were a long way from being completely 'professionalized.' The Canadian Welfare Council considered the senior staff of Montreal's English-language Catholic Welfare Bureau to be untrained and the Bureau's casework standards to be low.[49] Although the city's Protestant agencies increasingly articulated the importance of staff with some formal training in social work, levels of training varied widely among workers in different Protestant agencies, and sometimes within the same agency.[50] The records of the Baron de Hirsch Institute's Jewish Family Services show us social agencies attempting to professionalize. The Jewish Family Welfare Department, for instance, was anxious to be, and to be seen to be, more than simply a 'relief agency.'[51] It wanted to do more than dispense funds, and was concerned with social-work technique and with enhancing its expertise. Representatives of the department attended conferences for family agencies on the use of psychiatric consultation services and on marriage counselling.[52] The Jewish Child Welfare Bureau was likewise anxious 'to engage well trained and experienced case workers' in the wake of the war, and was eager to keep up with 'the most modern trends in child welfare work.'[53] But the records show clearly that such aims were far from realized in the 1940s. The fact that almost all providers of private welfare in the city were debating the merits of professional training suggests that they were anxious to maintain a role for themselves amid the state's new forays into social security. At the same time, the state itself was increasingly making use of trained social workers: the new federal services of the 1940s, including the National Selective Service, the Dependents Allowance Board, the Dependents Board of Trustees, and the personnel services of the armed forces, all relied on staff with social-work training.[54]

Denominational barriers meant that welfare organizations were sometimes unaware of what other institutions in the city were doing.[55] Sectarian conflict between social services also existed. The MCSA's Non-Catholic Juvenile Court Committee, for instance, found its relationship with 'the French committee' strained, and recorded in its minutes for 18 January 1946: 'Again the need to work harmoniously together was stressed, though the achievement was frought [sic] with many difficulties.'[56] The SSVP worried because some of its parishioners were turning to Protestant agencies for handouts and Christmas baskets, and were buying second-hand clothing at the Salvation Army depot instead of at the SSVP's Grenier du Pauvre.[57] Some of the city's private charitable organizations were anxious for the state to intervene in social welfare, at least in certain capacities.[58] Others, particularly Catholic institutions, were resistant to state intervention, especially that of the federal state.[59] Although the war had in many ways facilitated the development of a federally directed welfare state, provincial resentment of the wartime expansion of Ottawa's reach also made the building of this welfare state more difficult. Yet the reluctance of some francophone Quebecers to see the state intervene in family life was not just a case of anti-Ottawa sentiment: it was also rooted in ideas about who was best suited to help the poor and the needy, and about the importance, for Catholics, of performing good works.[60] Some SSVP volunteers, for instance, were disinclined to see the SSVP register with the provincial government as an institution eligible to receive QPCA funds, even though this would have considerably improved its precarious finances and helped its parishioners.[61]

Public Provisions

By the mid-1940s, the city of Montreal had a Social Welfare Department and Quebec had its provincial Department of Social Welfare and Youth.[62] Historians agree, however, that the initiative in public welfare came from Ottawa in the immediate postwar years.[63] In this section, I want to look briefly at two new federal measures – veterans' benefits and family allowances – in order to demonstrate the blending of private and public welfare that took place in the 1940s, and the ways in which private social agencies, the state, and recipients of social welfare negotiated private and public assistance. A coexistence of private and public provisions was not new in this period,[64] but the particular mix was new. The state's involvement in welfare was more visible than before, and recipients were especially conscious of new state intervention. Moreover, they developed a sense of entitlement to state welfare utterly unlike their sentiments toward private charity.[65] This sense of entitlement took different forms:

veterans' benefits and family allowances, as we will see, spoke to two distinct visions of citizenship in the 1940s. And yet these new public welfare measures did not entirely replace 'the private'; the private and the public continued to coexist.

Almost immediately after the Canadian government declared war in September 1939, it began planning measures for returned soldiers. The Cabinet Committee on Demobilization and Re-establishment was established by Order-in-Council in December 1939. The federal Advisory Committee on Reconstruction, headed by McGill University's Cyril James, was formed in March 1941. The Department of Pensions and National Health turned its veteran-related matters over to the newly created Department of Veterans' Affairs (DVA) in 1944; a Parliamentary Commission on Veterans' Affairs began sitting shortly thereafter. And as one First World War veteran noted in 1943, there was scarcely a department within the federal government that did not deal in some way with the rehabilitation of veterans. Furthermore, many of Canada's senators and elected members of Parliament were themselves Great War veterans with a particular interest in the well-being of discharged soldiers.[66] Veterans' benefits were thus rooted in war, but they were also integral to the federal welfare state emerging in the 1940s. They will be explored in depth in Chapter 3 for what they meant for gender and family during and immediately after the Second World War; in this chapter, I am interested in what they can tell us about the meeting of private and public welfare measures in Quebec in the 1940s, and in their implications for expanding senses of entitlement and citizenship.

Despite the fanfare that greeted returning war heroes, veterans were seen to be a potentially problematic group. Governments and private organizations were wary of antagonizing old soldiers. Veterans deserved government benefits, of course, as a reward for their contribution to the nation's safety. But they were also a force to be satisfied in order to prevent political unrest. The Canadian state had learned from the experience of the First World War and the nationwide labour protests of 1919 that unhappy veterans posed a threat to order.[67] One DVA employee, for instance, warned in 1943 that Montreal's 'scandalous' housing situation might lead to 'a sort of "POPULAR FRONT" radicalism on one side, and very marked MARXIST movements on the other.'[68] Rehabilitation benefits (considerably more generous than those allowed First World War veterans) were thus a means of thanking but also of appeasing returned soldiers.[69] In addition, they were a way of assisting military recruitment and of maintaining the morale of those still enlisted. Men would be more likely to volunteer and would make better soldiers, it was assumed, if they could rest assured that they would be provided for, once their services were no longer required. As one federal recruiting pamphlet promised francophones, 'Il n'y a pas lieu de vous inquiéter de l'après-guerre.'[70]

The state, then, willingly undertook the task of transforming the 'fighting man' into the 'peacetime citizen.'[71] Most of the initiative came from the Dominion government because veterans, like soldiers, were a federal responsibility. The 1944 Veterans Charter made provision for medical treatment, pensions, gratuities, transportation home, clothing allowances, life insurance, land purchases and, finally, a choice of university allowances, vocational training, or rehabilitation credits with which to purchase and furnish a home or establish a business. The centrepiece of rehabilitation, however, from the perspective of both federal officials and returned soldiers, was employment.[72] After August 1942, veterans could rely on the Reinstatement in Civil Employment Order, which promised them their old civilian jobs back, with seniority rights.[73] The government's dilemma was how to award veterans that to which they were entitled without undermining their sense of initiative and assuming them as permanent wards. As one civil servant noted pointedly, the Post Discharge Re-Establishment Order was not to 'degenerate into a dole or relief measure'; it was 'not the intention of the Government to subsidize idleness.'[74] This challenge was similar to that facing the state in its administration of other new welfare-state measures such as unemployment insurance. Although American scholar Theda Skocpol has questioned the appropriateness of grouping veterans' allowances – allocated to a specific group of 'morally worthy' people regardless of socioeconomic need – with social welfare measures, the benefits paid to Second World War veterans ought to be seen as part of Canada's emerging welfare state.[75] They were implemented at a particular moment in time, when Keynesian economic policies had considerable appeal in Ottawa, when federal coffers were full, and when the memory of the Great Depression was acute. Like family allowances, established in 1944, they were intended to maintain purchasing power in what was expected to be a difficult period of economic transition and reconstruction.[76] And yet they drew on older visions of citizenship, in that (like servicemen's assigned pay and dependents' allowances) it was necessary to prove loyalty to Canada through military service in order to receive them.

Veterans themselves clearly felt entitled to government benefits. This stemmed from their sense of their contribution to military victory, but also from their memory of post–First World War benefits and their knowledge of what other countries were doing for veterans. The Jeunesse Ouvrière Catholique noted relatively early in the war that while soldiers cherished their independence and did not want to be the objects of private charity, they were counting on help from the government in their postwar reestablishment. Indeed, the JOC argued, soldiers were sceptical of political leaders' promises and needed to be convinced of the government's sincerity. In 1945, one Montreal social and political reformer claimed that Canadian soldiers overseas were voting Liberal in the federal election because of their 'extreme approval' of the 'plans being made for their re-establishment in civilian life.' And in 1946, a Jewish family agency observed that veterans were accepting government grants without any sense of humiliation because they 'felt that they paid for this assistance by risking their lives.'[77]

Such was veterans' sense of entitlement to government benefits that they (and their advocates) were not in the least hesitant to complain when they found the amounts paid to be insufficient. In 1943, Montreal's Veterans' Welfare Officer noted that soldiers' discharge pay was not enough to carry them through until they had secured a job and received their first paycheque. As a consequence, veterans were resorting to the Poppy Day Fund for temporary help – a practice, the DVA worried, that would initiate the 'habit of receiving assistance' in veterans' families.[78] The Montreal Soldiers' Wives League expressed in February 1944 the 'widespread feeling' that the $65 clothing allowance 'was not sufficient for men discharged in winter time.'[79] Student-veterans at the Université de Montréal and McGill demanded an increase in their monthly allowances in 1946 and 1947. The government's establishment of a supplementary grants system in 1947 spoke to the real need of some veterans; the high cost-of-living of the immediate postwar years spurred an increase in pension rates for veterans and soldiers' widows by the end of 1947.[80] The Local Council of Women commended the Departments of National Defence and Veterans' Affairs in 1948 for establishing a benevolent fund of $9 million for 'needy veterans in receipt of pensions.'[81]

That some veterans were not able to make ends meet on government benefits or in an undeniably improved labour market serves as a useful check on the notion of immediate and widespread postwar prosperity. Veterans who found that discharge benefits, 'veteran preference' policies, and a general consensus that returned soldiers deserved a break were not enough to ensure their postwar well-being often turned to Montreal's private family and welfare agencies. Many perceived help from private agencies, unlike government benefits, to be charity.[82] Memories of piecemeal relief and means tests during the Depression explain some of the distaste felt by veterans for this private assistance. Nonetheless, at a moment when the state was just beginning to extend its tentacles into matters of social welfare, and in a place where federal measures such as family allowances were often administered by local, private, denominational agencies, such agencies were a logical source of assistance in times of need.

The DVA appears to have fully anticipated that its assistance would be supplemented by private agencies. It routinely referred veterans to private bodies when their situation required extra care, funds, or time.[83] Thus agencies and voluntary organizations such as the Family Welfare Department of the Baron de Hirsch Institute, the Jewish Vocational Service, organizations affiliated with the Conseil des Œuvres, Montreal's Citizens' Rehabilitation Committee and the welfare committees of regimental auxiliaries habitually undertook to help veterans in need of advice or material assistance.[84] Private bodies sometimes threw veterans back to the state, as when Montreal's Local Council of Women referred 'begging letters' from veterans to the DVA or when the Société de Saint-Vincent de Paul refused aid to a veteran's family living in Wartime Housing, arguing that the family was the responsibility of the (federal) government.[85] Conversely, private agencies, such as those affiliated with Montreal's Conseil des Œuvres, occasionally resented the federal government's interference in their veteran-clients' cases.[86]

Family allowances, established in 1944, targeted a broader cross-section of citizens. Universal in nature, allocated regardless of income or of 'moral worth,' and paid in cash, not in kind, family allowances assumed that parents were legitimately entitled to a regular supplement to their wages.[87] As we will see in Chapter 4, Catholic workers' organizations had lobbied the Quebec government for family allowances for years on the grounds that men's salaries were inadequate to support large families.[88] Once secured, Quebec women's groups campaigned to have federal family allowance cheques sent to mothers, as they were in every other province.[89] The fact that this campaign was successful was an acknowledgment of women's role in managing family budgets. Yet their financial authority was not uncontested. La Presse's advice columnist, Colette, received at least two letters from wives whose husbands were trying to expropriate their family allowance cheques, one husband arguing that the cheque was rightfully his because deductions were made from his salary for income taxes and social programs. These women's letters show clearly that they regarded the family allowance cheques as their own money, to be spent for the good of the family.[90] Women used their family allowances for milk for babies and children, extra and better food, clothing, children's pocket money, laundry bills, household equipment, medical care, and dental care.[91] Families and social welfare agencies reported that the benefits of the family allowance program were healthier and better-clothed children, increased school attendance, fewer children being taken into institutional or foster care, and in some cases, children being removed from institutions and reunited with their parents. Social workers and civil servants also anticipated that the greater financial security provided by allowances would mean less physical neglect of children and fewer marital difficulties.[92]

Although most observers claimed that family allowances had raised the standard of living of ordinary Montreal families, others argued that they had simply allowed it to keep pace with the rising cost-of-living in the immediate postwar period.[93] There is no doubt that state welfare payments and private agency allowances often fell considerably short of the increased cost-of-living in the late 1940s. The rates established by the QPCA and the provincial needy mothers' allowances were notoriously inadequate.[94] Families, then, made do by combining sources of state assistance. The universal nature of the family allowance program added stability to the lives of those who had been dependent on social welfare provisions with strict eligibility requirements. Long-standing recipients of needy mothers' allowances, for instance, now added family allowances to the household budget.[95] Families newly able to draw unemployment insurance could also count on their family allowance cheques each month. But in this era of a still-nascent welfare state, private assistance persisted. Families supplemented inadequate government cheques with aid from private agencies. As the Montreal Council of Social Agencies noted in 1949, a mother could not raise three children in Montreal on the $37 per month she received from needy mothers' assistance. Even when this was supplemented by family allowances to $54 per month, the council argued, she could not 'keep herself and three children properly fed, clothed and healthy.'[96] Social workers, Catholic organizations, and government bureaucrats debated what to do with families who drew on more than one private agency, more than one government department, or both private and public assistance, in this era of considerable flux in Quebec social welfare.[97] The SSVP, for example, discovered a family drawing on three different sources of private aid in February 1946: the SSVP, the Bureau d'assistance sociale aux familles, and the Family Welfare Association.[98] Social welfare organizations worked out ways of incorporating family allowances into agency and family budgets, and of collecting allowances for children under their care.[99] A survey of fourteen private family agencies across the country in 1946 found that most felt 'public agencies should have the responsibility to do case work with families who were misusing the funds, rather than the private agencies.'[100] At the same time, private agencies discovered that the development of public welfare measures such as family allowances made it more difficult for them to raise money through community fund-raising drives.[101] The SSVP defended itself against accusations that it was old-fashioned or obsolete by pointing to its importance for recipients of the new public welfare measures; the SSVP was frequently asked to help its parishioners register for the new benefits by filling out forms and notarizing documents.[102] The point here is that the new, much-heralded public welfare measures did not sweep 'the private' away before them. There were points of resistance to the expanding public in the 1940s, and the private and the public continued to coexist.

The provision of childcare in Montreal serves as a final illustration of the mixed private-public economy of family welfare in the late 1940s. The lack of comprehensive childcare services in the city speaks to the kind of family desired by most postwar commentators: one with 'la mère au foyer.' Wartime critics were given to loud laments that negligent mothers (particularly the wives of servicemen) were running off to work in factories, abandoning their children to the hazards of the street and the dubious hands of barely older siblings. Such lax supervision, they claimed, was resulting in skyrocketing juvenile delinquency rates.[103] Concerns that children be better supervised in a peacetime nation underlay the occasional call for the continuation of government-run wartime day nurseries after the end of hostilities. Six Dominion-provincial wartime day nurseries had been established in Montreal. Located on Coursol, Willibrord, Grand Trunk, Jeanne Mance, Delisle, and Ontario East Streets, the nurseries targeted mothers employed in essential war industries. In August 1943, enrolments ranged from twenty-five children at the Jeanne Mance daycare to sixty-two children at the daycare on Willibrord; the range of enrolments was roughly the same a year-and-a-half later.[104] Observers agreed that the wartime day nursery project enjoyed less success in Montreal than in Ontario. There were far fewer daycare spaces in Quebec than in Ontario (185 compared with 1,085 in July 1945), and yet the Ontario spaces were more rapidly and easily filled.[105] Administrators claimed that French-Canadian parents were resistant to the idea of placing their children in the government-run daycares because of unfamiliarity with daycares generally, because of the bad press given to Montreal's privately run nurseries, and because of a wariness of state involvement in childcare. Francophone parents tended to regard the state-run daycares, one observer noted, as the 'government nurser[ies]' and not 'our nurser[ies].'[106] This despite the fact that Day Nursery No. 5, located on Delisle Street, was staffed by nuns: a blend of state and private administration familiar to Montreal parents in the 1940s.[107] Enrolment was lowest at Day Nursery No. 6, in the largely francophone east-end district of Maisonneuve and near the Cherrier munitions plant. This nursery closed ten months earlier than the other five, on 31 December 1944, because of consistently poor attendance.[108] It was anticipated that the nursery in Montreal's Hertzl Institute, catering largely to Jewish industrial workers, would be more successful.[109] Those parents who did try out the nurseries seemed pleased with them.[110] Some requested that they be allowed to leave their children there on Saturdays as well as on weekdays.[111] Many of the children enrolled in the nurseries had mothers who were not working in the essential war industries for which the daycares had been designed, demonstrating a broader need.[112]

The closing of the government day nurseries in October 1945 was met with dismay by the small minority of parents who had used them. Montreal mothers and their supporters dispatched petitions to various levels of government requesting that the nurseries remain open. They argued that the nurseries had provided children with reliable care and a good education, had improved their health, and had saved them from the perils of juvenile delinquency. Without the nurseries, mothers claimed, they would have had to leave their children in other institutions (orphanages, for instance) or on the street. Many mothers, the petitions noted, would have to continue working in the postwar period due to the loss of their husbands, their husbands' inadequate wages, or the high cost-of-living. Keeping the daycares open, the mothers pleaded, 'would be a great help in enabling us to get our home life back to a stable basis.'[113] Committees were formed to lobby for the re-opening of government daycares, and local organizations recommended their establishment 'as a permanent peace measure.'[114]

Such calls, however, were relatively isolated. This was because of the common assumption that mothers would return home when the war ended, and it was because many spokespersons for Quebec continued to uphold the 'private' against a federal 'public.' Provincial submissions to the Canadian Youth Commission in 1945 claimed that French-Canadian mothers did not like daycares, had not used them during the war, and would certainly not use them in peacetime, when they returned to their homes.[115] Wartime commentators remarked that francophone mothers felt more comfortable leaving children with relatives or neighbours than with strangers.[116] In the wake of the war, Montreal mothers continued to turn to kin and community for childcare; complaints that working parents frequently left their children 'to provide for themselves' also persisted in the postwar period.[117] The choice of family and friends as providers of childcare was due partly to tradition and preference, but was no doubt also shaped by a lack of reliable and affordable alternatives in the postwar period.[118]

After the 1945 closure of the government-administered wartime day nurseries, there remained in Montreal a network of private day nurseries run by social agencies, religious communities, and stay-at-home mothers in search of extra income.[119] The Montreal Day Nursery, which provided for both pre–school- and school-age children, served 158 families in 1945 and 162 families the following year. Parents used the nursery because both husband and wife were working outside the home, because the father was absent from the home or unemployed, because a parent was ill or because housing was inadequate.[120] Various religious orders also administered nurseries for pre–school- and young school-age children. The Garderie Ste-Anne, in Griffintown, and the Garderie St-Enfant-Jésus, for instance, took in Catholic children (French-Canadian and Irish-Canadian) on a daily basis, while the Asile pour jeunes enfants, a private kindergarten, occasionally took in pre–school-age children whose parents were seeking daycare. Fees ranged from fifteen cents a day to fifty cents per week per child; the Garderie St-Enfant-Jésus frequently accepted children for free. Some daycares, such as the Garderie Ste-Anne, took no more than thirty-five children at a time; the Asile pour jeunes enfants, in contrast, took up to two hundred children at once. Children were provided with lunch, sometimes with snacks, and occasionally with training in cleanliness and proper behaviour. Their mothers tended to work in factories, as charwomen, or as office workers, or were women at home who were pregnant or overworked and in need of a break from their children.[121] Finally, some private individuals ran nurseries in their homes for the children of neighbours or for the sons and daughters of strangers. The fact that such informal nurseries flourished in the city's crowded neighbourhoods indicates clearly that they served the needs of many Montreal parents. Yet they were also subject to bad press, accused of not providing children with a safe, clean, or healthy environment.[122]

Parents used a variety of other institutions as babysitting services: after-school programs, summer camps, foster homes, and even longer-term institutions such as crèches and orphanages. After-school programs gained popularity during the war, as more mothers took on paid work. In 1942, the Commission des écoles catholiques de Montréal resolved to provide space in schools for noon meals and after-school care for 'latch-key' children. Two years later, the Montreal Parks and Playgrounds Association established an After-School Programme in Rosemount for 'the children of mothers working in war industries.' The Parks and Playgrounds Association described the program as 'a very successful experiment': fifty children aged five to thirteen registered, and each session saw an average of thirty children in attendance.[123] During the summer, camps took on the functions of schools and daycares, providing working parents with a supervised environment in which to leave their children. The Montreal Council of Social Agencies noted in 1944 that 'with the father in the Forces or the mother in industry, camps have had to assume some of the functions of a summer nursery.'[124] This function may well have continued after the war's end, and some mothers appeared appreciative of the camps' services.[125]

Sometimes parents chose longer-term options than after-school programs and summer camps. Convents, for example, boarded Catholic children.[126] Some working mothers in Montreal's Jewish community resorted to foster-care by the day or for longer periods of time.[127] Classified advertisements in *La Presse* reveal an exchange of children, as parents sought placements 'en pension' for their sons and daughters, while other families expressed their willingness to provide children with bed and board.[128] The city's Children's Aid Society reported in 1951 the occasional temporary placement of children because of their mothers' need to take on paid employment.[129] And occasionally, unmarried mothers entrusted their infants to religious crèches, paying a monthly fee and then taking them back once they were too old to remain in the crèche.[130] Summerhill House, meanwhile, sometimes took in non-Catholic girls whose mothers needed to work for pay and whose fathers were unavailable or unable to look after their daughters.[131]

What we see in this chapter, then, is a large and diverse industrialized city, with a complicated array of provisions for families in need. Private provisions varied according to religion and language, and were distributed by both religious and lay workers. Public welfare was supplied, to varying degrees, by the federal, provincial, and municipal governments. Prior to the Second World War, the Quebec government had, like the governments of most other Canadian provinces, begun to provide means-tested mothers' allowances and old age pensions. Quebec began participating in the federal-provincial pension scheme, however, a decade after the other provinces; its needy mothers' allowances were established fifteen to twenty years later than those of most other provinces. On the surface, the QPCA arrangement appeared unique to Quebec. It helped to alleviate need while respecting the long-standing institutional presence of the Catholic Church in the province (and taking advantage of its resources – in particular, its real estate and the unpaid labour of female members of religious communities). Yet recent studies emphasize the mixed public-private economies of the English-speaking provinces, calling into question the distinctiveness of the QPCA.[132] Moreover, despite a lag in the delivery of some state welfare programs, the provincial government had begun to incur significant welfare costs by the beginning of the Second World War.[133] And at least some of Quebec's civil servants were caught up in the 1940s spirit of welfare-state building: J.R. Forest, president of Quebec's Old Age Pension Commission, for instance, wrote to Ottawa in March 1943 requesting a copy of Leonard Marsh's report on social security.[134]

The 1949 pension debate gives us some idea of the new purchase of public welfare in the wake of the war. In 1947, the rates for federal-provincial means-tested pensions had been increased and eligibility had been broadened.[135] In 1949, rates for recipients of old age and blind pensions were once again increased, this time from thirty dollars to forty dollars per month. In May 1949, Paul Sauvé, Quebec's minister of social welfare and youth, sent a letter to all pension recipients in Quebec, claiming, on behalf of Duplessis and the Union Nationale, full responsibility for the recent increase. An irate Paul Martin, federal minister of national health and welfare, responded with a letter of his own a month later, stating that 'the Parliament of Canada passed the law providing for the increase from $30 to $40' and reminding Quebec pensioners of the fact that Ottawa paid 75 per cent of the pension: 'In other words, $3 out of every $4 of your pension is paid by the Federal Government.' Sauvé followed up within days with a third letter, denouncing what he called Martin's 'political propaganda.' Both pensions for the elderly and pensions for the blind, he reminded recipients of the letter, had been implemented in Quebec in the 1930s under Duplessis's UN government.

The recent increase, he noted rather disingenuously, had been adopted following an order-in-council signed by Duplessis.[136] The *Montreal Gazette* headlined its analysis of the issue 'Pensioners Confused by Propaganda.' The *Windsor Daily Star*, meanwhile (published in Paul Martin's constituency), denounced Sauvé's claim as a 'Cheap Trick.'[137] What this episode shows us is a historical moment markedly different from that of the Depression a decade earlier, when all three levels of government had rushed to deny, rather than assert, their responsibility for social welfare.

Duplessis himself was not a public welfare pioneer, and his lack of initiative in this regard created an administrative vacuum that allowed Ottawa to move in with its postwar, nation-building social programs. Bernard Vigod and Lucia Ferretti are perhaps right to suggest that the *grande noirceur* was an aberration – a departure from the earlier twentieth-century history of Quebec – rather than simply the culmination of a long record of what Michel Brunet called, in 1953, 'anti-étatisme.'[138] What we see in Montreal in the 1940s is not 'anti-étatisme,' but a continued mixed private-public economy. We see tensions between Ottawa and Quebec City over what the particular mix ought to be, and we see them vying to claim credit for ensuring the well-being of their citizens.[139]

Members of Montreal families, then (working-class and increasingly middle-class as well), were part of a postwar web of private and public welfare. Cheques sent out from Ottawa and Quebec City established relationships between the state and citizens. This web was woven, moreover, by new and more frequent conversations and correspondence among the men and women who worked in welfare in the postwar years: federal and provincial civil servants, professional social workers, the volunteers and paid staff of charitable associations, and the members of religious communities.[140]

'Pour que bientôt il me revienne': Sustaining Soldiers, Veterans, and Their Families

The narratives of homecoming told in Canada during the last years of war and the first months of peace included many of the elements of a literary romance. Like a romance, these war stories had young, valiant heroes and loyal, virtuous heroines who had suffered through a period of trial and tribulation. As in a romance, these heroes and heroines had vanquished evil and been vindicated by victory. These narratives of reunion, like romances, ended with the welcoming embrace between the returning hero and the girl he'd left behind.[1] And, like romances, these stories had great popular appeal. 'Integrating' myths, aimed at all classes and cultures, they were told in fiction and film, in song, in advertisements, and in magazine articles. They were also told in photographs: a couple embracing at a train station, or children on the knee of a father in uniform.[2]

Historians have also told this tale. V-E Day and V-J Day meant the return of the armed forces. North America settled down into domesticity, the suburbs, and relative affluence. And, one is left to assume, everyone lived happily ever after. Although more recent historical literature has challenged assumptions of postwar prosperity, suburban homogeneity, and contented nuclear families, and has begun to paint a more complex picture of 'the Fifties,'[3] historians of Canada have remained largely silent about the period of transition in family life that was the late 1940s.

The metaphor of reunion resonated even with those who did not themselves have loved ones overseas. Indeed, governments and communities, as well as individuals and families, participated in the romance with Canadian veterans. But the moment of reunion, while it may have been the ending to one story, was the beginning of another. Veterans found that returning home was often difficult, and that readjusting to family life and civilian status required considerable work. The sense of entitlement to a fair deal promoted by the Dominion government resonated with veterans' own feelings of sacrifice and the necessity of making up for lost time. Veterans were told that they were special kinds of citizens, deserving of special treatment. Upon their return, however, they discovered that not all members of their communities felt indebted to them. The warm reception extended by some civilians contrasted with the indifference and even hostility exhibited by others. Moreover, veterans' sense of entitlement was not always well received by their families. Soldiers' wives and parents had experienced their own wartime difficulties, and were not necessarily willing to subordinate their own interests to those of returning heroes. The gap between expectations and experience, aggravated by the fact that war had sometimes soured relationships, was harder to bear given the rhetorical force of the reunion narrative for soldiers and their families.

In this chapter, I examine the ways in which the war affected relationships between Montreal's enlisted men and their families – in particular, their wives and their mothers. I explore the construction and experiences of these wives and mothers as soldiers' dependents. I end by considering the various measures established in order to reintegrate veterans into Montreal society. This chapter argues that the wartime experiences of soldiers and their dependents imbued them with a sense of entitlement, both as citizens and as members of families. The postwar conceptions of citizenship espoused by veterans and their dependents, I suggest, grew out of their negotiation of federal wartime allowances and the gendered assumptions built into dependents' allowances and the Veterans Charter.

Soldiers, Wives, and Mothers

Soldiers seldom left the armed forces unscarred. Suffering from wounds, illness, 'battle exhaustion,' or anxiety about the future, they looked, with their governments and their communities, to the family as an agent of postwar healing. Women, as wives, girlfriends, or mothers, were to ensure the 'mental reestablishment of soldiers.'[4] Men posted overseas, single and married, had had plenty of time in which to romanticize ideas of marriage and parenthood. Veterans were returning to start their own homes, while girls and women were assumed to be eagerly anticipating weddings and children now that the boys were back. As one Quebec sergeant told his chaplain in September 1944, 'J'ai bonne [*sic*] espoir que tout cela sera fini bientôt et que je pourrai enfin reprendre la vie tranquille que je menais avec ma chère épouse avant la guerre.'[5]

Yet social service agencies, in Montreal and across Canada, discovered to their dismay that the soldiers' return produced 'intimate and complex' domestic problems.[6] Veterans suffering from 'shattered nerves' found it difficult to readjust to family life.[7] The fact that so many of these unions were 'mariages éclairs' – whirlwind weddings that had taken place immediately before enlistment, during wartime leaves, or in the first flush of homecoming – was part of the problem. The explosion of marriages after September 1939 has been attributed by one historian of Britain to a 'last dance' mentality that saw sexual tension heightened by the excitement of war and a reckless and romantic attitude in the face of an unknown future.[8] In Canada, other factors no doubt forced the formalization of relationships that might otherwise have remained unsolemnized: hopes of avoiding conscription, for instance, or the opportunity to allocate and receive dependents' allowances. The improved economy, moreover, meant that couples who had courted in the depths of the Depression could finally afford to establish their own households. In these cases, the usual strains of new relationships were exacerbated by problems of inadequate housing, lodging with in-laws, and the attendant lack of privacy. Yet even long-established relationships suffered from the strains of separation. Many husbands found wives changed by the time apart: imbued with a new sense of independence and self-sufficiency.[9] Other wives had suffered from loneliness and a lack of leisure activity while their husbands were away. Both parties had experienced serious problems of morale. Women were stretched thin by years of managing households and children alone, men by long periods of time away from home and family.[10]

Separation by time and distance meant that a great deal of weight had been placed on letters that crossed the Atlantic, with consequent problems of miscommunication. Wives and mothers worried about a lack of news from husbands and sons in action.[11] Military officials noted that the only thing as bad for soldiers' morale as discouraging news from home was no news from home. Women were encouraged to write frequently to their companions, to eschew complaints and to fill letters with good news.[12] Not all couples wrote regularly to one another, however. Even among frequent correspondents, there was room for misinterpretation and for fretting over silences and omissions. The most potent source of worry had to do with infidelity. Wives and girlfriends worried about soldiers' references to women met overseas.[13] Friends and relatives took it upon themselves to keep soldiers and their partners informed of any misbehaviour, often without much evidence. As one young sergeant overseas wrote to his Montreal priest in June 1944, 'J'ai été les plus sincères avec R— et il me semble avoir fait tous les sacrifices pour me la garder, on est si loin l'un de l'autre! Je ne comprends pas encore qui a bien pu lui mettre dans la tête que j'étais attaché de quelque façon que ce soit à une autre fille. *C'est parfaitement faux* et vous pouvez me croire.'[14] The morale of servicemen and of their dependents was adversely affected, the Artillery Branch of the Montreal Soldiers' Wives League noted, by 'anonymous letters containing malicious information.'[15]

Tales of wartime infidelity were common currency in 1940s Canada. Military Lotharios and ungrateful women who refused to wait for soldier-sweethearts had become stock characters in public discourse.[16] The enforced mobility of married men and the increased visibility of women living alone fuelled the narratives of unfaithfulness. Determining how often rumours of infidelity were founded was difficult enough then; any attempt by the historian to quantify infidelity in the past is foolhardy. It is likely that war, through spousal separation, increased geographic mobility, and new work opportunities for women (which provided a measure of independence as well as new possibilities for romantic partners), did hasten the breakdown of some relationships. War also seems to have provided an escape from those relationships that were already rocky: there is a great deal of evidence to indicate that unhappy home lives were one spur to military enlistment.[17] Although it is probably safe to assume that anxiety about infidelity was more common than actual instances of adultery, those instances that did come to light were enough to fuel a larger discourse of disloyalty.[18]

A public concern about infidelity was paralleled by policy-makers' more private negotiation of its consequences. The personal lives of soldiers were open to scrutiny in a way that those of most civilians were not. Candidates for military enlistment submitted their health, finances, and family relationships to examination by the various military bureaucracies; they were thoroughly 'administered' citizens.[19] At the same time, they had access to sources of state assistance that many civilians did not. Activities that had always taken place, then, came to the attention of state and private agencies more frequently during the war. The application process for dependents' allowances, in particular, uncovered 'irregular' relationships such as common-law marriages, adulterous unions, and illegitimate children.[20] Social service agencies in Montreal and elsewhere, long used to dealing with the problems of unmarried mothers, now discovered the wives of soldiers giving birth to the children of men other than their husbands.[21] Frequently, women in such a situation attempted to place their children for adoption, often before their husbands returned or learned of the situation. Other wives came to the attention of family agencies because they were deliberately neglecting their illegitimate children out of 'guilt and anxiety over the husband's re-action.'[22] Wives' infidelity was attributed to loneliness, to 'disreputable' leisure pursuits such as frequenting dance halls and beer parlours, and to retaliation for their husbands' own extramarital encounters overseas.[23]

The Dependents' Allowance Board (DAB) frequently suspended allowances to wives on evidence of their sexual infidelity. It was, the board's chairman argued, 'a general practice in welfare legislation to demand fidelity on the part of the wife in receipt of public funds.'[24] Even questionable leisure activities, such as wives entertaining men in their homes, were cause for the DAB to assign the family to the supervision of a social agency. Part of the concern over disloyal and 'immoral' wives was that they were perceived to be abdicating their 'domestic responsibility.'[25] The children of adulterous wives were sometimes removed to the care of relatives or institutions, particularly when wives were living with their new male companions.[26] If the wife promised to mend her ways, her children were allowed to remain in the home, and their dependents' allowances were increased in order to compensate for the loss of their mother's allowance.[27]

The unfaithfulness of soldiers and their partners inspired considerable comment. Gossip played an important role in the public and private negotiation of disloyalty. In addition to affecting the relationships in question, gossip frequently had a tangible effect on wives' and children's material well-being. The DAB relied heavily on rumours and innuendo to pinpoint unfaithful husbands and especially wives. Although complaints to the DAB often came from husbands themselves, neighbours and in-laws also took it upon themselves to inform the board of sexual disloyalty.[28] The board insisted that the allowances of unfaithful wives whose soldier-husbands were overseas were not suspended without prior investigation. In the case of wives whose husbands were posted in Canada, however, a husband's request was sufficient to have his wife's allowance suspended until allegations of her infidelity were disproven.[29] Moreover, private citizens used the dependents' allowance system as a means of condemning disloyalty. One Montreal woman whose husband was having an affair with the wife of a soldier, for instance, reported this 'other woman' to the DAB in order to have her dependents' allowance cut off.[30] Such tattling reflected personal grudges, but also pointed to the larger question of who was perceived to be entitled to state support. For the public, as for the DAB, the criterion for receiving military allowances was clearly loyalty: men's loyalty to their country, and women's loyalty to the men who were loyal to their country. As Nora Lea of the Canadian Welfare Council emphasized, the unfaithful wife who was not remorseful had 'forfeited her right to consideration as the soldier's wife.'[31]

Yet gossip concerning sexual infidelity occasioned a certain backlash. The DAB was criticized by representatives of some family agencies on a number of grounds, one of which was its reliance on gossip as sufficient evidence for withholding allowances.[32] When it did undertake to investigate claims of immorality and infidelity, these agencies charged, the DAB and affiliated public bodies used 'Gestapo' and 'bullying' techniques. Montreal agencies complained 'that information secured in this way was not treated as confidential and that before the investigation was completed a large sized scandal was public property in the neighbourhood.'[33] A family agency elsewhere in Canada likewise accused the Department of Pensions and National Health of taking 'a murky satisfaction in the sexual delinquencies of the soldiers' wives.'[34] Furthermore, critics noted, the suspension of allowances harmed the soldier's children as much as his wife by decreasing the family's income.[35] Married women pregnant with 'illegitimate' children, moreover, were avoiding seeking medical care for fear that their allowances would be suspended.[36] Certain Montreal welfare agencies were accused of keeping wives' adultery a secret from the DAB so that allowances would not be withheld.[37] Others applied to the board for the reinstatement of wives' allowances where they thought it warranted.[38]

Clearly, the reaction to women's infidelity was not monolithic. A concern for the morale of soldiers overseas, and a desire to preserve family units for the postwar period, meant that certain social agencies were willing to turn a blind eye, or at least a forgiving one, to sexual indiscretions. Across Canada, certain family agencies tried to prevent official reports from going to husbands overseas, particularly when wives appeared repentant. As one female worker from the Kitchener Children's Aid Society explained, 'Not that we wish to excuse them whatsoever, but we feel too, that if the matter could be kept quiet, we might be able to keep the family together for the sake of the husband who is Overseas.'[39] Many social workers, including some employed by public bodies, agreed that 'a definite family break could be avoided' if husbands were not informed of wives' illegitimate children until the couple had a chance 'to meet and talk things over.'[40] At the very least, family agencies pleaded, wives should be given the opportunity to tell their husbands themselves rather than have them receive the news from the DAB.[41]

The DAB also professed concern for the soldier's morale, but it took a different tack. Wives would 'have greater peace of mind' if they confessed all, the board argued, but regardless, husbands ought to be informed of wives' illegitimate children as soon as possible. As R.O.G. Bennett, chairman, explained, 'Careful as one tries to be in covering up the situation, the chances are the man will get word at some future time and distressing as the news will be to him now, it is thought by the Board that it is better for him to know when he has time to think over things while away rather than to return home and find out later. It is the attitude of the Board that to be fair to the soldier overseas, he should be informed how things are going at home.'[42]

The differing attitudes of the DAB and the private family agencies represented, in part, the distinction between those who formulated policy and those faced with implementing it. But there were other reasons for the contrasting approaches. Veterans of the First World War often filled key positions in federal departments such as the DAB and the Department of Veterans' Affairs.[43] The 'clients' of the DAB were members of the armed forces; in a sense, the board was standing in for the absent husband and father.[44] Social agencies were concerned with the needs of various family members, and there is considerable evidence that agency workers felt torn between their commitment to client confidentiality and their responsibility to inform the board of wives 'misbehaving' while in receipt of allowances.[45] Local agencies had roots in their communities that predated the war, and intended to continue serving their clients once peace was secured. Federal bodies such as the Dependents' Allowance Board and the Dependents' Board of Trustees (DBT), on the other hand, took their direction from Ottawa and were intended to function only 'for the duration.'

In general, agency workers appear to have been more willing to give erring wives a second chance, to keep in mind the difficulties of surviving without an allowance, and to think of the long-term consequences of confession. From the perspective of the DAB, women who chose not to remain faithful were traitors to their country as well as to their menfolk. The men they took up with were, furthermore, those who were not overseas: those who had either not enlisted, or who had volunteered but had failed to make the grade. The masculinity of such men, from the

point-of-view of soldiers, veterans, and the board, was undoubtedly somewhat suspect.[46]

Women's infidelity was interrogated to a far greater degree than
men's. The occasional lapse of judgment by men far from loved ones was
not ideal, but it was tolerated and perhaps even expected.[47] As Ruth
Jamieson has shown for Britain, for the military bureaucracies, the
sexual fidelity of a soldier's wife 'was also taken to be an index of her
commitment to the national interest.'[48] The question of soldiers' own
loyalty was slightly more ambiguous. Their loyalties to their families, to
the nation, and to comrades-in-arms may have been reinforcing, but
perhaps, as Susan Hartmann suggests, fidelity to fellow soldiers took
precedence. The result, she argues, was that in the United States, 'The
sexual double standard was reinforced on the grounds that the horrors
of war both excused male infidelity and required female faithfulness.'[49]

There is no doubt that, as Jamieson and Hartmann show for Britain
and the United States respectively, women's infidelity was denounced in
both public discussion and public policy. But the exposure of Canada's
welfare workers and government bureaucrats to wartime adultery may
have developed in them a greater tolerance of 'irregular' sexual relations – or at least, a pragmatic recognition that few marriages were
uncomplicated.[50] There was considerable debate within the DAB and
the Department of National Defence over how to handle marital infidelity,[51] as well as occasions on which the DAB demonstrated more flexibility than usual. As the war in Europe drew to a close and the soldiers'
return appeared imminent, for instance, the board shifted its focus from
the punishment of wives to the preservation of households. The 'necessity of considering the deterrent effect of Board decisions which existed
in the past has now largely disappeared with the approach of partial
demobilization,' the board noted. Past decisions revoking wives' allowances might be reconsidered more sympathetically, 'providing the Dependent does her part.' Like the family agencies, the board increasingly
counselled forgiveness and reconciliation, and insisted upon the importance of maintaining 'home and family circles' for the postwar period.[52]

How, then, did postwar couples deal with relationships that were at
the very least strained, and often fractured? Most married couples probably stuck it out. It is possible, as one social service agency argued, that
the impact of their wives' infidelity on soldiers' morale was less than
might be supposed. Certainly some soldiers, despite 'rather desperate'
first reactions, took the news of wives' infidelity in stride. The DAB
claimed that a serviceman's reaction would 'depend a good deal on their

marital relationship before he enlisted, on his behaviour since they have parted, and on the point of view of his relatives and their influence upon him.'[53] Some soldiers accepted their wives' 'illegitimate' children as their own. One French-Canadian woman, for instance, gave birth to her eighth child during the war, a child fathered by someone other than her soldier-husband. The soldier and his wife were reconciled, however, and the family stayed together.[54] Soldiers could request that dependents' allowances be reinstated to their unfaithful wives and/or allocated to their wives' illegitimate children. The DAB would agree to these requests if the wife showed signs of changing her ways, and if the soldier agreed to raise the children in question as his own.[55]

Evidence of formal or de facto postwar marital breakdown is nonetheless substantial. Divorce, for instance, increased in Quebec in the immediate postwar period, particularly among servicemen's families. Petitions to the Dominion government from Montreal residents rose steadily through the war years and jumped sharply in the immediate postwar period.[56] Yet in a predominantly Catholic province with no divorce courts, where a divorce required the delay, expense, and notoriety involved in petitioning the Dominion government, legal divorce was but one, minor, form of marital dissolution. More common, especially for French Canadians, were legal separations of bed-and-board or informal separations. Catholic organizations warned Quebecers that civil divorce was not a valid way of dissolving Christian marriages, while agencies that catered primarily to non-Catholic clients, such as Montreal's Society for the Protection of Women and Children (SPWC), also advised judicial separation rather than divorce in 'cases of marital discord.'[57] Some soldiers simply chose not to return to their relationships. Social service agencies noted the large number of wives abandoned by soldier-husbands; military enlistment was occasionally tantamount to desertion.[58] Some married Canadian soldiers formed second families in Europe and elected to stay with them – a precedent established during the First World War a generation earlier.[59]

The arrival in Canada of close to 45,000 war brides and their more than 21,000 children encapsulates many of the difficulties of postwar marital adjustment.[60] The immigration of British brides began midway through the war and was largely completed by 1947.[61] Some arrived while their husbands were still fighting overseas; many came with young children.[62] Brides were greeted by spouses and by in-laws: the publicity accorded these reunions was extensive. The photograph of 'Jane-Margaret et son papa' that appeared in *La Presse* in March 1946, for instance, depicted the reunion at Montreal's Bonaventure Station of M. Bérubé, former member of the Fusiliers Mont-Royal, his English bride, and their one-year-old daughter, Jane-Margaret. Newspaper articles gushed about 'heureuses Canadiennes' and 'nouvelles citoyennes du Canada': young Englishwomen who were being received with open arms and who would create comfortable homes for their veteran-husbands.[63]

In addition to the usual resources offered by an urban centre, the Englishwomen who settled in Montreal found special provisions made for them, largely by the city's Anglo-Protestant community. CN Rail and the Red Cross set up a canteen, a rest-area, and a nursery for British mothers and children arriving at Bonaventure Station. The Acorn Club, established 'to welcome and help in any way possible all British brides arriving in Montreal,' sent 'a letter of welcome to every member two weeks after her arrival' in the city. Members of the Local Council of Women were requested to do everything in their power 'to help the British war brides to become happy and useful Canadian citizens.' The YWCA, meanwhile, offered to arrange French lessons for them.[64]

Not everyone was caught up in the romance of the British brides, however. The Association catholique de la jeunesse canadienne-française (ACJC) argued that English women were morally unworthy of young French-Canadian men, despite their often superior education. The ACJC warned that French-Canadian families would not necessarily extend a warm welcome to these brides, and it wondered aloud whether the children of these unions would be 'French' or 'English.'[65]

War brides themselves found much to adjust to. Local observers expressed surprise at reports of unhappy British wives, and tended to attribute their discontent to Montreal's postwar housing crisis. The Victoria Rifles Ladies Association of Montreal felt it essential that the housing shortage be rectified so that 'no Canadian or British bride will feel like returning home to mother just because we have failed to provide liveable homes for them.'[66] Others blamed marital unhappiness on conflicts with in-laws. Montreal's Society for the Protection of Women and Children reported in 1945 and 1946 that it was seeing an increased number of cases involving 'marriages contracted overseas by service personnel,' including 'numerous cases in which the War-bride is not accepted by the soldier's family.' The SPWC noted 'more or less acute marital difficulties' related to 'culture, religion and race,' to the transition to urban living, and to situations where 'the soldier has reverted to an attachment made prior to his departure for overseas service.'[67] One woman's story captures war brides' frustrations with both housing and in-laws. The woman's husband, a veteran, worked the nightshift, and the couple and their two children lived with the husband's married sister in Verdun. Not long after her arrival in the city, the woman wrote to the Montreal Soldiers' Wives League (MSWL): 'Please can you refer me how to find out about returning home. I have two children and I am expecting another. We have one room here, and have been told that we must find another place. Whereas we can't – places are hard to get and I wish to return to England.'[68]

Other war brides were also prepared to return home. Montreal service clubs such as the Oak Society for British War Wives perceived 'this inability to settle down' to be widespread and problematic.[69] Newspapers noted that English wives were returning to Britain because they found Canadians cold and unfriendly.[70] Meanwhile, numerous instances of abandoned war brides were coming to the attention of social service agencies. A few women deserted by Canadian husbands overseas decided nonetheless to come to Canada.[71] The conclusions to some of these stories can be found in the *Statutes of Canada*: each year between 1945 and 1949 saw parliamentary divorces granted to Montreal residents whose marriages had taken place in wartime England.[72] Yet as observers were quick to point out, those war brides who returned to Britain were the exception rather than the rule.[73]

Although married veterans and their wives were often depicted as the heroes and heroines of the postwar romance of reunion, most Canadian veterans appear to have been young and single.[74] Veterans were referred to in the popular press as 'boys' (often 'our boys'): in a sense, they were everyone's sons. Parents, and often siblings, were expected to contribute to the task of rehabilitation. The Department of Veterans' Affairs noted approvingly that Montreal parents were encouraging their sons to get 'back to work.'[75] The Jeunesse Ouvrière Catholique Féminine reminded families and friends that young working-class men were returning much changed by their military experiences, often nervous and irritable. Women were to help them to readjust by reintroducing them to good habits, notably religious practice.[76]

Those veterans who were young and unmarried but whose adolescence had ended abruptly with their period of service found the return to the nest frustrating after several years of absence and mobility. Montreal's severe postwar housing shortage meant that veterans frequently moved back into overcrowded parental homes. Friction ensued as parents were forced to adjust to their young sons' independence and resistance to parental authority.[77] With regard to female veterans, the

Canadian Youth Commission thought it likely that 'once the first plea-sure of returning home is over, the standards of the parents will appear more rigid than ever and the advice and restrictions more irksome than before.'[78] Readers of the daily press were exposed to grim examples of the difficulties of rehabilitation. Twenty-five-year-old Laurent Leduc, for instance, a Montreal navy veteran, was charged in February 1946 with knifing his father in the back in a fit of hysteria, and with attempting to attack his mother and sisters.[79]

Well-known Canadian psychologist Brock Chisholm noted: 'Many people still speak of our soldiers as "boys"' but insisted 'It is very impor-tant that we should not regard our soldiers as boys but rather that we should see them clearly as they are – grown-up responsible men.'[80] Nowhere was this more evident than in the fact that parents often relied upon young soldier-sons for dependents' allowances.[81] This was not necessarily a new situation, given Montreal's history of child and teen labour and given the working-class background of many soldiers.[82] Par-ents of soldiers and veterans, used to depending on sons' earnings, had a clear sense of entitlement to state-administered allowances. As one woman reminded the MSWL in January 1946, 'After all, I am a veteran's mother and entitled to my check ...'[83] Moreover, parents across the country exhibited a marked preference for soldiers' and veterans' allowances over other forms of social welfare; military allowances were a source of pride rather than stigma.[84]

War's function as a rite of passage was highlighted by the fact that young soldiers often returned with new family responsibilities.[85] The transfer of assigned pay and dependents' allowances from mothers to new brides suggests one way in which the war transformed (and often strained) filial relationships. As soldiers and veterans transferred their primary allegiances and allowances from mothers to wives, mothers not only felt displaced, but suffered tangible consequences. Social service agencies noted the financial hardship caused to mothers by this switch, and by the fact that allowances to mothers were less than those to wives. Widowed mothers, in particular, appear to have relied on their allow-ances to cover the costs of medical care.[86] Conflict was aggravated in situations where new brides were living with their in-laws. Housing short-ages, the increased cost-of-living, fixed incomes, and perceptions of respectable living arrangements meant that families often doubled up, particularly while soldier-husbands were overseas. Catherine Stuart Vance, the general secretary of Montreal's YWCA, observed that in such situa-tions, 'Disagreements often start regarding allowances, discipline of children, etc., between the mothers-in-law and wives, both of whom may be the official responsibility of the enlisted men.'[87] The heroine of an advertisement for Castoria, a young mother living with her mother-in-law while her soldier-husband was overseas, presumably spoke to a receptive audience when she complained, 'J'ai un emploi de guerre ... et des ennuis avec belle-maman.'[88]

One of the biggest sources of controversy in the administration of dependents' allowances had to do with the different amounts allocated to wives and mothers respectively.[89] The wives of enlisted men were allocated $35 per month as a matter of right – that is, without financial means tests. The mothers of enlisted men could also apply for allowances. If their sons had supported them prior to enlistment, and they were found to be truly needy, they could be allocated payments of up to $20 (later $25) a month, depending on how much the son had contributed to his mother's home prior to joining up.[90] An avalanche of criticism was heaped upon the federal government from soldiers' advocates, members of Parliament, women's groups, and mothers themselves. Elderly mothers, their champions argued, needed at least as much financial support as wives, who were presumably healthier, had fewer medical expenses, and could take on paid work if need be. Why should the rights of wives be 'inviolate' while mothers who had raised sons and given them to the service of their country were reduced to applying for 'charity'? The campaign for increased rates for soldiers' mothers produced results – although never rates equal to the allowances of wives.[91] Such a campaign served as a reminder to the government that children continued to be a major source of support for aging parents (and sometimes for siblings). It also suggests that other familial relationships competed with the marriage bond for loyalty during the war years. In the context of war, women who had raised healthy sons and offered them up to the service of their country enjoyed widespread public respect and a certain political purchase, enabling their voices, and the voices of their supporters, to be raised and listened to in a variety of public forums.[92]

The DAB insisted throughout the war that assigned pay and dependents' allowances were not a wage; rather, they were designed to encourage recruitment and sustain morale among the troops by assuring servicemen that their wives, children, and other dependents would be cared for by the federal state.[93] Many wives felt entitled to their dependents' allowances.[94] This sense of entitlement, more usually associated with the universal measures of the postwar period, extended to demanding cost-of-living bonuses and increases in their allowances. One woman from Montreal North wrote to the DAB in 1941, saying that she was 'hoping to get an answer to the question that is being asked by hundreds everywhere, that being, *When* are we soldiers *wives* going to get a rise in our pay, the factory workers have all had their pay increased to keep up with the rise in the cost of living, also all Civil Servants are getting a bonus to help them out, But we Soldiers wives are still having to carry on the best we can with the same pay as we got when war started, and that is no easy job now that the cost of living has doubled, we are not complaining all we want is a square deal and a chance to live properly.'[95] Dependents had their advocates in Parliament: one MP argued that a cost-of-living bonus to soldiers' wives would mean that 'these women would take care of their children, look after their homes, devote themselves to their domestic duties instead of feeling impelled to take part in public movements to save their standards of living.'[96]

The investigations that accompanied the administration of dependents' allowances uncovered real need in these families (temporarily) without male breadwinners. Cramped and deteriorating housing was common, and poor health was frequent in these days before health and hospital insurance. The establishment of the Dependents' Board of Trustees (DBT) in 1941, to deal with financial needs above and beyond those covered by dependents' allowances, testified to the poverty of many of these families of enlisted men.[97] Over 90 per cent of DBT expenditures were related to costs incurred by illness.[98] A 'disproportionately large' number of applications for DBT assistance came from Quebec and were attributed to the many large families in the province, as well as the 'small number of Welfare Agencies operating in Quebec' and the 'abnormal incidence of sickness and attendant expense, resulting inevitably from many large families in poor circumstances.'[99] The poverty of many francophone families, in particular, was evident in the considerable costs incurred by the Bureau d'assistance sociale aux familles (BASF), the social agency charged with administering dependents' allowances for French-Canadian families whom the board thought needed to be supervised. The DAB believed these costs to be out of all proportion to costs incurred by agencies elsewhere. The BASF justified its expenditures by pointing to the severe need of many of the city's French-Canadian families, as well as the fact that many of these families had more children than the number provided for by the DAB (which increased from two children to six between September 1939 and January 1943).[100] Ottawa, the BASF charged, needed a better understanding of the workings of welfare in Montreal. Moreover, it needed to appreciate the fact that in administering allowances for the board, the BASF was unfairly neglecting the civilian cases under its care.[101]

Elsewhere in Canada, investigations for the DAB were generally carried out by local social agencies.[102] In Montreal, this was the practice for Protestant and Jewish families. The city's francophone families, however, were investigated not by the BASF (which was overburdened with work), but by the Department of Pensions and National Health, the Montreal Unemployment Relief Department (especially in 'tough' cases) and occasionally, the RCMP.[103] What this meant was that federal allowances to French-Canadian families were often accompanied by federal intrusions into family life. And yet, dependents' most vigorous complaints were reserved for City of Montreal investigators, who were criticized for being rude, 'unethical and indiscreet.'[104]

The evidence of need unearthed by DAB and DBT investigations may well have increased support for family allowances a few years later. As Susan Pedersen has argued about First World War separation allowances in Britain, some of the basic characteristics of wartime dependents' allowances reappeared in the welfare state of the 1940s.[105] Dependents' allowances created a relationship between the federal state and some wives that would be echoed, to some degree, in family allowances. Like family allowances, dependents' allowances for wives and children were exempt from means tests (although wives' behaviour was still open to moral scrutiny).[106] Like family allowances, dependents' allowances were calculated according to a diminishing rate after the first child.[107] Dependents' allowances, then, were a rehearsal for more expansive kinds of welfare-state measures, such as family allowances, that would be universal and not contingent on notions of loyalty and propriety. Moreover, family allowances, which were paid to all parents, probably defused the jealousy provoked by dependents' allowances – federal money allocated only to the dependents of servicemen. Paradoxically, one might also see the call for universal social provisions – expanded public measures – as an appeal for privacy, as these would be measures delivered without intrusive and humiliating means tests. When Montreal social agencies, 'both Protestant and French,' likened the investigations of dependents' allowances recipients carried out by municipal employees to 'Gestapo procedure,' they were arguing that a degree of privacy was essential in a democratic society in the 1940s.[108] In a number of ways, then, the federal family allowance program implemented in 1945 built and improved upon the system of wartime dependents' allowances. Yet in reaffirming a heterosexual, nuclear family consisting of a breadwinning husband, a stay-at-home wife, and dependent children, family allowances ignored the alternative conceptions of family – such as sons supporting dependent parents and siblings – lived out by many Canadians and discovered by DAB and DBT personnel during the war.

Rehabilitating Veterans

Roughly a quarter of Quebec men between the ages of eighteen and forty-five had served in the armed forces; the veterans' return, then, could not have gone unnoticed.[109] Yet, with the notable exception of an insightful chapter in Béatrice Richard's recent *La mémoire de Dieppe: Radioscopie d'un mythe*, there is a resounding historiographical silence surrounding Quebec's Second World War veterans.[110] Despite the considerable scholarly attention paid to francophone Quebecers' responses to conscription, we know very little about French-Canadian soldiers or veterans.[111] In the absence of an extensive secondary literature, it seems safe to assume that the insistence on society's obligation to its veterans came above all from the federal government. Ottawa had allies, of course, in the Canadian Legion and in local organizations such as the MSWL, which emphasized the 'need for a hearty welcome to returned men.'[112] Volunteer Citizens' Committees were established in Montreal, as elsewhere in Canada, in order to greet and rehabilitate local heroes.[113] Service clubs such as the Rotarians, the Kiwanis, the Chamber of Commerce, and the Advertising Club – none of which catered to francophones – offered their assistance to Montreal veterans seeking employment or simply company. Local French-language radio programs such as CKAC's 'Au Service des Vétérans' featured discharged soldiers as guest speakers.[114] Branches of the Action catholique attempted to reintegrate French-Canadian veterans into community and family life. Priests were encouraged by DVA officials and military officers to interview soldiers and their families as soon as the former returned to their parishes.[115] Mainstream newspapers such as *La Presse* called on citizens and employers to help veterans reintegrate into society and find jobs. Rehabilitation, the newspaper reminded its readers, could not be left entirely to the government.[116]

The federal government was, however, the veterans' biggest supporter. Despite the official fanfare that greeted returning war heroes, the political cleavages that structured Montreal were evident in the mixed reactions evoked by the veterans' return. Montreal's assistant veterans' welfare officer noted in 1942 that 'much unnecessary feeling exists as to the limits of a citizen's obligation to service in war.'[117] Certainly Quebec had contributed a smaller percentage of its eligible men to the armed services than had other provinces.[118] The Jeunesse Ouvrière Catholique alluded in 1945 to a 'méfiance' of veterans, suggesting that they had earned a bad name in certain circles.[119] As men who had risked their lives for Canada and for Christianity, veterans were – the youth organization argued – in need of friends, assistance, and public sympathy.[120] Historian Béatrice Richard has remarked upon the uneasy reception accorded French-Canadian veterans; drawing on interviews with former members of the Fusiliers Mont-Royal, she argues that some veterans were ignored, ostracized, or even considered dupes for having enrolled in the armed services.[121] For their part, certain anglophone organizations appear to have discriminated between volunteers and conscripts: the Women's Auxiliary of the Royal Canadian Corps Signals, for instance, was reluctant to take gifts to draftees in hospital.[122] The DVA itself did not idealize veterans: Montreal's veterans' welfare officer worried that 'shiftless and unstable men' would try to take advantage of their veteran status in order to secure concessions and charity from receptive members of the public.[123]

Veterans' own feelings about the society to which they returned were equally ambivalent. They disliked the complacency of those on the home front and were impatient with what Major-General Brock Chisholm called the 'little certainties of civilians.'[124] Many had grievances against those who had not gone overseas and who appeared to have profited by wartime employment. As one DVA official observed, veterans were not likely to look upon civil service or munitions workers as having made sacrifices comparable to their own.[125] Such distinctions were especially sharp in times of unemployment. A Montreal DVA official noted in 1944, for instance, that veterans laid off before younger men who had been exempted from service for three or four years were particularly bitter.[126] The sense that civilians were unable to understand the experience of those who had served in the armed forces, combined with a resentment of civilians who appeared to have done well by the war, meant that veterans often felt 'more at home with other veterans.'[127] Interviews conducted by Béatrice Richard underline the importance of the Legion and of veterans' groups as places of sociability for francophone veterans, where common histories could be shared and where no explanations were required.[128] For this reason, Brock Chisholm claimed that returned soldiers needed a sense of importance and belonging. He urged that soldiers be 'absorbed into the civilian community' immediately, rather than segregated and made to feel as though their interests were 'separate from and then in conflict with those of the rest of the people.'[129]

Ottawa was eager to use the Veterans Charter to transform the 'fighting man' into the 'peacetime citizen.'[130] Such an undertaking meant both de-masculinizing and re-masculinizing the former soldier, who was generally assumed to be male. Men had to be taken out of the homosocial, combative milieu of the armed services and re-acclimatized to heterosexual relations and domestic life.[131] Theda Skocpol has suggested that in the early-twentieth-century United States, soldiers and mothers were most likely to benefit from state-administered social policies – far more likely, she argues, than men claiming rights as breadwinners.[132] In Canada, the Veterans Charter was aimed at soldiers, naturally, but it was in fact designed to rehabilitate male breadwinners.[133] In the wake of a war during which large numbers of women and children had worked for pay, the male breadwinner was seen to need some help from the state. As one female observer commented in 1945, veterans whose wives had obtained paid employment during the war worried that 'their manly, breadwinning status [was being] whittled down.'[134] Thus the centrepiece of rehabilitation, from the perspective of both federal officials and returned soldiers, was employment.[135] Former servicemen had to shake off the regimentation and supervision of the services and stand on their own two feet; as the Department of Pensions and National Health reminded soldiers, sailors, and members of the air force in 1943, 'The aim of the whole re-establishment program is to help a man to help himself.'[136] Veterans enjoyed a sense of entitlement, then, as men who had served their country, but also as family men.[137]

Measures for veterans and, more broadly, the attention to veterans, gendered notions of entitlement and of public welfare as masculine. To bestow provisions on old soldiers was to give men in particular significant opportunities in the realms of work, housing, and education. As Linda Kerber has argued, when women are exempted from the obligations of citizenship (such as military service), their rights of citizenship are commensurately diminished.[138] In Quebec, moreover, the Veterans Charter was a sharp reminder that certain obligations of citizenship – such as bearing arms in defence of Canada – were amply rewarded. Thus older conceptions of citizenship involving military duty persisted amid new nods to universal entitlement.

Re-making former soldiers as men was most difficult in the case of those who had suffered serious wounds or illness during the war and were thus, at least temporarily, incapable of being breadwinners or 'productive' citizens. Many Montreal men had gone off to war suffering from poor health and years of inadequate diets (and many had been turned down by the services as 'medically unfit').[139] Montreal's veterans' welfare officer observed in 1943, 'The appalling number of substandard people (depression victims) who have old war, or new war service, who simply cannot do any kind of hard work, and who seem to have limited physical stamina, cannot be realized unless one "sits in" on placement work.'[140] Hospitals such as Sainte-Anne-de-Bellevue's Military Hospital, the Queen Mary Military Hospital, and the Saint-Hyacinthe DVA Hospital had been established during the war by the federal government to care for Montreal soldiers afflicted with injuries or disease. After the war, these hospitals, along with a service ward at the tuberculosis sanatorium in Sainte-Agathe, became the purview of veterans. Understaffed, dilapidated, and ill-prepared for the influx of soldiers and veterans in the last months of the war, the hospitals were overcrowded and the target of numerous complaints. The irate mother of a veteran hospitalized with a spinal wound wrote a four-page letter in October 1944 detailing the 'deplorable conditions existing at the St. [sic] Anne's Military Hospital.' Montreal's veterans, she concluded, were 'deserving of better treatment and should not be obliged to put up with conditions such as these.'[141]

Women's voluntary groups carried out hospital visiting for years after the war had ended, taking candy, cigarettes, and reading material to hospitalized veterans. The Local Council of Women reported in 1947–48 that its members were still regularly visiting veterans at the Sainte-Anne's, Queen Mary, and Saint-Hyacinthe hospitals. The MSWL observed in 1949 that there were more veterans in hospital in the region than at any time since 1945. Hospitalized veterans, the MSWL noted, were battling 'pain and desease, depression and sometime despair [sic].'[142] Most difficult to treat were those veterans suffering from mental illnesses defined variously as 'nerves,' 'battle exhaustion,' and 'psychopathic' or 'neuropsychiatric' disorders.[143] The Johns-Manville Company issued a notice in La Presse in 1947 asking Montrealers not to forget the veterans still languishing in military hospitals, while the Community Garden League and the Diggers and Weeders Garden Club offered to plough land near the Queen Mary Road Veterans Hospital in order that psychiatric patients might benefit from the 'therapeutic value of gardening.'[144]

For healthy veterans, jobs were priorities. Gallup polls conducted early in the war found that most Canadians wanted to see veterans treated better than their fathers had been at the end of the First World War and that this improved treatment should extend to finding employment for discharged soldiers.[145] Montreal's veterans' welfare officer reported that many employers thought that veterans deserved 'a "break" upon discharge' and were willing to '"try a veteran first."'[146] Yet returned men fretted about potential postwar unemployment. The Comité d'action trade-unioniste appealed explicitly to veterans in November 1945. 'Du FRONT DE COMBAT A LA CRISE ECONOMIQUE? Est-ce là ce que signifie "reconversion"?' it warned.[147] Veterans who were among the last contingents to return from overseas worried that they might already have lost their chance to secure employment in postwar Montreal. One veteran interviewed by Barry Broadfoot, for example, recalled that he had returned to Montreal in February 1946 and had been unable to find work because 'all the jobs were taken by those guys who were sent home in July and August of '45 and believe me, there were no jobs.'[148]

After August 1942, veterans could rely on the Reinstatement in Civil Employment Order, which promised them their old civilian jobs back, with seniority rights.[149] Those who had been unemployed or in school when they enlisted or who had no wish to return to their former jobs could visit the Veterans' Welfare Officers who had set up shop at the Unemployment Insurance Commission's local Employment and Claims Offices.[150] Returned soldiers who visited Montreal's Veterans' Welfare Bureau, located on Notre-Dame Ouest, obtained jobs as acetylene welders, warehousemen, metallurgists, stationary engineers, engine mechanics, parks men, teamsters, stokers, and chefs.[151] One of the welfare officer's tasks was to persuade the private sector to adopt 'veteran preference' policies and 'adjusted employment' for injured and disabled men; employment in the federal civil service and in work secured through government war contracts already operated according to this affirmative action policy.[152] By June 1944, Montreal's veterans' welfare officer was able to report that the 'preference' campaign was working and that employment conditions for the city's veterans were good. Nonetheless, in September 1946, the DVA still felt the need to advertise Canadian employers' endorsements of their good relations with 'leurs employés invalides.'[153] Some employers apparently viewed men discharged early in the war 'as though they had contagious diseases' and were reluctant to hire them.[154] Moreover, in their attempt to place veterans in positions with seniority rights, DVA and National Selective Service officials confronted the rights of civilian workers inscribed in unions' collective agreements. Michael Stevenson has shown that in Ontario the Ford Motor Company was eager to grant seniority rights to veterans as a way of replacing unionized workers hired during the war. The failure of the

Ford scheme, Stevenson argues, suggests that veterans' entitlement was not untouchable nor necessarily preeminent.[155]

Those veterans who wanted to improve their postwar opportunities through further education could take advantage of the university education credits allowed discharged soldiers, or could enrol in vocational training and apprenticeship programs. All Second World War veterans were eligible for retraining, in contrast to the First World War, when only the approximately 20 per cent who were disabled were eligible. The federal government presented educational and vocational training as part of its attempt to provide 'opportunity combined with security' to veterans. It emphasized manly independence, however: training grants were 'intended for those who are willing to help themselves.'[156] Discharged men and women in Montreal could take apprenticeship and 'improvement' courses offered by the Aid to Youth service, which was administered by Quebec's newly established Department of Social Welfare and Youth in conjunction with the federal government.[157]

University credits were intended to prepare veterans for employment in the postwar job market, but were also a way of delaying the entry of large numbers of veterans into that market until economic reconversion was stabilized.[158] Quebec's francophone universities, however, such as the Université de Montréal and Laval, never came close to enrolling the number of veterans that flocked to McGill.[159] The Jeunesse Ouvrière Catholique argued that anglophone veterans benefited to a greater degree from their university credits than francophones because it was easier to meet the admission standards of anglophone universities, and this appears to have been the case.[160] Peter Neary speculates, moreover, that the discretionary character of education credits (in order to be eligible for them, veterans had to be recommended by DVA counsellors) may have worked against francophones.[161]

Female veterans also faced a job search upon their return. The 4.64 per cent of Canadian veterans who were female had been paid less than men while enlisted and had not been able to allocate dependents' allowances until July 1943. After January 1945, however, they were entitled to the same pensions, discharge benefits, and rehabilitation credits as men.[162] They were also eligible for retraining schemes: for instance, as practical nurses and nurses' aides.[163] At least one bureaucrat within the DVA, however, argued that ex-service women were not receiving appropriate or adequate training for postwar employment.[164] Female veterans were trained for, and appear to have secured work in, traditionally feminine fields of employment. *La Presse* reported in 1944 that most female veterans hoped to work as stenographers after the war, with others preferring careers in nursing, teaching, bookkeeping, and office work.[165] A female speaker at a Training Conference on Women's Rehabilitation in 1946 felt that DVA counsellors should 'advise ex-service women generally to go into work accepted as women's work,'[166] while the National Council of Women noted that same year that the 'tendency for discharged service women is to go into commercial courses and hair dressing.'[167] In February 1945, Montreal's district superintendent of rehabilitation noted that the demand from employers for ex-service women was 'negligible.' Those women who had obtained jobs through the Veterans' Welfare Bureau had found them in clerical work. By April 1946, the Montreal superintendents were able to report that female veterans were securing employment without undue difficulty, but were finding it tough to 'adjust their income to civilian needs.'[168]

Women discharged from the services faced other difficulties in their transition to civilian life. The DVA, for instance, argued that homeowners preferred to rent to men than to women.[169] One social worker observed, 'Some girls look forward eagerly to returning home and are disappointed at what they find. Others openly admit they do not wish to leave the Service and for these too, return to civilian life is difficult.' A YWCA worker likewise noted that 'some girls come to the "Y" who felt like nobodies after discharge.'[170] Female veterans occupied an ambiguous position in public perceptions. Alongside provisions for training for postwar employment was the expectation that former servicewomen would marry and leave the workforce. Marriage, one army spokesman remarked, 'would appear to simplify the rehabilitation problems,' as 'the marriage of a woman in the Defence Forces will result in there being one less competitor for post-war employment.'[171] Yet not all commentators were sure that these women, who had enjoyed some economic and personal independence within the structures of the armed services, would settle for marriage, homemaking, and financial dependency in the postwar period.[172] Female veterans were an awkward fit with breadwinner policies; moreover, it was difficult to reconcile their wartime mobility, military experience, and (albeit limited) degree of sexual freedom with conventional narratives of postwar reunion. The returning military hero was supposed to be male; women's role was to wait loyally at home.[173]

By the end of 1947, the veteran-oriented work of social agencies such as the Jewish Vocational Service was coming to an end. Montreal's Citizens' Rehabilitation Committee, likewise, was effectively 'moribund.'[174]

During and immediately after the Second World War, train stations were the backdrop for farewells and reunions between servicemen and their loved ones. This photo was taken in Montreal's Bonaventure Station on 15 September 1942.

Montreal's downtown streets were the site of mass celebrations on VE-Day, 8
May 1945.

Montreal's mass marriage, 23 July 1939. Many of the couples shown here would be tracked by the press, and by organizers of the Jeunesse Ouvrière Catholique and the Ligue Ouvrière Catholique, for up to fifteen years after the wedding.

Montreal photographer Conrad Poirier entitled this picture, taken 21 May 1944, 'New Babies Everywhere.' The rapid increase in birth rates associated with the postwar baby boom actually began during the war.

These children lived in a Wartime Housing complex of 400 homes built for the families of war workers employed by Noorduyn Aviation Ltd., in Ville Saint-Laurent.

Line-ups were a common sight in Montreal in the context of wartime and postwar rationing and shortages. Here, men and women wait their turn in front of the Quebec Liquor Commission store at the corner of Bleury and Ste-Catherine.

Some married women objected to the closing of federal-provincial Wartime Day Nurseries after the end of hostilities. Here, a group of Quebec mothers and children gather to meet with Premier Maurice Duplessis in October 1945, in all likelihood to demand the creation of new day nurseries.

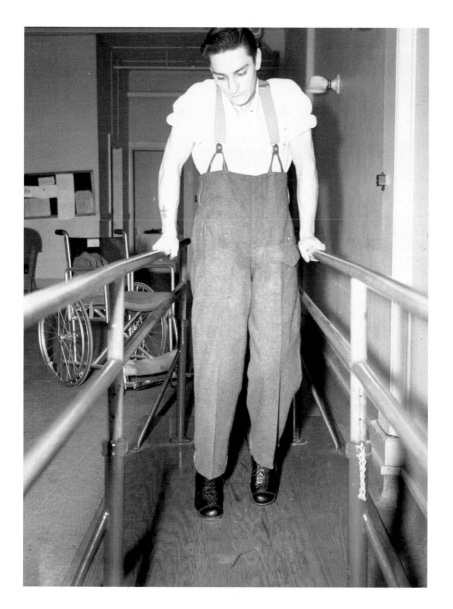

The physical and emotional rehabilitation of men who had fought overseas was a lengthy process. Montreal hospitals such as Ste Anne's Military Hospital, shown here in 1946, were busy with Second World War veterans until the end of the 1940s.

A restaurant in Saint-Henri, the Montreal neighbourhood made famous by Gabrielle Roy's wartime novel *Bonheur d'occasion* (translated as *The Tin Flute*), published in 1945.

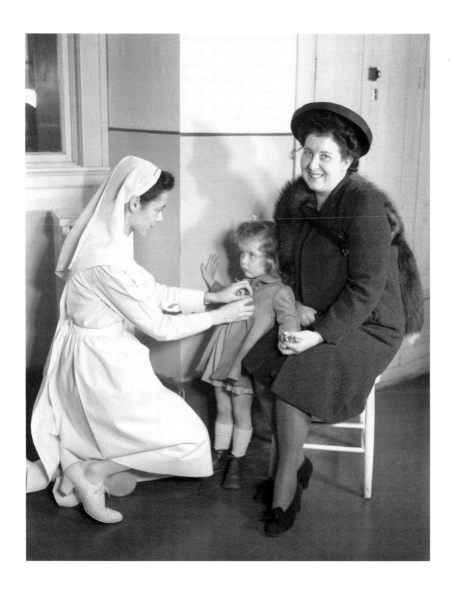

Since the beginning of the twentieth century, Montreal children and parents had been able to count on the expertise of doctors, nurses, and volunteers affiliated with the Hôpital Sainte-Justine, specializing in children's health and shown here in 1945.

The farmers' stalls at the Bonsecours Market (shown here ca. 1950) were among those seriously affected by the grocery boycotts carried out by Montreal housewives in 1947–8.

Ville de gratte-ciel

Montréal est véritablement une ville de gratte-ciel comme le démontre cette photo aérienne prise de l'ouest en regardant vers le sud-est. On distingue au premier plan les appartements "Le Château", l'hôtel Ritz-Carlton, puis les hôtels Mont-Royal, Windsor et Laurentien, l'imposant édifice de la Sun Life, la basilique, etc. Au loin, le mont Saint-Bruno et le mont Beloeil. *(Photo Armour Landry, Montréal)*

By the end of the 1940s, Montreal looked like the metropolis that it was – what *La Patrie* in its Sunday edition of 13 November 1949 called a 'City of Skyscrapers.'

Many of the veterans dealt with by such organizations – men at loose ends, or men suffering from illness or depression, or men who had returned to face significant family problems – had figured only occasionally in the reunion tales told during the war.[175] By the later 1940s, however, rosy narratives of reunion occasionally ran up against postwar portrayals of disillusionment. Consider, for example, the tale told in Gratien Gélinas's smash-hit *Tit-Coq*. First performed at the Monument National in May 1948, the play ran for over a year in Montreal and Quebec City. Playwright Gélinas, who also acted in the title role, published a written version in 1950. An English version of the play was performed to an extremely favourable reception across Canada and in Chicago and (less successfully) New York. In 1952 *Tit-Coq* was made into a film starring Gélinas and most of the original stage actors. It is now considered to be one of the most important works in the history of Quebec theatre.[176]

Tit-Coq was structured around a number of elements common to wartime narratives of reunion. Arthur Saint-Jean, nicknamed Tit-Coq, is a Montreal soldier of unknown parentage, raised in an orphanage, and alone in the world. On leave at Christmas 1942, he falls in love with Marie-Ange, the sister of his army buddy Jean-Paul. Their romance flourishes until Tit-Coq and Jean-Paul are sent overseas in June 1943. Although Tit-Coq and Marie-Ange write faithfully to one another for some time, Tit-Coq eventually notices a change in the tone of Marie-Ange's letters. Shortly before returning to Canada at the end of the war, he discovers that she has succumbed to loneliness and the influence of friends and family, and married another man. Upon his arrival in Montreal, Tit-Coq confronts a tearful Marie-Ange. She admits that she still loves him, but there is nothing to be done: divorce is next to impossible for Catholic Quebecers and, even were she to abandon her husband to run away with Tit-Coq, any child they might have would be illegitimate, like Tit-Coq himself. Both the play and the film end with the former couple parting for good. In the film, their farewell takes place at the train station – an ironic twist on the photographs of joyful reunions in Bonaventure Station that peppered Montreal newspapers at the end of the war.[177]

Tit-Coq was a wartime narrative in some ways particular to Quebec, capturing local specificities of language, politics, and political economy. Its unhappy ending, however, was what differentiated it most dramatically from most wartime narratives. This unhappy ending may well have been due to the fact that the play was first performed in 1948: postwar disenchantment and cynicism had replaced wartime optimism and romance. Similar sentiments are evident in Marcel Dubé's *Un simple soldat*, another play set in Montreal in the immediate wake of the war. First aired on Radio-Canada television in 1957, it was performed at Gratien Gélinas's own theatre, La Comédie Canadienne, in 1958.[178] In it we see Joseph Latour, a Second World War veteran who never made it to the front and who is unable to readjust to civilian life after the war. He spends his days quarrelling with family members and drifting aimlessly from job to job, and his nights drinking in pubs and gambling away his pay. Finally shown the door by his father, he reenlists in the army in 1949. The play ends with his death, two years later, in Korea.[179]

Narratives of demobilization had a certain timeless quality, harking back to a mythical golden age of Ulysses and Penelope, and were no doubt told in the wake of other military conflicts such as the First World War a generation earlier. Indeed, the strength of these narratives can be attributed partly to their familiarity. But the length of the war, Canada's 'total war' effort, the widespread nature of married women's paid work, and the homosocial nature of life for many Canadians in wartime, ensured that these reunion narratives had a particular resonance in the 1940s. Family strains were deeply felt, given that soldiers had been encouraged to fight to preserve Home and Family, and given that the postwar years witnessed an intense pressure to rebuild households disrupted by war. Widespread evidence of troubled marriages and of women's sexual autonomy was, in part, what lay behind the push for conjugal domesticity in the postwar period.[180]

There were other ways, too, in which Montrealers incorporated private wartime experiences into postwar expectations. The experience of receiving regular (if sometimes inadequate) federal allowances – as soldiers, as wives, or as mothers – informed many Montrealers' visions of citizenship and their demands of the state under reconstruction. Although in many cases these allowances had created a sense of entitlement, recipients had also learned to be critical of state measures and to demand improvements when they considered them to be inadequate.

chapter four

Commemorating the Cent-Mariés : Marriage and Public Memory

The Wedding

On 23 July 1939, six weeks before Canada entered the Second World War, 105 Catholic, francophone, working-class couples were married in a baseball stadium on the east side of Montreal. More than 25,000 observers crowded the stands on this sunny Sunday morning. Local dignitaries and public officials were present, as were reporters from more than 150 Canadian and American newspapers, and numerous newsreel companies filmed these extraordinary events.[1]

The mass wedding was the project of the Jeunesse Ouvrière Catholique (JOC), one of the specialized movements of the Action catholique canadienne (ACC). The Action catholique canadienne, modelled after its Belgian predecessor, had been established in Quebec in the early 1930s by Oblate priests wishing to re-spiritualize everyday life amid what appeared to be rapid secularization.[2] The JOC (founded, in Canada, in 1932) was an organization within which young, unmarried, working-class French-Canadian men and women could address everyday matters that concerned them both as Catholics and as workers.[3] In response to the papal encyclical *Casti Connubii* of 1931, which had called for an effort to emphasize the sacred nature of marriage, the JOC established marriage preparation courses for Catholic working-class couples. All 210 participants in the mass wedding had taken the marriage preparation courses for over a year; the wedding was thus a kind of graduation ceremony as well.[4] Over one hundred other couples had apparently applied to participate in the wedding but had been refused. Many observers considered the mass wedding a kind of publicity stunt for the JOC; its organizers insisted, however, that it was a public celebration of

Christian marriage and of the benefits of carefully considered marital unions.

Like the working-class weddings in early twentieth-century Halifax described by historian Suzanne Morton, this wedding combined the sacred and the secular, and twinned an infatuation with romance with a concern for economic realities. The marriage ceremony was preceded by communion at Montreal's Notre-Dame cathedral, and followed by a picnic for the celebrants and their guests on Île Sainte-Hélène. Although clearly a religious event designed to celebrate Christian marriage, it reflected broader North American concerns of consumption. Young couples on tight budgets worried about paying for dresses, bouquets, and honeymoons. Moreover, unlike most working-class women who married in 1930s Montreal, all 105 brides wore white. White wedding gowns, popular among brides belonging to the Montreal bourgeoisie, were becoming the norm elsewhere in mid-twentieth-century North America, and were, as both Morton and British historian John Gillis point out, part of the promotion of a classless ideal of romance.[5] Yet these elements of romance that were supposed to transcend class and ethnicity were incorporated into a wedding that was all about the specificity of French-Canadian and working-class experiences.

In this chapter, I look first at the public celebration of the couples' fifth, tenth, and fifteenth wedding anniversaries by the press, provincial politicians, and the Catholic Church. I then turn to the ways in which the Ligue Ouvrière Catholique (LOC) used surveys and questionnaires to keep track of the couples (known as the 'Cent-Mariés') well into the postwar period. The LOC itself traced its birth to the mass wedding. Calling itself 'le mouvements [sic] des papas et des mamans,' it was an offshoot of the JOC intended for married, working-class, francophone Quebecers. I examine the LOC's postwar projects for what they can tell us about family and reconstruction, and I situate the Cent-Mariés and the LOC within the broader context of a Catholic 'mouvement familial.' The commemoration of the mass marriage provides insight, I argue, into the visions of family and postwar reconstruction espoused by one branch of the Catholic Church. In contrast to the insistence by Prime Minister Mackenzie King and his 'Ottawa men' that class, ethnicity, and religion didn't matter – that all Canadians were citizens of a common federal state – the JOC and the LOC offered an alternative vision of reconstruction that insisted on the specificity of francophone families and the importance of acknowledging differences of religion and class.

The Marriages

Public Remembering

The mass marriage merits a mention in several histories of twentieth-century Quebec. Some scholars have viewed it as a last gasp of clerical nationalism, others as heralding the advent of 'personalist feminism' and as helping to sow the seeds of the Quiet Revolution.[6] My own interest is not so much the wedding itself as the ways in which the marriages of these 105 couples were both celebrated and monitored, in public and in more private forums, five, ten, and fifteen years after the wedding. It is not likely that the fanfare and hoopla of this wedding would have quickly disappeared from public memory, and journalists would probably have periodically revisited the couples as a human-interest story anyway, as they did, for instance, with the Dionne quintuplets.[7] What interests me here are the efforts taken by the LOC to ensure that the couples would not be forgotten, by organizing very public celebrations of their wedding anniversaries. Both the wedding and the anniversary celebrations spoke volumes about the LOC's conceptions of family and nation. More than a tribute to romantic love, the anniversary celebrations, like the wedding, reflected and shaped ideas of class, community, and patriotism.

The LOC held picnics for some of the anniversaries,[8] but it reserved the major celebrations for the fifth, tenth, and fifteenth anniversaries. These celebrations involved masses at St Joseph's Oratory and pilgrimages to Cap-de-la-Madeleine, both popular sites of religious worship. Seventy of the 105 couples showed up for their fifth anniversary, and forty-nine couples for their fifteenth; moreover, thousands of curious onlookers crowded the grounds of the Oratory on each occasion in order to observe the festivities.[9] The strong religious component of the anniversaries is not surprising, but there were other dimensions to the celebrations. The fifth anniversary celebration, in 1944, included a large-scale pageant about the material problems facing working families. For, as the LOC's publicist Léo-Paul Turcotte asked the provincial Leader of the Opposition Maurice Duplessis, 'Le relèvement de la famille ouvrière, n'est-ce pas le second front sur lequel il faut à tout prix gagner la guerre[?]'[10] The LOC also took the opportunity to present its 'Charte de l'Oratoire' (Oratory Charter), which called on workers, employers, and the state to address the needs of working families. Obviously patterned on the 1941 Atlantic Charter, Roosevelt's and Churchill's declaration of postwar principles that incorporated Roosevelt's Four Freedoms (freedom from want and fear, freedom of speech and religion), the Charte de l'Oratoire spoke to the context of war, to a new international awareness, and to an emerging sense of entitlement among ordinary citizens.[11] The fifteenth-anniversary pilgrimage to Cap-de-la-Madeleine took place in an 'année mariale'; this tribute to the Virgin Mary, however, included a Rally for Working Families.[12] Clearly, the spiritual and the material were closely intertwined.

The anniversaries drew attention from both church and state. Provincial politicians, including Liberal Premier Adélard Godbout, Leader of the Opposition Maurice Duplessis, and leader of the Bloc Populaire André Laurendeau, published messages of congratulations in the LOC's newspaper. Laurendeau also dispatched a personal telegram apologizing for not being able to attend the anniversary celebrations but thanking the LOC for its efforts on behalf of Quebec families.[13] Meanwhile, French-Canadian businesses, such as the Dupuis Frères department store, offered best wishes to the couples.[14]

The LOC's commemorative efforts were an attempt to insist upon the religious dimension of an ideal marriage, the importance and effectiveness of marriage preparation, and those factors that set Catholic and francophone workers apart from continental norms. To some degree, its motives reflected those ascribed by American historian John Bodnar to 'cultural leaders,' who, he claims, 'orchestrate commemorative events to calm anxiety about change in political events, eliminate citizen indifference toward official concerns, promote exemplary patterns of citizen behavior, and stress citizen duties over rights.'[15] Bodnar's analysis has some applicability to LOC organizers, who celebrated the Cent-Mariés in the context of war, growing secularization, and competing models of marriage and family offered by both popular culture and the official culture of the federal state. Aimé Carbonneau, the président-général of the LOC, declared that the July 1944 reunion was essential in a context where everyone was claiming to save the family, and where the state was busy making plans for postwar social security. No policy would be truly family-centred, Carbonneau argued, unless it took into account the perspective of the Church and, more specifically, the LOC, as the embodiment and representative of working-class families.[16]

In the speeches and press releases that accompanied the wedding anniversaries, the LOC emphasized above all the happiness of the couples and the speed with which they were producing children. The LOC found itself having to defend the mass marriage experiment to critics, denying charges that the experiment had turned out to be a 'fiasco' or that many of the marriages had ended in divorce.[17] A year after the marriage, the LOC informed the *Montreal Standard* that 'not one single case of marital discord' had been discovered among the couples; on the occasion of the fifth anniversary, the LOC claimed that the couples continued to enjoy 'perfect harmony' in their relationships.[18] The insistence upon the couples' marital happiness was an argument that preparation worked. The LOC claimed that the Action catholique's marriage preparation courses had provided these young couples, who had reached adulthood in the dark years of the Depression, with as many chances at happiness as possible.[19]

Faith in the value of marriage preparation was certainly not unique to the LOC. Marriage preparation courses were offered elsewhere in Montreal: the Young Women's Hebrew Association and various synagogues, for example, offered lecture series in the late 1940s on marriage and the family, the psychology of marriage, and marriage counselling. Moreover, as historian Mona Gleason demonstrates, marriage preparation courses were popular elsewhere in Canada in these years – integrated, for instance, into university curricula.[20] This emphasis on adequate preparation was part of a twentieth-century reliance on 'experts,' as historians such as Katherine Arnup, Veronica Strong-Boag, and Cynthia Comacchio have argued. It also anticipated the postwar passion for planning.[21] But preparation for marriage was seen to be especially important in a period when war was believed to have wreaked havoc with many relationships or, at least, when the fragility of relationships had been brought to light by war. In a period of continent-wide gender disruptions – married women's paid work; a certain geographic mobility for women; husbands away; rising divorce rates outside Quebec – people were seen to need reminding of the necessity of heterosexual marriage and of the best ways in which to ensure its stability.

The couples' fertility was also remarked on ceaselessly – in a context where Quebec's birth rate had been dropping more-or-less steadily since the late nineteenth century and would fall to the Canadian average within two decades. Montreal's birth rates between 1945 and 1948 were in fact lower than those of both the province of Quebec and Canada as a whole.[22] The LOC noted in 1944 that the Cent-Mariés had produced 204 children to-date, including two sets of twins. Twenty-three couples had given birth to three or more children in the first five years of their marriage, while only eight of the 105 couples had no children as yet.[23]

The insistence upon the Cent-Mariés' numerous children was a political claim. LOC organizers argued that large families were what had traditionally set Quebec apart from other provinces. That cultural differences regarding the ideal number of children were perceived to exist was reflected in the LOC's claim that the Cent-Mariés' fertility 'fait l'admiration de tous et même des protestants.'[24] Some commentators deployed the 'revanche des berceaux' argument; a contributor to the LOC's newspaper *Le Mouvement Ouvrier*, for instance, argued that francophones could exert their influence across Canada only by increasing their numbers.[25] At the same time, the LOC noted pointedly that the provincial government had not always given large families the material support they had a right to expect.[26] In underlining the material costs of numerous children, the LOC departed from the traditional celebration of fertility found in clerical nationalist rhetoric.

If the family idealized by the LOC in its commemoration of the mass marriage was one with numerous children, it was also one where wives and mothers confined their work to the home. Thirteen of the 105 wives worked for pay a year after their marriage; by 1944, the LOC noted approvingly, only three wives worked for pay, and none of these women had children.[27] The LOC's disapproval of married women's waged labour was neither a new nor an isolated sentiment in 1940s Quebec and Canada, but it acquired a particular resonance in a wartime context where the paid work of married women was highly visible and highly publicized. Alongside other organizations in Montreal and elsewhere in Canada, the LOC hoped to rectify the disruptions in gender roles occasioned by the Second World War and what it perceived to be the consequences of these disruptions, including unhappy marriages and smaller families. Mothers' paid employment, a *lociste* claimed in 1944, was destroying working-class homes more surely than the war itself.[28] In particular, the LOC objected to the National Selective Service's registration of women for war-work, which it called 'la conscription des femmes' and which it viewed as an example of federal intrusions into French-Canadian homes.[29] Thus as the Cent-Mariés celebrated their fifth anniversary, the LOC lobbied federal and provincial authorities in an attempt to prohibit mothers with children under the age of sixteen from working in factories, and called for family allowances so that married women could stay home where they belonged.[30] 'Réclamez plutôt les allocations familiales,' the LOC told married working-class women, 'et vous pourrez RESTER CHEZ VOUS.'[31]

The Cent-Mariés were portrayed by the LOC as both ordinary and special: both representative couples and model couples. They were described as 'Comme tout le monde,' and yet they were warned that both within Canada and beyond its borders, they were the standard by which French-Canadian working-class families would be judged.[32] They were both something for other working-class francophones to emulate and couples with which others could empathize. From the beginning, the couples were intended to be 'exemples' or 'échantillons.'[33] On their fifth anniversary, the Cent-Mariés crowned their own 'model couple': a couple who owned their own home, had savings in the bank, and 'a much easier time making the budget balance now than when they were married.'[34] *Le Mouvement Ouvrier* featured another couple in its June 1944 issue, describing the pair as 'Un couple ordinaire mais uni,' and insisting that theirs were not the sensational lives of modern novels.[35] The LOC declared that all the couples set a good example, 'dans un monde et à une époque où le mariage perd de son caractère sacré.'[36] Moreover, the LOC encouraged the couples to think of themselves as one large 'family,' or community.[37] There is evidence that some of the Cent-Mariés took this to heart. More than one couple stated that they felt linked to the others by bonds akin to family ties. Other couples proposed business ventures and cooperative schemes exclusively for the Cent-Mariés.[38]

Not everyone commemorated the Cent-Mariés for the same reasons. Provincial politicians, for instance, did not necessarily have the same interest in religion as the LOC. But the Cent-Mariés phenomenon offered them an alternative to the vision of reconstruction promoted by the expanding federal state. At the heart of Ottawa's postwar reconstruction program was a federally directed welfare state, scaffolded on family allowances, veterans' benefits, and an unemployment insurance program that reinforced traditional notions of gender and family.[39] One of the reasons that a reconstruction program centred on family had so much appeal for Prime Minister Mackenzie King and his Liberal government was that it promised to paper over the bitter cleavages of class, ethnicity, and politics recently exacerbated by the Second World War and the conscription crisis. Just as individual families would heal the physical and emotional wounds of servicemen and servicewomen,[40] so a federally directed welfare state geared to families would help to create an allegiance to the federal government and a sense of citizenship in a common 'nation.'

In opposition to Mackenzie King's desire for a public forgetting, the LOC's anniversary celebrations were attempts at public remembering, at inserting differences of language, religion, and class into the public consciousness and the public memory.[41] The fifth anniversary celebrations, in particular, took place amid the tensions engendered by war and conscription and in the context of other types of commemoration that celebrated English-Canadian patriotism and wartime sacrifice.[42] Patriotic celebrations of war were countered by anti-commemorations such as anti-conscription riots. The summer of 1944 found André Laurendeau, for example, simultaneously congratulating the couples on their fifth wedding anniversary and protesting the federal government's internment of former Montreal mayor Camillien Houde and its proposal to implement military conscription for overseas service.[43] Duplessis's congratulations to the couples in July 1944 might be seen as part of a larger campaign to capitalize on the groundswell of nationalist sentiment in Quebec in order to return to power in the provincial election two weeks later. Liberal Premier Adélard Godbout's words of congratulations were notably more restrained, and unlike those of Laurendeau or Duplessis, made no mention of distinctly 'French-Canadian' experiences.[44] But as Dominique Marshall has observed, because the August 1944 election was the first provincial election in which Quebec women would vote, all three political parties took care to elaborate and articulate 'une politique familiale.'[45]

Attention to the anniversaries was not simply local. Just as journalists and magazine writers from across Canada and the United States had descended upon the wedding in 1939, so they remarked upon the anniversaries. Toronto newspapers such as the *Globe and Mail* and the *Daily Star* assessed the couples' first five years together in terms similar to those of the LOC itself, commenting on the couples' happiness, their children, and the degree to which they kept in touch with members of their extended families.[46] 'Foreign' newspapers' interest in the Cent-Mariés reflected a widespread celebration of heterosexuality, domesticity, and conjugal bliss across North America in the immediate postwar years.[47] Yet at the same time, the foreign interest in this local phenomenon reflected some sense that here was a quaint relic of 'traditional' Quebec: a mythical place that was devout, family-centred, and populated by what historian Ian McKay has called 'the folk.'[48] Thus the mass marriage appealed to outside observers both because it spoke to their own postwar interests and because it appeared to hark back to simpler, more traditional values.

By keeping the Cent-Mariés in the public eye in the late 1940s, the LOC, the press who advertised them, and the provincial politicians who congratulated them argued (implicitly and sometimes explicitly) that the family was an integral part of postwar reconstruction. But in doing so, they suggested an alternative vision of reconstruction to the one proffered by the federal government. Ottawa had accrued a great deal of power and authority during the Second World War, and it continued to do so in the postwar period, with its new social programs and what some have called its 'revanche administrative' or its New National Policy.[49] Unlike the vision of family offered by the expanding federal state, the celebration of the Cent-Mariés acknowledged the specific experiences of French-Canadian families, and made the Church a public player in postwar reconstruction.

Private Tracking

The LOC kept extensive records on the Cent-Mariés. At semi-regular intervals for at least fifteen years, it sent questionnaires to the couples. Many couples not only responded to the questionnaires, but also took the initiative to write letters to the LOC to give additional news, request advice, or ask for help. In 1954, fifteen years after the wedding, the LOC was in contact with seventy of the couples; the files on these seventy couples have survived, and I've relied especially on the files of those couples who lived in Montreal at some point in the 1940s.[50] These documents, used carefully, can give us some sense of the ways in which relatively ordinary francophone Quebecers imagined their postwar lives.

   In one sense, the LOC's tracking of these couples can be seen as a justification of the enormous effort that had gone into planning the mass marriage, a desire to see how the experiment had worked out. It was also an effort to build a Catholic working-class 'family' or community, just as was done through the LOC's newspapers, *Le Mouvement Ouvrier* and then *Le Front Ouvrier*. But in keeping track of its community, the LOC was also gathering information for its own reconstruction project. The Cent-Mariés who wrote to the LOC described daily wartime and postwar urban life: births, illness, death, jobs, unemployment, moving. Much of this news must have informed the LOC's various postwar projects for better and more affordable housing, consumer cooperatives, and a family budget. As the work of Jean-Pierre Collin, Lucie Piché, and others has demonstrated, the specialized Action catholique movements emphasized the importance of knowing their constituency (through first-hand observation) before taking action to improve that constituency's lot in life.[51] The social survey, conducted in workplaces and working-class neighbourhoods, and the collection of 'facts,' were central to their methods.[52] The LOC was concerned with urban-industrial life, with 'familles ouvrières.' That it was well aware of working-class realities was indicated by its chaplain's prescriptions for a happy marriage, which were, in fact, remarkably material: 'good health, freedom from debt, and prospects of saving enough money to care for a rainy day.'[53] In compiling 'facts' about working-class Quebecers, the LOC paralleled the work of sociologists such as Maurice Lamontagne and Jean-Charles Falardeau, whose empirical studies of urban French-Canadian families were a departure from earlier rural studies by Quebec sociologist Léon Gérin and were also an attempt to counter the rural, pastoral myth propagated by Lionel Groulx and other conservative clerical nationalists.[54] The LOC's project was in some ways truly radical: working-class citizens – normally the 'observed' – were not only doing the observing themselves, but were interpreting and disseminating what they discovered, whether that was low incomes, poor health, or inadequate housing.

Lucie Piché notes that the ACC's belief in la 'primauté méthodologique du réel' – the importance of first-hand observation of everyday realities – was inspired by the methods of French scholars such as Frédéric LePlay, Gustave LeBon, and Charles Péguy.[55] In keeping tabs on the Cent-Mariés, the LOC may also have drawn on developments among Quebec sociologists in the 1940s. These developments included the work of Father Georges-Henri Lévesque and other scholars at Laval University's School of Social Sciences, which became an autonomous faculty in 1943. They also included the important influence of the Chicago school of sociology, which favoured field empiricism and a focus on industrialization, urbanization, and class structure. The University of Chicago's Everett C. Hughes taught at McGill in the 1920s and 1930s and at Laval in 1942–43; his studies of Quebec were translated into French and influenced a generation of francophone sociologists, including Laval's Jean-Charles Falardeau, who had himself studied at the University of Chicago.[56]

The LOC may also have been influenced by broader North American developments, where social scientists were beginning to take an interest in focus groups and longitudinal studies that traced subjects over time. American historian Elaine Tyler May, for instance, has drawn on the records of the Kelly Longitudinal Study, a series of surveys of 300 middle-class American couples that also began in the late 1930s and continued until the mid-1950s.[57] Closer to home, psychologists were undertaking longitudinal studies in Toronto schools in the interwar years.[58] *Locistes* were not necessarily plugged in to these academic trends. But such scholarly developments had echoes in the media and public culture, where newspapers regularly reported the results of polls conducted by the Gallup-affiliated Canadian Institute of Public Opinion after 1941, and by Britain's Mass Observation during the war, and provided periodic updates on the scientific observation of the Dionne quintuplets.[59] The LOC's tracking of the Cent-Mariés, in fact, can be seen as one way in which certain elements of the Church attempted to 'modernize' in the wake of the war.[60]

What, then, can these letters tell us about the private lives of the Cent-Mariés, and by extension, about other French-Canadian, working-class couples in the wake of the war? We know that in 1944 half of the couples lived in Montreal. According to the LOC's records, the men worked as mechanics, machinists, drivers, clerks, grocers, and bakers. Before their marriage, the women had worked as domestic servants, dressmakers, and factory operatives.[61] The couples reflected the constituency of the JOC and the LOC, of course, in that they were largely working class. Wives reported on their husbands' success, or lack thereof, in finding work; on the kinds of hours they worked; and on whether the couple felt itself to be financially stable.[62]

Many of the Cent-Mariés who wrote to the LOC insisted on the happiness of their marriages.[63] News of children dominated the letters, at least in part because the LOC specifically asked for details on children's names, ages, and birthdays. Parents reported on their children's ill-health and expressed pride when their children were healthy.[64] Couples without children who felt obliged to respond to the LOC's requests for their children's names and ages articulated their disappointment at being childless. As one woman told the LOC eight years after the mass wedding, 'C'est bien malheureux, nous n'avons pas encore d'enfant.'[65] Clearly the LOC was not simply interested in knowing its subjects, but was also attempting to shape behaviour. Its emphasis on children was intended to remind the couples of what they ought to be doing, even if they were not (or could not). Asking whether wives worked for pay, and taking care to find out who was looking after these women's household duties, was another way of prescribing family.[66]

In all likelihood, the Cent-Mariés emphasized marital happiness and children in their letters because they thought that this was what the LOC was interested in hearing. Certainly these elements of the marriages were what turned up in the LOC's press releases and anniversary updates. On the other hand, the Cent-Mariés also confided other truths, which did not show up in the official celebrations, such as severe poverty and the inability to find work or housing. Some letters point to the existence of real poverty, both before the wedding (at the tail end of the Depression) but also after their marriage, during the years of supposed wartime and postwar prosperity. Some of the couples were on relief; some husbands lost jobs or worked irregularly; many suffered from serious problems of health and poor housing related to low or no income.[67] These harsher realities of working-class existence turned up, instead, in the LOC's community action: in its demands for family allowances or affordable housing.

The Cent-Mariés did not write simply in response to the LOC's requests for information: they also wrote for advice and for tangible aid. Couples wrote to ask if the LOC knew of available jobs or housing; they requested advice on how to secure a housing loan; they asked for monetary assistance in order to pay hospital bills and rent and to buy toys and clothing for their children.[68] Turning to the LOC for assistance was in a sense invoking an older model than turning to the state – but at a time when much social welfare was private and denominational, and when the provincial government's welfare initiatives were limited, this was a logical strategy. There may have been a sense, too, in which the Cent-Mariés saw the LOC as implicated in their fates. The JOC had organized the wedding and sent them off to embark upon married life: did the Action catholique not bear some responsibility for how that married life turned out?

The letters written by the Cent-Mariés reveal their own concern for reconstruction, for what they hoped their lives would look like in a victorious postwar democracy. Their reconstruction dreams involved family, children, decent housing – in some cases, home ownership. One couple, for instance, had had a very difficult first few years of marriage marked by poverty, illness, and the death of their infant son. But by 1945, things were looking up. The couple had three healthy young children, the husband (a streetcar driver) had more work than he could handle, and as his wife explained, 'Surtout quand nous aurons notre petit 'home' à nous avec une grande cour ce sera le bonheur rêvé.'[69] Other couples wrote to the LOC at the end of the war, describing their plans to build their own house or to provide their young children with a decent future.[70] The war had clearly improved the financial situation of many of these couples, especially where husbands had secured steady employment in the city's munitions factories and aircraft plants.[71] At the same time, their letters serve as a check on easy notions of postwar security and prosperity. In this era of a still-nascent welfare state, before state-administered health and hospital insurance, illness especially cast a dark shadow on these young families, bringing worry, sorrow, and debt.[72] Moreover, enthusiasm for domesticity and child-rearing had its limits. The Ligue Ouvrière Catholique Féminine (LOCF), for instance, acknowledged that fear of another pregnancy was a common sentiment among working-class wives.[73] One Granby woman who married in the mass wedding explained in 1947 that she and her husband loved their children but, with the seventh baby on the way, were beginning to find the task of child-rearing burdensome and expensive, especially given the high cost-of-living.[74] Her words contrasted rather sharply with the LOC's celebration of fertility, and were a reminder that this fertility was not always freely chosen.

The problems and possibilities experienced by the Cent-Mariés were undoubtedly shared by other working-class families in postwar Montreal. Unemployment, housing shortages, infant mortality, illness, and a sky-rocketing cost-of-living were concerns evident in the letters written by the Cent-Mariés but also in Montreal union newspapers such as *Le Monde Ouvrier*. A broad public of newspaper readers and radio listeners was exposed to the celebration and commemoration of this mass wedding through the 1940s and 1950s; some elements of the married lives of these couples must surely have resonated with them. In translating the Cent-Mariés' private experiences into the basis of political or community action through lobbying governments, through services such as l'Entr'aide familiale, and through its newspaper, the LOC helped to shape new definitions of what was fit for public discussion. Moreover, in supporting 'une politique vraiment familiale,' the LOC explicitly acknowledged the ways in which family and politics were intertwined in visions of postwar reconstruction.[75]

A 'mouvement familial'

The Cent-Mariés experiment, and the specialized movements of the ACC more broadly, were projects that took place within the context of increasing secularization, marital disruptions occasioned and brought to light by war, the expansion of married women's paid work, and falling birth rates.[76] The LOC, one of the most active of the ACC's specialized movements, adopted as its particular cause the well-being of francophone, Catholic, working-class husbands and wives. It operated under the assumption that in order to re-spiritualize these couples' daily lives, it had to address the material context in which they lived. It was impossible, the LOC argued, to create truly Christian spouses and parents without first effecting considerable improvements in their housing, incomes, budgets, and health. The LOC's advice to married couples, then, was an amalgam of the spiritual and the mundane, combining an analysis of men's and women's 'true natures' with an emphasis on marriage contracts and family budgets.[77]

The Action catholique's slogan, 'Voir, Juger, Agir,' indicated the various elements of its mission: observing its community carefully, deciding what needed to be done, and then acting to change the world around it. The LOC attempted to transform marriage and family in Quebec in three ways: through education (for example, its Forum Populaire, its Service d'orientation des foyers, and its newspaper), through its community services (such as l'Entr'aide familiale, summer camps, and a family budget), and through lobbying various levels of government for changes in legislation (among them a *crédit ouvrier*, family allowances, and legislation restricting married women's employment in factories). Publicizing and commemorating the Cent-Mariés was one way of educating the city's workers about marriage and family.

The LOC's choice of what to celebrate in the lives of the Cent-Mariés spoke to working-class experiences. Its determination to teach couples how to be happy in their conjugal life reflected, among other things, the difficulty of escaping an unhappy marriage in Quebec – a province with no divorce courts, where divorce was forbidden by Catholic teachings and required a petition to the Dominion government.[78] Its celebration of marriage took place at a time when Quebecers, like citizens elsewhere on the continent, were marrying at unprecedented rates.[79] Its emphasis on children reflected the North American baby boom and postwar fascination with domesticity.[80] But it was also a reaction to the long-term decline in Quebec's birth rates, particularly in urban areas. The Action catholique–sponsored Service de préparation au mariage took it upon itself to teach the Ogino-Knauss (rhythm) method of birth control in part because Montrealers were clearly learning about other forms of contraception elsewhere: from mothers and mothers-in-law, co-workers, the armed services, some private social agencies, and back-alley abortionists.[81] The Montreal Council of Social Agencies' Committee on Unmarried Parenthood observed in 1949, in fact, that 'a large section of society' was familiar with contraceptives.[82] The LOC's insistence that married women confine their work to the home, hardly a new idea, was articulated more vociferously in the wake of a war when married women had worked for pay in unprecedented numbers and, indeed, had been encouraged by many to do so.[83] Finally, the Action catholique's faith in the redemptive powers of a family budget (an example of the postwar faith in planning) built on an understanding of the minimal incomes with which many of its constituents made do, but was also a recognition of the fact that money was a frequent source of conflict in marriages. A 'ménagère prévoyante économe et industrieuse' was seen to be essential to a happy marriage, and husbands were not to upset the family budget with unnecessary spending.[84]

In its celebration and tracking of the Cent-Mariés, and in its community projects more generally, the LOC exemplified the conflict of ideologies that historians such as Jean Hamelin, Jean-Pierre Collin, and Gaston Desjardins argue existed within the Catholic Church in the postwar period. On the one hand, the LOC's position was defensive: a rearguard action in the face of considerable changes in the lives of Quebecers. On the other hand, the LOC wanted to respond in positive ways to these changes and to demonstrate the Church's adaptability to the real lives of its parishioners.[85] The LOC argued for the distinctiveness of French-Canadian families in the wake of the war, but these were not the rural, preindustrial French Canadians whose virtues were lauded in conservative clerical nationalist rhetoric. Rather, the LOC made new kinds of claims, on behalf of modern, urban, working-class French Canadians with material concerns. Its religious and its social missions thus coexisted uneasily. But if, as Collin has argued, the LOC was generally progressive on matters of class, its record on gender was more conservative. Although Collin maintains that the LOC espoused a 'familial feminism,' I would contend that this was an ideology more steeped in the familial than in the feminist.[86] Like many secular postwar organizations in Quebec and elsewhere in North America, the LOC's vision of women's roles was circumscribed by traditional conceptions of family and gendered conceptions of work.

The extent to which the Action catholique was able to combat the problems it perceived around it is another question altogether. By 1950, the LOC claimed to have effected transformations in a considerable number of working-class households by teaching Christian family values.[87] But despite the fact that Montreal's LOC federation was relatively large and active, the Action catholique movements, and the LOC in particular, only ever engaged a small minority of the city's population.[88] The beliefs of those who joined the LOC were not necessarily representative of those of other francophone Quebecers, nor of the sentiments of Montrealers of other ethnic backgrounds. Moreover, by the early 1950s, according to Jean-Pierre Collin, the LOC was turning away from community and class-based activism, and began instead to look inward, focusing on relations within families and matters of personal and spiritual improvement. This shift observed by Collin reflected a larger turn to the right that Jean Hamelin argues took place within the Catholic Church in Quebec in the 1950s.[89] If the LOC failed to fulfil its democratic potential in the later postwar years, it was not alone: many other community organizations, unions, and consumer groups also appear to have turned inward and away from the utopian projects they had launched in the 1940s.

The LOC was by no means the only organization in postwar Montreal concerned with the well-being of the city's families. In particular, it needs to be examined in the context of the *mouvement familial* – an ensemble of organizations for working- and middle-class families that had begun to emerge in the late 1930s but that seemed poised for expansion at the end of the war.[90] Marie-Paule Malouin, the historian of Quebec's *mouvement familial*, describes the movement as encompassing institutions including the LOC, the École des parents, the Service d'éducation familiale, and the Associations parents-maîtres (Parent-Teacher Associations).[91] All of these groups had links with the Catholic Church, but to different degrees. Some, like the JOC and the LOC, were member organizations of the (Oblate-dominated) Action catholique; others, like the Institut familial, were affiliated with the Franciscans, and still others (for example, the Foyers Notre-Dame) were founded by Sulpicians. Malouin notes the lack of unity among these organizations, citing differences of approach, class cleavages, and varying degrees of attachment to the church hierarchy.[92] Jean-Pierre Collin, in fact, maintains that it is inappropriate to consider the LOC part of the *mouvement familial*; more important than its interest in families, he claims, were its urban and sociopolitical concerns.[93] Yet despite diverging methods and priorities, all of these organizations were concerned with the same kinds of issues at the same time – and at the same time as other organizations across North America. Although André Laurendeau claimed in 1950 that Quebec was still waiting for a unified and articulate 'mouvement des familles,' he acknowledged that recent years had seen an explosion of associations and publications devoted to the province's families.[94]

All of these organizations argued that men and women needed to learn how to be members of a postwar family.[95] They shared a sense that the family had undergone a prolonged crisis through the years of depression and war. Working wives, absent husbands, marital breakdown, adultery, juvenile delinquency: all were cited as signifiers of widespread familial distress.[96] For the organizations that made up Quebec's *mouvement familial*, the solution was twofold: improving the day-to-day functioning of families, and doing so with some eye to Christian teachings.[97] These organizations argued that parents needed answers, and from reliable sources. Future spouses should be educated through marriage prepara-tion courses; mothers and fathers could seek assistance in the École des parents.[98] In teaching domestic skills, budgeting, birth control, and parenting, these church-affiliated organizations were, in effect, usurping parents' own role.[99] Indeed, they often complained that young men and women had not received proper training in their own homes. Yet the active role played by clerics varied considerably from one organiza-tion to the next. One fundamental tenet – perhaps *the* fundamental tenet – of the specialized Action catholique movements was the central role played by laypeople.[100] This gave working-class participants in the JOC and the LOC some space in which to contest and depart from the teachings of the church hierarchy. In some organizations, such as the École des parents, the initiative in sustaining the group and setting the agenda came from young parents themselves.[101] Many of these groups subscribed to an ethos of mutual aid. Their names (École des parents, Équipes de ménages) reflected a sense of teamwork and a conviction that they were educating one another. In this way they pro-vided postwar Quebecers, as Jean-Pierre Collin has argued about the LOC, with an education in democracy.[102] Clearly, Ottawa was not the only postwar player calling for the cultivation of democracy by individual citizens: parents' groups and some Catholic organizations were also in-volved in teaching citizens how to participate in the public sphere.[103]

Although various orders of the Catholic Church had long assumed responsibility for social welfare provisions in Quebec, the emergence of a widespread *mouvement familial* in this period was something different. It aimed to educate families, and sometimes speak for them, rather than simply assisting them with their most immediate needs. The emergence of the *mouvement familial* suggests, first, that a variety of social groups in Quebec were in search of new models of family.[104] Its blossoming after the war also suggests that various branches of the Catholic Church had an interest in postwar reconstruction, and, possibly, a desire to counter-act other models of marriage and family present in Quebec in the late 1940s.

Competing models of family ranged from that structured by the expanding federal welfare state[105] to an increasingly prosperous, suburban, and secular North American norm propagated by the popular culture of movies, magazines, and advertisements.[106] All these models advocated, to some degree, a new 'democratic' ideal of family in the wake of the war. Like the Catholic Church, most secular marriage experts were fully aware that many unions were far from idyllic, and like their religious counterparts, many blamed unhappy marriages on the privations of the Depression and the turmoil of war and separation. Commentators fretted about the lingering after-effects of these major crises on Canadian families.[107] But they were also optimistic that a return to peace and a stable economy would permit families to rebuild and to flourish. This optimism was rooted in part in North America's postwar faith in democracy: families, observers agreed, should operate on the same democratic principles that had been recently vindicated on the battlefields of Europe.[108] Thus Montreal liberal reformer Renée Vautelet declared at the dawn of 1947 that a modern family was 'no longer the husband with his chattel goods but a union of two partners.'[109] *La Presse* likewise claimed in 1949 that the French-Canadian family was making the transition from an 'authoritarian' to an 'egalitarian' institution, and that children were now recognized to have certain rights.[110]

The Canadian Youth Commission found, however, that its inquiry into the family lives of young Canadians elicited mixed responses. In its handbook for postwar youth, entitled *Jeunesse vs. Après-Guerre*, the commission described the currency enjoyed in Canada by a new democratic (rather than patriarchal) conception of the family and an improved status for women. Yet its 1948 publication *Youth, Marriage and the Family* called for still more democracy in family relationships. In the opinion of the commission, this need was particularly acute in Quebec. While family size was steadily diminishing in that province, the commission argued, family status would probably 'retain much of its patriarchal character.'[111] This ambivalence was evident in the JOC's 1945 submission to the commission. At the same time that the Catholic youth organization claimed that fathers and mothers should hold authority within the family together, it observed that if families were assured of some economic security, wives would stay home where they belonged.[112]

In part this ambivalence reflected the confusion of a transitional era in family relations. But it was also an indication of the particular meanings ascribed to democracy: most observers saw no lapse in logic in simultaneously advocating democratic families and stay-at-home wives. Indeed, the postwar democratic family was in many instances predicated on a stay-at-home wife and mother: its essence was 'spousal cooperation, not equality.'[113] Women's unpaid contributions to the family's well-being were to be recognized and lauded, but there was very little question that this unpaid labour was women's work. As Mona Gleason has convincingly argued, prescriptions for modern democratic marriages drew heavily on the much older ideal of separate spheres for women and men. Postwar psychological discourse commended, and recommended, families based on emotional bonds wherein fathers were the 'rightful "heads" of families' and wives were responsible for the 'emotional climate' of the marriage. The 'legitimization of traditional gender roles,' Gleason claims, 'hierarchized the spousal relationship in postwar marriages.'[114] Like secular experts, the Action catholique movements attempted to reconcile democracy and sex-specific roles – sometimes with difficulty. Most Catholic commentators continued to insist that the father was the 'chef de famille' and the rightful source of authority within the family.[115] But they also suggested that he exercise this authority with benevolence. Leaders of the ACC movements, then, emphasized husbands' and wives' respective roles – different but complementary.[116]

Alongside the pronouncements of secular experts such as psychologists and marriage counsellors were other ways in which the family lives of ordinary people were made public in this period: the opinion polls that were beginning to turn up regularly in the press, such as the results of the Gallup-affiliated Canadian Institute of Public Opinion and Britain's Mass Observation; and the advice columns, or 'chroniques sentimentales,' that appeared in most daily and weekly newspapers in Montreal.[117] Gaston Desjardins has explored the advice columns of Montreal newspapers between 1940 and 1960 and argues that they played a significant role in constituting discourses of youth and sexuality in Quebec in this period.[118] Montrealers who wrote to Colette, or Fadette, or Françoise, or Josette, made their private matters public, albeit behind the anonymity of initials or a pseudonym.[119] In the 1940s, advice columnists were frequently forced to juggle with new ideas of democratic families.[120]

Quebec's postwar church saw itself as attempting to address, and sometimes counteract, such secular models of family through the Action catholique and other organizations affiliated with the *mouvement familial*. But in doing so, it revealed the ways in which it was in fact similar to secular institutions in postwar North America. Like other postwar institutions, the church saw proper families as integral to reconstruction. At the dawn of 1945, for instance, the Canadian episcopate urged wives and mothers to return home as soon as possible so that families torn apart by the exigencies of war could be mended.[121] This message was part of a larger (and well-documented) North American push to return both newlywed and long-married women to their homes at the close of the war.[122] In the immediate postwar period, the Catholic Church's long-standing interest in keeping wives at home converged with the renewed effort by secular institutions to do the same.[123] Leaders of the *mouvement familial* participated, moreover, in what amounted to a postwar consensus concerning the value of experts, marriage counselling, good parenting, and education for democracy.[124] Like other institutions, the church was optimistic about the potential of planning as a solution to social problems. But the model of family promoted by the Action catholique movements was not the hegemonic Anglo-Celtic, middle-class model that historians have claimed was universally lauded in the 1950s.[125] The Action catholique promoted an ethnically specific (francophone and Catholic) family, and in the case of the JOC and the LOC, a working-class family. The tensions between the exaltation of a Catholic 'reine du foyer' and the realities of working-class budgets in 1940s Montreal help to explain some of the ambivalence in the LOC's thinking. Its calls for 'un salaire familial' and family allowances were so vociferous because it was attempting to bring into being a working-class family that consistently adhered to the model of a breadwinning husband and a dependent wife and children.

Conclusions

The commemoration of Montreal's mass marriage and the postwar efforts of the LOC more generally point, first, to competing visions of reconstruction in Canada in the wake of the Second World War. The federal Liberals' vision, centred on a federally directed welfare state, clearly did not go unchallenged. There were, of course, similarities between this federal vision and that promoted by the LOC. Both the federal state and the LOC were constructing 'family' in a context where married women had recently worked for pay in large numbers. Both the Catholic Church and Mackenzie King argued that a wife and mother should be 'la reine du foyer.'[126] The LOC campaigned for family allowances using the argument that they would allow mothers to stay home; as Ruth Pierson has demonstrated, there were numerous federal incentives to encourage married women to return home, including family allowances, the closing of wartime day nurseries, and amendments to the federal Income Tax Act.[127] The primary difference was that Ottawa promoted a homogeneous Canadian family; the LOC, in contrast, insisted upon the specificity of the experiences of French-Canadian and of working-class families. This story is thus significant for a second reason: it points to competing definitions of family. The popular conception of a postwar North American family – prosperous, suburban, secular, and nuclear – clearly coexisted with other familial realities.[128] Third, this story supports recent work that highlights the pluralism and ideological flux of 1940s Quebec, the Catholic Church's responses to the social, economic, and intellectual changes taking place around it, and the conflicting strands of thought within the church itself.[129]

Finally, I would argue that the celebration of the Cent-Mariés in the postwar years had implications for understandings of the public. During the war, citizens had been encouraged to think in terms of a public interest, a civic community. In the postwar years, more people, and more kinds of people, claimed access to this public: to public provisions, and to public spheres of discussion. Hence the number of issues that could be appropriately discussed in public also multiplied. The German philosopher Jürgen Habermas has argued that the development of liberal, capitalist societies in the eighteenth and nineteenth centuries was accompanied by the growth of a public separate from the state; indeed, the public, in Habermas's conception, was a sphere of discussion that acted as a check on the state.[130] A Habermasian conception of the public is useful here if we think of the LOC as raising public awareness of social welfare issues that the provincial state was dragging its heels on or that the federal state was addressing, but in ways that the LOC found inadequate or inappropriate for Quebec. The LOC argued, for instance, that a family allowances program ought to be administered by the provincial government so as to safeguard provincial autonomy. Once federal family allowances were implemented in 1945, the LOC maintained that the program should at least take into account Quebec's larger families and not drop its rates after the fourth child.[131] The public thus became a forum for competing conceptions of family, and despite the many private functions of the Catholic Church, the Action catholique served as a 'counterpublic,' in the 1940s, to the expanding federal state.

chapter five

A Politics of Prices: Married Women and Economic Citizenship

> Mrs. Conroy said that every woman in Canada was thinking of prices at the present time and if we intended to reach the heart of Canadian women we should give some indication that we are going to study prices very carefully.
>
> Canadian Association of Consumers, 29 September 1947[1]

> Every Canadian is either a consumer or dead.
>
> Brief by Kathleen M. Jackson to the Royal Commission on Prices, 1948[2]

A concern with prices, and a politics centred on purchasing, figured prominently in Canada's urban centres in the 1940s. As Mrs Patrick Conroy, the Canadian Congress of Labour's representative to the all-women Canadian Association of Consumers, suggested, this politics of prices was thoroughly gendered. In cities across the country, women used their intimate knowledge of their household finances to demand better social welfare measures and a reasonable cost of living in the context of the Second World War and postwar reconstruction.

This chapter explores the ways in which Montreal women drew on a sense of economic citizenship cultivated over the war years to organize around consumer issues in the immediate postwar period. The federal government had encouraged a wartime consumer consciousness as part of its efforts on the home front. Rationing, price controls, salvaging and recycling drives, and the black market made the availability and distribution of goods a popular topic of discussion through the 1940s. After the war, continuing government controls, consumers' groups, and labour newspapers encouraged both middle- and working-class families to maintain their interest in prices, standards, consumer choice, and the availability of products. Montrealers, grown accustomed to the equity of rationing and worried about the rising cost of living, demanded the ability to purchase household necessities at reasonable prices as one of the rights of economic citizenship.[3]

Household management and daily shopping had long been considered the work of married women – the so-called Mrs Consumers or Purses on Legs.[4] Consumer activism, then, allowed women in particular to carve out significant space in the public sphere. These women, acting in the name of wives and mothers, targeted the state as well as shopkeepers, and thus claimed gendered citizenship rights using what American historian Susan Porter Benson has called the 'trope of the good manager.'[5] Their efforts made the family visible in public; indeed, these women used the claims of family as a key basis for citizenship. As historian Sylvie Murray argues, a concern for issues that affected home and family was not the same thing as a 'retreat' to the nuclear family.[6] Moreover, in Montreal, women's articulation of economic citizenship took place in the context of their newly acquired political citizenship: Quebec women had secured the provincial suffrage in 1940. This chapter argues, then, that a reasonable cost of living and economic citizenship were essential aspects of Montreal families' visions of postwar reconstruction. It also argues that consumer activism was one way in which both women and gender configured the political and the public in this period.

An examination of consumer organizing, in fact, nuances our understanding of the balance of 'private' and 'public' in the 1940s. The federal government's intervention in the running of households during the war, through its regulations on what and how much people could buy, what they could eat, and what they ought not to discard, threw wide open what had once been private. North American historians have argued that at the end of the war, some citizens called for a restoration of privacy; they retreated to domesticity in an attempt to avoid engagement with public matters.[7] Yet as we shall see in this chapter, others took the lessons that they had learned over the course of the war and used them to transform their private household and financial situations into a kind of politics. They made a public, political statement out of what might once (during the Depression, for instance) have been regarded as a shameful situation, to be hidden at all costs.[8] In making the private public, individuals and groups who took action as consumers were taking the promise of Freedom from Want seriously, and were attempting to craft a more democratic public sphere. Women's consumer actions traversed the boundaries of private and public, and in fact threw into question the utility of such distinctions.

At issue here was the limited consumption of necessities such as groceries, not the high consumption of automobiles and expensive consumer durables commonly associated with postwar North America. I begin this chapter by exploring the dimensions and implications of the consumer consciousness developed during the war – particularly among women. I then turn to two examples of Montreal residents organizing as consumers in the immediate postwar years: women's boycott of grocers and butchers in 1947–8; and women's battle to secure the legalization of margarine as a cheaper substitute for butter. Such basic aspects of 'private' life made headlines in the late 1940s; the margarine debate in fact made it to the Supreme Court. Middle-class families had long been units of consumption as well as production; by the 1940s this was increasingly true of Montreal's working class as well.[9] These two consumer campaigns thus had cross-class appeal and involved both French- and English-speaking Montrealers. Moreover, while such campaigns had particular class and ethnic dimensions in Montreal, they were part of a larger phenomenon in these years. Local newspaper reports on 'militant housewives' in Toronto, Chicago, and Paris, France, lent legitimacy and increased importance to the activities of housewives at home.[10]

The prominent role played by women in these battles is not surprising: women around the world had a long history of public protests about consumption, ranging from pre-industrial bread riots to cost-of-living rallies at the close of the Great War.[11] What distinguishes the following episodes from such precedents is, first, the degree to which this consumer consciousness had been encouraged over the course of the Second World War; and second, women's growing sense that an expanding state was accessible to them and that they were entitled to make certain demands on it. The public claims of consumers point to some of the things that citizens thought they deserved in a victorious, welfare-state democracy and reveal sites where the family met the public in the reconstruction period. They also reveal a variety of responses to the federal state's new interventionist role: responses shaped by everyday experiences of a rising cost-of-living, occasionally by liberal convictions, and often by the particular features of Quebec's political economy. Such responses reflected contemporary debates over the ideal size, shape, and purpose of the postwar public. While some citizens called for an expanded federal state, others called for a larger role for Quebec City in structuring the public. Still others envisioned a liberal public: that is, a public sphere that allowed for rights to privacy and the rights of property.

Gaining Consumer Consciousness during the Second World War

In an attempt to manage the war and build a consensus on the home front, Ottawa crafted a relationship with its citizens premised on preserving scarce materials for the war effort and avoiding the inflation that might result from having more money than goods in circulation. Canadians were to save, salvage, and reuse; they were to accept rationing so that goods could be equitably distributed. They were to ensure that shopkeepers adhered to price ceilings, and they were to curb their own desires to spend.[12] Victory Bond campaigns catered to patriotic sentiment while siphoning off 'excess' purchasing power and also satisfying citizens' Depression-bred instincts to put money away in case of future need. Constant public monitoring of the cost-of-living meant that, despite the improved wages of the war years, Canadians were keenly aware of fluctuating costs and of the fine balance between income and expenditures.

The work of rationing, recycling, salvaging, saving, and spending wisely was seen to belong to women.[13] The Consumer Branch of the Wartime Prices and Trade Board (WPTB) in fact secured the official cooperation of 16,000 women across the country, all of whom agreed to monitor prices and report back to the board. These women, the state and the press insisted, were contributing to an Allied victory and were ensuring that the country their men came home to would be in sound economic health.[14] Women were reminded, moreover, that in wartime Canada, unlike war-torn Europe, government controls were 'inconveniences,' not '"hardships" or "sacrifices."'[15] On V-E Day, the government congratulated women on their wartime efforts: thanks to them, Canadians had managed to keep inflation to reasonable levels. Now, the task was to win the peace. Citizens and consumers were reminded that the worst inflation associated with the First World War had come *after* the end of hostilities.[16] The 'danger of inflation' was 'more real now than at any time since the war commenced'; the 'homemakers of the Nation should be on the alert, more than ever ...'[17] Price controls would be lifted only gradually. Slowly, the production of peacetime consumer durables would resume and goods would return to store shelves: in the meantime, anxious consumers were to be patient.[18] Certain items would remain rationed, since Canada was allocating some of its food supplies for export to Europe.[19] Victory Bond campaigns continued through the late 1940s. As long as wages and savings exceeded supplies of consumer goods, inflation remained a threat and the black market tempting.

Historian Jeff Keshen reminds us that cheating, 'gouging,' and black-marketing coexisted with civilian compliance with wartime regulations. Black-marketing was, he claims, 'most prevalent in Montreal,' a phenomenon that he attributes to 'Quebec's lukewarm support for the war.'[20] Opinions about military participation were undeniably mixed. Yet many francophone Quebecers took pride in their cooperation with the state. Quebec women participated in the WPTB's price-watching campaign during the war, and the women of Montreal's Fédération nationale Saint-Jean-Baptiste (FNSJB) reprinted Donald Gordon's letter thanking them for their assistance with price controls in the May 1947 issue of their newsletter.[21] Mariana Jodoin, who was awarded the OBE for her war-work with the WPTB's Consumer Branch, thanked the FNSJB for its congratulations 'en son nom personnel et au nom de toutes les Canadiennes françaises, dont cette décoration représente le dévouement pendant la guerre.'[22] Nonetheless, the federal propaganda machine may have had to work harder in Quebec than elsewhere, especially since the administrators of federal wartime bodies such as the WPTB and the Department of Munitions and Supply included very few francophones.[23] Maurice Duplessis's return to provincial power in August 1944 suggests significant resentment of federal policy and the purchase of Quebec nationalism as the war drew to a close. Duplessis himself regularly attacked Ottawa's wartime regulations, deriding them as 'Restrictions, vexatoires, stupides, inopportunes, intempestives,' and claiming that 'La BUREAUCRATIE remplace la démocratie.'[24]

Canada-wide opposition to government restrictions intensified once the war was won and controls remained in place; the 'orderly decontrol' campaign led by Donald Gordon and the WPTB required persistent and strategic marketing.[25] The immediate postwar period in fact witnessed conflict between those who wanted Ottawa to reduce its new interventionist role now that peace had been secured, and those who felt that citizens stood to benefit from continued and substantial state intervention. Montreal poet and legal scholar F.R. Scott, a member of the latter camp, satirized the postwar priorities of federal Liberals with the words, 'Above all, we must have orderly decontrol / No foolish rush and scramble to renounce / The prime functions of government.'[26] Those desiring a less significant role for Ottawa included not only advocates of provincial autonomy and a decentralized federalism, but also liberal believers in 'small government' and free enterprise.[27] In Montreal, although producers, consumers, and shopkeepers alike appear to have welcomed the end of rationing,[28] the decontrol of prices met with mixed reactions. *La Presse* noted at the end of 1945 that price controls, not surprisingly, continued to enjoy a popularity that wage controls did not.[29] Landlords, manufacturers, and some shopkeepers rejoiced as controls were lifted, but tenants, workers, and consumers soon began lobbying for their reestablishment.[30] The Canadian Institute of Public Opinion claimed in 1947 that price controls were most popular among women, poor people, and unionized workers and their families. Yet it also found that Quebec was less eager for a reimposition of price controls than other regions.[31] High taxes also remained a source of grievance in the postwar period: as Gabrielle Roy's fictional bank-teller Alexandre Chenevert noted in the late 1940s, 'taxes, taxes on all sides, and the cost of living was soaring.'[32] Regular reports in the daily press on Canadians' battle with inflation, and frequent updates on price indexes, kept readers aware of the continued importance of prices in peacetime. As *La Presse* concluded in 1947, the public had learned a great deal about inflation over the past three years.[33]

Most Canadians had had their consumer consciousness raised by the war effort, but the fact that this effort had so frequently been framed as women's work had consequences for the gendered nature of postwar consumer activism. In the late 1940s, household consumers were invariably assumed to be women.[34] More specifically, they were assumed to be married women; the purchasing power of single women was largely ignored. Many Canadian wives argued that they deserved recognition for their wartime cooperation with the government's fiscal policy. Mrs Leslie Hodges, involved with both Montreal's Local Council of Women and the WPTB, claimed in 1944 that Canada was 'the only country in the World where Price Ceilings are really effective, chiefly through the co-operation of the housewives and the Government.'[35] Another woman, proposing the establishment of a Women's Centre in Montreal in 1946, declared that it would be 'a tribute to the excellent work done on the home front by the ordinary housewife during the past six years': in voluntary war work, in the home, and 'as a consumer when she co-operated to maintain price ceilings.'[36] Women were aware that their ordinary work had acquired new worth during the war. As the National Council of Women remarked a half-dozen years after the war had ended, thrift had 'national importance' because of its role in combating inflation. Housewives, Montreal liberal reformer Renée Vautelet observed astutely, enjoyed a new importance as citizens of an economic democracy.[37]

Many women used the construct of the price-watching housewife to make new claims in the public sphere. I have shown elsewhere, for instance, that recipients of military dependents' allowances meticulously itemized their household budgets in letters to Ottawa demanding increased allowances in the context of a rising wartime cost of living.[38] Alongside such solitary letter-writers were the women who organized. The Canadian Association of Consumers (CAC), an exclusively female association formed in 1947, was one example of women building on public recognition of their wartime achievements. The CAC carried on some of the work of the WPTB's Consumer Branch and represented the determination of some women to maintain a role in public life and to keep their unpaid labour in the public eye.[39] Described by one journalist as 'a permanent consumers' organization of women who "cannot sit idly by" and watch rising prices and production bottlenecks disrupt the economy of the home,'[40] the CAC declared its realm of interest to be 'tout ce qui peut améliorer le statut social de la famille canadienne.'[41] It met regularly with federal politicians and civil servants, and asked members to protect housewives' interests by scrutinizing prices and adhering to government controls.[42] Like the Consumer Branch and the Councils of Women that dotted the country, the CAC consisted of a national council overseeing provincial and local chapters. The Quebec division drew on institutional structures particular to the province, recruiting at the parish level.[43]

Middle-class women, both English- and French-Canadian, initiated the CAC. Its francophone organizers were social and political activists such as Renée Vautelet, Thérèse Casgrain, Mariana Jodoin, and Mme Gérard Parizeau.[44] The CAC made some effort to ally with working-class organizations, notably the Canadian Congress of Labour and affiliates of the Action catholique such as the Ligue Ouvrière Catholique (LOC). According to Claire Aubin, national president of the LOC Féminine and the CAC's liaison with women workers, the CAC's goal was to maintain 'un certain standard de vie pour les ouvriers.'[45] Another member of the CAC insisted with reference to male unionists that it was 'the wives of these men whom we [are] representing and trying to help.'[46]

Although the CAC was the largest and most prominent of the many consumers' leagues formed in the wake of the war, some working-class women chose instead to participate in consumers' leagues and cooperative movements affiliated with unions and union auxiliaries.[47] The union movement's consumer activism was not the exclusive purview of women: union men also organized around prices. The Montreal Labour Council, for example, protested the increased cost-of-living and the lifting of price controls by the federal government; called for union-label shopping; demonstrated enthusiasm for consumers' cooperatives; and invited the female representatives of the city's consumer leagues to speak at its meetings. Male members of the council made a point of inviting their wives to their 1947 conference on the cost-of-living, and, as breadwinners, claimed an interest in prices on behalf of their families.[48] The Confédération des travailleurs catholiques du Canada (CTCC) likewise insisted in 1947 that the federal government's decision to abandon controls had seriously diminished the purchasing power of working families.[49]

Behind Quebec unions' objections to spiralling prices and vanishing controls was the conviction that Ottawa did not understand French-Canadian experiences: low wages, meagre budgets, and families that were sometimes larger than the English-Canadian norm. A cartoon printed in *Le Monde Ouvrier* (published by the Trades and Labor Congress–affiliated Fédération provinciale du travail) in January 1948, for instance, shows a tired couple sitting in the living room of a house in disarray, surrounded by eleven rowdy children. The wife reassures her husband: 'Ne te décourage pas, vieux, le docteur Pett, d'Ottawa, dit qu'on peut les nourrir pour 15½ cents par repas!'[50] In reaction to this same federal statistic, Saint-Henri's newspaper *La Voix populaire* conducted an informal survey of the neighbourhood's housewives, asking them if they could feed their families on fifteen and a half cents each per meal. The journalist was greeted with laughter and jeers, the women insisting that it was impossible to feed their husbands well enough on that sum for them to properly carry out their jobs.[51] The rickety household economies of many Montreal families in the 1940s bear little resemblance to the 'mass consumption society' assumed by most historians of postwar North America. Accustomed to frugality, many Montrealers continued to restrain themselves to careful, minimal spending for some time.[52]

Finally, the Action catholique adopted consumer efforts similar to those of labour unions. The LOC built on the heightened awareness of prices by holding study groups on cooperative movements and consumers' leagues and by teaching its working-class participants how to budget in the context of the increased cost-of-living.[53] Unlike most unions in this period, the Action catholique was somewhat wary of state involve-

ment. Consumers' cooperatives, for instance, were praised as a response
to the high cost-of-living that embodied the Christian principle of cooperation; they were an alternative, not simply to unfettered capitalism,
but also to socialism or communism.[54] But in publishing editorials,
articles, and cartoons about high prices, price controls, and rationing,
both the LOC's *Le Front Ouvrier* and union newspapers such as *Le Monde
Ouvrier* fostered a consumer consciousness and took it upon themselves
to teach their working-class readers *how* to consume in the early postwar
years. They were echoed by advice columnists such as *La Presse*'s Colette
(actually Édouardine Lesage), whose daily columns provided another
site for women to discuss prices in public.[55] Readers wrote in describing
their families' income and expenditures, wondering how to cut costs.[56]
The detailed attention given to family budgets in Colette's column made
the minutiae of running a household (often on very small incomes)
public, and gave readers the opportunity to compare their own household management with the examples that appeared in print.

Consumer Activism: Two Case Studies

In November 1947 shoppers across Canada loaded their baskets with
fresh and canned fruits and vegetables. The federal government had
recently imposed an embargo on the importation of certain goods in an
effort to conserve its supply of American dollars, and consumers feared
an imminent produce shortage.[57] Montreal housewives' initial response
to the embargo appeared to vary by class and ethnicity. The west side of
the city (more English Canadian and more affluent) witnessed a 'course
des acheteurs' (buyers' race), as shoppers made massive purchases of
goods that might soon be unavailable. On the east side of Montreal
(largely French Canadian and poorer), women with less money, and
more likely to have ice-boxes than refrigerators, made small daily purchases and watched prices carefully.[58] Yet as panic buying across the
country led to speculation and skyrocketing prices, housewives implemented 'buyers' strikes,' refusing to purchase fruits and vegetables at
outrageous prices. From Toronto, the president of the CAC, Blanche
Marshall, urged Canadian women to use their purchasing power to put
an end to inflation in the produce trade. Don't pay twenty-five cents for a
cabbage worth ten cents, she advised. Prices would fall, she predicted, as
soon as housewives stopped buying.[59] Montreal housewives took note
and stayed home, 'eating the products bought in panic earlier this week
and last week.'[60] Newspapers described deserted produce stands across

the city; at the Bonsecours Market, women asked prices and moved on without purchasing when they heard the responses. *La Presse* reported that buyers' strikes were making farmers and merchants gloomy and that the market for fruits and vegetables was '*mort, tout à fait mort!*'[61]

The housewives' strike worked, at least in the short term. Some farmers dropped the prices of their fruits and vegetables almost immediately. By the end of November, for instance, the cost of carrots and onions was falling daily. The federal government's reimposition of price ceilings on certain tinned foods and fresh produce at the end of the month contributed to the stabilization of prices.[62] By late February 1948, *La Presse* noted, Montreal housewives were loosening their purse strings as essential foods were becoming more affordable. Cabbages that had been left on grocers' shelves at thirty cents a pound were now selling for five cents a pound. Shoppers' 'silent strikes' had had a serious impact, the newspaper claimed, and butchers, as well as produce vendors, had been hard hit. Meat prices had peaked in early January: although they had dropped somewhat after the federal government threatened to impose a price ceiling, shoppers continued to exercise restraint in their purchases of bacon, beef, and sausages. By late February, butchers' ice-boxes were reported to be overflowing, and meat was selling for approximately 10 per cent less than at the beginning of the month.[63] Meat consumption was especially likely to drop in times of high prices. As one labour journalist discovered, working-class mothers with numerous mouths to feed and few groceries stockpiled in their pantries could not stop buying food altogether, but tended to avoid purchasing expensive items such as meat and butter.[64] Class and cultural differences were also evident in the choice of scapegoats for high food prices. While Montreal's mainstream press pointed to farmers and shopkeepers as the culprits, *Le Front Ouvrier*, a Catholic labour paper, indignantly defended rural producers and suggested that the speculation and attempted profiteering of importers, wholesalers, and distributors were more likely the cause of increased prices.[65]

The boycott of grocers and butchers in 1947–8 crossed lines of class and ethnicity and straddled the divisions between organized and informal consumer activism, between private needs and public action. In this sense it was both more widespread and more diffuse than other postwar consumer campaigns, such as the battle to secure the legalization of margarine as a cheaper alternative to butter. Margarine became news across Canada in the late 1940s, but as a city of a million consumers, Montreal was a key player in this campaign. In his legislative history of

margarine, W.H. Heick argues that Canada's 1886 ban on the manufacture, importation, and sale of margarine was the result of the leverage
exercised by dairy farmers and butter producers in a largely rural nation.[66] By the 1940s, a more urban country faced with food rationing and
a high cost of living called for margarine as a less expensive and more
easily available butter substitute. Canada's political centre of gravity had
shifted: in Heick's words, 'the wishes of 150,000 producers of milk had to
give way to the desires of 13 million consumers.'[67] But they were not to
give way without a fight. The seemingly mundane margarine issue sparked
debate not only between rural producers and urban consumers, but also
between Ottawa and the provinces.

In Quebec, Premier Maurice Duplessis, mindful of rural voters, chose
to present the demand for margarine as an attack on the province's
agrarian traditions and farmers' livelihoods. He drew support from the
Union catholique des cultivateurs (UCC), who argued that the manufacture and sale of margarine in Quebec would deal a death blow to the
province's dairy industry and, by extension, to its entire agricultural
sector.[68] Yet the massive wartime migration of rural Quebecers to industrial jobs in cities meant that within Quebec the balance between food
producers and consumers had shifted dramatically.[69] While Duplessis
catered to rural electors, the growing number of urban-dwellers who
called for the right to purchase margarine drew support from unions,
social welfare agencies, and voluntary associations including the
Fédération nationale Saint-Jean-Baptiste, the Montreal Labour Council,
Montreal's Family Welfare Association and its Local Council of Women,
the Canadian Welfare Council, and the Canadian Association of Consumers.[70] At stake were questions of class and entitlement: clearly, those
most in need of margarine were low-income families.[71]

Margarine advocates targeted governments rather than farmers or
shopkeepers,[72] and invoked free enterprise, free choice, healthy competition, and family needs in a victorious democracy. In the early postwar
years, amid butter rationing and high food prices, Montreal's Local
Council of Women protested the 'prohibition on the manufacture,
Import and sale of Margarine,' because 'a vitamin fortified substitute for
butter should be available for needy Canadian families.'[73] Le Front Ouvrier
noted in January 1948 that the cost of butter had risen steadily since
price controls had been lifted; with what, the newspaper asked, would
workers replace it?[74] By early 1948, polls showed that the margarine
movement was gaining ground in Canada: with the notable exception of
farmers, most people now opposed the ban on margarine. Although
polls found that opinions on margarine did not vary much by sex, La

Presse claimed that housewives felt the scarcity of butter most acutely.[75] Mariana Jodoin of the Fédération nationale Saint-Jean-Baptiste underlined the issue's gendered dimensions when she informed the FNSJB that, at a public assembly on margarine held in Montreal in September 1948, 'Mme [Thérèse] Casgrain a su, mieux que tous ces Messieurs, traiter la question.'[76]

The Supreme Court's widely reported December 1948 decision – that the federal government did not have the right to prohibit the manufacture or sale of margarine – was upheld by the Judicial Committee of the Privy Council in 1950 and appeared to many to confirm the consumer's right to choose.[77] Margarine lobbyists then turned their efforts to provincial authorities. In Duplessis, they faced a formidable opponent: provincial antimargarine legislation was enacted in March 1949, and margarine would remain illegal in Quebec until 1961.[78] Montreal's Local Council of Women dispatched a series of telegrams to Duplessis, arguing for the consumer's right to 'free choice in the purchase of a healthful substitute for butter.' Antimargarine legislation, the clubwomen claimed, 'encroached on personal liberty.' How ironic that 'a government which has stood for provincial autonomy,' the women commented, should 'deny the autonomy of the individual in his home and household.'[79] In emphasizing free choice, personal liberty, and individual autonomy, the Local Council of Women articulated assumptions about citizenship and entitlement increasingly common in the late 1940s. As the Canadian Association of Consumers and the National Council of Women argued in 1948, 'If we are entering upon a period of free enterprise, we feel that consumers are entitled to the protection of individual competition, by manufacturers, wholesalers, and retailers.'[80] Or, as popular Montreal performer Peter Barry sang in his postwar calypso hit, 'Margie Margarine':

My mother go to the grocery store,
To buy a pound of butter or more
But the butter price is much too high
So mother sit at home and cry ...
This is democracy, I am told,
So why can't margarine be sold?[81]

Economic Citizenship

Consumer activism had considerable purchase in the postwar years in part because Montrealers, like residents of other Canadian cities, were reshaping their sense of citizenship. Dominique Marshall has argued persuasively that in the postwar years, Quebec residents came to adopt a sense of 'economic citizenship' that included new welfare state measures such as unemployment insurance and family allowances.[82] These new measures were intended, in part, to paper over the cleavages of ethnicity and politics exacerbated by war and conscription, and to build allegiance to the federal state and a common 'nation.' What Marshall calls economic citizenship has been described by other historians and sociologists as 'social citizenship' – that is, a sense of citizenship rooted, in part, in state welfare measures.[83] In this chapter I have used the phrase 'economic citizenship' to mean the conviction that one was entitled to participate in a capitalist economy on reasonable terms, and, furthermore, that the state had a role to play in facilitating this participation.[84] This sense of economic citizenship had been fuelled by wartime propaganda that insisted that being a good citizen meant spending wisely, and it was encouraged by early Cold War rhetoric that touted the superiority of democratic capitalism. Consumer spending was seen to be important to the health of Canada's postwar economy.[85] In turn, Canadians increasingly expected the rewards of citizenship to include such tangible benefits as an acceptable cost of living. As Mrs F.E. Wright of the Canadian Association of Consumers and Mrs R.J. Marshall of the National Council of Women declared before the Royal Commission on Prices in 1948, 'We shall continue to work for the maintenance of an adequately high standard of living for our people at prices they can afford to pay, with fair play towards all interests in the economy, and to co-operate with all those who are concerned with the economic well-being of the Canadian family, so that together we may share the privileges and responsibilities of our democratic way of life.'[86]

Through the years of war and reconstruction, unions, working-class branches of the Action catholique, and unorganized men and women – members of working-class families – attempted to maintain their standards of living by calling for continued price and rent controls and for more generous state-welfare measures. Yet there existed competing visions of economic citizenship. By the later 1940s and certainly by the 1950s, dominant understandings of democracy and economic citizenship often assumed the superiority of a more or less 'free' market.[87] Numerous voices argued that the security provided by a healthy economy and publicly funded social welfare programs would prevent Communism from taking root among the nation's citizens; economic, social, and political citizenship were linked.[88] Citizens had a role to play in fighting the Cold War and arresting Communism by being disciplined consumers. In its 1950 publication *Why Be Thrifty?* the National Council of Women warned that Communism grew amid 'economic collapse' but also amid regimentation and rigid controls; conversely, 'Democracy's strength lies in a sense of individual responsibility and the exercise of individual initiative.'[89] Democracy needed to be carefully cultivated; citizens, including women, had responsibilities as well as rights.[90] The liberal strand of economic citizenship that seems to have won out by the 1950s drew explicit links between (gendered) consumption and political participation in a democracy. Montreal liberal reformer Renée Vautelet, for example, spoke of women's votes 'going to market,' of 'shop[ping] on election day at the store of experience in government,' of 'buying' the future.[91] In this liberal political culture, conscientious consumer activists (demanding lower prices, greater quantities of goods, and more choice in products) were seen to help, not hinder, the smooth operation of the postwar economy.[92]

A grassroots politics scaffolded on prices had the potential to rally large numbers of people around issues commonly thought private, ranging from margarine to monthly rent payments. Consumer activism could be seen as bringing shoppers of all classes together in a common effort to win the peace. Although working people were harder hit by the increase in the cost-of-living, middle-class citizens also publicly deplored increases in prices. Vautelet, for instance, declared consumption to be 'the only economic interest in Canada that speaks for all Canada ... our common denominator ... the only shared Interest of the land.'[93] Yet class differences were in fact embedded in consumer activism in Montreal. A politics of prices highlighted the fragility of working-class budgets in a city grappling with the rising cost-of-living. It resonated with Montreal citizens precisely because, in many cases, every penny mattered. Working-class women participated in the budget projects of the Ligue Ouvrière Catholique Féminine, in the consumer activities of union auxiliaries, and in consumer cooperatives. Above all, they scrimped and saved at home – in non-organized forms of consumer 'activism.' For working-class families, an emphasis on prices was clearly inadequate on its own. As Susan Porter Benson reminds us, consumption 'was always tightly tethered to earning': in a province where low wages were endemic, attempts to lower prices could only accomplish so much.[94]

The middle-class women who had forged partnerships with the federal government during the war years through the Consumer Division of the WPTB also continued their consumer efforts in the wake of the war. In insisting that governments and citizens listen to housewives, the

Fédération nationale Saint-Jean-Baptiste, the Local Council of Women, and the Canadian Association of Consumers made women's unpaid work public.[95] In subscribing to what historian Sylvie Murray has called an ethos of 'active citizenship,' these women joined other postwar North Americans involved in such family-centred causes as Home and School organizations, Parent-Teacher Associations, the École des Parents, and battles for daycare.[96] As part of the practice of active citizenship, members of Montreal's Notre-Dame-de-Grâce Women's Club, for instance, taught each other parliamentary procedure and held study sessions on 'Canadian Democracy in Action,' took field trips to City Hall and to Parliament Hill, and invited guest speakers to lecture on such topics as 'Women Face a Changing World' and 'Education for a New Day.'[97] Their outlook was neatly summarized in the 1948 declaration by the president of the Local Council of Women that 'as politics today have to do with the home and family politics should be our business.'[98] This claim had particular resonance in a place where women had only recently secured the provincial vote. These women certainly defined themselves as active citizens; their actions call into question assumptions about postwar women's insular domesticity, and suggest broader definitions of politics for this period. Moreover, they support an extensive literature demonstrating that the 'great darkness' that is supposed to have descended over Quebec during the Duplessis years was punctuated by numerous points of protest.[99]

Examining the politics of prices in a city under reconstruction points to one way that 'family' and families were mobilized in pursuit of postwar citizenship rights. Both family and consumer activism could be deployed on behalf of a variety of political beliefs and to a multitude of ends: the maternalist argument was articulated in sites as diverse as the largely middle-class Canadian Association of Consumers and the Catholic labour paper *Le Front Ouvrier*.[100] Yet while organizations as different as the Local Council of Women and the Ligue Ouvrière Catholique often had different visions of family, the families invoked by these disparate bodies were increasingly ones that purchased, rather than produced, their basic needs. And although the particular notions of family marshalled in support of consumers' rights were not always identical, 'family' as an abstract concept had remarkable persuasive power in these years.

Women's consumer activity traversed the boundaries between private and public. Consumer boycotts – tellingly referred to as 'grèves silencieuses' – were markedly different from strikes, for instance, which were public, vocal, and occasionally violent. Not only did consumer activism target lower-profile establishments, but also, like much of women's domestic labour, decisions about what and what not to purchase were made quietly, often in private, and were acts of restraint, most noticeable in their absence.[101] Most of women's consumer 'activism,' in fact, was probably informal and unorganized: simply not buying when prices were too high.[102] Consumers' delegations and marches of women on City Hall were important exceptions: visible and newsworthy, attracting public attention similar to that garnered by strikes and men's occupation of the streets.

What we see in Montreal in the 1940s are calls by both working- and middle-class citizens for a role in shaping the postwar public. In the wake of a war when the duties of citizenship had been paramount, Montrealers demanded the rights of citizenship. Many worked to make the public sphere more democratic by attempting to expand its membership and to translate public presence into political impact. In particular, the working-class families who exposed their meagre incomes and expenditures to public view were unveiling the private in an attempt to see the democratic rhetoric of wartime realized. In claiming and negotiating new postwar citizenship rights – economic citizenship, but also, for women, political citizenship in the form of the provincial suffrage, and for working-class families, especially, social citizenship in the form of new welfare-state measures – some Montrealers pushed for a broader and more inclusive public, and they used the rhetoric of 'family' to strengthen their claims. At the same time, Montrealers concerned with the liberal values of privacy and property, and with the particular needs of Quebec, attempted to ensure that the postwar 'public' consisted of more than simply an expanding federal state.

chapter six

In the Streets: Fatherhood
and Public Protest

This chapter explores two instances of household politics being played out in the streets of Montreal in the 1940s: postwar calls for affordable housing and, specifically, the Squatters' Movement of 1946–7; and the Catholic schoolteachers' strike of January 1949. It focuses particularly on the role of fathers in these episodes. The Squatters' Movement shows us men taking to the streets as fathers to demand better housing for their families. The teachers' strike reveals both male teachers striking as fathers, and pupils' fathers passing judgment on the strike in the name of their children's needs and rights. While fathers were by no means the only actors in these dramas, their 'gendered interventions'[1] in public life are telling in a context in which the state was increasingly stepping in to regulate households and families. These examples of household politics bore the imprint of fathers' desire to retain authority and influence despite a new and increasing role for the state. The chapter argues that these men's visions of reconstruction, and of social citizenship, included the right to decent housing for their family, their children's right to education, and the right to a voice in their children's education.

Some contemporaries worried that government intervention into family life – through compulsory schooling or family allowances, for instance – meant the usurping of fathers' authority. A paternalistic state would replace real fathers in caring for wives and children. And yet these developments also meant new, legal obligations for parents to support their children: in Quebec, the provincial compulsory schooling act of 1942 was accompanied by legislation restricting child labour. These acts were an attempt to ensure the prolonged dependence of all children, including working-class children, upon their parents; as historians Dominique Marshall and Susan Pedersen remind us, it is essential to consider both generation and gender in studies of social policy.[2] In the two episodes discussed in this chapter, we see men articulating their rights as parents as much as, or more than, their rights as husbands. Fathers appear to have felt that they had less decision-making power than before, but in some ways greater responsibility.[3] The particular weight of such responsibility in Quebec is suggested by the fact that, throughout the 1940s, Montreal workers and welfare advocates repeatedly claimed that new social policies needed to take into account Quebec's 'familles nombreuses.'

This chapter thus adds to the growing Canadian literature on postwar fatherhood, but differs from most recent studies in its focus on the relationships fathers crafted with the public sphere.[4] Furthermore, both of the episodes discussed here shed light on the renegotiation of relationships between citizens and the state in the reconstruction period. Responses to the 1949 teachers' strike reveal occasionally ambivalent attitudes to new forms of state intervention in family life, in this case compulsory schooling. And yet what we see here is hardly the unequivocal 'anti-étatisme' that was once seen as the hallmark of pre-Quiet Revolution Quebec.[5] The postwar campaign for affordable housing, for instance, points to one place where many Montrealers insisted that the state had not sufficiently intervened.[6]

Fathers, Veterans, and the Squatters' Movement of 1946–1947

Then we must care for the housing needs of our people,
The Family being so sacred. What we need here
Is the freeing of private contractors, a secure five per cent
For insurance and mortgage companies. Thus we achieve
Incentives to build the luxury homes and apartments
Fit for heroes to look at.

F.R. Scott, 'Orderly Decontrol: 1947'[7]

As we saw in Chapter 1, postwar Montreal (like many other Canadian cities) experienced a severe housing crisis exacerbated by wartime shortages of materials, in-migration to the city and a high rate of family formation. Faced with this crisis, Montrealers doubled up with friends and relatives, lodged in strangers' spare rooms and according to the Action catholique, were more likely to use birth control.[8] Some of them campaigned for more housing and more affordable housing, using tactics ranging from letter-writing to the occupation of public buildings.

Those citizens who called for low-cost housing and continued postwar rent controls framed their demands in the language of democracy and family needs. The Jeunesse Ouvrière Catholique's protests to Ottawa regarding poor housing conditions, for instance, were made in the name of working families.[9] The Ligue Ouvrière Catholique (LOC) saw housing as a basic right of citizenship; the state should do everything in its power to see that decent housing was accessible to all.[10] This was a cause upon which the classes could agree: working- and middle-class Montrealers undertook parallel campaigns, and sometimes worked together, to demand affordable housing.[11] As early as 1944, the city's Local Council of Women (LCW) and the Canadian Legion passed resolutions requesting the prolongation of rental controls.[12] The Montreal Labour Council lobbied vigorously for rental controls and low-cost housing through the late 1940s.[13] Advocates of rent control came in various political, ethnic, and religious stripes and included the Canadian Welfare Council, the Montreal Section of the National Council of Jewish Women, consumers' leagues in NDG and Snowdon, the Next-of-Kin Association, the Ligue des électrices catholiques, the Ligue des locataires de Montréal, the Société de protection du locataire, the Ligue Ouvrière Catholique, and the Communist-led Ligue des Vétérans sans logis.[14]

It is essential, however, to distinguish between those who wanted the state to play a central role in the provision of housing and those who merely wanted it to facilitate the efforts of hard-working individuals, between those who sought help from Ottawa and those who turned to Quebec City. While the Montreal Labour Council denounced the federal government in November 1949 for lifting rental controls and at the same meeting called upon Duplessis to enact provincial rent control legislation,[15] other lobbyists, such as the Action catholique movements, were less consistently enthused by state intervention. When the Action catholique did look to the state, it turned to the provincial government more frequently than to Ottawa.[16] For the Action catholique, and for some Quebec unions, a key housing-related demand was a *crédit ouvrier*. The Fédération provinciale du travail du Québec argued that a provincial *crédit ouvrier* to help workers build their own homes would assist men with numerous children who had difficulty securing adequate rental housing.[17]

While campaigns by Quebec unions and by the LOC for housing cooperatives and a *crédit ouvrier* for single-family homes depended on provincial assistance, they were also a form of self-help and mutual aid.[18] The LOC's attempt to put home ownership within the reach of working-class French Canadians met with a favourable response from its constituents. One father of five children wrote to the LOC in March 1948 requesting information about the *crédit ouvrier* in order that he might provide a suitable house for his family. Another father, a carpenter-builder, wrote six months later to say that he was interested in building a house through the LOC's cooperative movement and would also like to contribute his expertise to the movement. He and his three children lived in an apartment consisting of a small bedroom and a small kitchen.[19] The men who wrote to the LOC to find out how to secure decent housing or to offer their construction skills to other *locistes* in need of shelter clearly understood it to be the duty of a man, as a father and breadwinner, to ensure that his family had a roof over its head. Their interest in a cooperative form of consumption reflected and responded to the Action catholique's efforts to promote cooperatives among French-Canadian workers. Their willingness to contribute their skills and labour to building their homes demonstrates, meanwhile, that they continued to view their families as units of production as well as consumption. Cooperation was an attractive option for families on the margins of consumption, with earnings insufficient to allow them to consume at going prices. Yet the type of home envisioned by the *crédit ouvrier* was a dramatic departure from the Montreal norm. The LOC's campaign for single-family home ownership broke with a long tradition of tenancy, extended families, and 'doubling up' in Montreal's brick triplexes. The LOC's slogan, 'À chaque famille sa maison' claimed decent housing as a right for every family, but also spoke to new norms of consumption, property ownership, and privacy emerging across North America in the postwar years.[20]

Among the most vocal proponents of affordable housing were war veterans. Veterans' feelings of entitlement, seen in Chapter 3, extended to their quest for lodging. Veterans' housing was assumed to be family housing, and veterans became a target market: classified advertisements, for instance, pitched household appliances and furniture to recently demobilized men.[21] Confronted with housing shortages and high rents, veterans turned to the state to demand affordable homes for their families. The problem, Montreal's Local Council of Women noted, was that housing had become a political 'football tossed between the Federal and Municipal Governments, with local organizations trying to give the ball a shove in the right direction.'[22] Under Section 92 of the British North America Act, which included 'property and civil rights,' housing was generally a provincial responsibility. With the establishment of War-

time Housing Ltd., a Crown corporation, the federal government entered the housing domain in order to house wartime munitions workers.
After the war, veterans were eligible for Wartime Housing in such Montreal
neighbourhoods as Ville Saint-Laurent, Rosemont, and Montreal North.
Concerned citizens, notably clubwomen from the LCW, visited the homes
for veterans constructed by the federal government and found them to
be 'liveable and attractive' and 'ideal for the young married couple just
starting up housekeeping.'[23] Yet while the LCW was pleased with the 843
Wartime Houses for veterans built and occupied by 1946–7, it claimed
the next year that there were still four hundred veteran families in
emergency shelters in the Montreal region.[24] It was up to municipalities,
the LCW noted, to petition the Dominion government for more Wartime Housing projects. Meanwhile, Montreal navy veterans demanded
housing aid from the city and from the federal government, and
Montreal's municipal councillors requested that the Department of
National Defence put military barracks at the disposal of homeless
families.[25]

In their search for housing, veterans met with considerable sympathy.
Associations including the LCW, the Montreal Soldiers' Wives League,
the Jeunesse Ouvrière Catholique, and the Ligue Ouvrière Catholique
decried the local housing crisis and blamed various levels of government
for failing to see that veterans were properly housed.[26] The Legion
complained that rents at the new Benny Farm housing project were too
high for veterans.[27] The federal government, meanwhile, sought assistance from local citizens who might be willing to rent to returned
soldiers. 'Ceci vous a été épargné,' it reminded readers of La Presse in an
advertisement depicting Nazi atrocities. 'Soyez reconnaissants. LOUEZ A
UN VETERAN.' Equally evocative was an ad portraying a veteran walking
with a cane, his wife, and their young daughter. 'NOUS AVONS BESOIN
D'UN LOGIS!' the family exclaimed.[28]

The most dramatic manifestation of Montreal men's postwar housing
discontents was the Squatters' Movement of 1946–7.[29] Primarily a movement of Second World War veterans, the episode was spearheaded by
the Ligue des vétérans sans logis, led by Henri Gagnon, an electrician,
union activist, and provincial francophone organizer of the Labour-
Progressive Party. Gagnon and his Ligue demanded the preservation of
rent controls, a halt to evictions and the construction of low-rent housing. In doing so, they relied on gendered perceptions of the right and
obligation of a man to house his family. Gagnon demanded that the
federal government 'PROVIDE DECENT SHELTER FOR THESE EVICTED VET-

ERANS THEIR WIVES AND CHILDREN.' Overcrowded housing meant that 'Aucune vie familiale n'est plus possible.' Quebec families were particularly hard hit by landlords who refused to rent to families with numerous children. As a Ligue pamphlet asked, was having children a crime? 'Les chefs de famille,' the Ligue observed, were employed and could afford to pay their rents – if only there were houses to rent.[30] Montreal war veterans in search of adequate housing could take inspiration from squatters movements elsewhere: in Ottawa, Vancouver, Chicago, New York City, Great Britain, and France.[31] War veterans were particularly 'entitled' citizens: they had fought for their country, and decent housing was recognized to be one of the rights and freedoms for which they had fought.[32] Moreover, as men used to receiving army pay and federal allowances, they did not hesitate to demand their due from Ottawa. Finally, as family men and notably as fathers, they garnered considerable sympathy from a public that acknowledged the rights of children and the plight of fathers attempting to do their best under difficult conditions.

The first volley in this war was fired during the night of 23 October 1946. Henri Gagnon, a number of veterans, including Napoléon Auger, David Durocher, and Roland Mongeau, and their families, took possession of an empty four-storey house on downtown McGill-College avenue.[33] These families had previously been living in single rooms, in unheated tourist cabins, in basements, and in one case, in a shed. In this last case, two of the children were apparently suffering from tuberculosis.[34] Five days later, three more veterans' families moved into a house on Saint-Denis street, at the corner of Mont-Royal avenue. One Montreal newspaper investigated the former living conditions of the two sets of squatters and found that 'Rheumatism and tuberculosis are rampant among both the squatters and the people whose homes they were sharing before the squatting began.'[35] Readers of the local press soon learned, moreover, that the houses on McGill-College and on Saint-Denis had previously been used as gambling dens – members of the police force who arrived to deal with the squatters discovered playing cards, gambling chips, square tables, and telltale green lampshades in the basement of each house.[36] This discovery added a new dimension to the squatters' story. On the one hand, the veterans were both breaking the law and associating with Gagnon, a well-known Communist. On the other hand, Communist or not, war veterans with wives and children were surely more deserving of these houses than gamblers and those who lived off the spoils of gambling. Newspapers proclaimed the conflict to be one between 'Squatters' and 'Barbottes.'[37] Gagnon and his Ligue asked whether Montreal's vacant houses would be 'Des "barbotes" [sic]? Ou des foyers de veterans?' and called in members of the Canadian Seamen's Union to protect the squatters from the gamblers.[38] One newspaper claimed that the veterans were winning the publicity battle because the 'Robin Hood legend' was dear to the hearts of the people.[39]

Gagnon and the Ligue struck again on 4 November with a third house in Snowdon, on Décarie Boulevard. Three French-Canadian war veterans and their families – including sixteen children in all – moved into the two-storey brick house. All three families had been lodging in rooms on the Plateau Mont-Royal. The sixteen children were described by the *Herald* as being 'well and cleanly dressed'; some, however, 'had pinched features which their parents attributed to living in overcrowded and poorly ventilated rooms.'[40] The three families were aided in their move by members of the Snowdon section of the Canadian Legion.[41] The Legion, which had played an important role in bringing veterans' housing difficulties to public attention,[42] was itself split on the squatters issue. The provincial branch of the Canadian Legion condemned the illegal seizure of private property, while Montreal's Snowdon and Outremont sections supported the veterans in their quest for housing and felt that their actions were morally justified.[43] The mixed reactions of Legion members in some ways paralleled the views found in the editorials and articles of local newspapers. *La Patrie*, for instance, condemned the squatters' illegal actions, the violation of private property rights, and the Communist influence of Gagnon et al., but repeatedly expressed sympathy for war veterans in their search for homes for themselves and their families. 'Un logement,' the newspaper argued, 'ce n'est pas un luxe, c'est une nécessité. Et une nécessité pressante.'[44] Émile-Charles Hamel, editor of *Le Canada*, agreed that 'ceux qui ont risqué leur vie pour la défense de la patrie ont droit à un toit, pour eux et leurs familles.'[45]

Although the autumn 1946 phase of the squatters' campaign involved private houses,[46] Montreal veterans also squatted in former military barracks and military hospitals. The movement took on renewed life in the summer of 1947, after veterans and their families were evicted from barracks on Île Sainte-Hélène and a former military hospital in Longueuil.[47] At least one public rally was held in downtown Montreal in support of the eighteen families (including seventy-five children) evicted from the Île Sainte-Hélène shelters.[48] Newspapers accorded significant coverage to the families sleeping outdoors or under tarpaulins or in tents after being denied access to the barracks. They focused on fathers gone to Montreal to look for proper housing or for food, mothers attempting to 'keep house' in the mud, and sick children coughing or being sent to stay with relatives in town after spending nights sleeping in the rain.[49] Sympathetic journalists and editorialists used photographs to make their point. In addition to showing readers mattresses, household goods, and baby carriages piled up outside the off-limits barracks, these photographs focused on children – lined up in neat rows, counted, and identified by name and by age.[50] Newspapers took particular note of families of five, six, or eight children, and this was surely not accidental. The argument that fathers of 'familles nombreuses' faced a particularly difficult challenge finding adequate housing was widespread in Montreal at this time and was used to suggest the particular burdens of parenthood in Quebec in the wake of the war.[51]

The men in these stories were portrayed in various ways: as war veterans, as illegal squatters, and as possible or potential Communists. Always, however, they were presented as family men, responsible for wives and children who were depicted, in these articles, as dependent and as 'menacés d'être jetés dehors par la police.' As La Patrie noted, the squatters on McGill-College avenue 'sont tous pères de familles.'[52] Roland Dinelle, war veteran and publicist for the Ligue des vétérans sans logis, declared 'Que je sois communiste ou non, tout ce que je demande au gouvernement, c'est qu'il me donne un logement pour ma famille, après sept ans de service dans les forces armées.'[53] Thomas Desmaresq explicitly denied communist sympathies and underlined his responsibility as a father, saying, 'Je ne suis pas communiste et personne ne m'a approché. Je ne connais même pas Henri Gagnon, qu'on dit chef des squatters. Mais, ce que je sais, c'est que ma femme et mon bébé d'un mois ne pouvaient vivre dans ce taudis de Ville La Salle.'[54] Photographs in the Ligue pamphlet 'Éviction! QUI SERA LE SUIVANT?' depicted parents and their numerous children.[55] The story of the relatively small group of war veterans involved in the Squatters' Movement struck a chord with the much larger number of people attempting to negotiate inadequate and/or unaffordable housing in the wake of the war. By taking the law into their own hands in order to provide for their families, these fathers could be seen as doing the responsible – indeed, the manly – thing. As one letter-writer to the editor of the Herald asked, 'Is it so very "stupid" for a man to do what he can to improve the lot of his family, even if it's against the law. Ill-advised perhaps, but certainly not "stupid." Isn't it about time we quit passing the buck by yawping about communism and make an effort to give our veterans their elemental and richly deserved right – decent living quarters.'[56] As Jill Wade demonstrates in her study of veterans' 1946 occupation of the Hotel Vancouver, public tolerance of homeless veterans squatting in public buildings was high; the general attitude appeared to be that if the federal government were not able to house its veterans, then it ought to let them sleep in federal buildings.[57]

On more than one occasion, however, the veteran-squatters were presented as dupes – poor veterans, men simply trying to find a roof for their family, the innocent victims of a political campaign orchestrated by Henri Gagnon and his fellow Communists. The mainstream press suggested that a revolt was brewing *within* the Squatters' Movement. Some veteran-fathers, for instance, went on record as stating that they didn't want to stay in these houses against the will of their owners.[58] *La Patrie* claimed that both veteran-squatters and the Canadian Legion resented having been 'infiltrated' by Gagnon and other Communist sympathizers.[59] Yet some veteran-squatters professed not to care about Gagnon's politics: 'le principal, pour eux était d'avoir obtenu un toit pour leur famille.'[60] Émile-Charles Hamel pointed out that the best way to undercut Communist efforts was to respond to veterans' very real needs with decent, affordable housing.[61] In the months following the Squatters' Movement, organizations ranging from the relatively conservative housing committee of the Canadian Legion to the relatively progressive Conseil des métiers de Montréal continued to deploy the argument (presumably in an effort to push various levels of government to action) that people unable to afford adequate shelter would be easy targets for Communist and 'subversive' elements.[62] And André Laurendeau, provincial leader of the Bloc populaire canadien, blamed the Squatters' Movement on both the federal and the Quebec governments' lack of initiative in the area of housing.[63]

Veterans, accustomed to receiving federal allowances and possessed of a sense of entitlement earned through military service, were not afraid to ask for the government's help in housing their families. They sought action principally from Montreal or from Ottawa – in one evicted veteran's words, from 'la Ville ou le Gouvernement' – rather than from Quebec City.[64] The federal government, officially responsible for veterans, received the lion's share of the blame. Ottawa, Gagnon charged after veterans were evicted from the Île Sainte-Hélène barracks, was guilty of 'callous inhuman indifference' and of poor treatment of 'those who served our country during wartime.'[65] Yet C.D. Howe, the federal minister of reconstruction, declared that Ottawa was responsible only for veterans who had served overseas. The rest, he claimed, was up to cities, provinces, and private industry.[66] Indeed, the municipal government could not help but get involved, responsible as it was for questions of local property and policing.[67] The urgent issue of veterans' housing, then, continued to be tossed back and forth between Ottawa and Concordia.[68]

As for the squatters, those who had moved their families into the three Montreal houses were required to appear before the courts.[69] While awaiting their hearings, some were released on bail, others held in municipal police cells.[70] The wives of three of these veterans, who appeared at the Palais de Justice with their young children, were described as sobbing and as using 'violent words' as their husbands were escorted back to their cells in handcuffs.[71] The charges against the three veterans who had moved into the house on Saint-Denis street (accused of using violence to illegally take possession of a building) were dropped.[72] In the end, none of the squatters were convicted of any crime; even the charges of conspiracy against Gagnon were eventually dropped.[73] Two families were given rooms at the former Hôtel Viger, which Wartime Housing Ltd. had begun to renovate for the use of war veterans in October 1946, before the Squatters Movement had even started.[74] Several veterans and their families obtained a permanent place to live in new homes built by Wartime Housing. Almost all of the families evicted from the Île Sainte-Hélène barracks were found other shelter by the Central Mortgage and Housing Corporation, by the City of Montreal, 'or by generous citizens.'[75]

Parents, Pupils, and the 1949 Teachers' Strike

In January 1949, for one cold week in the middle of a Montreal winter, the city's Catholic lay teachers went on strike. Across the metropolis, the classrooms normally run by these teachers remained empty, although nuns and teaching brothers continued to go to work. Children hung about school playgrounds or stayed home; parents listened to radio reports on the strike in order to decide whether to send their children to school. Nearly fifteen hundred francophone teachers congregated daily in a downtown hall to listen to speeches and strategize; more than three hundred English-speaking Catholic lay teachers joined them in solidarity.[76]

This strike by Montreal teachers was unprecedented.[77] Since the teachers were considered public service workers, it was also illegal.[78] Although the teachers ultimately achieved some of their salary demands from the school board, their union's certification was suspended by Premier Maurice Duplessis and the Quebec Labour Relations Board, and was not restored until 1957.[79] The strike has thus attracted some attention from scholars interested in labour relations and Duplessiste politics.[80] A dimension of the strike that has not been dealt with by labour historians or industrial relations scholars, however, is the role played by parents – and, to a lesser extent, children – in the dispute.

This was principally a strike about wages. The union representing Montreal public-school teachers, the Alliance des professeurs catholiques de Montréal (APCM), had been trying to negotiate better wages with the school board, the Commission des écoles catholiques de Montréal (CECM), for almost two years. Wages for lay teachers in Quebec had historically been low, particularly in rural areas. In part, this was because lay teachers competed with nuns and teaching brothers, who were paid very little on the assumption that they had taken vows of poverty and had few expenses. The APCM, led by Léo Guindon, pointed out that Montreal's Catholic teachers earned less than teachers in other provinces and, particularly grating, far less than Protestant teachers in the city itself.[81] When arbitration failed to resolve the problem, members of the APCM voted to strike and, on the morning of 17 January, refused to show up to work.

By all accounts, the teachers enjoyed a great deal of public support. The school board complained that newspapers and radio stations were biased in favour of the teachers. Union files overflow with telegrams of support from the city's Protestant teachers, from teachers elsewhere in Quebec and Canada, from other unions, from the Co-operative Commonwealth Federation (CCF), and from concerned individuals. Likewise, the school board archives are filled with telegrams urging commissioners to take the teachers' needs seriously and to act responsibly in order to end the strike. The Canadian Congress of Labour, the Confédération des travailleurs catholiques du Canada, and the Fédération provinciale du travail du Québec all backed the APCM's stand, offering financial assistance if need be. Prominent Montreal activists such as Thérèse Casgrain and Frank Scott also offered the union financial support.[82] Streetcar drivers, students at the Université de Montréal, and, as we will see, public school pupils, rallied to the teachers' support.[83] Teachers were seen to be fighting for the city's children, a perception that teachers capitalized on by publicly expressing their concern for their 'dear students.'[84] Commentators spoke of children's 'right' to education[85] – a right that was, of course, only recently acquired.

The majority of these striking Catholic lay teachers were women, and the central role played by female teachers in the strike was acknowledged and commended by the press. A reporter for *Le Devoir* noted that women had assumed leadership roles in this strike, and had played a large part in sustaining morale and solidarity. The commitment of the striking female teachers to their cause had earned them, this journalist claimed, the support of 'des mères de famille.'[86] *Le Front Ouvrier* also highlighted women's importance to this strike by publishing a photograph of picketing female teachers, alongside a photograph of an empty classroom with the caption 'La maîtresse n'y était pas.'[87]

Because of the particular mix of lay teachers and teaching brothers and nuns in Montreal's Catholic school system, most schools were not shut down completely. Those with lay principals and a preponderance of lay teachers were much more affected by the strike than those run and taught primarily by members of religious orders. Religious personnel continued to teach during the strike. As Sœur Marie-Anne-Françoise of the Sisters of Sainte-Anne told the school board president six months after the strike, 'Nos religieuses, il me semble, ont donné, comme les autres communautés, une preuve tangible de leur zèle héroïque, de leur absolue fidélité à votre cause, lors de la suspension du travail des instituteurs laïques.'[88] Yet there is little evidence of hostility on their part toward the lay teachers. Religious and lay personnel had a long tradition of working together in the city's schools, and knew that they would once again be sharing the school corridors after the strike was resolved.[89] Religious directors of schools appeared reluctant to report striking teachers to the board. Sœur Sainte-Anne-des-Miracles, the principal of École Ville-Marie, neglected to inform the school board about the actions of two militant female lay teachers during the strike because, as she explained to the CECM's president, Eugène Simard: 'Vraiment, je n'ai pas pensé que les incidents qui se sont produits pouvaient être considérés comme des faits saillants. Souvent dans notre vie d'éducatrice, nous avons affaire à des jeunes filles nerveuses ou surrexcitées et nous pensons que la meilleure attitude à prendre dans la circonstance est le calme et l'oubli. C'est pourquoi, en recevant la feuille du rapport le 19 janvier, j'ai omis de mentionner les faits du 17 janvier.'[90]

Another female member of a religious community, the director of l'École Ste-Jeanne-d'Arc, met with eighty pupils and five homeroom teachers on the first morning of the strike. Called to the telephone, she returned to find that all eighty students had vanished. Yet in her report to the school board she refused to blame the female lay teachers and instead attributed the students' disappearance to 'une manœuvre extérieure.'[91]

Once the strike began, the union and the school board reached an agreement on wage demands relatively quickly, but the teachers refused to return to work until the board agreed not to inflict reprisals on the teachers who had participated in the strike.[92] Seven days into the strike, it ended when, at a meeting of the teachers that lasted through the evening and into the early hours of the next morning, Archbishop Joseph Charbonneau and two Catholic parents' groups, the École des Parents and the Catholic Parents' League, promised the teachers that they would lobby for wage increases for them and would attempt to ensure that no reprisals were taken, if only they would return to their classrooms later that day.[93]

But what of the pupils? On the Monday that had marked the first day of the strike, children had appeared at a loss as to what to do: they hung around schoolyards and crowded around teachers' cars for information. As it became clear that classes run by lay teachers would not be held, most children stayed home. The APCM reported on the first day of the strike that 'les classes laïques sont vides, les élèves sont repartis.'[94] Activist pupils, or simply restless ones (those the assistant director of the city police called 'quelques écoliers turbulents')[95] participated in the strike. *Le Devoir* described children parading in front of their school with banners reading, 'Nous appuyons nos professeurs.'[96] Boys from Le Plateau and Saint-Stanislas schools travelled in packs to other schools, encouraging fellow students to leave class and to rally behind striking teachers. In the wake of the strike, the school board claimed that two hundred to three hundred pupils had marched in the streets and had demonstrated in front of the school board offices and various schools. Madeleine Vézina, a ninth-year student at the École Baril, organized a sympathy strike and led one hundred fellow students from school to school gathering support for the teachers.[97]

Students at over a dozen schools, including St-Paul de la Croix, Le Plateau, and St-Barthélemy, sent telegrams to the union expressing their support. Pupils at St-Louis de Gonzague, for instance, dispatched a telegram to the APCM that read: 'SUPPORTONS VOTRE GREVE IL EST TEMPS QUE VOUS AYEZ JUSTICE A VOS REVERENDICATIONS [*sic*] NOUS VOULONS L'EGALITE DE VOS SALAIRES COMME LES PROFESSEURS DE LANGUE ANGLAISE AINSI QUE LES AUTRES PROVINCES. NOUS SOMMES EN ARRIERE DE VOUS ET VOUS SOUHAITONS LA VICTOIRE.' Other students sent telegrams to their particular teachers. Marcel Patenaude, of St-Louis de Gonzague, wrote to his teacher, Mlle Lafrance: 'VOUS SOUHAITE BONNE

CHANCE DUN ELEVE QUI VOUS AIME.' Bernard Binette drafted a telegram from his fellow fourth-year students at Ste-Bernadette to their teacher, Marcel Pelletier: 'A NOTRE SEUL ET DEVOUE PROFESSEUR TOUT LE SUCCES POSSIBLE.'[98]

The role played by the École des Parents and the Catholic Parents' League in ending the strike, which I will address later in this chapter, was but the tip of the iceberg – they were the most visible, articulate, and organized of parents. Unorganized parents, or parents organized in ways *other* than as parents, also expressed their support for the teachers. Fathers, in particular, sent letters and telegrams to the union in support of the strike. Henri Véronneau, for instance, wrote to the teachers on the first day of the strike. 'Mesdames, Mesdemoiselles, Messieurs,' he began. 'J'accomplis ce matin mon devoir dans ma faible capacité en gardant mes deux filles d'âge scolaire à la maison.' Roland Barrette wrote to the APCM president, Léo Guindon, 'Je suis père de trois enfants qui vont à l'école St-Barthélemy, et je sais tout le dévouement de nos instituteurs et institutrices laïques, et je souhaite que votre cause triomphe. Nul doute que l'immense majorité des parents sont avec vous de tout cœur.'[99] Joseph Moncel explained his position in a letter to the Révérend Frère Amédée-Stanislas, the principal of his son's school:

Cher Frère Amédée,

A la suite de votre demande de raisons sur l'absence de l'École de mon petit garçon, je dois vous dire que mon garçon, Jean, ne fait pas acte de présence ces jours-ci sur mes ordres.

Je suis de tout cœur avec la position prise par l'Alliance des Instituteurs et Institutrices dont Monsieur Leroux, le maître de Jean, est un membre et qui doit faire front uni, par une grève, avec environ 1,700 de ses confrères pour obtenir la revendication de leurs droits et réclamations.

En refusant de laisser mon garçon paraître à l'école où sa classe est sans maître, je veux montrer mon approbation de ce geste de Monsieur Leroux. Et ceci continuera tant que le différend ne sera pas réglé.

Je pourrais plonger dans une discussion sur les mérites de la grève en question, mais ceci ne règlerait rien. Je vous dirai, seulement, ma réaction ce matin à la suite des nouvelles de l'approbation unanime des Instituteurs et Institutrices aux bons offices de Monseigneur Joseph Charbonneau. J'admire la dignité personnelle de Léo Guindon dans tous ses agissements. Quant à Eugène Simard, C.R., well – 'a plague on his house.'

Avec mes cordiales salutations, veuillez me croire, Frère Amédée,

Votre tout dévoué,

Joseph P. Moncel[100]

Members of other unions wrote to advise the teachers that they were keeping their children home from school. André Plante and L. Perreault, of La Fraternité canadienne des employés civiques, told the APCM that they were recommending that their Montreal members not send their children to school until the school authorities showed a willingness to come to an agreement.[101] This support from members of local unions, acting as parents, made a difference in the 1940s, when unionization was widespread and memberships were relatively militant.

Parents also wrote to the school board to defend the strikers. One mother told the board, 'Mon mari & moi, nous opposons fermement à la manière dont vous traitez actuellement le corps proffessoral [sic] de Montréal et nous vous obligeons à garder dans nos classes nos proffesseurs respectifs [sic] si non [sic] nous garderons nos enfants un temps indéfini.'[102] The principal of l'École Dollier-de-Casson stated that most of the neighbourhood fathers were union members who refused to send their children to school during the strike. Certainly the majority of children attending CECM schools came from working-class or lower-middle-class families; wealthier parents tended to send their children to private, Church-run schools.[103] Yet even those parents who may not have approved of unions appear to have heeded the requests of striking teachers, broadcast across the local radio waves, to keep children at home rather than sending them to unsupervised classrooms.[104]

Not all parents supported the teachers' actions, however. The files of the school board (unlike those of the union) contain a few letters from parents who opposed the strike.[105] One father wrote to Eugène Simard, the president of the school board, to say:

> C'est plus fort que moi, ça me commande, il faut que je vous écrive pour vous dire que la plus part [sic] des parents sont avec vous et vous appuient dans votre tenacité [sic]. Je suis un père d'une famille de 5 enfants et je gagne $40.00 pour 55 heures de travail dur, je dis dur parce que c'est de *nuit*, et pourtant je suis satisfais [sic] et je suis seul pour gagner. Pour mon opinion je serais plus que satisfais [sic] avec un salaire d'instituteur. Ils ont tort. Continuez de tenir votre bout et je suis sur [sic] qu'avec le temps et l'organisation et l'aide du public vous pourrez avoir le succès sur votre côté.
>
> Je suis âgé de 38 ans et j'ai déjà passé par un [sic] grève, *fini*, pour moi les unions, telles qu'elles soient.[106]

Another father wrote to advise Simard of his opposition to the strike. In abandoning their classrooms, teachers were, he argued, neglecting their responsibilities.[107] Quebec Premier Duplessis likewise expressed his regret that people in charge of young minds should exhibit such a lack of respect for law, order, and properly constituted authority. Children, he argued, were the strike's main victims.[108]

The resonance of parenthood in the immediate postwar years is suggested by the fact that the striking teachers themselves articulated their interests as parents. They claimed, understandably, that they were unable to meet the needs of their own families on their current salaries and in the context of the high cost of living. A union representative told Montrealers gathered around their radios during the strike, 'C'est justement de 1944 que date le début des difficultés actuelles. Devant l'inflation qui se faisait déjà sentir à ce moment, les instituteurs ont voulu, au même titre que tous les pères de familles, que tous les citoyens conscients de leurs responsabilités, assurer à leurs familles un rampart contre l'insécurité.' This speaker hoped that Montreal parents would understand that 'en menant leur propre lutte, les instituteurs mènent en même temps la lutte de toutes les familles qui sont actuellement aux prises avec le coût de la vie.'[109] Striking teachers, not surprisingly, kept their own children home from school.[110] Invoking family could be a prudent way to defuse hostility to strikes.[111] Implicitly, however, this was an argument that applied only to married *male* teachers. The needs of female teachers – who were, of necessity, unmarried and therefore unable to make the claims of parents – were overshadowed.[112] The union's wage demands, for instance, maintained a gendered wage discrepancy, requesting salaries of up to $2,500 per year for women and up to $3,500 per year for men.[113] Female teachers were, it seemed, among the few actors in this dispute unable to claim the rights of parents.

Teachers were seen to have returned to work on 24 January both 'for the good of the children' and because they recognized the desires of Montreal parents.[114] The decisive intervention of the École des Parents and the Catholic Parents' League, in a successful bid to resolve the strike, speaks to parents claiming a voice in public matters in the wake of the Second World War and in the context of Quebec children's new universal rights. In a resolution distributed to the teachers, the school board, and the press, the École des Parents insisted that parents were 'les premiers responsables de leurs enfants,' who had merely delegated their power to other authorities. As parents, members of the École des Parents felt compelled to demand that the parties involved resolve the strike as quickly as possible.[115]

Begun by a group of young, francophone, Catholic parents in 1940, the Montreal-based École des Parents du Québec was a cornerstone of Quebec's *mouvement familial*, and by the end of the decade claimed more than one thousand members. The École described itself as 'une association fondée par un groupe de parents, convaincus comme beaucoup de leurs compatriotes, que pour donner à leurs enfants la préparation à la vie à laquelle ils ont droit, il leur fallait faire l'effort de mieux comprendre leurs enfants, d'adopter les méthodes les plus susceptibles d'en faire des personnalités fortes, efficientes et bien équilibrées. Ils ont compris aussi l'importance de conserver à la famille canadienne-française ce qui lui a donné à date la force de lutter : sa foi, ses traditions, ses mœurs, tout en lui permettant de suivre le progrès.'[116]

Its early members included Montrealers active in intellectual, political, and union circles in the postwar years, many of whom had been involved with the Action catholique youth movements.[117] The École invited speakers – including Thérèse Casgrain, Florence Martel, Germaine Parizeau, and Édouard Montpetit – to share their thoughts on parenthood and parenting techniques.[118] It offered courses, held study groups, screened documentary films and, beginning in 1943, spoke to an even broader audience through its Radio-Canada series called RADIO-PARENTS.[119] The École des Parents had a particular interest in building bridges between parents and schools.[120]

The intervention of the École des Parents, alongside Montreal Archbishop Joseph Charbonneau and the English-language Catholic Parents' League (led by Dr Magnus Seng and Dr J.G. Howlett), played upon the loyalties of Catholic teachers to the postwar Church. But their entreaties to the strikers were made principally in the name of parents and children.[121] The irony is that although the École des Parents and the Catholic Parents' League supported the teachers, by pressuring them to return to work for the children's sake, they were, in effect, putting the needs of parents and children ahead of the needs of wage-earners – including, in this case, many unmarried female wage-earners. In promising the teachers that they would lobby for their interests if they would only go back to work, they exercised a moral pressure that encouraged workers to subordinate their own rights to those of parents and children.[122] As Léo Guindon, president of the APCM, noted after the teachers returned to work, 'L'Alliance des Professeurs se trouvait en présence d'un dilemne [*sic*] . D'un côté, elle voyait une commission scolaire se réservant le droit de sévir. De l'autre, elle voyait des parents, des enfants qui subissaient les inconvénients d'un geste dont les causes ne venaient pas d'eux.'[123] Or as a female Trois-Rivières teacher noted to *Le Devoir*, teachers bore the burden of representing a 'triple authority': the Church, the State, and the Family.[124] Children's (new) right to education was counterposed against teachers' right to a living wage. And the interests of parents – even parents supportive of the teachers' demands – could trump the interests of workers in an era that celebrated family.

André Laurendeau's columns in *Le Devoir*, written during and after the strike, provide insight into these debates.[125] Laurendeau, a well-known journalist and politician, certainly empathized with the striking teachers. Yet his principal concern was that children would be the first to suffer and that parents had no way of making their voices heard in the dispute. Laurendeau approved of the interventions of the École des Parents du Québec and the Catholic Parents' League, but noted that these organized groups of parents had only moral suasion, not direct authority, on their side. His columns reveal discomfort with the idea that parents were to relinquish control of their children's education to the state. Parents, he argued, bore the primary responsibility for the education of their children – before the state and the church. They thus needed an official role in the management of the schools. Although they paid school taxes, they had no voice in educational policy. The school board was responsible to the provincial government, not to Montreal parents. Parents received no recognition for their role in raising children, and were treated like minors. Laurendeau especially lamented the loss of authority of the 'chefs de famille' and, more precisely, the 'père de famille.' Civil authorities, he insisted, did not listen to fathers anymore. Was there no way to reintegrate them into 'la cité'?

This concern about the 'chefs de famille' and the 'pères de famille' was expressed at a time when the state was perceived to be stepping in to replace fathers and breadwinners through measures such as family allowances and compulsory schooling. It was shared by other commentators. *Le Devoir*'s Gérard Filion, for instance, commented several months after the strike but in the context of the ongoing dispute between the school board and the union:

> Il reste bien encore quelques pères de familles à Montréal. Mais les pères de famille, à quoi peuvent-ils bien servir de nos jours? Ils font des enfants, c'est tout. Pour le reste, on leur impose le silence.
>
> Que pensent les pères de famille de l'imbroglio actuel? Quelqu'un s'est-il donné la peine de les consulter? Sont-ils du côté de la Commission ou du côté de l'Alliance?
>
> Personne ne le sait. Ils ne le savent probablement pas eux-mêmes. La

seule chose certaine, c'est qu'ils vont, eux et leurs enfants, payer les pots cassés.

On parle d'opérer un rapprochement entre la Commission et les parents; on va même jusqu'à préconiser un programme radiophonique. C'est de la bouillie pour les chats. Le rapprochement, c'est entre l'école et la famille qu'il doit se faire d'abord, entre l'instituteur et le père de famille.

Filion ended his article by calling for parents to reclaim their right to the education of their children.[126] The Jesuit publication *Relations* likewise printed an article in the wake of the strike supporting the teachers and arguing that the labour dispute had demonstrated parents' desire for a greater role in their children's education. The provincial government appointed four of the seven commissioners on the Montreal school board, and the church appointed the other three. Yet 'les chefs de famille,' taxpayers all, had no representation on the board.[127]

Nadia Fahmy-Eid judiciously warns against assuming a consensus favourable to the implementation of compulsory schooling in 1943.[128] She is surely correct: only five years before the strike, Opposition leader Maurice Duplessis, in the context of wartime controls, had described provincial compulsory schooling legislation as the conscription 'des enfants pour l'école.'[129] We might, in fact, see the controversy over the teachers' strike as one way in which conflicting opinions over compulsory schooling were still being worked out, six years after the fact. Yet the strike also suggests that the view that schooling was a 'right' for Quebec's children had become quite quickly entrenched – indeed, it had probably existed in some form, and in certain circles, prior to the 1942 legislation.[130] The children of a victorious postwar democracy were seen to belong in school. The strike suggests, moreover, that compulsory schooling allowed parents to claim a public voice as parents, as they negotiated the terms of their children's education with the state. In the wake of the strike, for instance, the École des Parents demanded that parents be represented on the Montreal school board.[131] Such demands contrasted with a very recent past, when schooling was seen by many working-class parents to conflict with family needs and with their needs in particular. Indeed, Dominique Marshall's work demonstrates that for the poorest of Quebec families, such conflict continued to exist through the 1940s.[132]

While the École des Parents and the Catholic Parents' League were the most organized and vocal of parents, other parents also voiced their opinions (both for and against) the strike by writing letters to the teachers' union or to the school board. All parents spoke through their actions, choosing whether or not to send their children to school during the strike. Even parents who opposed the strike could be seen as claiming citizenship rights – in this case, children's (new) right to education. Thus the idea of family could be used to legitimate parents' claims to a public voice – but the use of family in this way could also have conservative results. In this case, the rights of children took priority over the rights of unmarried female wage-earners. Children were a particularly powerful argument in the immediate postwar years; it was difficult to respond to the critics of the strike who invoked children deprived of their right to education.[133]

Conclusions

The two episodes discussed in this chapter illustrate some of the ways in which household and familial politics could be played out in the streets in the wake of the Second World War. They also point to changing roles for both fathers and the state in the reconstruction years. The Squatters' Movement was one of the more dramatic examples of Montrealers calling for state intervention in the 1940s. The squatters expressed a clear sense of entitlement, both as war veterans and as fathers, to decent housing. The teachers' strike likewise suggests that the view that schooling was a right for Quebec's children had become quite quickly entrenched. It also demonstrates that compulsory schooling allowed some parents to claim a public voice, as they negotiated citizenship rights and the terms of their children's education with the state. And yet reactions to the strike also suggest that other fathers felt left out of the negotiations – as though there were no role for them in the new era of compulsory schooling.

It is well known that the wartime regulations imposed by the federal government frequently incurred resentment across Canada, and perhaps especially in Quebec. Premier Duplessis, for instance, who returned to power in 1944, was a vocal critic of military conscription, rationing, and federal taxes.[134] And yet, in the immediate postwar years, this opposition to state incursions into private life was not universally shared. While the middle- and working-class parents who intervened in the 1949 teachers' strike revealed a reluctance to entirely relinquish their children's education to the state, many Montrealers, as we saw in this chapter, lobbied persistently for state intervention in housing. Moreover, all three of Quebec's union federations, along with the Jeunesse Ouvrière Catholique and the Ligue Ouvrière Catholique, demanded continued price and rent controls in the years immediately following the war.[135] *Le Front Ouvrier*, for instance, while critical of postwar meat rationing, saw no contradiction in demanding continued peacetime price controls.[136] It is important to recognize, then, the lack of agreement in early postwar Quebec about new roles for the state. Canadian historians have for the most part avoided positing a wartime consensus, but they have been quicker to assume a postwar consensus centred on the reconstruction plans of federal Liberals. This chapter suggests that this assumption needs interrogation – for Quebec and, in all likelihood, more broadly.

Conclusion: City Unique?

The whole city lay spread out below him, enchanting in the sunlight of a late afternoon in June, mile upon mile of flat gray roofs half hidden by the light, new green of the trees; a few scattered skyscrapers, beyond the skyscrapers the long straight lines of the grain elevators down by the harbor, further up to the right the Lachine Canal, and everywhere the gray spires of churches, monasteries and convents. Somehow, even from here, you could tell that Montreal was predominantly French, and Catholic.

Gwethalyn Graham, *Earth and High Heaven*[1]

It is a curious city, Montreal, and in this story I keep returning to the fact that it is.

Hugh MacLennan, *The Watch That Ends the Night*[2]

In its particular configuration of language, religion, ethnicity, and class, mid-twentieth-century Montreal was, perhaps, a 'city unique,'[3] or as long-time resident Hugh MacLennan christened it, a 'curious city.' Canada's commercial and industrial metropolis, Montreal differed from other Quebec cities because of its significant English-speaking minority and its increasingly cosmopolitan nature. Yet its francophone majority, its role as the cultural and intellectual capital of French-speaking America ('l'Amérique française'), and the institutional importance of the Catholic Church meant that it was a city in certain ways distinct from its North American neighbours. Montreal's history, then, is not necessarily 'representative' of some Canadian or continental norm. As Natalie Zemon Davis argues, 'The singled-out case is not the world translated into a grain of sand, but a local power cluster, receiving influence and signals from – and sending them to – other clusters and authoritative power centers.'4 Rather, the 'local power cluster' that was 1940s Montreal offers us the opportunity to study a variety of responses to the end of the Second World War and the shaping of postwar society.

Household Politics explores the meanings of postwar reconstruction for Montreal families. It examines the ways in which members of both working-class and middle-class families took wartime promises, such as democracy, liberty, and freedom from want, seriously, and the ways in which they incorporated these promises into their postwar expectations. 'Social security,' for instance, was not just a political platitude: it had real meaning to families who had lived through the poverty of the Depression and the unsettled years of war. Montrealers chose security in their reconstruction campaigns. In seeking security, they called for and negotiated new kinds of citizenship. The rights and obligations of citizenship were up for discussion, in the context of federal wartime controls ranging from rationing to military conscription, Quebec women's winning of the provincial suffrage in 1940, and the Canadian Citizenship Act of 1946. Some Montrealers demanded that political citizenship be accompanied by social citizenship (new welfare-state measures) and by economic citizenship (the right to participate in a capitalist economy on reasonable terms). In doing so, they pushed at the boundaries of the public. They requested new kinds of public legislation that would be available to more members of the public. They made private troubles public in order to demonstrate the legitimacy of claims for enhanced citizenship. We hear, in this period, new voices in public spaces: union members, consumer activists, working-class participants in the Action catholique, recipients of state allowances.

Montrealers' reconstruction hopes, however, were not identical to the official policies and pronouncements emanating from Ottawa in these years. We have seen in this book that some citizens seeking new postwar measures turned to Quebec City rather than to the federal government. Other citizens, wary of an interventionist state, attempted to maintain a role for private associations and institutions in the postwar 'mixed social economy.' While the importance of family and of social and economic security was widely acknowledged in postwar Montreal, no similar postwar consensus seems to have emerged around the means of achieving this security.

This book contributes to the historical literature on reconstruction, the family, citizenship and the welfare state, the public, and postwar Quebec. It does so by examining a series of examples of what I call 'household politics' – Montrealers' attempts, in the 1940s, to place their households on a more secure footing while at the same time making family matters a subject for public (and political) discussion. These household politics took shape within a specific set of material conditions, described in Chapter 1: high rates of family formation; a serious housing shortage; a cost-of-living that had risen considerably since the late war years; a labour market that was relatively good for men, teenagers, and young, unmarried women, but less receptive to married women; and high rates of early school-leaving for both boys and girls. The household politics of the 1940s also took place within the context of new federal welfare-state measures, and were often a response to the particular combination of private and public welfare provisions analysed in Chapter 2. And they took a number of different forms. In Chapter 3, for instance, we see the ways in which soldiers, veterans, and their (generally, but not always, female) dependents translated their private wartime experiences into postwar expectations. Regular, if sometimes inadequate, allowances issued by Ottawa forged relationships between the state and servicemen, their wives, their children, and their parents. These allowances created a sense of entitlement among their recipients: while the entitlement articulated by soldiers and by veterans was rooted in their military service to the country and in masculine conceptions of breadwinning, that expressed by their dependents rested on claims gendered 'feminine,' such as marriage, motherhood, and sexual fidelity. Recipients of allowances also learned to be critical of state measures and to demand improvements when they considered them to be insufficient. Moreover, wartime negotiations between Ottawa and Montreal, the federal state and private welfare bodies, and social workers and family members bequeathed a legacy to the reconstruction period. The objections of Montreal's Bureau d'assistance sociale aux familles – that Ottawa did not understand the workings of welfare in Montreal, or the poverty of Montreal families, or the challenges facing French-Canadian families with more children than the number provided for by the Dependents' Allowance system – spoke to differences of perspective that would remain important throughout the postwar years.

The commemoration of Montreal's mass marriage and the postwar efforts of the Ligue Ouvrière Catholique on behalf of French-Canadian families, examined in Chapter 4, highlight an alternative vision of reconstruction to the one proposed by federal Liberals. There were, of course, similarities between this federal vision and that promoted by the LOC. Both Ottawa and the LOC were responding to a situation in which married women had recently worked for pay in large numbers. Both the Catholic Church and Mackenzie King argued that a wife and mother should be 'la reine du foyer.' Yet Ottawa promoted a pan-Canadian family that in some ways transcended class, whereas the LOC used the Cent-Mariés as a way of asserting, to a public audience and to various levels of government, the distinctiveness of working-class French Canadians and their needs. Gathering information on these families became a way for the LOC to marshal evidence for its reconstruction projects. Its findings were touted as evidence that Ottawa's new social programmes were inadequate or inappropriate for Quebec families. The Action catholique – a movement concerned that the Catholic Church remain relevant to the lives of its postwar parishioners – thus served as one counterpublic, in the 1940s, to the expanding federal state.

In Chapter 5, we see both working-class and middle-class citizens – women, in particular – attempting to shape the postwar public through their actions as consumers. In the wake of a war when the duties of citizenship had been paramount, Montreal women, newly endowed with the provincial vote, claimed additional rights of citizenship, notably economic citizenship. They demanded the ability to purchase household goods – groceries, in particular – at reasonable prices. By exposing their fragile household budgets to public view, some working-class wives and mothers heightened public awareness of the need for lower prices or better wages. Yet not all Montrealers were in favour of state intervention on all issues. Some citizens put their faith in a somewhat 'free' market and called for a greater choice of products, as a benefit of living in a capitalist democracy.

In Chapter 6, we glimpse some of the ways in which household politics were literally made public through being played out in the streets. The two episodes discussed here – the Squatters' Movement of 1946–7 and the Catholic schoolteachers' strike of 1949 – point to the intensity of discussions around proper roles for the state in the wake of the war. They also suggest that the meanings of fatherhood were being debated in the reconstruction years. The sense of entitlement to decent housing articulated by Montreal squatters was rooted in their identities as war veterans and as fathers. They had no qualms about turning to the government (and in particular, the federal government) in order to demand what they saw as a right of citizenship. The rhetoric of rights is also evident in public discussion of the teachers' strike; the opinion that Quebec's children had a right to education appears to have been accepted by parents and community members relatively quickly. The strike also illustrates the ways in which the compulsory schooling act gave some parents a basis on which they could negotiate with public bodies. Yet it is clear that some fathers felt as though their voice counted for very little in the negotiation of issues concerning their children's education. No clear consensus around state intervention existed in Montreal in these years. In the late 1940s, new state roles were being negotiated, tested, and contested by the beneficiaries and the targets of new public measures.

The devastation wrought by the Second World War meant that many countries, notably those in Europe and East Asia, spent the latter half of the 1940s literally rebuilding their physical infrastructure and their citizens. North American nations had been spared the mass destruction on the home front. But their commitment of human, economic, and bureaucratic resources to the war meant that they, too, were presented with the opportunity and the necessity of reimagining and reorganizing their societies for the postwar era. The 1940s were a sustained moment during which social change seemed, to many, both desirable and possible. Just what form that change would take was up for debate.

In many ways, the negotiations and debates that took place in the households and neighbourhoods of 1940s Montreal paved the way for the moment of rapid political change in the 1960s that has come to be known as Quebec's Quiet Revolution. The 1940s saw experiments and exercises in democracy at local and community levels (the École des Parents, the 'mouvement familial,' consumer movements, associations of clubwomen, unions, the Action catholique). These years also saw an interest in state intervention among many citizens, although this interest was neither unconditional nor uncontested, and it was accompanied by an interest in a renewed civil society (witness the activities of the Ligue ouvrière catholique).[5] The 1940s also involved first-hand experiences of state intervention: military allowances, dependents' allowances, veterans' benefits, unemployment insurance, family allowances. As Dominique Marshall has proposed, Quebec Liberals' state-centred reforms of the 1960s thus built upon the federal programs of the 1940s.[6] They also built upon the relationships that citizens had initiated and forged with their governments in the years of war and reconstruction. And their popularity can be explained, in part, by the expectations of family life nurtured by Montreal's women, men, and children during and in the years immediately following the Second World War.

The lessons learned over the course of the war and during the immediate postwar period also produced, however, a frustration with federal interference in areas assigned by the BNA Act to the provinces. This frustration helps to explain why most Quebec citizens were so receptive to the provincial reforms of the 1960s. The fact that the ground was prepared well before 1960 accounts, in part, for the speed and ease with which political reforms were put into place by Jean Lesage and his *équipe de tonnerre*. In the 1960s, as Paul-André Linteau argues, we see a reconciliation between nationalism and the interventionist liberalism of the Quebec Liberal Party: two ideological currents that had for many years run largely separate courses in Quebec.[7]

In 1949, however, the Quiet Revolution was still some years away, and no one could predict what the second half of the twentieth century would bring. What was certain was that in Montreal, the prolonged transition period after the war had been significantly marked by the household politics of men, women, and even children who took reconstruction seriously and demanded a place for family matters in the postwar public sphere.

Notes

Introduction

1 National Archives of Canada (NA), Dependents' Allowance Board (DAB), RG 36, Series 18, Vol. 29, File: DAB 5-6, Vol. 1, Mrs T.G. Hodge, Chairman, Welfare Committee, Royal Canadian Army Service Corps (ACA) Women's Auxiliary, Montreal, to Hon. J.L. Ralston, Minister of Defence, Ottawa, 21 July 1941.

2 NA, Montreal Council of Women (MCW), Vol. 3, File 1B, Minutes, Local Council of Women, 8 December 1948.

3 Royal Commission on Prices, *Minutes of Proceedings and Evidence*, No. 39 (Ottawa: King's Printer, 1948), 2081, Brief by Kathleen M. Jackson, Family Division of the Canadian Welfare Council.

4 'King, ET LA FAMILLE CANADIENNE,' *La Presse* (Montreal), 1 June 1945, 14.

5 J.L. Granatstein, *The Ottawa Men: The Civil Service Mandarins, 1935–1957* (Toronto: Oxford UP, 1982).

6 NA, Jewish Family Services of the Baron de Hirsch Institute (JFS), MG 28 V 86, Vol. 10, File: Minutes of Meetings of Case Committee, Family Welfare Department, 1944–45, Minutes, 28 October 1944; Summary for Case Committee – [K] family. David and Norma Klein are pseudonyms.

7 Gabrielle Roy, *Bonheur d'occasion* (Montreal: Beauchemin, 1965 [1945]), trans. Hannah Josephson as *The Tin Flute* (Toronto: McClelland & Stewart, 1969 [1947]).

8 Archives nationales du Québec à Montréal (ANQM), Mouvement des Travailleurs Chrétiens (MTC), P257, Vol. 11, File: Cent-Mariés – Couple 25. Albert Toupin, Rita Boucher, Lucien, Denis, and Gérard are pseudonyms.

9 I follow the Oxford *Guide to Canadian English Usage* in my use of 'Quebecer' to designate a resident of Quebec: Margery Fee and Janice McAlpine, *Guide*

to Canadian English Usage (Toronto: Oxford UP, 1997), 405. Although the term 'French Canadian' is less often used in present-day Quebec, it was commonly employed in the 1940s to refer to French-speaking residents of Quebec. In this book it is thus used interchangeably with the expression 'francophone Quebecers.' I refer to English-speaking residents of Quebec as, variously, 'English Canadians' and 'anglophone Quebecers.'

10 On women's relationship to welfare states see, e.g., Carole Pateman, 'The Patriarchal Welfare State,' in Joan B. Landes, ed., *Feminism, the Public and the Private* (Oxford: Oxford UP, 1998); Susan Pedersen, 'Gender, Welfare, and Citizenship in Britain during the Great War,' *American Historical Review* 95, 4 (1990): 983–1006; Seth Koven and Sonya Michel, eds., *Mothers of a New World: Maternalist Politics and the Origins of Welfare States* (New York: Routledge, 1993).

11 Greg Donaghy, ed., *Uncertain Horizons: Canadians and Their World in 1945* (Ottawa: Canadian Committee for the History of the Second World War, 1997); Peter Neary and J.L. Granatstein, eds., *The Veterans Charter and Post–World War II Canada* (Montreal and Kingston: McGill-Queen's UP, 1998); Gail Cuthbert Brandt, '"Pigeon-Holed and Forgotten": The Work of the Subcommittee on the Post-War Problems of Women, 1943,' *Histoire sociale / Social History* 15, 29 (May 1982): 239–59.

12 Kevin Brushett, '"People and Government Travelling Together": Community Organization, Urban Planning and the Politics of Post-War Reconstruction in Toronto 1943–1953,' *Urban History Review* 27, 2 (March 1999): 44–58.

13 L.B. Kuffert, *A Great Duty: Canadian Responses to Modern Life and Mass Culture, 1939–1967* (Montreal and Kingston: McGill-Queen's UP, 2003). See chap. 2, 'The Culture of Reconstruction.'

14 Brandt, '"Pigeon-Holed and Forgotten,"' 239.

15 In Britain, the immediate postwar period is generally considered separately from what followed. See, e.g., Michael Sissons and Philip French, eds., *Age of Austerity 1945–51* (London: Hodder and Stoughton, 1963); Stephen Brooke, ed., *Reform and Reconstruction: Britain after the War, 1945–51* (Manchester: Manchester UP, 1995). These dates corresponded, of course, with the Labour governments of 1945–51.

16 Nancy Christie and Michael Gauvreau, eds., *Cultures of Citizenship in Post-war Canada, 1940–1955* (Montreal and Kingston: McGill-Queen's UP, 2003). See 'Introduction: Recasting Canada's Post-war Decade.'

17 For Canada, see Ruth Roach Pierson, *'They're Still Women After All': The Second World War and Canadian Womanhood* (Toronto: McClelland & Stewart, 1986). The international literature includes Margaret Randolph Higonnet et al., eds., *Behind the Lines: Gender and the Two World Wars* (New Haven: Yale UP, 1987); Joy Damousi and Marilyn Lake, eds., *Gender and War: Australians at*

War in the Twentieth Century (Cambridge: Cambridge UP, 1995); Susan
Jeffords, *The Remasculinization of America: Gender and the Vietnam War* (Bloom-
ington: Indiana UP, 1989); Christine Gledhill and Gillian Swanson, eds.,
*Nationalising Femininity: Culture, Sexuality and British Cinema in the Second World
War* (Manchester: Manchest er UP, 1996); Ruth Jamieson, 'The Man of
Hobbes: Masculinity and Wartime Necessity,' *Journal of Historical Sociology* 9,
1 (March 1996): 19–42; Linda K. Kerber, '"I Hav Don ... much to Carrey on
the Warr": Women and the Shaping of Republican Ideology after the
American Revolution,' in Harriet B. Applewhite and Darline G. Levy, eds.,
Women and Politics in the Age of the Democratic Revolution (Ann Arbor: U of
Michigan P, 1990); Nancy A. Hewitt, 'Did Women Have a Reconstruction?
Gender in the Rewriting of Southern History,' *Proceedings and Papers of the
Georgia Association of Historians* 14 (1993): 1–11; Susan M. Hartmann, 'Pre-
scriptions for Penelope: Literature on Women's Obligations to Returning
World War II Veterans,' *Women's Studies* 5 (1978): 223–39; Sonya Michel,
'Danger on the Home Front: Motherhood, Sexuality, and Disabled Veterans
in American Postwar Films,' *Journal of the History of Sexuality* 3, 1 (July 1992):
109–28.

18 For example, Renée Morin, 'Women after the War,' *Canadian Affairs,*
Canadian Edition, Vol. 2, No. 4, 1 March 1945.

19 Pierson, *'They're Still Women After All'*; Deidre Rowe Brown, 'Public Attitudes
towards Canadian Women During and Immediately after World War Two'
(MA thesis, University of Toronto, 1992); Penny Summerfield, *Women
Workers in the Second World War: Production and Patriarchy in Conflict* (London:
Croom Helm, 1984); Susan M. Hartmann, *The Home Front and Beyond: Ameri-
can Women in the 1940s* (Boston: Twayne Publishers, 1982); Elaine Tyler May,
Homeward Bound: American Families in the Cold War Era (New York: Basic
Books, 1988). Scholarly interpretations of these issues have been written in
the shadow of American popular culture's views of postwar women: see, e.g.,
Betty Friedan's best-selling *The Feminine Mystique* (New York: W.W. Norton,
1963).

20 May, *Homeward Bound.*

21 Joanne Meyerowitz, ed., *Not June Cleaver: Women and Gender in Postwar
America, 1945–1960* (Philadelphia: Temple UP, 1994); Sylvie Murray, *The
Progressive Housewife: Community Activism in Suburban Queens, 1945–1965*
(Philadelphia: U of Pennsylvania P, 2003).

22 Pierson, *'They're Still Women After All.'* See esp. Conclusion.

23 Veronica Strong-Boag, 'Home Dreams: Women and the Suburban Experi-
ment in Canada, 1945–60,' *Canadian Historical Review* 72, 4 (1991): 471–504;
Doug Owram, *Born at the Right Time: A History of the Baby Boom Generation*
(Toronto: U of Toronto P, 1996); Mona Gleason, *Normalizing the Ideal:*

Psychology, Schooling, and the Family in Postwar Canada (Toronto: U of Toronto P, 1999); Mary Louise Adams, *The Trouble with Normal: Postwar Youth and the Making of Heterosexuality* (Toronto: U of Toronto P, 1997); Valerie J. Korinek, *Roughing It in the Suburbs: Reading* Chatelaine *Magazine in the Fifties and Sixties* (Toronto: U of Toronto P, 2000). See also Chris Dummitt, 'Finding a Place for Father: Selling the Barbecue in Postwar Canada,' *Journal of the Canadian Historical Association*, n.s., 9 (1998): 209–23.

24 Joan Sangster, *Earning Respect: The Lives of Working Women in Small-Town Ontario, 1920–1960* (Toronto: U of Toronto P, 1995); Susanne Klausen, 'The Plywood Girls: Women and Gender Ideology at the Port Alberni Plywood Plant, 1942–1991,' *Labour / Le Travail* 41 (Spring 1998): 199–235; Valerie Endicott, '"Woman's Place [Was] Everywhere": A Study of Women Who Worked in Aircraft Production in Toronto during the Second World War' (MA thesis, University of Toronto, 1991); Julie Guard, 'Fair Play or Fair Pay? Gender Relations, Class Consciousness, and Union Solidarity in the Canadian UE,' *Labour / Le Travail* 37 (Spring 1997): 149–77. For other studies that suggest postwar complexity, see Susan Prentice, 'Workers, Mothers, Reds: Toronto's Postwar Daycare Fight,' *Studies in Political Economy* 30 (Autumn 1989): 115–41; Franca Iacovetta, *Such Hardworking People: Italian Immigrants in Postwar Toronto* (Montreal and Kingston: McGill-Queen's UP, 1992). Joy Parr's edited collection, *A Diversity of Women: Ontario, 1945–1980* (Toronto: U of Toronto P, 1995), is for all intents and purposes the Canadian counterpart to Joanne Meyerowitz's *Not June Cleaver*.

25 Two exceptions are Geneviève Auger and Raymonde Lamothe, *De la poêle à frire à la ligne de feu: La vie quotidienne des Québécoises pendant la guerre '39–'45* (Montreal: Boréal Express, 1981); Sylvie Murray, 'À la jonction du mouvement ouvrier et du mouvement des femmes: la Ligue auxiliaire de l'Association internationale des machinistes, Canada, 1903–1980' (MA thesis, Université du Québec à Montréal, 1988).

26 On expanded definitions of politics, see Paula Baker, 'The Domestication of Politics: Women and American Political Society, 1780–1920,' *American Historical Review* 89, 3 (June 1984): 620–47.

27 Hewitt, 'Did Women Have a Reconstruction?'

28 Merrily Weisbord notes that Communist parents (both men and women) living in Montreal's Park Extension district in the 1950s attended home and school meetings, 'ran community nursery schools, and child-rearing seminars, started a library, petitioned for stop-signs, and presented a detailed, carefully researched brief to the Protestant School Board, asking that a high school be built in their underprivileged district.' Merrily Weisbord, *The Strangest Dream: Canadian Communists, the Spy Trials, and the Cold War*, 2nd ed. (Montreal: Véhicule, 1994), 204.

29 See, e.g., Joy Parr, *Domestic Goods: The Material, the Moral, and the Economic in the Postwar Years* (Toronto: U of Toronto P, 1999).

30 Denyse Baillargeon, *Ménagères au temps de la crise* (Montreal: Éditions du remue-ménage, 1991); Bettina Bradbury, *Working Families: Age, Gender, and Daily Survival in Industrializing Montreal* (Toronto: McClelland & Stewart, 1993); Terry Copp, *The Anatomy of Poverty: The Condition of the Working Class in Montreal, 1897–1929* (Toronto: McClelland & Stewart, 1974).

31 Veronica Strong-Boag, *The New Day Recalled: Lives of Girls and Women in English Canada, 1919–1939* (Toronto: Copp Clark Pitman, 1988); Cynthia R. Comacchio, *Nations Are Built of Babies: Saving Ontario's Mothers and Children, 1900–1940* (Montreal and Kingston: McGill-Queen's UP, 1993); Gleason, *Normalizing the Ideal.*

32 May, *Homeward Bound*; Gleason, *Normalizing the Ideal.*

33 For one discussion of the Citizenship Act, see Donald Creighton, *The Forked Road: Canada 1939–1957* (Toronto: McClelland & Stewart, 1976), 129–31.

34 Many Quebecers must also have been aware that women in France were granted the right to vote in 1944. For a perceptive analysis of the ways in which the Citizenship Act was couched in familial metaphors, see Annalee Gölz, 'Family Matters: The Canadian Family and the State in the Postwar Period,' *Left History* 1 (Fall 1993), 29–31, 48–9.

35 T.H. Marshall, 'Citizenship and Social Class,' in *Class, Citizenship, and Social Development* (New York: Anchor Books, 1965). See also Suzanne Mettler, 'Dividing Social Citizenship by Gender: The Implementation of Unemployment Insurance and Aid to Dependent Children, 1935–1950,' *Studies in American Political Development* 12 (Fall 1998): 303–42; Pedersen, 'Gender, Welfare, and Citizenship in Britain during the Great War'; Ann Shola Orloff, 'Gender and the Social Rights of Citizenship: The Comparative Analysis of Gender Relations and Welfare States,' *American Sociological Review* 58 (June 1993): 303–28; Alice Kessler-Harris, *In Pursuit of Equity: Women, Men and the Quest for Economic Citizenship in Twentieth-Century America* (New York: Oxford UP, 2001).

36 A federal Department of Health was also established in 1919. Harry M. Cassidy, *Social Security and Reconstruction in Canada* (Toronto: Ryerson P, 1943), 26; Harry M. Cassidy, *Public Health and Welfare Reorganization* (Toronto: Ryerson P, 1945), 8. On mothers' allowances, see Veronica Strong-Boag, 'Wages for Housework: Mothers' Allowances and the Beginnings of Social Security in Canada,' *Journal of Canadian Studies* 14 (1979): 21–34; Margaret Little, *No Car, No Radio, No Liquor Permit: The Moral Regulation of Single Mothers in Ontario, 1920–1997* (Toronto: Oxford UP, 1998).

37 Neary and Granatstein, *The Veterans Charter.* On the close historical relationship between war and welfare in Canada, see Dennis Guest, 'World War II

and the Welfare State in Canada,' in *The 'Benevolent' State: The Growth of Welfare in Canada*, ed. Allan Moscovitch and Jim Albert (Toronto: Garamond, 1987); Andrée Lévesque, 'Les Québécoises et les débuts de l'État providence,' in Brigitte Studer et al., eds., *Frauen und Staat / Les Femmes et l'État* (Basel: Schwabe & Co., 1998), 175.

38 Leonard Marsh, 'An Introduction,' in *Report on Social Security for Canada* (Toronto: U of Toronto P, 1975 [1943]), xvii. See also James Struthers, *No Fault of Their Own: Unemployment and the Canadian Welfare State, 1914–1941* (Toronto: U of Toronto P, 1983); Dominique Marshall, *Aux origines sociales de l'État-providence: Familles québécoises, obligation scolaire et allocations familiales 1940–1955* (Montreal: Presses de l'Université de Montréal, 1998); Brigitte Kitchen, 'The Introduction of Family Allowances in Canada,' in Moscovitch and Albert, *The 'Benevolent' State*.

39 Cassidy, *Social Security and Reconstruction in Canada*, 6 and chap. 6; Doug Owram, *The Government Generation: Canadian Intellectuals and the State, 1900–1945* (Toronto: U of Toronto P, 1986); Granatstein, *The Ottawa Men*. Canada's Leonard Marsh had in fact attended the London School of Economics in the 1920s when William Beveridge directed the School; Guest, 'World War II and the Welfare State in Canada,' 211.

40 Cassidy, *Public Health and Welfare Reorganization*, 1.

41 Lara Campbell, '"A Barren Cupboard at Home": Ontario Families Confront the Premiers during the Great Depression,' in Edgar-André Montigny and Lori Chambers, eds., *Ontario since Confederation: A Reader* (Toronto: U of Toronto P, 2000).

42 Jane Ursel, *Private Lives, Public Policy: 100 Years of State Intervention in the Family* (Toronto: Women's P, 1992); Marshall, *Aux origines sociales*; Dennis Guest, *The Emergence of Social Security in Canada*, 3rd ed. (Vancouver: UBC P, 1997).

43 Marshall, *Aux origines sociales*, 259–62.

44 James Struthers, *The Limits of Affluence: Welfare in Ontario, 1920–1970* (Toronto: U of Toronto P, 1994); Marshall, *Aux origines sociales*; Little, *No Car, No Radio, No Liquor Permit*.

45 Alvin Finkel, 'Paradise Postponed: A Re-examination of the Green Book Proposals of 1945,' *Journal of the Canadian Historical Association* 4 (1993): 120–42; Guest, 'World War II and the Welfare State in Canada'; James Struthers, 'Family Allowances, Old Age Security, and the Construction of Entitlement in the Canadian Welfare State, 1943–1951,' in Neary and Granatstein, *The Veterans Charter*.

46 Jill Wade, 'Wartime Housing Limited, 1941–1947: Canadian Housing Policy at the Crossroads,' *Urban History Review* 15, 1 (1986): 41–59; Alvin Finkel,

'Competing Master Narratives on Post-War Canada,' *Acadiensis* 29, 2 (Spring 2000): 190–1. For a recent review of Canadian welfare-state historiography, see Alvin Finkel, 'The State of Writing on the Canadian Welfare State: What's Class Got to Do With It?' *Labour/Le Travail* 54 (Fall 2004): 151–74.

47 Susan Porter Benson, 'Living on the Margin: Working-Class Marriages and Family Survival Strategies in the United States, 1919–1941,' in Victoria De Grazia with Ellen Furlough, eds., *The Sex of Things: Gender and Consumption in Historical Perspective* (Berkeley: U of California P, 1996), 222.

48 As Allan Moscovitch and Glenn Drover note, capitalist nation-states have historically implemented social welfare programs in order to make capitalism run more smoothly – that is, to facilitate the reproduction of a healthy, 'appropriately educated' labour force. Moscovitch and Drover, 'Social Expenditures and the Welfare State: The Canadian Experience in Historical Perspective,' 29, 13–14, in Moscovitch and Albert, *The 'Benevolent' State.*

49 Yves Vaillancourt, *L'évolution des politiques sociales au Québec 1940–1960* (Montreal: Presses de l'Université de Montréal, 1988). On 'the mixed social economy' as a longstanding institution in Canada, see Mariana Valverde, 'The Mixed Social Economy as a Canadian Tradition,' *Studies in Political Economy* 47 (Summer 1995): 33–60; and in the same issue: Lynne Marks, 'Indigent Committees and Ladies Benevolent Societies: Intersections of Public and Private Poor Relief in Late Nineteenth Century Small Town Ontario'; Margaret Little, 'The Blurring of Boundaries: Private and Public Welfare for Single Mothers in Ontario.' The findings of these three scholars suggest that the Quebec government was not unique in its funding of private charities.

50 Jane Lewis, 'Gender, the Family and Women's Agency in the Building of 'Welfare States': The British Case,' *Social History* 19, 1 (January 1994): 37–55; Valverde, 'Mixed Social Economy.'

51 Vaillancourt, *L'évolution des politiques sociales au Québec,* 230.

52 V.C. Fowke, 'The National Policy – Old and New,' *Canadian Journal of Economics and Political Science* 18, 3 (August 1952): 271–86; Michael D. Behiels, *Prelude to Quebec's Quiet Revolution: Liberalism versus Neo-Nationalism, 1945–1960* (Montreal and Kingston: McGill-Queen's UP, 1985).

53 Marshall, *Aux origines sociales,* 107.

54 Marshall, *Aux origines sociales;* Keith G. Banting, *The Welfare State and Canadian Federalism,* 2nd ed. (Montreal and Kingston: McGill-Queen's UP, 1987). On George Drew, see Finkel, 'Paradise Postponed'; Creighton, *The Forked Road,* 114–15.

55 Leonore Davidoff, 'Regarding Some "Old Husbands' Tales": Public and

Private in Feminist History,' in Landes, *Feminism, the Public and the Private*, 180.

56 Michelle Zimbalist Rosaldo, 'Women, Culture, and Society: A Theoretical Overview,' in Rosaldo and Louise Lamphere, eds., *Women, Culture and Society* (Stanford: Stanford UP, 1974); Carroll Smith-Rosenberg, 'The Female World of Love and Ritual: Relations between Women in Nineteenth-Century America,' *Signs* 1 (Autumn 1975): 1–29; Nancy F. Cott, *The Bonds of Womanhood: 'Woman's Sphere' in New England, 1780–1835* (New Haven: Yale UP, 1977); Leonore Davidoff and Catherine Hall, *Family Fortunes: Men and Women of the English Middle Class, 1780–1850* (London: Hutchinson, 1987); Linda K. Kerber, 'Separate Spheres, Female Worlds, Woman's Place: The Rhetoric of Women's History,' *Journal of American History* 75 (June 1988): 9–39.

57 Suzanne Lebsock, *The Free Women of Petersburg: Status and Culture in a Southern Town, 1784–1860* (New York: W.W. Norton, 1984); Christine Stansell, *City of Women: Sex and Class in New York, 1789–1860* (Urbana: U of Illinois P, 1987 [1986]); Mary P. Ryan, *Women in Public: Between Banners and Ballots, 1825–1880* (Baltimore: Johns Hopkins UP, 1990); Sarah Deutsch, *Women and the City: Gender, Space and Power in Boston, 1870–1940* (New York: Oxford UP, 2000); Donald F. Davis and Barbara Lorenzkowski, 'A Platform for Gender Tensions: Women Working and Riding on Canadian Urban Public Transit in the 1940s,' *Canadian Historical Review* 79, 3 (September 1998): 431–65.

58 Jürgen Habermas, 'The Public Sphere: An Encyclopedia Article (1964),' *New German Critique* 3 (Fall 1974): 49–55; Habermas, *The Structural Transformation of the Public Sphere: An Inquiry into a Category of Bourgeois Society*, trans. Thomas Burger with the assistance of Frederick Lawrence (Cambridge, MA: MIT P, 1989 [original German publication 1962]).

59 Joan B. Landes, *Women and the Public Sphere in the Age of the French Revolution* (Ithaca, NY: Cornell UP, 1988); Kerber, '"I Hav Don ... much to Carrey on the Warr"'; Landes, *Feminism, the Public and the Private*.

60 Denise Riley, '"The Social," "Woman," and Sociological Feminism,' in *'Am I That Name?' Feminism and the Category of 'Women' in History* (Minneapolis: U of Minnesota P, 1988), 49.

61 Lewis, 'Gender, the Family and Women's Agency'; Valverde, 'Mixed Social Economy.'

62 Struthers, *The Limits of Affluence*; Marshall, *Aux origines sociales*; Shirley Tillotson, *The Public at Play: Gender and the Politics of Recreation in Post-War Ontario* (Toronto: U of Toronto P, 2000).

63 Davidoff and Hall, *Family Fortunes*; Cecilia Morgan, *Public Men and Virtuous Women: The Gendered Languages of Religion and Politics in Upper Canada, 1791–1850* (Toronto: U of Toronto P, 1996).

64 T.H. Marshall, 'Citizenship and Social Class,' 78–9; Nancy Fraser and Linda Gordon, 'Contract versus Charity: Why Is There No Social Citizenship in the United States?' *Socialist Review* 22, 3 (1992): 46. Emphases in the original. T.H. Marshall is generally cited as the first scholar to elaborate a concept of 'social' citizenship.

65 See Tillotson, *The Public at Play,* for a study of one attempt to 'rearticulate' the relationship between public and private in the late 1940s.

66 T.H. Marshall, 'Citizenship and Social Class'; Fraser and Gordon, 'Contract versus Charity.'

67 Jean-Pierre Collin, *La Ligue ouvrière catholique canadienne, 1938–1954* (Montreal: Boréal, 1996).

68 Vaillancourt, *L'évolution des politiques sociales au Québec;* B.L. Vigod, 'History According to the Boucher Report: Some Reflections on the State and Social Welfare in Quebec Before the Quiet Revolution,' in Moscovitch and Albert, *The 'Benevolent' State.*

69 Jacques Rouillard, *Histoire du syndicalisme québécois* (Montreal: Boréal, 1989).

70 Patricia Smart, *Les femmes du Refus global* (Montreal: Boréal, 1998).

71 Collin, *La Ligue ouvrière catholique canadienne;* Lucie Piché, *Femmes et changement social au Québec. L'apport de la Jeunesse ouvrière catholique féminine, 1931–1966* (Quebec: Presses de l'Université Laval, 2003); Louise Bienvenue, *Quand la jeunesse entre en scène: L'Action catholique avant la Révolution tranquille* (Montreal: Boréal, 2003); Nicole Neatby, *Carabins ou activistes? L'idéalisme et la radicalisation de la pensée étudiante à l'Université de Montréal au temps du Duplessisme* (Montreal and Kingston: McGill-Queen's UP, 1999). Ramsay Cook reminds us, moreover, that Duplessis never won more than 51 per cent of the popular vote. *Canada, Quebec, and the Uses of Nationalism,* 2nd ed. (Toronto: McClelland & Stewart, 1986), 113.

72 Vaillancourt, *L'évolution des politiques sociales au Québec;* Behiels, *Prelude to Quebec's Quiet Revolution.*

73 Lucia Ferretti, *Brève histoire de l'Église catholique au Québec* (Montreal: Boréal, 1999).

74 Ferretti, *Brève histoire de l'Église catholique au Québec;* Jean Hamelin, *Histoire du catholicisme québécois. Le XXe siècle,* Vol. 2, *De 1940 à nos jours,* ed. Nive Voisine (Montreal: Boréal, 1989); Gaston Desjardins, *L'amour en patience: La sexualité adolescente au Québec, 1940–1960* (Sainte-Foy, QC: Presses de l'Université du Québec, 1995); Collin, *Ligue ouvrière catholique canadienne.*

75 For a summary of this literature, see, e.g., Paul-André Linteau, 'Un débat historiographique: l'entrée du Québec dans la modernité et la signification de la Révolution tranquille,' in *La révolution tranquille: 40 ans plus tard: Un bilan,* ed. Yves Bélanger et al. (Montreal: VLB Éditeur, 2000).

76 Fernande Roy, *Progrès, harmonie, liberté: Le libéralisme des milieux d'affaires
    francophones à Montréal au tournant du siècle* (Montreal: Boréal, 1988); Behiels,
    Prelude to Quebec's Quiet Revolution; Collin, *Ligue ouvrière catholique canadienne*;
    Desjardins, *L'amour en patience*; Michèle Dagenais, *Des pouvoirs et des hommes:
    L'administration municipale de Montréal, 1900–1950* (Montreal and Kingston:
    McGill-Queen's UP and the Institute of Public Administration of Canada,
    2000).
77 Roy, *Progrès, harmonie, liberté*, 278.
78 Marshall, *Aux origines sociales*, especially 286–7.
79 Banting, *The Welfare State and Canadian Federalism*, 140–44.
80 For an extended discussion of such sources and their problems, see Franca
    Iacovetta and Wendy Mitchinson, 'Introduction: Social History and Case
    Files Research,' in *On the Case: Explorations in Social History* (Toronto: U of
    Toronto P, 1998).
81 In the fact that they dealt with the members of a voluntary, self-selecting
    community, these records were perhaps closer to those kept by nineteenth-
    century Protestant churches or twentieth-century class-reunion committees
    than to modern case files. On church records, see Lynne Marks, 'Christian
    Harmony: Family, Neighbours, and Community in Upper Canadian Church
    Discipline Records,' in *On the Case*, ed. Iacovetta and Mitchinson. My thanks
    to Bettina Bradbury for suggesting the class-reunion analogy.
82 Early statements include Joan Wallach Scott, *Gender and the Politics of History*
    (New York: Columbia UP, 1988); Bryan D. Palmer, *Descent into Discourse: The
    Reification of Language and the Writing of Social History* (Philadelphia: Temple
    UP, 1990); Christine Stansell, Response to Joan Scott, *International Labor and
    Working-Class History* 31 (Spring 1987). For two thoughtful Canadian discus-
    sions of these issues, see Joy Parr, 'Introduction,' in *The Gender of Breadwin-
    ners: Women, Men, and Change in Two Industrial Towns 1880–1950* (Toronto:
    U of Toronto P, 1990); Joan Sangster, 'Introduction: Placing the Story of
    Women's Work in Context,' in *Earning Respect*.

Chapter 1

1 *La Patrie* (Montreal), 7–9 May 1945.
2 Ibid., 15–16 August 1945.
3 Hugh MacLennan, *Two Solitudes* (Toronto: Macmillan, 1945); Gabrielle Roy,
   The Tin Flute, trans. Hannah Josephson (Toronto: McClelland & Stewart,
   1969 [1947]); Mordecai Richler, *The Apprenticeship of Duddy Kravitz*
   (Harmondsworth, UK: Penguin, 1959).

4 Christine Stansell, *City of Women: Sex and Class in New York, 1789–1860* (Urbana: U of Illinois P, 1986).

5 The exact population was 1,139,921. *Eighth Census of Canada 1941*, Vol. 1, chap. 2.

6 Ibid., chap. 8.

7 Bettina Bradbury, *Working Families: Age, Gender, and Daily Survival in Industrializing Montreal* (Toronto: McClelland & Stewart, 1993), 39–43.

8 Pierre Anctil, *Tur Malka: Flâneries sur les cimes de l'histoire juive montréalaise* (Sillery, QC: Septentrion, 1997), esp. chaps. 1–3.

9 Bruno Ramirez, *Les premiers Italiens de Montréal: l'origine de la Petite Italie du Québec* (Montreal: Boréal Express, 1984), chaps. 1–2.

10 National Archives of Canada (NA), Montreal Council of Women (MCW), MG 28 I 164: Vol. 5, File 7, Local Council of Women, 54th Year Book and Annual Report 1947–1948, Report of the Migration Committee 1947–48; Vol. 8, File 9, 'Migration. Annual Report, Spring 1949'; Migration Report – 1949–50; Vol. 8, File 13, Mrs T.W. MacDowell, Convener of Migration, Montreal, to Conveners of Migration, 14 April 1947; Mrs T.W. MacDowell, Convener of Migration, NCW, to Conveners of Migration, 17 September 1947; Mrs T.W. MacDowell, Migration Convener, NCW, to Conveners of Migration, 7 September 1948. See also Paul-André Linteau et al., *Histoire du Québec contemporain*, Vol. 2, *Le Québec depuis 1930* (Montreal: Boréal compact, 1989), 219–23.

11 *Eighth Census of Canada 1941*, Vol. 1, chap. 10.

12 *Ninth Census of Canada 1951*, Vol. 1, Table 42.

13 Ibid., Vol. 3, Table 127. In both 1941 and 1951, 'family' was defined as 'husband and wife (with or without children) or a parent with an unmarried child (or children) living together in the same housekeeping community.' Ibid., Vol. 10, 304.

14 *La Presse* (Montreal): 'Pourquoi sévit la crise du logement,' 25 January 1945, 3; 'Mariages et naissances augmentent depuis 1939,' 5 January 1946, 20.

15 *Annuaire Statistique*, Quebec 1948, Table 74; *Annuaire Statistique*, Quebec 1950, Tables 60 and 58.

16 Renée Vautelet, *Post-War Problems and Employment of Women in the Province of Quebec* (Montreal: Published under the auspices of the Local Council of Women of Montreal, 1945). Located in NA, Montreal Soldiers' Wives League (MSWL), MG 28 I 311, Vol. 5, File: Local Council of Women of Montreal, 1945. See also Angus McLaren and Arlene Tigar McLaren, *The Bedroom and the State: The Changing Practices and Politics of Contraception and Abortion in Canada, 1880–1980* (Toronto: McClelland & Stewart, 1986), 127.

17 Archives nationales du Québec à Montréal (ANQM), Jeunesse Ouvrière Catholique (JOC), P104: C. 240, File: Commission Canadienne de la Jeunesse, Mémoires soumis par le comité central de l'ACJC à la CCJ, 27–8 janvier 1945, 'Jeunesse et Famille' by Armand Godin; C. 134, File: Rapport Enquête 1947, 'Les jeunes travailleurs et le problème de l'épargne.'

18 *Annuaire Statistique*, Quebec 1945–6, 148.

19 François Ricard, *The Lyric Generation: The Life and Times of the Baby Boomers*, trans. Donald Winkler (Toronto: Stoddart, 1994), 37, 42; McLaren and McLaren, *The Bedroom and the State*, 126.

20 Collectif Clio, *L'histoire des femmes au Québec depuis quatre siècles*, 2nd rev. ed. (Montreal: Le Jour, 1992), 417.

21 McLaren and McLaren, *The Bedroom and the State*, 125.

22 Hervé Gauthier, *Évolution démographique du Québec* (Quebec: Office de planification et de développement du Québec, 1977), chap. 2.

23 Danielle Gauvreau et Peter Gossage, '"Empêcher la famille": Fécondité et contraception au Québec, 1920–60,' *Canadian Historical Review* 78, 3 (September 1997): 487–8.

24 *Annuaire Statistique*, Quebec 1948, Table 78; *Annuaire Statistique*, Quebec 1950, Tables 64, 62.

25 Morley Callaghan, *The Loved and the Lost* (Toronto: Macmillan, 1977 [1951]), 1.

26 McGill University Archives (MUA), Montreal Parks and Playgrounds Association (MPAP), MG 2079: C. 2, File 53, Recreation Survey Report, Notre Dame de Grace Ward, December 1948; C. 3, File 101, William Bowie to Alan C. Macdougall, Esq., 16 February 1928.

27 MUA, MPAP, MG 2079, C. 3, File 101, William Bowie to Mr L.A. Cormier, 17 June 1953; President, Parents' Association, Westhaven Village, to Pierre DesMarais, Esq., 2 May 1955.

28 MUA, MPAP, MG 2079, C. 5, File 320, Report of the Executive Assistant, Summer Programme, 1948; NA, MCW, MG 28 I 164, Vol. 3, File 1A, Minutes, Sub-Executive Committee of the LCW, 9 April 1947; MUA, MPAP, MG 2079, C. 6, File 226, Minutes of Meeting of Districts' Council of the Community Garden League of Greater Montreal, 29 November 1945; MUA, MPAP, MG 2079, C. 7, File 252, Minutes of 42nd Annual Meeting of the Montreal Parks and Playgrounds Association Inc., 10 February 1944; MUA, MPAP, MG 2079, C. 5, File 136, Montreal Parks and Playgrounds Association Incorporated, Report of Executive Director for the Year 1944; Montreal Parks and Playgrounds Association Incorporated, Report of Executive Director for the Year 1945; NA, MCW, MG 28 I 164, Vol. 6, File 5, News clipping, 'Approval Voiced by Council Head on Visit to Typical Vets' House,' *Montreal Gazette*, 13 June 1946; NA, Canadian Council on Social Development (CCSD), MG 28 I 10, Vol. 236, File 236-9, Visite au 'Wartime Housing' de Cartierville,

Entrevue avec M. Labrie, 10 décembre 1943, par Marie Hamel.

29 MUA, MPAP, MG 2079, C. 3, File 101, William Bowie to Alan C. Macdougall, Esq., 16 February 1928.

30 Roy, *The Tin Flute*, 48–9.

31 MUA, MPAP, MG 2079, C.5, File 334, A brief Summary of Districts Studied in a preliminary survey by the Settlements Survey Committee, Memorandum submitted to the Education and Recreation Division, Montreal Council of Social Agencies, 10 October 1930; MUA, MPAP, MG 2079, C. 3, File 101, William Bowie to Alan C. Macdougall, Esq., 16 February 1928; MUA, Montreal Council of Social Agencies (MCSA), MG 2076, C. 9, File 556, Report of the Work of the Negro Community Centre, Publication XXI, MCSA, 1944; William Weintraub, *City Unique: Montreal Days and Nights in the 1940s and '50s* (Toronto: McClelland & Stewart, 1996), 128–30.

32 On Verdun, see Weintraub, *City Unique*, 158–60; Serge Durflinger, 'The Patriotism of Local Identity: Verdun, Québec Responds to the Second World War' (paper presented to the annual meeting of the Canadian Historical Association, Brock University, 31 May 1996).

33 MUA, MPAP, MG 2079, C.5, File 334, A brief Summary of Districts Studied in a preliminary survey by the Settlements Survey Committee, Memorandum submitted to the Education and Recreation Division, Montreal Council of Social Agencies, 10 October 1930; MUA, MPAP, MG 2079, C. 3, File 101, William Bowie to Alan C. Macdougall, Esq., 16 February 1928; MUA, MPAP, MG 2079, C.6, File 226, Community Garden League of Greater Montreal [1933]; MUA, MPAP, MG 2079, C. 5, File 136, Montreal Parks and Playgrounds Association Incorporated, Report of Executive Director for the Year 1944.

34 MUA, MPAP, MG 2079, C. 6, File 226, Minutes of Meeting of Districts' Council of the Community Garden League of Greater Montreal, 29 November 1945.

35 Pierre Vallières, *White Niggers of America*, trans. Joan Pinkham (Toronto: McClelland & Stewart, 1971 [1968]), 119; 'C'est le régime sec à Ville Jacques-Cartier,' *La Presse*, 24 August 1949, 9. One couple married in the 1939 mass wedding moved to Coteau Rouge, Longueuil, in 1947, however, and were very happy with their 'très beau petit logis.' ANQM, Mouvement des Travailleurs Chrétiens (MTC), P257, Vol. 11, File: Cent Mariés – Couple 103, Husband and wife to Mr and Madame Nap. Chayer, 16 May 1947. Both Protestants and Catholics worried about the lack of welfare services in Montreal's 'outlying areas' in the early postwar period: NA, CCSD, MG 28 I 10, Vol. 236, File 236-3, Isobel Woonton to Bessie Touzel, 10 March 1950; ANQM, Société Saint-Vincent-de-Paul de Montréal (SSVP), P61, Vol. 2, File 7, Réunion du Conseil Central de la SSVP, 24 novembre 1947.

36　NA, MCW, MG 28 I 164, Vol. 7, File 18, 'The Outremont School Problem,' by Louis Rosenberg, Research Director, Canadian Jewish Congress [1947].

37　Weintraub, *City Unique*, 198–9. Also NA, Jewish Family Services of the Baron de Hirsch Institute (JFS), MG 28 V 86: Vol. 12, File: Minutes of Meetings of Board of Directors, Jewish Child Welfare Bureau, 1947–9, Minutes, Meeting of Board of Directors of Jewish Child Welfare Bureau, 17 September 1947; Vol. 7, File: Minutes of Meetings of Board of Directors, Family Welfare Department (Baron de Hirsch Institute), 25 August 1947–5 November 1952, Minutes of Meeting of Board of Directors, 27 April 1948. And see Anctil, *Tur Malka*, 31.

38　Ramirez, *Les premiers Italiens*, chaps. 3–4.

39　MUA, MPAP, MG 2079, C. 5, File 315, Annual Report of the Executive Director to the Montreal Parks and Playgrounds Association Incorporated for the Year 1949.

40　On Mount Royal and Olmsted, see Witold Rybczynski, *A Clearing in the Distance: Frederick Law Olmsted and North America in the Nineteenth Century* (Toronto: HarperFlamingo, 1999); Terry Copp, *The Anatomy of Poverty: The Condition of the Working Class in Montreal, 1897–1929* (Toronto: McClelland & Stewart, 1974), 18.

41　Jeanne M. Wolfe and Grace Strachan, 'Practical Idealism: Women in Urban Reform, Julia Drummond, and the Montreal Parks and Playgrounds Association,' in Caroline Andrew and Beth Moore Milroy, eds., *Life Spaces: Gender, Household, Employment* (Vancouver: UBC P, 1988): 65–80.

42　MUA, MPAP, MG 2079, C. 6, File 226, Community Garden League of Greater Montreal [1933]; W.J. Tawse to J.O. Asselin, 3 December 1948.

43　Conflict between the two organizations can be glimpsed in MUA, MPAP, MG 2079, C. 5, File 188, Statement prepared by the Montreal Parks and Playgrounds Association, Incorporated, 28 June 1944; MUA, MPAP, MG 2079, C. 5, File 198, Jean Gadoury to A.S. Lamb, 1 July 1944. A list of the playgrounds in Montreal in April 1945 is in MUA, MPAP, MG 2079, C. 5, File 188, City of Montreal, Playgrounds List, 27/4/45.

44　*Ninth Census of Canada 1951*, Vol. 3, Table 10; also MUA, MPAP, MG 2079, C. 5, File 136, Montreal Parks and Playgrounds Association Incorporated, Report of Executive Director for the Year 1946; Archives de l'Université du Québec à Montréal (AUQAM), Fonds Henri-Gagnon, 54P 3g/2, Brochure: 'Éviction! Qui sera le suivant?' This brochure claimed that 96.5 per cent of Montreal's population were tenants. On Montreal 'plexes,' see Jason Gilliland, 'Visions and Revisions of House and Home: A Half-Century of Change in Montreal's "Cité-jardin,"' in *(Re)Development at the Urban Edges: Reflections on the Canadian Experience*, ed. H. Nicol and G. Halseth (Waterloo: Department of Geography, University of Waterloo, 2000), 140.

45 J.S. Hodgson, Quebec regional supervisor of the Central Mortgage and
    Housing Corporation, attributed Montreal's postwar housing crisis to the
    fact that 'people today, with more money to spend, are marrying in greater
    numbers.' *Montreal Herald*, '3,000 Vets' Homes to Be Ready Soon Hodgson
    Predicts,' 14 June 1947, 7.
46 *Ninth Census of Canada 1951*, Vol. 3, Table 118. In Canada's urban areas as a
    whole, 16.6 per cent of households were deemed 'crowded' in 1951 (Vol. 10,
    p. 393). The definition of crowding is also found on page 393.
47 ANQM, MTC, P257, Vol. 21, File: Habitation, Mémoire de la L.O.C. sur
    l'Habitation Ouvrière, préparé pour le Comité d'habitation de la Chambre
    de Commerce Senior de Montréal. Also MUA, MCSA, MG 2076, C. 21, File
    983, 'Some Highlights of the Curtis Report,' prepared by the Housing
    Committee of the Montreal Branch of the Canadian Association of Social
    Workers and the MCSA, March 1946.
48 NA, MCW, MG 28 I 164, Vol. 7, File 27, 'Housing – Their Problem: A Study
    of the Dwellings of 298 Montreal Families,' prepared by the Canada Com-
    mittee of the Montreal Branch of the Canadian Association of Social Work-
    ers, March 1947.
49 'La famille Doyon 'déménage' devant les démolisseurs,' *La Presse*, 24 October
    1949, 29; NA, CCSD, MG 28 I 10, Vol. 236, File 236-9, Service économique
    Ste-Justine, Entrevue avec Mlle Jeanne Baril, directrice, 1 décembre 1943,
    par Marie Hamel; NA, Dependents' Allowance Board (DAB), RG 36, Series
    18, Vol. 28, File DAB 4-7, Ruth Robertson, Supervisor of Investigations,
    DPNH, Montreal, to R.O.G. Bennett, Chairman, DAB, 15 March 1943.
50 ANQM, JOC, P104, C. 286, Unfiled, Rapport de la Semaine d'Étude tenu
    [*sic*] à Contrecoeur le 4–5–6 septembre 1948; ANQM, MTC, P257, Vol. 23,
    File: Habitation – À chaque famille sa maison, 'Montreal's Housing Problem
    and its Relationship to Urban Housing in Canada,' 34, Brief presented by
    J.O. Asselin, 8–11 July 1947.
51 ANQM, MTC, P257, Vol. 21, File: Habitation – Habitation ouvrière, Maurice
    Thérien to Commission nationale de l'habitation, 17 January 1948.
52 ANQM, MTC, P257, Vol. 21, File: Habitation – Habitation ouvrière, Adrien
    Malo to Maurice Thérien, 27 January 1948.
53 NA, DAB, RG 36, Series 18, Vol. 29, File: Inadequacy of Allowances, Com-
    plaints, Etc., DAB 5-6, Vol. 3, Mrs A. Stark to Mr McIvor, 27 February 1944.
54 NA, JFS, MG 28 V 86, Vol. 11, File: Minutes of Case Conferences: FWD and
    JCWB, 1944–46, Summary for Jewish Child Welfare Bureau, 5 November
    1945.
55 *La Presse*, 26 February 1948, 26.
56 NA, MCW, MG 28 I 164, Vol. 7, File 27, 'Housing – Their Problem: A Study
    of the Dwellings of 298 Montreal Families.' Prepared by the Canada Com-

mittee of the Montreal Branch of the Canadian Association of Social Workers, March 1947; NA, JFS, MG 28 V 86, Vol. 10, File: Minutes, Case Committee, Family Welfare Dept, 1947, Presentation for Case Committee Meeting, 13 January 1948.

57 AUQAM, Fonds Henri-Gagnon, 54P 3g/2. Brochure: 'Éviction! Qui sera le suivant?'; ANQM, MTC, P257, Vol. 11, File: Histoire de la LOC - documents, 'Rerum Novarum au service de la Ligue Ouvrière Catholique.'

58 'Propriétaire agressive et trop bruyante,' *La Presse*, 20 May 1949, 11.

59 ANQM, MTC, P257, Vol. 16, File: Journée d'Etude Nationale, avril 1949, *L.O.C. – Programme de notre Journée d'Etude, printemps '49 - L.O.C.F.*

60 MUA, MCSA, MG 2076, C. 19, File 44, MCSA, Child Care Agencies, Policies and Practices in Collections and Budgetting [*sic*] (from meeting held 29 October 1948); NA, CCSD, MG 28 I 10, Vol. 236, File 236-7, Annual meeting of the Conseil des Œuvres, 28 May 1947; Archives de l'Université de Montréal (AUM), Fonds de l'Action catholique canadienne (ACC), P16/H3/18/24, Conseil des Œuvres, Commission diocésaine des œuvres de charité et de service social de Montréal, Rapport annuel 1946–47.

61 NA, Summerhill Homes, MG 28 I 388, Vol. 4, File 4-1, Minutes, General Meeting of the L.B.S., 11 September 1945. Also NA, CCSD, MG 28 I 10, Vol. 234, File 234-16, Fifth Annual Meeting of the Children's Aid Society of Montreal, Report of the Executive Director, 7 March 1951.

62 ANQM, MTC, P257, Vol. 21, File: Habitation, Forum sur l'habitation ouvrière; 'L'étude en classe crée un problème,' *La Presse*, 24 August 1949, 9; NA, MCW, MG 28 I 164, Vol. 7, File 27, 'Housing – Their Problem: A Study of the Dwellings of 298 Montreal Families,' Prepared by the Canada Committee of the Montreal Branch of the Canadian Association of Social Workers, March 1947.

63 Bradbury, *Working Families*, 23–24; Paul-André Linteau et al., *Histoire du Québec contemporain*, vol. 1, *De la Confédération à la crise (1867–1929)* (Montreal: Boréal compact, 1989).

64 *Ninth Census of Canada 1951*, Vol. 4, Table 6, Table 17.

65 Robert Bothwell, Ian Drummond, and John English, *Canada since 1945: Power, Politics, and Provincialism*, rev. ed. (Toronto: U of Toronto P, 1989), 73, 68.

66 *Labour Gazette* 45, 9 (September 1945): 1376–7; 46, 8 (August 1946): 1151–2. On transitional unemployment and economic uncertainty, see Bothwell et al., *Canada since 1945*, 68; Desmond Morton, *Working People: An Illustrated History of the Canadian Labour Movement*, 3rd ed. (Toronto: Summerhill P, 1990), 187. For a more optimistic view of Montreal's postwar economy, see

Paul-André Linteau, *Brève histoire de Montréal* (Montreal: Boréal, 1992) and Paul-André Linteau, *Histoire de Montréal depuis la Confédération* (Montreal: Boréal, 1992).

67 Bryan D. Palmer, *Working-Class Experience: Rethinking the History of Canadian Labour, 1800–1991*, 2nd ed. (Toronto: McClelland & Stewart, 1991), 268–9, 282–84, 336–39; Don Wells, 'The Impact of the Postwar Compromise on Canadian Unionism: The Formation of an Auto Worker Local in the 1950s,' *Labour/Le Travail* 36 (Fall 1995): 147–73.

68 *Ninth Census of Canada 1951*, Vol. 4, Table 6, Table 17.

69 Morton, *Working People*, 215.

70 Linteau, *Histoire de Montréal*, chap. 16; Palmer, *Working-Class Experience*, 308. The *Labour Gazette* contended in March 1947 that, in the province of Quebec, 'general manufacturing was on the upswing': 47, 3 (March 1947): 418. A decade later, in 1961, 31.6 per cent of Montreal's total labour force was still employed in manufacturing. Donald Kerr and Deryck W. Holdsworth, eds., *Historical Atlas of Canada*, Vol. 3, *Addressing the Twentieth Century, 1891–1961* (Toronto: U of Toronto P, 1990), Plate 51.

71 *La Presse*: 'Au jour le jour,' 4 September 1947, 13; 'Au jour le jour,' 5 December 1947, 11; 'L'activité ne fait pas défaut,' 5 janvier 1948, 6. See also Linteau et al., *Histoire du Québec contemporain*, vol. 2, *Le Québec depuis 1930*, chap. 20; Linteau, *Histoire de Montréal*, chap. 18.

72 For Canada, see Ruth Roach Pierson, *'They're Still Women After All': The Second World War and Canadian Womanhood* (Toronto: McClelland & Stewart, 1986); for the United States, see Elaine Tyler May, *Homeward Bound: American Families in the Cold War Era* (New York: Basic Books, 1988).

73 Pierson, *'They're Still Women*,' 215–16; Veronica Strong-Boag, 'Canada's Wage-Earning Wives and the Construction of the Middle Class, 1945–60,' *Journal of Canadian Studies* 29, 3 (Fall 1994): 6–7; Joan Sangster, *Earning Respect: The Lives of Working Women in Small-Town Ontario, 1920–1960* (Toronto: U of Toronto P, 1995), 221–4; Francine Barry, *Le travail de la femme au Québec: L'évolution de 1940 à 1970* (Montreal: Les Presses de l'Université du Québec, 1977), 23.

74 *Ninth Census of Canada 1951*, Vol. 10, 6, 248.

75 NA, CCSD, MG 28 I 10, Vol. 51, File 456, 'What the Census Says About Families' by F.G. Boardman, Chief, Family Unit, Dominion Bureau of Statistics, 14 January 1954.

76 NA, Renée Vautelet papers, MG 30 C 196, Vol. 1, 'Le droit de vote pour les femmes [n.d. but post-1945]'; ANQM, JOC, P104, C. 213, File: Semaine d'Étude (Long. 48), Programme – rapport – Correspondance, etc. Rapport

du Congrès des Responsables locaux du S.P.M., 23–29 août 1948; NA, MCW, MG 28 I 164, Vol. 8, File 1, Causerie donnée à Radio-Canada, CBF Montréal, 6 février 1947, par Mme Pierre Casgrain, O.B.E., Présidente du Comité conjoint du Statut légal de la femme mariée.

77 *Ninth Census of Canada 1951*, Vol. 10, 286; Vol. 10, Table 8.

78 Ibid., Vol. 1, Table 29; Vol. 4, Table 8.

79 Ibid., Vol. 4, Table 7.

80 Ibid., Vol. 1, Table 29; Vol. 4, Table 8.

81 Ibid.

82 Collectif Clio, *L'histoire des femmes au Québec*, 402.

83 ANQM, MTC, P257, Vol. 13: File: Campagne de Propagande – Travail féminin, Réunions, Réunion du 4 octobre 1943 re: conscription des femmes.

84 NA, MCW, MG 28 I 164, Vol. 8, File 4, 'Situation in regard to the Employment of Women as seen in Verdun at end of October 1945.'

85 Barry, *Le travail de la femme au Québec*, 14, 11. In Montreal, 20,612 women worked in the clerical sector in 1941; by 1951, 38,159 Montreal women worked in this sector. *Eighth Census of Canada*, Vol. 6, Table 7; *Ninth Census of Canada 1951*, Vol. 4, Table 6.

86 'Retour au foyer,' *La Presse*, 26 October 1945, 5; Pierson, *'They're Still Women.'*

87 NA, MCW, MG 28 I 164: Vol. 5, File 8, 56th Year Book and Annual Report 1949–50, Unemployment Insurance Commission, National Employment Service, Quebec Region; Vol. 8, File 4, 'Situation in regard to the Employment of Women as seen in Verdun at end of October 1945.'

88 NA, MCW, MG 28 I 164, Vol. 6, File 13, Report of the Trades, Business and Professions Committee of the MCW on the problem of the Older Woman Worker, 1949–50.

89 *Ninth Census of Canada 1951*, Vol. 4, Table 6.

90 NA, MCW, MG 28 I 164, Vol. 5, File 9, Resolution on Income Tax Regulations (Married Women), March 1947; and 'Working Wives, Their Income, and the New Income Tax,' *Labour Gazette* 47, 3 (March 1947): 293–7.

91 *La Presse*, 3 May 1947, 24.

92 NA, MCW, MG 28 I 164, Vol. 8, File 4, 'Situation in regard to the Employment of Women as seen in Verdun at end of October 1945'; Trades and Professions for Women Committee, Minutes, 7 February 1946. Francine Barry notes that the service sector (domestic service, in particular) became less significant for working women in the 1940s. See *Le travail de la femme au Québec*, 14, 11. The number of women employed in personal service in Montreal dropped from 22,063 in 1941 to 20,612 in 1951 – during a decade when the city's population rose considerably. *Eighth Census of Canada 1941*, Vol. 6, Table 7; *Ninth Census of Canada 1951*, Vol. 4, Table 6.

93 See, e.g., Agnes Calliste, 'Canada's Immigration Policy and Domestics from the Caribbean: The Second Domestic Scheme,' in Jesse Vorst et al., eds., *Race, Class, Gender: Bonds and Barriers* (Toronto: Garamond and Society for Socialist Studies, 1989). On the extent to which women and girls found service an unappealing option in the postwar period, see 'Employment of Women and Girls in Restaurants,' *Labour Gazette* 49, 1 (January 1949): 36.

94 Collectif Clio, *L'histoire des femmes au Québec*, 415.

95 *La Presse*, 28 January 1947, 22.

96 *Labour Gazette*, 47, 3 (March 1947): 296; NA, MCW, MG 28 I 164, Vol. 8, File 4, 'Situation in regard to the Employment of Women as seen in Verdun at end of October 1945.'

97 NA, CCSD, MG 28 I 10, Vol. 236, File 236-9, Garderie Ste-Anne, Entrevue avec Sister Magdeline, 4 novembre 1943.

98 NA, Summerhill Homes, MG 28 I 388, Vol. 14, File 14-27, Summerhill House, Superintendent's Report for the Year 1950; NA, JFS, MG 28 V 86, Vol. 12, File: Minutes of Meetings, Case and Adoption Committee, JCWB, 1944–8, Minutes, 11 November 1946.

99 *Royal Commission on Prices, Minutes of Proceedings and Evidence* (Ottawa: King's Printer, 1949), No. 41, Brief submitted by Mrs Rae Luckock, National President, Housewives and Consumer Federation of Canada, 2194. See also *Royal Commission on Prices, Minutes of Proceedings and Evidence* (Ottawa: King's Printer, 1948), No. 39, Brief submitted by Kathleen M. Jackson, Secretary of the Family Division, Canadian Welfare Council, 2080.

100 Dominique Marshall, *Aux origines sociales de l'État-providence: Familles québécoises, obligation scolaire et allocations familiales 1940–1955* (Montreal: Les Presses de l'Université de Montréal, 1998); Thérèse Hamel, 'Obligation scolaire et travail des enfants au Québec: 1900–1950,' *Revue d'histoire de l'Amérique française* 38, 1 (Summer 1984): 39–58.

101 Marshall, *Aux origines sociales*, 168.

102 *Royal Commission on Prices, Minutes of Proceedings and Evidence* (Ottawa: King's Printer, 1948), No. 39, Brief submitted by Kathleen M. Jackson, Secretary of the Family Division, Canadian Welfare Council, 2080.

103 NA, CCSD, MG 28 I 10, Vol. 234, File 234-11, Memo: Baron de Hirsch, 24 January 1947.

104 See Tamara Hareven, *Family Time and Industrial Time: The Relationship between the Family and Work in a New England Industrial Community* (Cambridge: Cambridge UP, 1982), for examples of the intrafamily conflict produced by children's labour; see also Marshall, *Aux origines sociales*, 184–5.

105 NA, Department of Labour, RG 27, Vol. 610, File 6-52-2, Vol. 2, Chief, Legislation Branch, Dept of Labour to Marion Royce, 23 September 1943.

106 Marshall, *Aux origines sociales*, 231.
107 NA, CCSD, MG 28 I 10, Vol. 218, File: Quebec: Dept of Social Welfare and Youth (5), 1940–62, Nora Lea to Maud Morlock, 26 April 1943.
108 NA, CCSD, MG 28 I 10, Vol. 234, File 234-24, André M. Guillemette to Nora Lea, 6 April 1944. The Ligue des droits de la femme, which included both francophone and anglophone members, claimed in 1943 that the paid labour of children under the age of 16 'a atteint des proportions assez déplorables ici.' NA, Fonds Thérèse-Casgrain, MG 32 C 25, Vol. 7, File: Ligue des droits de la femme – Minutes des assemblées 1941–6, Rapport de la Secrétaire pour l'année 1942–43, présenté à l'Assemblée annuelle tenue le 17 mai 1943.
109 *Ninth Census of Canada 1951*, Vol. 10, 312. See also Hamel, 'Obligation scolaire et travail des enfants.'
110 NA, MCW, MG 28 I 164, Vol. 8, File 4, Resolution [n.d.].
111 Marshall, *Aux origines sociales*, esp. chap. 5; and NA, Dept of National Health and Welfare, RG 29, Vol. 136, File 266-5-49, Annual Report 1949–50. Family Allowances Division, Dept of National Health and Welfare, Annual Report of Expenditures and Administration in connection with the Family Allowances Act, for the Fiscal Year ended March 31st 1950.
112 Canadian Youth Commission (CYC), *Youth, Marriage and the Family* (Toronto: Ryerson P, 1948), 39, 85–6.
113 Hamel, 'Obligation scolaire et travail des enfants.'
114 ANQM, MTC, P257: Vol. 13, File: Campagne de Propagande – Allocation familiale, Comités généraux de la JOC et de la JOCF to Marcel Labrie, 2 février 1943; Vol. 11, File: Discours du Congrès, 5e anniversaire 1944, Discours de Léo Turcotte, 1944 – 5e anniversaire; AUM, ACC, P16/G5/8/3, Manifeste de la JOC sur la situation économique des jeunes travailleurs [1948].
115 AUM, ACC, P16/G5/8/4, Mémoire présenté par la JOC canadienne à l'Honorable Paul Martin, Ministre du Bien-Être Social, autour de l'établissement des Jeunes Travailleurs [August–September 1948].
116 ANQM, SSVP, P61, Vol. 5, File 32, Assemblée 18 décembre 1944; MUA, MCSA, MG 2076, C. 1, File 874, Memorandum concerning the employment of children in the Province of Quebec [May 1944]. Thérèse Hamel notes that the problem in Montréal was not a complete lack of school attendance, but rather, '*l'abandon précoce* de l'appareil scolaire.' One of the principal goals of compulsory schooling 'est donc de *prolonger* la fréquentation scolaire.' See 'Obligation scolaire et travail des enfants,' 48. Emphases in the original.

117 NA, JFS, MG 28 V 86, Vol. 11, File: Minutes of Case Conferences, FWD and JCWB, 1944–46, Summary for Jewish Child Welfare Bureau, 26 March 1947.
118 *La Presse*: 21 October 1944, 55; 22 April 1944, 43.
119 *Ninth Census of Canada 1951*, Vol. 4, Table 7.
120 Bradbury, *Working Families*, chap. 4.
121 Marshall, *Aux origines sociales*, esp. 219–28.
122 *Ninth Census of Canada 1951*, Vol. 3, Table 135; and see Bradbury, *Working Families*, 133–4; Copp, *The Anatomy of Poverty*, 29. Thérèse Hamel observes that girls' unpaid domestic work 'est totalement évacué dans les recensements.' 'Obligation scolaire et travail des enfants,' 53.

Chapter 2

1 La Loi de l'assistance publique, 1921.
2 Harry M. Cassidy, *Public Health and Welfare Reorganization* (Toronto: Ryerson P, 1945), 365–66, 375–76; Yves Vaillancourt, *L'évolution des politiques sociales au Québec 1940–1960* (Montreal: Presses de l'Université de Montréal, 1988), chap. 5; Marie-Paule Malouin, ed., *L'univers des enfants en difficulté au Québec entre 1940 et 1960* (Montreal: Bellarmin, 1996), chap. 1; B.L. Vigod, 'Ideology and Institutions in Quebec: The Public Charities Controversy 1921–1926,' *Histoire sociale / Social History* 11, 21 (May 1978): 167–82.
3 Vaillancourt, *L'évolution des politiques sociales*, chap. 6; Malouin, *L'univers des enfants en difficulté*, chap. 5.
4 Paul-André Linteau et al., *Histoire du Québec contemporain*, Vol. 2, *Le Québec depuis 1930* (Montreal: Boréal compact, 1989), 327–8.
5 Denise Riley, '"The Social," "Woman," and Sociological Feminism,' in *'Am I That Name?' Feminism and the Category of 'Women' in History* (Minneapolis: U of Minnesota P, 1988).
6 Mariana Valverde, 'The Mixed Social Economy as a Canadian Tradition,' *Studies in Political Economy* 47 (Summer 1995): 33–60. Jane Lewis, describing the British case, has used the expression 'mixed economy of welfare.' See Lewis, 'Gender, the Family and Women's Agency in the Building of "Welfare States": The British Case,' *Social History* 19, 1 (January 1994): 37–55.
7 Vaillancourt, *L'évolution des politiques sociales*.
8 National Archives of Canada (NA), Canadian Council on Social Development (CCSD), MG 28 I 10, Vol. 238, File 238-9, Welfare Federation Campaign Post-Mortem in Outline, 10 October 1945. The Welfare Federation likewise noted in 1949: 'The giving is good because the need is more

urgent than in most cities – the absence of a public assistance program and low government subsidies impose a special burden on private welfare agencies in Montreal.' NA, CCSD, MG 28 I 10, Vol. 238, File 238-11, Campaign Organization Review, Welfare Federation of Montreal, December 1949. An American child-welfare worker noted in 1946, 'An observer from outside Montreal is struck by the lack of provincial or local governmental services.' McGill University Archives (MUA), Montreal Council of Social Agencies (MCSA), MG 2076, C. 1, File 871, Howard W. Hopkirk to Charles H. Young, 31 January 1946.

9 Alvin Finkel, 'Paradise Postponed: A Re-examination of the Green Book Proposals of 1945,' *Journal of the Canadian Historical Association* 4 (1993): 120–42. An indication of a Drew-Duplessis alliance in the early postwar years is in York University Archives (YUA), Maurice Duplessis Fonds, 1980–008/ 001, Reel 1, Note de l'hon. Geo. Drew à Hon. Duplessis à une conférence fédérale-provinciale, à Ottawa, 1945.

10 NA, CCSD, MG 28 I 10, Vol. 237, File: Montreal, Fédération des œuvres de charité canadiennes-françaises, 1935–44, Charlotte Whitton to Paul A. Béique, 4 February 1941.

11 Cited in Jean Hamelin, *Histoire du catholicisme québécois: Le XXe siècle*, Vol. 2, *De 1940 à nos jours*, ed. Nive Voisine (Montreal : Boréal Express, 1984), 38–39. The designation o.p. stands for *ordre des prêcheurs*, i.e., the Dominican order.

12 NA, CCSD, MG 28 I 10, Vol. 234, File 234-24, Statement by André-M. Guillemette, o.p., Executive Director, Conseil des Œuvres, Montreal, 17 November 1943; Le Conseil des Œuvres, par Marie Hamel [n.d.]. On the FOCCF and the Conseil des Œuvres, see also Lionel-Henri Groulx, *Le travail social. Analyse et évolution: Débats et enjeux* (Laval, QC: Éditions agence d'Arc, 1993), 13.

13 The SSVP described itself as 'une institution purement laïque mais soumise à l'autorité ecclésiastique,' Archives nationales du Québec à Montréal (ANQM), Société Saint-Vincent-de-Paul (SSVP), P61, Vol. 3, File 17, Rapport de la première assemblée régulière du Conseil Particulier St-Joseph de Bordeaux de la SSVP, 13 November 1947. The SSVP's objectives and organization are described in: Vol. 7, File 54, Rapport du Conseil Central de Montréal, 1848–1948; Vol. 7, File 54, Discours à l'Hôpital Notre Dame de la Merci, 1er Dimanche du Carême, 6 March 1949; Vol. 2, File 6, Réunion du Comité des Finances de la SSVP de Montréal, 9 August 1944; Vol. 2, File 6, Réunion du Conseil Central de la SSVP de Montréal, 28 August 1944; Vol. 2, File 7, Réunion de la SSVP, 25 March 1946; Vol. 3, File 19. Assemblée générale de tous les membres des conférences du conseil particulier Saint-Georges, 15 April 1945; Vol. 5, File 33, Minutes, Conférence Notre-Dame, Assemblée du 9 septembre 1946.

14 ANQM, SSVP, P61, Vol. 2, File 6, Réunion du Conseil Central de la SSVP de Montréal, 26 February 1945.

15 NA, CCSD, MG 28 I 10: Vol. 236, File 236-9, Visite faite à la St-Vincent de Paul Féminine, 7 March 1944; Vol. 237, File 237-13, Federation of French Charities, Twelfth Annual Appeal, 21 February – 2 March, *War or Peace – Share!*

16 NA, CCSD, MG 28 I 10: Vol. 234, File 234-24, Œuvres Membres du Conseil des Œuvres, Section d'Étude 'Assistance Familiale,' December 1944; Vol. 237, File 237-13, Federation of French Charities, Twelfth Annual Appeal, 21 February–2 March, *War or Peace – Share!* Also *La Presse* (Montreal): 15 December 1945, 28; 11 August 1948, 16. Also Archives de l'Université de Montréal (AUM), Fonds de l'Action catholique canadienne (ACC), P16/O4/52, Deuxième partie, chap. 2, 'La santé dans la famille.' Also ANQM, SSVP, P61, Vol. 7, File 54, Rapport du Conseil Central de Montréal, 1848–1948. For an analysis of l'Assistance maternelle and the Gouttes de lait, see Denyse Baillargeon, 'L'encadrement de la maternité au Québec entre les deux guerres: les gardes de la Métropolitaine, les Gouttes de lait et l'Assistance maternelle,' *Bulletin du Regroupement des chercheurs-chercheures en histoire des travailleurs et travailleuses du Québec* 16, 2–3 (Summer/Fall 1990): 19–45.

17 NA, Dept of Labour, RG 27, Vol. 611, File 6-52-5-2, Vol. 1, 'La Crèche d'Youville, Côte de Liesse, Direction des Soeurs Grises,' Rapport soumis par Renée Morin, Service Sélectif National; NA, CCSD, MG 28 I 10, Vol. 234, File 234-24, H.-H. Dansereau to Révérend Père A.M. Guillemette, 8 March 1944. And see Malouin, *L'univers des enfants en difficulté;* Andrée Lévesque, *Making and Breaking the Rules: Women in Quebec, 1919–1939,* trans. Yvonne M. Klein (Toronto: McClelland & Stewart, 1994).

18 NA, CCSD, MG 28 I 10: Vol. 236, File 236-7, Annual Meeting of the Conseil des œuvres, Montreal, 28 May 1947; Vol. 237, File: Montréal; Service Social Ville-Marie; Hôpital général de la Miséricorde; Service Social de la Miséricorde, 1949–1966, Marie Hamel, 'Report of a Field Visit to the Service Social de la Miséricorde, Montréal,' 16 April 1953. Also AUM, ACC, P16, File: P16/H3/18/24, Le Conseil des Œuvres, Rapport Annuel 1946–47.

19 ANQM, Jeunesse Ouvrière Catholique (JOC), P104, C. 134, File: Bureau d'Assistance aux Familles – Documentation, Bureau d'Assistance Sociale aux Familles, 8e Assemblée Annuelle, 3 juin 1948. And see Vaillancourt, *L'évolution des politiques sociales,* 221; Malouin, *L'univers des enfants en difficulté,* 416.

20 NA, CCSD, MG 28 I 10: Vol. 237, File: Montreal, Fédération des œuvres de charité canadiennes-françaises, 1935–44. Albert Doyen [*sic*] to Marie Hamel, 23 February 1943; Vol. 238, File 238-4, Memo for Bureau d'Assistance Sociale aux Familles File, 6 May 1943, by Nora Lea. NA, Dependents' Allowance Board (DAB), RG 36, Series 18, Vol. 28, File: DAB 4-7, Reports by Administra-

tion Section DAB on Cases Submitted by the Bureau d'Assistance Sociale aux Familles; Memoranda [*sic*] to R.O.G. Bennett from Board of Directors, Bureau d'Assistance Sociale aux Familles, Montreal [May 1944]; Mémoire from Jeanne Barabé-Langlois to R.O.G. Bennett, 23 December 1942.

21 NA, CCSD, MG 28 I 10, Vol. 238, File 238-4, Memo re: Bureau d'Assistance Sociale aux Familles, Montreal, 31 May 1945. Conflict between BASF workers and the Catholic sisters running the service for unwed mothers at the Miséricorde is described in NA, CCSD, MG 28 I 10, Vol. 238, File 238-4, Field Visit to the Bureau d'Assistance Sociale aux Familles, 14–15 February 1946, by Marie Hamel.

22 ANQM, SSVP, P61, Vol. 2, File 6, Minutes de la réunion du Conseil Central de la SSVP de Montréal: 31 January 1944, 28 February 1944, 27 March 1944, 26 June 1944.

23 AUM, ACC, P16, File: P16/H3/18/24, Le Conseil des Œuvres, Rapport Annuel 1946–47.

24 NA, Thérèse Casgrain Papers, MG 32 C 25, Vol. 8, File: 25e anniversaire du suffrage féminin – 1965, '25e anniversaire du droit de vote des femmes au Québec. Résumé de l'exposé de Mme Jeanne B. Langlois.'

25 NA, CCSD, MG 28 I 10: Vol. 236, File 236-7, Field Visit to the Conseil des Œuvres, 14–15 February 1946; Interview with Father Caron, Conseil des Œuvres, 20 October 1948; Annual Meeting of the Conseil des œuvres, Montreal, 28 May 1947; Vol. 238, File 238-1, Mémoire, 'La Société d'Adoption et de Protection de l'Enfance,' 3 June 1946; Vol. 238, File 238-1, Report of Field Visit to Father Contant, Société d'Adoption, Montreal, 8 September 1950; Vol. 238, File 238-4, Memo re: Bureau d'Assistance Sociale aux Familles, Montreal, 27 February 1945. See Groulx, *Le travail social,* 53–55, on conflict between social workers and nuns and between social workers and volunteer charity workers.

26 MUA, MCSA, MG 2076, C. 19, File 54, Memorandum Reporting on Conversation with Father Guillemette Re: the Position of the Conseil des Œuvres on the Proposed Independent Welfare Agency (21 January 1944). The Conseil des Œuvres also expressed the need for a 'système d'assistance familiale [qui protègerait] mieux la vie familiale' in its annual report of 1946–7. AUM, ACC, P16, File: P16/H3/18/24, Le Conseil des Œuvres, Rapport Annuel 1946–47.

27 AUM, ACC, P16, File: P16/H3/18/24, Le Conseil des Œuvres, Rapport Annuel 1946–7.

28 NA, CCSD, MG 28 I 10, Vol. 236, File 236-7, Interview with Father Caron, Conseil des Œuvres, 20 October 1948. The SSVP's 'alarming' financial situation is described in ANQM, SSVP, P61, Vol. 2, File 7, Réunion du Conseil Central de la SSVP, 30 May 1949.

29 NA, CCSD, MG 28 I 10, Vol. 237, File 237-14, News clipping, 'A Call to the Whole Community.' *Montreal Gazette*, 21 February 1944.

30 NA, CCSD, MG 28 I 10, Vol. 234, File 234-15, Catholic Welfare Bureau [1938].

31 MUA, MCSA, MG 2076, C. 19, File 21, 'An aid to the doctor in guiding unmarried mothers to social services for help'; NA, DAB, RG 36, Series 18, Vol. 50, Report on the Visit to the Montreal Agencies, March 29 and 30 [1943], by Ruth Harvey; ANQM, SSVP, P61, Vol. 3, File 16, 'Cinéma,' Brief prepared by the Boys' Bureau of the Federation of Catholic Charities, 13 January 1943.

32 Cassidy, *Public Health and Welfare*, 376.

33 MUA, MCSA, MG 2076, C. 14, File 1000, MCSA, Annual Report for 1945.

34 MUA, MCSA, MG 2076, C. 14, File 1001, Annual Report for 1946. Also C. 14, File 1002, MCSA, Annual Report 1947, Report of the Board of Governors for the Year 1947; Annual Report 1948; Annual Report 1949, Health Section; Annual Report 1950, Report of the Board of Governors for the Year 1950.

35 MUA, MCSA, MG 2076, C. 14, File 1002, MCSA, Report of the Board of Governors for the Year 1947.

36 MUA, MCSA, MG 2076, C. 19, File 54, Report of a Special Committee of the Montreal Council of Social Agencies Concerning the Proposal to Establish an Independent Agency – the Montreal Public Welfare Bureau – to Care for Long Term and Borderline Cases, 5 January 1944; 'Why the Family Welfare Association Needs So Much Money' [September 1942].

37 MUA, MCSA, MG 2076, C. 14, File 1002, Annual Report 1950, Report of the Board of Governors for the Year 1950.

38 MUA, MCSA, MG 2076, C. 14, File 1002, MCSA, Annual Report 1949, Report of the Board of Governors for the Year 1949.

39 NA, CCSD, MG 28 I 10, Vol. 237, File 237-2, Basic Facts on which to develop article re Federation of Jewish Philanthropies, Montreal.

40 MUA, MCSA, MG 2076, C. 14, File 1000, MCSA, Annual Report for 1945.

41 NA, Jewish Family Services of the Baron de Hirsch Institute (JFS), MG 28 V 86, Vol. 10, File: Minutes of Meetings of Case Committee, Family Welfare Dept, 1944–45, Review of purpose and activities of case committee [n.d.]. Donald Hurwitz, appointed to the head of the Federation of Jewish Philanthropies in 1946, was likewise 'appalled by deficiencies in public welfare and child welfare in Quebec.' NA, CCSD, MG 28 I 10, Vol. 237, File 237-1, Memo re: Jewish Federation, Montreal, 23 September 1946, by K. Jackson, CWC.

42 NA, JFS, MG 28 V 86, Vol. 10, File: Minutes of Meetings of Case Committee, Family Welfare Dept, 1946–47, Minutes of Case Committee Meeting, 20 March 1946.

43 NA, CCSD, MG 28 I 10, Vol. 238, File 238-1, Visit to Father Paul Contant, Executive Director, La Société d'Adoption et de Protection de l'Enfance, Montreal, 12 October 1949. Emphasis in the original.

44 NA, CCSD, MG 28 I 10: Vol. 219, File: Quebec Gov't General (2), 1930, 1942–52, 'Public Welfare Services in the Province of Quebec,' 16 May 1946; Vol. 234, File 234-24, Mémoire au Révérend Père Guillemette sur les Œuvres visitées à Montréal au cours des mois d'octobre, novembre et décembre 1943; Marie Hamel to Révérend Père A.M. Guillemette, o.p., 6 January 1944; Marie Hamel to Révérend Père André M. Guillemette, o.p., 23 May 1945; Vol. 236, File 236-7, Interview with Father Caron, Conseil des Œuvres, 20 October 1948; Vol. 238, File 238-1, Nora Lea to Laura L. Noya, 9 November 1945; Memo on field visit to La Société d'Adoption et de Protection de l'Enfance, 21 January 1948, by Marie Hamel; Vol. 238, File 238-4, Memo for Bureau d'Assistance Sociale aux Familles File, 6 May 1943, by Nora Lea. The social service branch of the Ste-Justine children's hospital, meanwhile, felt that municipal welfare investigators were similarly lacking in social work training. NA, CCSD, MG 28 I 10, Vol. 236, File 236-9. Service économique Ste-Justine, Entrevue avec Mlle Jeanne Baril, directrice, le 1er décembre 1943, par Marie Hamel.

45 ANQM, SSVP, P61, Vol. 3, File 19, Rapport de la dernière assemblée tenu [sic] au sein de la Conférence St-Enfant-Jésus, 14 juin 1948.

46 NA, Thérèse Casgrain Papers, MG 32 C 25, Vol. 7, File: Ligue des droits de la femme – Minutes des assemblées 1941–46, Rapport de la Secrétaire pour l'année 1942–43, présenté à l'Assemblée annuelle tenue le 17 mai 1943.

47 Groulx, Le travail social, 13, 33.

48 NA, CCSD, MG 28 I 10, Vol. 237, File: Montréal; Service Social Ville-Marie; Hôpital général de la Miséricorde; Service Social de la Miséricorde, 1949–66, Marie Hamel, 'Report of a Field Visit to the Service Social de la Miséricorde, Montréal,' 16 April 1953. Jeanne Barabé-Langlois, a well-known Montreal social worker, stated in 1965 that, in the 1940s, 'les autorités religieuses reconnurent la valeur des techniques du service social professionnel en envoyant, à ce moment-là, plusieurs membres du clergé étudier dans des universités européennes ou américaines: les abbés Lucien Desmarais (premier directeur de l'École de Service social) et Gérald Berry (son assistant) de même que les révérends Pères André-M. Guillemette o.m.i. [sic] et Émile Bouvier, s.j.' NA, Thérèse Casgrain Papers, MG 32 C 25, Vol. 8, File: 25e anniversaire du suffrage féminin – 1965, '25e anniversaire du droit de vote des femmes au Québec. Résumé de l'exposé de Mme Jeanne B. Langlois.'

49 NA, CCSD, MG 28 I 10, Vol. 234, File 234-15, K.M. Jackson's comments [confidential] on Catholic Welfare Bureau, Montreal, 1 August 1950.

50 NA, CCSD, MG 28 I 10, Vol. 234, File 234-16, Memo for Children's Service
    Association, 6 April 1943, by N.L. [Nora Lea]. One American child-welfare
    worker claimed in 1946, 'The scarcity of professionally trained social workers
    is perceptible in Montreal.' MUA, MCSA, MG 2076, C. 1, File 871, Howard
    W. Hopkirk to Charles H. Young, 31 January 1946. See also Vaillancourt,
    L'évolution des politiques sociales, 221.

51 NA, JFS, MG 28 V 86, Vol. 11, File: Minutes of Staff Meetings, Sept. 1945–
    Jan. 1947, Minutes of Staff Conference, 20 February 1946.

52 NA, JFS, MG 28 V 86, Vol. 10, File: Minutes of Meetings of Case Committee,
    Family Welfare Dept, 1946–47, Minutes of Case Committee Meeting, 29 Oc-
    tober 1946.

53 NA, JFS, MG 28 V 86, Vol. 12, File: Minutes of Meetings, Staff Committee,
    J.C.W.B., 1942–47, Minutes, Meeting of Staff Committee of Jewish Child
    Welfare Bureau, 21 October 1945; Memo re: salary standards for social
    agency employees [n.d.]; NA, CCSD, MG 28 I 10, Vol. 237, File 237-1,
    An Affair of Honour, 1917–1941: The Story of Canada's First Financial
    Federation.

54 NA, CCSD, MG 28 I 10, Vol. 237, File 237-8, Stuart K. Jaffary to Charles H.
    Bland, 24 November 1942.

55 NA, CCSD, MG 28 I 10: Vol. 218, File 17, Interview with Miss Laurette Hetu
    by Maud Morlock, 24 March 1944; Vol. 234, File 234-11, K.M. Jackson to
    Anna H. Sacks, 28 January 1946.

56 MUA, MCSA, MG 2076, C. 47, File 435, Juvenile Court Committee Meeting,
    18 January 1946. See also, in the same file, Minutes of Meeting of the Juve-
    nile Court Committee, 4 May 1949; Minutes of a Special Meeting of the
    Juvenile Court Committee, 23 June 1949.

57 ANQM, SSVP, P61: Vol. 2, File 7, Réunions du Conseil Central: 27 January
    1947, 30 August 1948, 28 March 1949; Vol. 3, File 19, Rapport de la réunion
    du Conseil Particulier St-Georges, 28 September 1948.

58 NA, CCSD, MG 28 I 10, Vol. 238, File 238-9, News clipping, 'Dollar Hobbles
    on Welfare.' *Montreal Gazette*, 28 March 1946. By the late 1940s, even the
    SSVP advised its councils to send the unemployed to the city's social welfare
    department. ANQM, SSVP, P61: Vol. 2, File 7, Réunions du Conseil Central
    de la SSVP, 29 April 1946, 29 March 1948; Vol. 3, File 17, Rapport de l'as-
    semblée tenue conjointement par les Conseils Particuliers St-Georges et
    St-Joseph de Bordeaux le 22 février 1948.

59 NA, CCSD, MG 28 I 10, Vol. 234, File 234-24, André-M. Guillemette, o.p., to
    Nora Lea, 6 April 1944; AUM, ACC, P16, File: P16/R57, Institutions d'assis-
    tance aux familles.

60 See Vigod, 'Ideology and Institutions in Quebec,' 171.

61 ANQM, SSVP, P61, Vol. 2, File 7, Réunions du Conseil Central, 27 January
    1947, 31 May 1948, 30 May 1949.
62 NA, CCSD, MG 28 I 10: Vol. 134, File 600 (II), Response to questionnaire
    from N.R. Beaudet, 8 June 1942; Vol. 218, Files 13, 14, 17; Michèle Dagenais,
    Des pouvoirs et des hommes: l'administration municipale de Montréal, 1900–1950
    (Montréal and Kingston: McGill-Queen's UP and the Institute of Public
    Administration of Canada, 2000), 75–76; Vaillancourt, *L'évolution des
    politiques sociales*, 133.
63 Vaillancourt, *L'évolution des politiques sociales*; Marshall, *Aux origines sociales de
    l'État-providence: Familles québécoises, obligation scolaire et allocations familiales
    1940–1955* (Montreal: Presses de l'Université de Montréal, 1998); John A.
    Dickinson and Brian Young, *A Short History of Quebec*, 2nd ed. (Toronto:
    Copp Clark Pitman, 1993), 278–80.
64 Valverde, 'Mixed Social Economy.'
65 For a different view, see ibid., 36.
66 Robert England, *Discharged: A Commentary on Civil Re-establishment of Veterans
    in Canada* (Toronto: Macmillan, 1943), 115, 78; Desmond Morton, *A Military
    History of Canada: From Champlain to the Gulf War*, 3rd ed. (Toronto:
    McClelland & Stewart, 1992), 176, 182.
67 NA, Dept of Veterans' Affairs (DVA), RG 38, Vol. 184, File: Rehabilitation -
    Confidential Letters, Vol. 1, Walter S. Woods [for Minister] to Alex Walker,
    Dominion President, Canadian Legion of the B.E.S.L., Ottawa, 18 August
    1941; England, *Discharged*, 28; Craig Heron, ed., *The Workers' Revolt in
    Canada, 1917–1925* (Toronto: U of Toronto P, 1998).
68 NA, DVA, RG 38, Vol. 193, File 65-47-A, Monthly Report, 2 February 1943.
    See also ANQM, JOC, P 104, Container 216, File: Soldats (Service). Memo-
    randum of the JOC To the Canadian Government in Favour of Demobilized
    Young Men [n.d. but after October 1946].
69 On First World War veterans, see Desmond Morton and Glenn Wright,
    *Winning the Second Battle: Canadian Veterans and the Return to Civilian Life,
    1915–1930* (Toronto: U of Toronto P, 1987).
70 ANQM, JOC, P 104, Container 216. File: Soldats (Service). DND recruiting
    pamphlet: 'Notre armée a besoin de bons canadiens.' This message was
    followed by a list of nine ways in which veterans would be helped by the
    state. Also NA, DVA, RG 38, Vol. 184, File: Rehabilitation – Confidential
    Letters, Vol. 1, Confidential Letter No. 1, 22 July 1941.
71 NA, DAB, RG 36, Series 18, Vol. 12, File: Local Committees – General Corre-
    spondence, Vol. 1, Article [no author, n.d. but probably December 1944], 7.
72 AUM, Fonds Édouard-Montpetit, P 8/1, Comité de Reconstruction, 1941–
    43, Memorandum for the Committee on Reconstruction by F. Cyril James,

27 March 1941; Memorandum regarding the activities of local committees in the field of Post-War Reconstruction, 17 August 1942. See also Peter Neary and J.L. Granatstein, eds., *The Veterans Charter and Post–World War II Canada* (Montreal and Kingston: McGill-Queen's UP, 1998).

73 England, *Discharged*, 201–2.

74 NA, DVA, RG 38, Vol. 184, File: Rehabilitation – Confidential Letters, Vol. 1, Confidential Letter No. 11, 24 January 1942. Also NA, DAB, RG 36, Series 18, Vol. 12, File: Local Committees – General Correspondence, Vol. 1, Article [no author, n.d. but probably December 1944], 4.

75 Theda Skocpol, *Protecting Soldiers and Mothers: The Political Origins of Social Policy in the United States* (Cambridge, MA: Belknap P of Harvard UP, 1992), 151.

76 Family allowances and purchasing power are discussed in NA, CCSD, MG 28 I 10, Vol. 58, File 490, Nora Lea to Col. H.E. Pense, 20 March 1945; Nora Lea to Col. H.E. Pense, 13 February 1946.

77 ANQM, JOC, P 104, Container 216, File: Soldats (Service), Untitled memorandum [n.d. but 1941–2]; NA, Renée Vautelet papers, MG 30 C 196, Vol. 1, 'Federal election' [1945], 6; NA, JFS, MG 28 V 86, Vol. 11, File: Minutes of Staff Meetings, September 1945–January 1947, Minutes of Joint Meeting, Family Welfare Dept and Jewish Child Welfare Bureau, 30 January 1946.

78 NA, DVA, RG 38, Vol. 193, File 65-47-A, Monthly Report, Montreal, 3 May 1943.

79 NA, Montreal Soldiers Wives League (MSWL), MG 28 I 311, Vol. 1, File 91, Association Meeting, 11 February 1944.

80 NA, Montreal Council of Women (MCW), MG 28 I 164, Vol. 3, File 1A, Minutes, 21 May 1947; *La Presse*, 3 January 1947, 6; 20 December 1947, 47. One of the JOC's topics for discussion in 1945 was veterans who were 'rehabilitated' but irregularly employed. ANQM, JOC, P 104, Container 170, File: Divers (Amour-Guerre-Chômage), Forum Populaire: 'Guerre ou Chômage.'

81 NA, MCW, MG 28 I 164, Vol. 3: File 1A, Minutes, 19 February 1947; File 1B. Minutes, 21 January 1948.

82 NA, MSWL, MG 28 I 311, Vol. 5, File 24, Montreal War Services Co-Ordinating Council – Welfare Committee. Minutes, 8 February 1946; NA, DVA, RG 38, Vol. 197, File: Rehabilitation, Statistics: Women's Division, Proceedings: Training Conferences on Women's Rehabilitation, 83.

83 NA, MSWL, MG 28 I 311, Vol. 5, File 24, Montreal War Services Co-Ordinating Council – Welfare Committee, Minutes, 8 February 1946; ANQM, SSVP, P 61, Vol. 2, File 7, Réunion du Conseil Central, 30 September 1946; NA, CCSD, MG 28 I 10, Vol. 234: File 234-16, George F. Davidson to Miss Muriel Tucker, 18 December 1942; File 234-24, André-M. Guillemette, o.p., to Nora Lea, 24 July 1945.

84 NA, JFS, MG 28 V 86, Vol. 10: File: Minutes of Meetings of Case Committee, Family Welfare Dept, 1944–5, Minutes, 28 October 1944; File: Minutes of Meetings of Case Committee, Family Welfare Dept, 1946–47, Minutes, 20 March 1946; NA, MCW, MG 28 I 164, Vol. 5, File 7, 53rd Year Book and Annual Report 1946–47, Report of the Committee for the Welfare of Members of National Defence Services and their Dependents; NA, DAB, RG 36, Series 18, Vol. 12, File: General Correspondence Re: Citizens' Committees, 'A' District – Montreal, Letter from H.M. Hague, 25 July 1947; MUA, MCSA, MG 2076, C. 17, File 67, Jacob Tuckman, 'Vocational Guidance – A Community Responsibility,' 7 April 1949.

85 NA, MCW, MG 28 I 164, Vol. 3, File 1A, Minutes of Meeting of Sub-Executive Committee, 12 February 1947; ANQM, SSVP, P 61, Vol. 2, File 7, Réunion du Conseil Central, 26 May 1947.

86 NA, CCSD, MG 28 I 10, Vol. 234, File 234-24, André-M. Guillemette, o.p., to Nora Lea, 24 July 1945.

87 For the most thorough treatment of Canadian family allowances to-date, see Marshall, *Aux origines sociales*.

88 ANQM, JOC, P104, C. 181, File: Commission Canadienne de la Jeunesse (Congrès – Janvier 1945), Mémoire de la JOC, Jeunesse vs. après-guerre, 'Jeunesse et famille.' And see Marshall, *Aux origines sociales*; Vaillancourt, *L'évolution des politiques sociales*.

89 Thérèse F. Casgrain, *A Woman in a Man's World*, trans. Joyce Marshall (Toronto: McClelland & Stewart, 1972), chap. 10; Andrée Lévesque, 'Les Québécoises et les débuts de l'État providence,' in Brigitte Studer et al., eds., *Frauen und Staat / Les Femmes et l'État* (Basel: Schwabe & Co., 1998), 183.

90 *La Presse*: 2 November 1946, 34; 26 October 1948, 15.

91 *La Presse*, 14 February 1949, Courrier de Colette, 18; NA, JFS, MG 28 V 86: Vol. 10, File: Minutes of Meetings of Case Committee, FWD, 1944–45, Follow-Up re: L. family, 30 October 1945; Vol. 10, File: Minutes of Meetings of Case Committee, FWD, 1946–47, Follow-Up Case No. 12, 8 May 1946; Vol. 11, File: Minutes of Staff Meetings, Family Welfare and Child Welfare Depts, July–December 1947. Minutes of Staff Meeting held 30 July 1947. Also NA, Dept of National Health and Welfare, RG 29, Vol. 1283, File: 266-5-46, Mae Fleming, Chief Supervisor, Welfare Services, 'Annual Report of Welfare Services,' 31 May 1947. On the uses to which Quebec families put their family allowances, see also Marshall, *Aux origines sociales*, chaps. 4 and 5.

92 MUA, MCSA, MG 2076, C. 14, File 1001, Chairman's Remarks, 1946; also NA, CCSD, MG 28 I 10, Vol. 58, File 490, 'Family Allowances – from the National Point of View' by Mae Fleming, Paper presented at 10th Biennial Meeting, Canadian Conference on Social Work, 25–8 June 1946; Statement by Cana-

dian Welfare Council, Ottawa, 16 February [1949?]; Nora Lea to Nora J. Rowe, 5 December 1944; also NA, Dept of National Health and Welfare, RG 29, Vol. 1283, File 266-5-49, L.H. Senez, Supervisor of Welfare Services, Quebec, Welfare Annual Report – Fiscal Year 1949–50, to R.B. Curry, National Director, Family Allowances, Ottawa, 5 April 1950.

93 NA, MCW, MG 28 I 164, Vol. 5, File 7, 53rd Year Book and Annual Report 1946–47, Report of Child Welfare Committee 1946–47; AUM, ACC: P16/H3/18/24, Le Conseil des Œuvres, Rapport Annuel 1946–47; P16/R64, 'Vers l'Edification de la famille de demain,' Rapport des premières journées d'étude de la Commission française du Conseil canadien du Bien-être social, Hôpital de la Miséricorde, Montréal, 9–10 mars 1951: Mme Kaspar Fraser, présidente générale du Conseil canadien du Bien-être Social, 'La famille canadienne en 1951.'

94 NA, JFS, MG 28 V 86, Vol. 10, File: Minutes of Meeting of Case Committee, FWD, 1947, Memo to Mr Weiss, Montreal, 22 October 1947; AUM, ACC, P16/H3/18/24, Le Conseil des Œuvres, Rapport Annuel 1946–47.

95 NA, JFS, MG 28 V 86, Vol. 10, File: Minutes of Meetings of Case Committee, FWD, 1944–45, Minutes, 31 October 1945. In 1948, more than 450,000 Quebec families received family allowances, whereas only 12,000 families benefited from the provincial Needy Mothers' Assistance. NA, CCSD, MG 28 I 10, Vol. 58, File 490, Statement by Canadian Welfare Council, Ottawa, 16 February [1949?].

96 MUA, MCSA, MG 2076, C. 14, File 1002, Annual Report of MCSA, 1949, Report of the Board of Governors for 1949. Also C. 19, File 54, 'Why the Family Welfare Association Needs So Much Money' [September 1942]. On state expectations that family allowances would be supplemented with private aid in cases of dire need, see Marshall, *Aux origines sociales*, chap. 5.

97 ANQM, SSVP, P61, Vol. 2, File 6. Réunions du Conseil Central de la SSVP de Montréal, 28 February 1944, 27 November 1944; Vol. 2, File 7. Réunion du Conseil Central, 29 March 1948; Vol. 5, File 32. Minutes, Conférence Notre-Dame, 5 June 1944, 2 October 1944; MUA, MCSA, MG 2076, C. 14, File 1002. MCSA, Annual Report 1949, Health Section; MCSA, Annual Report 1950, Report of the President. Also NA, Dept of National Health and Welfare, RG 29, Vol. 136, File 208-5-4, Part 4, J.W. MacFarlane to J.R. Forest, 14 July 1950.

98 ANQM, SSVP, P61, Vol. 2, File 7, Réunion du Conseil Central, 25 février 1946. See also Réunion du Conseil Central, 31 octobre 1949.

99 NA, JFS, MG 28 V 86: Vol. 7, File: Minutes of Meetings of Board of Directors, Family Welfare Dept (Baron de Hirsch Institute), 25 August 1947–5 November 1952, Memorandum to Members of the Board of Directors, 20 August 1947; Vol. 11, File: Minutes of Staff Meetings, Sept. 1945–Jan. 1947, Minutes

of Staff Meeting, 26 August 1947. NA, CCSD, MG 28 I 10: Vol. 236, File 236-2, Nora Lea to Chas. H. Young, 15 May 1945; Vol. 238, File 238-1, La Société d'Adoption et de Protection de l'Enfance, Montreal, Field visit [by Marie Hamel], 24 August 1946. MUA, MCSA, MG 2076, C. 14, File 1002, MCSA, Report of the Board of Governors for the Year 1947. ANQM, SSVP, P61, Vol. 2, File 7, Réunion du Conseil Central de la SSVP, 29 October 1945.

100 NA, JFS, MG 28 V 86, Vol. 11, File: Minutes of Staff Meetings, September 1945–Jan. 1947, Minutes of Staff Meeting, 12 March 1947.

101 NA, CCSD, MG 28 I 10, Vol. 238, File 238-9, Charles H. Young to Nora Lea, 6 October 1945; Welfare Federation Campaign Post-Mortem in Outline, 10 October 1945; Welfare Federation of Montreal, Report on 1945–46 campaign, September 24th to October 2nd.

102 ANQM, SSVP, P61, Vol. 3, File 16, Historique de la Société Saint-Vincent-de-Paul de Montréal depuis sa fondation en mars 1848 jusqu'à nos jours [1948?].

103 AUM, ACC, P16/R219, R.P. Valère Massicotte, O.F.M., 'La Délinquence [sic] juvénile et la guerre' (Montreal: L'Oeuvre des Tracts, 1944); NA, DAB, RG 36, Series 18, Vol. 28, File: DAB 4-5, Vol. 4, Margaret H. Spaulding to R.O.G. Bennett, 21 November 1942.

104 NA, Dept of Labour, RG 27, Vol. 611, File 6-52-5-2, Vol. 1, Quebec Dominion-Provincial Wartime Day Nurseries – Monthly Report, Month of August 1943; Quebec Dominion-Provincial Wartime Day Nurseries – Monthly Report, Month of February 1945.

105 NA, Dept of Labour, RG 27: Vol. 609, File 6-52-1, Vol. 2, Memorandum to Miss Norris from Margaret Grier, Ottawa, 7 July 1945; Vol. 610, File 6-52-2, Vol. 1, Memorandum to Mr A. MacNamara from Mrs Rex Eaton re: Progress of Day Nursery Plan, 29 January 1943; Vol. 611, File 6-52-5-1, Florence F. Martel to Margaret Grier, 18 December 1943.

106 NA, Dept of Labour, RG 27, Vol. 611, File 6-52-5-2, Vol. 1, Memorandum to Margaret Grier, NSS, Ottawa, from Renée Morin, NSS, Montreal, re: Meeting at the Maisonneuve Day Nursery, 23 April 1944; Miriam Chapin to Mrs Rex Eaton, 18 February 1943; Florence Martel to Margaret Grier, 14 January 1944.

107 NA, Dept of Labour, RG 27, Vol. 611, File 6-52-5-2, Vol. 1, A. Lapierre to Margaret Grier, 10 January 1945.

108 NA, Dept of Labour, RG 27, Vol. 611, File 6-52-5-2, Vol. 2, Memorandum to Arthur MacNamara from Margaret Grier re Wartime Day Nurseries – Montreal, 8 November 1945; NA, MCW, MG 28 I 164, Vol. 5, File 6, 51st Year Book and Annual Report 1944–45. Report of Child Welfare Committee.

109 NA, Dept of Labour, RG 27, Vol. 610, File 6-52-2, Vol. 1, Memorandum to

Mr A. MacNamara, Deputy Minister of Labour, from Mrs Rex Eaton, re: Establishment of Day Nursery in Montreal, 1 March 1943.

110 NA, Dept of Labour, RG 27, Vol. 611, File 6-52-5-2, Vol. 1, Memorandum to Margaret Grier, NSS, Ottawa, from Renée Morin, NSS, Montreal, re Meeting at the Maisonneuve Day Nursery, 23 April 1944.

111 NA, Dept of Labour, RG 27, Vol. 611, File 6-52-5-2, Vol. 1, Margaret Huskins to Dr Lalande, 7 September 1944.

112 NA, Dept of Labour, RG 27, Vol. 611, File 6-52-5-2, Vol. 1, Memorandum to Mr A. MacNamara from Mrs Rex Eaton, re: Wartime Day Nurseries – Montreal, 4 July 1944.

113 NA, Dept of Labour, RG 27: Vol. 611, File 6-52-5-2, Vol. 1, Mothers of Day Nursery No. 1, Montreal, to Dept of Day Nurseries, Ministry of Health and Social Welfare, 20 April 1945; Vol. 3538, File 3-2—45, Requête auprès du Gouvernement fédéral en faveur des garderies, octobre 1945.

114 NA, Dept of Labour, RG 27: Vol. 3538, File 3-26-45, James P. Anglin to Hon. Humphrey Mitchell, 12 October 1945; Vol. 611, File 6-52-5-2, Vol. 1, Florence F. Martel to Margaret Grier, 30 December 1943; *La Presse*, 26 October 1945, 4; NA, MCW, MG 28 I 164, Vol. 5, File 6, 51st Year Book and Annual Report 1944–45, Report of Child Welfare Committee. For an analysis of the Dominion-Provincial Wartime Day Nursery scheme, see Ruth Roach Pierson, *'They're Still Women After All': The Second World War and Canadian Womanhood* (Toronto: McClelland & Stewart, 1986), chap. 1.

115 AUM, ACC, P16/O4/52, Commission Canadienne de la Jeunesse, Comité provincial du Québec, Mémoire sur la famille, Deuxième partie, chap. 2, 'La santé dans la famille.'

116 NA, MSWL, MG 28 I 311, Vol. 5, File 24, MSWL to Mr E.I. Smit, March 1942; NA, Dept of Labour, RG 27, Vol. 611, File 6-52-5-2, Vol. 1, Florence Martel to Margaret Grier, 14 January 1944. But see also Marion V. Royce, *The Effect of the War on the Life of Women: A Study* (Geneva: World's YWCA, 1945), 47: Royce comments that this mistrust of wartime day nurseries was shared by women in various countries.

117 NA, Summerhill Homes, MG 28 I 388, Vol. 6, File 6-12, Letter, 5 November 1945.

118 Montreal women's complaints about the lack of reliable babysitters can be found in ANQM, Mouvement des Travailleurs Chrétiens (MTC), P257: Vol. 11, File: Cent Mariés – Couple 20; Vol. 10, File: Cent Mariés – Couple 11; ANQM, Église catholique, Diocèse de Montréal, Service de préparation au mariage (SPM), P116, Boite 60-0-002-13-06-001B-01, File: 1949: Semaine des fiancés. Responses to SPM questionnaire, December 1948; *La Presse*, 6 April 1948, 15.

119 NA, Dept of Labour, RG 27, Vol. 611, File 6-52-5-2, Vol. 1, Memorandum to Margaret Grier, Director, Wartime Day Nurseries, Ottawa, from Florence F. Martel, NSS, Montreal, re: Visit to two Day Nurseries, 12 July 1943. Some of these were long-standing: see Micheline Dumont, 'Des garderies au 19e siècle: les salles d'asile des Soeurs Grises de Montréal,' in Nadia Fahmy-Eid and Micheline Dumont, *Maîtresses de maison, maîtresses d'école: Femmes, familles et éducation dans l'histoire du Québec* (Montreal: Boréal Express, 1983).

120 MUA, MCSA, MG 2076, C. 17, File 84, 'The Montreal Day Nursery: A Study of Services and Facilities,' September 1947.

121 NA, CCSD, MG 28 I 10, Vol. 236, File 236-9, Asile pour jeunes enfants, 1471 rue Fullum, Entrevue avec Soeur Berthe-Cécile, directrice, 5 novembre 1943; Garderie Ste-Anne, Entrevue avec Sister Magdeline, 4 novembre 1943; Garderie St-Enfant-Jésus, 28 octobre 1943.

122 'La garderie était dans un état de malpropreté,' *La Presse*, 5 November 1945, 3. In 1943, the Ligue des droits de la femme noted the recent death of several children placed in private nurseries. NA, Thérèse Casgrain Papers, MG 32 C 25, Vol. 7, File: Ligue des droits de la femme – Minutes des assemblées 1941–1946, Assemblée spéciale du Comité exécutif tenue le 15 novembre 1943; Assemblée publique tenue sous les auspices de la Ligue pour les droits de la femme le 19 novembre 1943.

123 NA, Dept of Labour, RG 27, Vol. 611, File 6-52-5-2, Vol. 1, Florence F. Martel to Mrs Rex Eaton, 25 September 1942; MUA, Montreal Parks and Playgrounds Association (MPAP), MG 2079, C. 5, File 136, Montreal Parks and Playgrounds Assn Incorporated, Report of Executive Director for the Year 1944.

124 MUA, MCSA, MG 2076, C. 9, File 556, Camp Survey, Publication XIX, 1944.

125 A woman whose twelve-year-old daughter had attended Summerhill House's Camp Carowanis, for instance, telephoned the House in 1949 to express her thanks and noted that her daughter had gained six pounds at camp. NA, Summerhill Homes, MG 28 I 388, Vol. 14, File 14-27, Report on Camp Carowanis, 1949.

126 NA, Dept of Labour, RG 27, Vol. 611, File 6-52-5-2, Vol. 1, Miriam Chapin to L. Austin Wright, 9 April 1942.

127 NA, JFS, MG 28 V 86, Vol. 12, File: Minutes of Meetings, Case and Adoption Committee, Jewish Child Welfare Bureau, 1944–48, Minutes, 11 November 1946.

128 See, e.g., *La Presse*, 7 March 1944, 19.

129 NA, CCSD, MG 28 I 10, Vol. 234, File 234-16, Fifth Annual Meeting of the Children's Aid Society of Montreal, Report of the Executive Director, 7 March 1951.

130 NA, Dept of Labour, RG 27, Vol. 611, File 6-52-5-2, Vol. 1, 'La Crèche
d'Youville, Côte de Liesse, Direction des Soeurs Grises,' Rapport soumis
par Renée Morin, Service Sélectif National.

131 NA, Summerhill Homes, MG 28 I 388, Vol. 15, File 15-2, Case Committee
Meeting, 25 February 1948; Case Committee Meeting, 27 April 1949.

132 Valverde, 'Mixed Social Economy,' and in the same issue: Margaret Little,
'The Blurring of Boundaries: Private and Public Welfare for Single Mothers
in Ontario'; Lynne Marks, 'Indigent Committees and Ladies Benevolent
Societies: Intersections of Public and Private Poor Relief in Late Nineteenth Century Small Town Ontario.'

133 B.L. Vigod, 'History According to the Boucher Report: Some Reflections
on the State and Social Welfare in Quebec Before the Quiet Revolution,'
in Allan Moscovitch and Jim Albert, eds., *The 'Benevolent' State: The Growth
of Welfare in Canada* (Toronto: Garamond P, 1987); Vigod, 'Ideology and
Institutions in Quebec'; Dickinson and Young, *A Short History of Quebec*, x.
Father Gerald Berry, former director of Montreal's Catholic Welfare
Bureau, noted in 1948 that religious communities across the country were
saving governments large sums of money through their charitable and
social service work. 'Nos lois sociales,' *La Presse*, 13 May 1948, 3.

134 NA, Dept of National Health and Welfare, RG 29, Vol. 136, File 208-5-4,
Part 3, J.-R. Forest to J.W. MacFarlane, 27 March 1943.

135 NA, Dept of National Health and Welfare, RG 29, Vol. 136, File 208-5-4,
Part 3, Memorandum from J.W. MacFarlane to Mr. D.G. Emerson, 20
December 1948.

136 NA, Dept of National Health and Welfare, RG 29, Vol. 136, File 208-5-4,
Part 4, Paul Sauvé aux bénéficiaires d'une pension de vieillesse ou
d'aveugles de la Province de Québec, le 12 mai 1949; Paul Martin to all
those living in the Province of Quebec who receive old age or blind pension, 10 June 1949; Paul Sauvé aux bénéficiaires d'une pension de vieillesse
ou d'aveugles de la province de Québec, le 15 juin 1949. A similar propaganda war had occurred with the 1947 rate increase. NA, Dept of National
Health and Welfare, RG 29, Vol. 136, File 208-5-4, Part 3, Paul Martin to
Honourable Louis St. Laurent, 20 October 1947.

137 NA, Dept of National Health and Welfare, RG 29, Vol. 136, File 208-5-4,
Part 4, News clipping, 'Cheap Trick,' *Windsor Daily Star*, 13 June 1949; News
clipping, 'Pensioners Confused by Propaganda,' *Montreal Gazette*, 30 June
1949.

138 Vigod, 'History According to the Boucher Report'; Lucia Ferretti, *Brève
histoire de l'Église catholique au Québec* (Montreal: Boréal, 1999), 144. On
Brunet, see Vigod, 'Ideology and Institutions in Quebec,' 168.

139 Duplessis claimed that in the realm of social security, 'Québec n'a de leçons à recevoir de personne. Notre législation sociale est avancée et avancée plus que partout ailleurs.' Rather than providing any evidence for this claim, he remarked, 'Il serait trop long d'énumérer ici ce que nous avons fait. Nous sommes à la page et j'éprouve beaucoup de fierté à le déclarer.' YUA, Duplessis Fonds, 1980-008/001, Reel 7, Summary of Duplessis's speech to federal-provincial conference in Quebec City [Sept. 1950?], 4. In the same speech, Duplessis called for scrupulous adherence to the division of powers set out in the BNA Act.

140 For the opinion that contacts between the federal civil service and the field of private welfare had been rare before the 1940s, see NA, CCSD, MG 28 I 10, Vol. 237, File 237-8, George F. Davidson to Alice L. Taylor, 30 March 1943.

Chapter 3

1 'Pour que bientôt il me revienne ...' Victory Bond poster reproduced in Marc H. Choko, *Canadian War Posters 1914–1918, 1939–1945* (Laval, QC: Éditions du Méridien, 1994), 14.

2 For reunion photographs see e.g., *La Presse* (Montreal), 30 April 1945, 3. On the romance in literature, see Northrop Frye, *The Secular Scripture: A Study of the Structure of Romance* (Cambridge, MA: Harvard UP, 1976). Kate Darian-Smith has argued that Australian women interviewed decades after the Second World War described their wartime experiences using the structure and language of 'conventional romantic narratives.' 'Remembering Romance: Memory, Gender and World War II,' in Joy Damousi and Marilyn Lake, eds., *Gender and War: Australians at War in the Twentieth Century* (Cambridge: Cambridge UP, 1995), 117–29.

3 Susan Prentice, 'Workers, Mothers, Reds: Toronto's Postwar Daycare Fight,' *Studies in Political Economy* 30 (Autumn 1989): 115–41; Franca Iacovetta, *Such Hardworking People: Italian Immigrants in Postwar Toronto* (Montreal and Kingston: McGill-Queen's UP, 1992); Line Chamberland, *Mémoires lesbiennes: Le lesbianisme à Montréal entre 1950 et 1972* (Montreal: Éditions du Remue-ménage, 1996); Joanne Meyerowitz, ed., *Not June Cleaver: Women and Gender in Postwar America, 1945–1960* (Philadelphia: Temple UP, 1994).

4 NA, MSWL, MG 28 I 311, Vol. 3, File 64, Speech by Brock Chisholm, 13 November 1944, 'Women's Responsibility for Mental Reestablishment of Soldiers'; Terry Copp and Bill McAndrew, *Battle Exhaustion: Soldiers and Psychiatrists in the Canadian Army, 1939–1945* (Montreal and Kingston: McGill-Queen's UP, 1990).

5 Archives nationales du Québec à Montréal (ANQM), Mouvement des Travailleurs Chrétiens (MTC), P 257, Vol. 11, File: Cent Mariés – Couple 92, Sgt. [Husband], 12 Cdn Amd Regt., Cdn Army Overseas, Italie, to Rév. Père Victor-M. Villeneuve, Aumônier général de la JOC et de la LOC, 11 September 1944.

6 NA, Marion Creelman Savage papers, MG 30 C 92, Vol. 3, File: Council of Women, Montreal Local, 1948–51, 1947 Report of the Convener for the Welfare of Members of National Defence Services and their Dependents. Also NA, Society for the Protection of Women and Children (SPWC), MG 28 I 129, Vol. 5, File: Minutes of Board Meetings, June 1943 to March 22 1945, Minutes of Meeting of the Board of Directors of the SPWC, 20 September 1944.

7 NA, Jewish Family Services of the Baron de Hirsch Institute (JFS), MG 28 V 86, Vol. 12, File: Minutes of Meetings, Case and Adoption Committee, Jewish Child Welfare Bureau, 1944–48, Minutes of Meeting of Placement Committee, 28 March 1944; also Vol. 10, File: Minutes of Meetings of Case Committee, Family Welfare Department, 1944–45, Minutes, 28 October 1944.

8 Raynes Minns, *Bombers and Mash: The Domestic Front, 1939–45* (London: Virago, 1980), 180.

9 NA, Dependents' Allowance Board (DAB), RG 36, Series 18, Vol. 12, File: Committees Local – General Correspondence, 'Volunteer Citizens' Committees'; Marion V. Royce, *The Effect of the War on the Life of Women: A Study* (Geneva: World's YWCA, 1945), 71; Canadian Youth Commission (CYC), *Youth, Marriage, and the Family* (Toronto: Ryerson P, 1948), 46; Renée Morin, 'Women after the War,' *Canadian Affairs* 2, 4 (March 1945): 3.

10 Archives de l'Université de Montréal (AUM), Action catholique canadienne (ACC), P16/ R219, R. P. Valère Massicotte, O.F.M., 'La délinquence [*sic*] juvénile et la guerre' (Montreal: L'Oeuvre des Tracts, 1944); NA, MSWL, MG 28 I 311, Vol. 5, File 25, Women's Auxiliary of the R.C.C.S., Annual Report, 1944. A soldier-husband's perspective on 'personal family trouble brought upon by discouragement and loneliness and war bastard that prey on soldier wifes [*sic*]' is in NA, DAB, RG 36, Series 18, Vol. 29, File: Inadequacy of Allowances, Complaints, Etc. DAB 5-6, Vol. 3, Letter from C.E.N. to DAB, n.d.

11 NA, MSWL, MG 28 I 311, Vol. 5, File 25, Report of Victoria Rifles Ladies Association [1944–5?].

12 Robert England, *Discharged: A Commentary on Civil Re-establishment of Veterans in Canada* (Toronto: Macmillan, 1943), 325; *La Presse*, 22 April 1944. See also John S. Sonnen, 'Out of the Attic, or What Price Memorabilia? A Minnesota Couple's World War II Letters,' *Minnesota History* 53, 2 (Summer 1992): esp. 60.

13 NA, Canadian Council on Social Development (CCSD), MG 28 I 10, Vol. 134, File 600, Response to Questionnaire from Welfare Convener, Royal Montreal Regiment; NA, DAB, RG 36, Series 18, Vol. 29, File: Children of Unmarried Mothers, DAB 5-5, G.F. Thompson to DAB, 6 March 1943.

14 ANQM, Jeunesse Ouvrière Catholique (JOC), P 104, Container 250, File: Militaires, Sgt. L. to R.P. Victor Villeneuve, 24 June 1944. Emphasis in the original.

15 NA, CCSD, MG 28 I 10, Vol. 134, File 600, Response to questionnaire from MSWL, Artillery Branch, June 1942. Also NA, DAB, RG 36, Series 18, Vol. 28, File: Reports on Conferences and Inspections, DND Memorandum by Ruth Harvey, 16 December 1941.

16 ANQM, MTC, P 257, Vol. 24, File: Divers – Faits. 'Faits' [n.d.]; ANQM, JOC, P 104, Container 170, File: Divers (Amour – guerre – chômage), Forum populaire: 'L'Amour est-il aveugle?'; *La Presse*, 15 August 1945, 18.

17 NA, JFS, MG 28 V 86, Vol. 10, File: Minutes of Meetings of Case Committee, Family Welfare Dept., 1946–47, Case of the T. family, 3 May 1946; NA, CCSD, MG 28 I 10, Vol. 134, File 600 (II), Response to questionnaire from David G. Stevenson, Children's Aid Society for the County of Ontario and the City of Oshawa, June 1942.

18 NA, DAB, RG 36, Series 18, Vol. 50, File: Procedure 43, Gwyneth Howell to Ruth Harvey, 30 April 1943; Charles H. Young to R.O.G. Bennett, 20 October 1942. Young claimed that the number of unfaithful wives was 'small compared with the total number of enlisted men,' but noted that 'nevertheless such problems loom very large to the local groups who have to deal with them.'

19 On the more general lack of privacy for American families during the Second World War, see Perry R. Duis, 'No Time for Privacy: World War II and Chicago's Families,' in Lewis A. Erenberg and Susan E. Hirsch, eds., *The War in American Culture: Society and Consciousness during World War II* (Chicago: U of Chicago P, 1996).

20 NA, DAB, RG 36, Series 18, Vol. 36, File: Petitions of Unmarried Applicants, DAB 7-24-117, R.O.G. Bennett to Colonel Ralston, 8 August 1942; Memorandum to Deputy Adjutant-General from H.T. Cook, 21 October 1942.

21 NA, MSWL, MG 28 I 311, Vol. 2, File 33, E.I. Smit to C.H. Young, 5 May 1943; J.F. Chisholm to Children's Service Association, 10 November 1943; NA, SPWC, MG 28 I 129, Vol. 5, File: Minutes of Board Meetings, April 18 1945 to January 15 1947, Executive Secretary's Report, Annual Meeting, 22 March 1946.

22 NA, DAB, RG 36, Series 18, Vol. 28, File: Reports on Conferences and Inspections, Children's Aid Society Meeting [Ottawa], 1 December 1941.

23 NA, DAB, RG 36, Series 18, Vol. 28, File DAB 4-5, Vol. 4, General Correspondence with Welfare Agencies; NA, Department of Veterans Affairs (DVA), RG 38, Vol. 184, File: Rehabilitation, Confidential Letters, Vol. 2, Counsellors' Reference Book, April 1945, 'Collaboration of Social Welfare Agencies with Ex-Service Personnel and the DVA'; NA, CCSD, MG 28 I 10, Vol. 134, File 600, Responses to questionnaire, 1942; CYC, *Youth, Marriage, and the Family*, 44–5.

24 NA, DAB, RG 36, Series 18, Vol. 50, File: Procedure 43, Suspension of Allowances for Wife on Ground of Improper Conduct, R.O.G. Bennett to Charles H. Young, 27 October 1942. The chairman added that 'Even in needy Mothers' Allowance Regulations, where in most cases, the mother is a widow, the procedure is to declare her ineligible for a Government allowance is [*sic*] she has irregular relations with a man.' It appears that mothers' allowances in other provinces were also cut off upon news of recipients' 'illegitimate' pregnancies. 'Report on the Visit to the Montreal Agencies, March 29 and 30,' by R. Harvey, DAB, 3 May 1943, in the same file. See also Margaret Little, *No Car, No Radio, No Liquor Permit: The Moral Regulation of Single Mothers in Ontario, 1920–1997* (Toronto: Oxford UP, 1998).

25 NA, DAB, RG 36, Series 18, Vol. 50, File: Procedure 43, R.O.G. Bennett to Charles H. Young, 27 October 1942; R.O.G. Bennett to Miss R. Robertson, 3 December 1943.

26 NA, DAB, RG 36, Series 18, Vol. 50, File: Procedure 43, Memo re D.A.B. & C.W.C. by Nora Lea, 14 June 1941; Vol. 28, File: Montreal Welfare Department, DAB 4-7, 'Families referred by D.A.B. to the Bureau d'Assistance Sociale aux Familles for supervision and re-education,' 31 July 1944.

27 NA, DAB, RG 36, Series 18, Vol. 50, File: Procedure 43, R.O.G. Bennett to Charles H. Young, 27 October 1942.

28 NA, DAB, RG 36, Series 18, Vol. 28: File: DAB 4-5, Vol. 4, General Correspondence with Welfare Agencies, R.O.G. Bennett to Miss Elizabeth Wallace, 25 January 1944; File: Montreal Welfare Department, DAB 4-7, MCSA, Meeting to discuss services provided by certain Montreal Social Agencies to Dependents' Allowance Board Cases, 10 October 1941; File: Reports on Conferences and Inspections, DND, Memorandum by R. Harvey, 16 December 1941; File: DAB 4-3, Vol. 1, Investigations, Department of Pensions and National Health, K.M. Jackson to R.O.G. Bennett, 24 August 1945; NA, CCSD, MG 28 I 10, Vol. 134, File 600 (II), Response to questionnaire from Local Superintendent, Children's Aid Society of Huron County, Goderich, 15 June 1942.

29 NA, DAB, RG 36, Series 18, Vol. 50, File: Procedure 43, R.O.G. Bennett to Charles H. Young, 27 October 1942.

30 NA, JFS, MG 28 V 86, Vol. 11, File: Minutes of Case Conferences: Family Welfare Department and Jewish Child Welfare Bureau, 1944–46, Case History to be presented at conference between Child Welfare Bureau and Family Welfare Department, 26 December 1944. See also NA, CCSD, MG 28 I 10, Vol. 134, File 600 (I), Response to questionnaire from Family Service Bureau, Hamilton.

31 NA, DAB, RG 36, Series 18, Vol. 50, File: Procedure 43, Memo re D.A.B. and C.W.C. by Nora Lea, 14 June 1941.

32 NA, DAB, RG 36, Series 18, Vol. 28, File: Report on Conferences and Inspections, DND, Memorandum by R. Harvey, 16 December 1941; Frances Barr to Chairman, DAB, 27 June 1944; Vol. 50, File: Procedure 43, Gwyneth Howell to Ruth Harvey, 30 April 1943.

33 NA, DAB, RG 36, Series 18, Vol. 28, File: DAB 4-7, Montreal Welfare Department, 'Conference on Working Relationships Between the Dependents' Allowance Board and Protestant Welfare Agencies of Montreal,' 15 October 1941.

34 NA, DAB, RG 36, Series 18, Vol. 28, File DAB 4-5, Vol. 4, General Correspondence with Welfare Agencies, K.M. Jackson, Edmonton Family Welfare Bureau, to Ruth Harvey, 16 November 1943.

35 NA, DAB, RG 36, Series 18, Vol. 50, File: Procedure 43, MCSA, Memorandum on Problems caused by Stoppage of Pay, or Reductions in Allowances paid to Dependents of Enlisted Men, October 1942; Vol. 28, File: DAB 4-5, Vol. 4, General Correspondence with Welfare Agencies, Elisabeth Wallace to R.O.G. Bennett, 6 January 1944; NA, CCSD, MG 28 I 10, Vol. 134, File 600, Response to questionnaire from G.B. Clarke, General Secretary, Family Welfare Association, Montreal, 12 June 1942.

36 NA, DAB, RG 36, Series 18, Vol. 28, File: Report on Conferences and Inspections, Children's Aid Society Meeting [Ottawa], 1 December 1941.

37 NA, DAB, RG 36, Series 18, Vol. 28, File: Montreal Welfare Department, DAB 4-7, Lt. Col. J.G. Raymond to Mr. Charles Young, n.d. [22 September 1941]; and 'Conference on Working Relationships Between the Dependents' Allowance Board and Protestant Welfare Agencies of Montreal,' 15 October 1941 for the SPWC's denial of these charges.

38 NA, MSWL, MG 28 I 311, Vol. 5, File 18, Report of Welfare Committee, Women's Division, Black Watch (R.H.R.) of Canada, 1942.

39 NA, DAB, RG 36, Series 18, Vol. 28, File: DAB 4-5, Vol. 4, General Correspondence with Welfare Agencies, Olive M. Snyder to R.O.G. Bennett, 3 May 1943.

40 NA, DAB, RG 36, Series 18, Vol. 28, File: Reports on Conferences and Inspections, Report on Canadian Conference of Social Workers, May 1944.

Also NA, DAB, RG 36, Series 18, Vol. 29, File: Children of Unmarried Mothers, DAB 5-5, B.W. Heise to R.O.G. Bennett, 5 August 1942.

41 NA, DAB, RG 36, Series 18, Vol. 50, File: Procedure 43, F.N. Stapleford to Joseph E. Laycock, 24 June 1941; Vol. 28, File: DAB 4-5, Vol. 4, General Correspondence with Welfare Agencies, George F. Davidson to R.O.G. Bennett, 28 June 1944.

42 NA, DAB, RG 36, Series 18, Vol. 28, File: DAB 4-5, Vol. 4, General Correspondence with Welfare Agencies, R.O.G. Bennett to Olive M. Snyder, 28 May 1943.

43 England, *Discharged*, 78; Desmond Morton, *A Military History of Canada: From Champlain to the Gulf War*, 3rd ed. (Toronto: McClelland & Stewart, 1992), 176, 182.

44 NA, DAB, RG 36, Series 18, Vol. 50, File: Procedure 43, R.O.G. Bennett to Miss R. Robertson, 11 March 1944.

45 NA, DAB, RG 36, Series 18, Vol. 28, File: DAB 4-5, Vol. 4, General Correspondence with Welfare Agencies, Mrs E.A. Richardson to Chairman, DAB, 25 January 1943; Report on the Children's Aid Societies' Conference and Toronto Social Agencies Held May 20th to 22nd, 1943, by V.M. Parr, 25 May 1943.

46 On returned Australian soldiers' views of 'the shirker' as a 'non-man,' see Stephen Garton, 'Return Home: War, Masculinity and Repatriation,' in Damousi and Lake, eds., *Gender and War*, 191–204.

47 Susan Hartmann, 'Prescriptions for Penelope: Literature on Women's Obligations to Returning World War II Veterans,' *Women's Studies* 5 (1978): 230–1.

48 Ruth Jamieson, 'The Man of Hobbes: Masculinity and Wartime Necessity,' *Journal of Historical Sociology* 9, 1 (March 1996): 33.

49 Hartmann, 'Prescriptions for Penelope,' 231, 236.

50 Royce, *Effect of the War*, 59.

51 NA, DAB, RG 36, Series 18, Vol. 50, File: Procedure 43, Memorandum from the Office of the Deputy Minister of National Defence to R.O.G. Bennett, Chairman, DAB, 30 August 1943; Memorandum re Erring Wives of Soldiers, 20 May 1941.

52 NA, DAB, RG 36, Series 18: Vol. 28, File: Report on Conferences and Inspections, Typed statement re: the DAB [no title, n.d.]. The DAB's claim that its aim was to preserve 'home and family circles' can be found in Vol. 49, File: Procedure 33, Watson Sellar to A. MacNamara, 30 September 1940; Vol. 28, File: DAB 4-5, Vol. 4, General Correspondence with Welfare Agencies, R.O.G. Bennett to Olive M. Snyder, 28 May 1943; George F. Davidson to R.O.G. Bennett, 28 June 1944. Margaret McCallum argues that in the First

World War, the Canadian Patriotic Fund likewise demonstrated a degree of flexibility regarding 'immoral' soldiers' wives, especially in Montreal. Margaret E. McCallum, 'Assistance to Veterans and Their Dependants: Steps on the Way to the Administrative State, 1914–1929,' in W.W. Pue and B. Wright, eds., *Canadian Perspectives on Law and Society: Issues in Legal History* (Ottawa: Carleton UP, 1988), 161.

53 NA, CCSD, MG 28 I 10, Vol. 134, File 600: Questionnaire, Service Men's Families, Morale and Security, 1942, Commissioner, Bureau of Child Protection, Saskatchewan, to Dr George F. Davidson, 15 June 1942; NA, DAB, RG 36, Series 18, Vol. 28, File: DAB 4-5, Vol. 4, General Correspondence with Welfare Agencies, R.O.G. Bennett to Olive M. Snyder, 28 May 1943.

54 NA, DAB, RG 36, Series 18, Vol. 28, File: Montreal Welfare Department, DAB 4-7, 'Families referred by DAB to the Bureau d'Assistance Sociale aux Familles for supervision and re-education,' 31 July 1944.

55 NA, DAB, RG 36, Series 18: Vol. 29, File: Children of Unmarried Mothers, DAB 5-5, R.O.G. Bennett to G.F. Thompson, 14 April 1943; Vol. 28, File: DAB 4-5, Vol. 4, General Correspondence with Welfare Agencies, R.O.G. Bennett to Olive M. Snyder, 28 May 1943. The Dependents' Board of Trustees likewise observed in 1945, 'In respect to children born to a dependent whose husband is alleged not to be the father, the attitude of the husband should be the criterion for action by the Board; if the member of the Forces accepted the child as a member of his family (and in many cases this is done and even an application is made for an allowance for the child as the enlisted man's dependent) the Board would be prepared to consider granting assistance.' NA, Department of National Defence (DND), RG 24, Vol. 1596, File: Dependents' Board of Trustees – Reference Manual for Regional Dependents' Advisory Committees, DND, the Dependents' Board of Trustees, Information Circular No. 46, 3 May 1945. Also File: Dependents' Board of Trustees, Index and Minutes of Meetings, Minutes, Regular Meeting of the Executive Committee, 12 April 1944, 351.

56 *La Presse*, 6 April 1946, 32; CYC, *Youth, Marriage and the Family*, 52; NA, DAB, RG 36, Series 18, Vol. 36, File: Permission to Marry (Army) – DAB 7-24-102g, Vol. 1, Circular No. 103, 3 April 1944; *Statutes of Canada* 1944-5; 1945; 1946; 1947; 1948; 1949 (8 George VI–13 George VI).

57 AUM, ACC, P16, P16/H3/18/84, 'Le Mariage Chrétien' (1946); NA, SPWC, MG 28 I 129, Vol. 6, File: SPWC Minutes, February 19 1947 to March 24 1950, Minutes of Meeting of Board of Directors, 19 October 1949. Approximately 20 per cent of the parliamentary divorces awarded to Montreal couples between 1944 and 1946 went to couples where at least one of the partners had a French surname; clearly French Canadians were underrepresented. *Statutes of Canada* 1944-5; 1945; 1946 (8 George VI–10 George VI).

58 NA, Savage papers, MG 30 C 92, Vol. 3, File: Council of Women, Montreal Local, 1948–51, Local Council of Women, Vancouver, BC, Annual Report of Convener of Armed Forces. See also David A. Kent, '"Gone for a Soldier": Family Breakdown and the Demography of Desertion in a London Parish, 1750–91,' *Local Population Studies* 45 (1990): 27–42.

59 James Snell, *In the Shadow of the Law: Divorce in Canada, 1900–1939* (Toronto: U of Toronto P, 1991).

60 Desmond Morton, *1945: When Canada Won the War* (Ottawa: Canadian Historical Association, 1995), 11; Joyce Hibbert, *The War Brides* (Toronto: Peter Martin Associates, 1978).

61 *La Presse*: 3 October 1946, 4; 2 November 1946, 28; 8 February 1947, 35.

62 NA, MSWL, MG 28 I 311: Vol. 5, File 25, Annual Report of the Recording Secretary, Women's Auxiliary of the R.C.C.S. (Montreal) [1944]; Vol. 3, File 54, Canadian Red Cross Society, Quebec Provincial Division, Lists of Dependents (Army) Arriving from Britain for Montreal.

63 *La Presse*: 7 March 1946, 4; 27 November 1944, 4; 27 March 1944, 4; 2 November 1946, 63.

64 *La Presse*, 6 December 1944, 4; NA, MSWL, MG 28 I 311, Vol. 3, File 65, Letter to all Auxiliary Presidents from Mary Elder, Hon. Corresponding Secretary, 1 June 1945; NA, Marion Creelman Savage Papers, MG 30 C 92, Vol. 3, File: Council of Women – National – 1940–48, Letter from Marion D. Savage, National Convener, to Local Conveners, 13 October 1945; NA, MSWL, MG 28 I 311, Vol. 1, File 91, Association Meeting and Directors' Meeting, 12 October 1945.

65 ANQM, JOC, P 104, Container 240, File: Commission Canadienne de la Jeunesse, Mémoires soumis par le comité central de l'ACJC à la Commission Canadienne de la Jeunesse, 27–28 janvier 1945. Also AUM, ACC, P16/04/52, Commission Canadienne de la Jeunesse, Comité provincial du Québec, Mémoire sur la famille, for similar worries about the linguistic and religious problems posed by war brides.

66 NA, MSWL, MG 28 I 311, Vol. 5, File 25, Victoria Rifles Ladies' Association, Report of Welfare Committee [1946?]. Also NA, MSWL, MG 28 I 311: Vol. 1, File 91, Executive Meeting, 5 January 1945; Vol. 3, File 54, Letter from Chairman of Oak Society for British War Wives, n.d.; Vol. 3, File 66. Letter from President of Royal Montreal Regiment Ladies Committee, 19 November 1945.

67 NA, SPWC, MG 28 I 129: Vol. 6, File: Minutes, February 19 1947 to March 24 1950, Report of the Executive Secretary for the Year 1946; Vol. 5, File: Minutes of Board Meetings, April 18 1945 to January 15 1947, Executive Secretary's Report, Annual Meeting, 22 March 1946; also Minutes of Meeting of Board of Directors, 16 May 1945.

68 NA, MSWL, MG 28 I 311, Vol. 3, File 54, Mrs V. to MSWL, September 1945 and n.d.; also Canadian Red Cross Society, Quebec Provincial Division, List of Dependents (Army) who arrived in Montreal Ex. Vessels W933 and W934 on 29 August 1945.

69 NA, MSWL, MG 28 I 311, Vol. 3, File 54, Letter from Chairman of Oak Society for British War Wives [n.d.].

70 *La Presse*, 2 November 1946, 28. Barry Broadfoot's interviews with veterans also uncovered evidence of the poor reception given to some English wives and he notes that many returned to England after a very short time in Canada. See *The Veterans' Years: Coming Home from the War* (Vancouver: Douglas & McIntyre, 1985), 87, 134.

71 NA, CCSD, MG 28 I 10, Vol. 58: File 489, K.M. Jackson, Secrétaire de la Division d'Assistance familiale, to Monsieur L. Désilets, C.R., Assistant-procureur-général, Québec, 25 février 1948; File 489A, Memorandum Re: Wives of Canadian Servicemen Overseas Proceeding to Canada but either Widowed or Deserted, 1946; File 489A, Letter from Reverend S.A. Yeo, Department of Social Service, PEI to Miss Lillian Thompson, National Council, YWCA, Toronto, 4 December 1946.

72 *Statutes of Canada* 1944–5; 1945; 1946; 1947; 1948; 1949 (8 George VI–13 George VI). See also NA, CCSD, MG 28 I 10, Vol. 58, File 489A, Memorandum re: Wives of Canadian Servicemen Overseas Proceeding to Canada but either Widowed or Deserted, 1946.

73 *La Presse*, for instance, claimed in November 1945 that only 29 of the 9000 British war brides in Canada had requested a return to England. *La Presse*, 28 November 1945, 4.

74 England, *Discharged*, 152. The Montreal Soldiers' Wives' League also claimed that after the first year of war, during which the married unemployed enlisted in great numbers, the average soldier tended to be single. NA, MSWL, MG 28 I 311, Vol. 5, File 24, MSWL to Mr E.I. Smit, Chairman, Committee on Provision of Care for the Children of Working Mothers, March 1942. Married men were not called up under the National Resources Mobilization Act until December 1942. C.P. Stacey, *Arms, Men, and Governments: The War Policies of Canada, 1939–1945* (Ottawa: Queen's Printer, 1970), Appendix 'N,' 586.

75 NA, DVA, RG 38, Vol. 193, File 65-47-A, Monthly Report on Activities, 1 August 1944. Robert England's massive rehabilitation manual, *Discharged*, was written to reassure servicemen and their parents: see 376.

76 ANQM, JOC, P 104, Container 28, File: Bulletins des Chefs de la J.O.C.F. 1945–1946–1947, Bulletin mensuel J.O.C.F. Mars 1946. 'Le retour de nos vétérans.'

77 'Idéal à mettre à la portée de nos combattants,' *La Presse*, 5 November 1945, 4; ANQM, JOC, P 104, Container 216, File: Soldats (Service), Memorandum of the J.O.C. To the Canadian Government in Favour of Demobilized Young Men [n.d.]; CYC, *Youth, Marriage, and the Family*, 43.

78 ANQM, JOC, P 104, Container 58, File: Émissions Radiophoniques – Campagne des loisirs – 1946, 3ème émission, Semaine de propagande de la J.O.C. 16 au 23 juin 1946; CYC, *Youth, Marriage, and the Family*, 62–3.

79 'Accusé d'avoir tenté d'assassiner son père,' *La Presse*, 6 February 1946, 3.

80 NA, MSWL, MG 28 I 311, Vol. 3, File 64, Speech by Brock Chisholm, 13 November 1944: 'Women's Responsibility for Mental Reestablishment of Soldiers.' See also England, *Discharged*, 329–30.

81 NA, MSWL, MG 28 I 311, Vol. 1, File 91, Executive Committee Meeting, 19 January 1940; NA, JFS, MG 28 V 86, Vol.10, File: Minutes of Meetings of Case Committee, Family Welfare Department, 1944–45, Follow-Up, H.P., 9 May 1945.

82 On Montreal soldiers' class background: ANQM, JOC, P 104, Container 170, File: Organisation. Projet d'un service de soldat, Organisé par la J.O.C. et la L.O.C. 2e copie. On child and teen labour in mid-twentieth-century Montreal, see Dominique Marshall, *Aux origines sociales de l'État-providence: Familles québécoises, obligation scolaire et allocations familiales 1940–1955* (Montreal: Presses de l'Université de Montréal, 1998).

83 NA, MSWL, MG 28 I 311, Vol. 2, File 33, Mrs C to MSWL, January 1946; also NA, DAB, RG 36, Series 18, Vol. 29, File: Mothers' Allowance, DAB 5-1, Gertrude C[?], Secretary to the Child Welfare Board, Department of Health and Public Welfare, Winnipeg, to R.O.G. Bennett, 19 March 1942.

84 NA, DAB, RG 36, Series 18, Vol. 29, File: Mothers' Allowances, DAB 5-1, C.W. Lundy, Superintendent of Welfare, Department of the Provincial Secretary, Social Assistance Branch, B.C., to R.O.G. Bennett, 26 July 1943.

85 NA, MSWL, MG 29 I 311, Vol. 2, File 33, 'Clothing Allowance for Discharged Officers [n.d.].'

86 NA, MSWL, MG 28 I 311, Vol. 2, File 33, Janet Bennett, Welfare Committee, Black Watch of Canada, Women's Division, to MSWL, 23 May 1944; Report of Sub Committee on Need of Soldier's Widows and Widowed Mothers for Supplementary Grants [n.d.]. One of the original purposes of the Dependents' Board of Trustees was to provide financial assistance to 'a mother whose Dependents' Allowance has been reduced by reason of the prior claim of more immediate dependents of the son.' NA, DND, RG 24, Vol. 1596, File: Dependents' Board of Trustees, Index and Minutes of Meetings, Minutes, Regular Meeting of the Executive Committee, 12 April 1944, pp. 352–3.

87 NA, DVA, RG 38, Vol. 193, File 65-47-A, Monthly Report on Activities, 2 February 1943; NA, CCSD, MG 28 I 10, Vol. 134, File 600 (2), Catherine Stuart Vance, General Secretary, Montreal YWCA, to Charles H. Young, Executive Director, MCSA, 10 June 1942.

88 *La Presse*, 7 April 1945, 15.

89 As Nancy Christie notes about dependents' allowances, 'The privileges of wives were distinctly superior to those of mothers of soldiers ...' Nancy Christie, *Engendering the State: Family, Work, and Welfare in Canada* (Toronto: U of Toronto P, 2000), 254.

90 The DAB's rationale for this difference is in NA, DAB, RG 36, Series 18, Vol. 29, File: DAB 5-1, Mothers Allowance, Memorandum by A.H. Brown, 7 June 1940.

91 Bessie Touzel of Toronto's Welfare Council attributed increases in DAB rates to popular demand and public opinion. NA, DAB, RG 36, Series 18, Vol. 29, File: DAB 5-6, Vol. 3, Inadequacy of Allowances, Complaints, etc., Bessie Touzel to The Rt. Hon. William L. Mackenzie King, Prime Minister, 22 December 1942. There is evidence that DAB Chairman R.O.G. Bennett passed along certain kinds of letters (e.g., those from elderly mothers and women with numerous children) to Canada's Department of Finance. NA, DAB, RG 36, Series 18, Vol. 29, File: DAB 5-6, Vol. 2, Inadequacy of Allowances, Complaints, etc., R.O.G. Bennett, Chairman, DAB, to Dr. W.C. Clark, Deputy Minister of Finance, 23 October 1941; R.O.G. Bennett, Chairman, DAB, to Mr Walter Gordon, Department of Finance, 6 November 1941.

92 On the First World War mythology of the Canadian soldier's devotion to his mother, see Jonathan F. Vance, *Death So Noble: Memory, Meaning, and the First World War* (Vancouver: UBC P, 1997), chap. 5.

93 NA, DAB, RG 36, Series 18, Vol. 29, File: Mothers' Allowance, DAB 5-1, A.H. Brown to Arthur MacNamara, 15 April 1940; Christie, *Engendering the State.* For an excellent article on the role of American Civil War pensions in sustaining soldiers' morale, making up for the loss of a male breadwinner, providing for the elderly, and supervising widows, see Megan J. McClintock, 'Civil War Pensions and the Reconstruction of Union Families,' *Journal of American History* 83, 2 (September 1996): 456–80.

94 Women's and children's sense of entitlement to their dependents' allowances was suggested in the advertisement that appeared in the *Canadian Unionist* 19, 9 (September 1945): inside front cover.

95 NA, DAB, RG 36, Series 18, Vol. 29, File: Complaints, DAB 5-6, Vol. 2, Mrs E. Wiltshire to DAB, 5 September 1941. Emphases in the original.

96 Canada, House of Commons *Debates*, 12 November 1941, p. 4334; also *Debates*, 28 April 1942, pp. 1935, 1939.

97 Canada, House of Commons, *Debates*, 14 November 1941, pp. 4424–6; 28 April 1942, pp. 1932–3.

98 NA, DND, RG 24, Vol. 1596, File: Dependents' Board of Trustees, Index and Minutes of Meetings, DND, the Dependents' Board of Trustees, Confidential Memorandum re: The Dependents' Board of Trustees, 1 March 1946. The DBT considered applications for assistance 'when the need is due to: size of family, illness, death, change of domicile, educational assistance, social problems or other hardships.' NA, DND, RG 24, Vol. 1596, File: Dependents' Board of Trustees – Reference Manual for Regional Dependents' Advisory Committees, Part 10, Applications, 2.

99 NA, DND, RG 24, Vol. 1596, File: Dependents' Board of Trustees, Index and Minutes of Meetings, Minutes, Regular Meeting of the Executive Committee, 8 November 1944, 402.

100 Canada, House of Commons, *Debates*, 28 April 1942, 1923.

101 NA, DAB, RG 36, Series 18, Vol. 28, File: Montreal Welfare Department, DAB 4-7, Eveline P. Laporte, pour Mlle Françoise Marchand, to Capitaine J.M. Campeau, 29 June 1946; Mme Jeanne Barabé-Langlois to M. R.O.G. Bennett, 23 December 1942; Memoranda [*sic*] from Board of Directors, Bureau d'Assistance Sociale aux Familles, to R.O.G. Bennett, DAB, 6 May 1944; R.O.G. Bennett to Mr Charles E. Geoffrion, 31 July 1944. The Montreal Council of Social Agencies also pointed out to the DAB, 'The Montreal Social Agencies have their particular difficulties in that as there is no Public Welfare Department functioning here, the voluntarily supported agencies are overloaded with work at all times, and therefore find it particularly difficult to add extra work and costs to continually overburdened staffs and inelastic funds.' In the same file, MCSA, Meeting to discuss services provided by certain Montreal Social Agencies to Dependents' Allowance Board Cases, 10 October 1941.

102 NA, DAB, RG 36, Series 18, Vol. 28: File: DAB 4-5, Vol. 4, General Correspondence with Welfare Agencies, J. Pembroke, Chairman, DBT, to R.O.G. Bennett, Chairman, DAB, 4 November 1942; File: DAB 4-3, Investigations, Department of Pensions and National Health, R.O.G. Bennett to Kathleen M. Jackson, 12 July 1945.

103 NA, DAB, RG 36, Series 18: Vol. 28, File: Montreal Welfare Department, DAB 4-7, MCSA, Meeting to discuss services provided by certain Montreal Social Agencies to Dependents' Allowance Board Cases, 10 October 1941; Lt. Col. J.G. Raymond to Mr Charles Young, n.d. [22 September 1941]; R.O.G. Bennett to Colonel G.S. Currie, 12 August 1944; Vol. 50, File: Procedure 43, Suspension of Allowances for Wife on Ground of Improper Conduct, Ruth Robertson to R.O.G. Bennett, 29 November 1943.

104 NA, DAB, RG 36, Series 18: Vol. 28, File: DAB 4-3, Investigations, Department of Pensions and National Health, J.W. McKee to R.O.G. Bennett, 10 November 1941; Vol. 29, File: DAB 5-6, Inadequacy of Allowances, Complaints, Etc., Vol. 2, R.O.G. Bennett to Brigadier General Edouard de B. Panet, 24 November 1941.

105 A reading of Pedersen's article suggests a number of similarities between separation allowances in First World War Britain and dependents' allowances in Second World War Canada. The former, she argues, were characterized by the 'privileging of the status of the citizen-soldier as a consequence of the pressures of war; the development of a state administration that incorporated the work of private charities; and the enforcement of the sexual and economic rights of men through the operation of moral tests of wives' eligibility for benefits.' Susan Pedersen, 'Gender, Welfare, and Citizenship in Britain during the Great War,' *American Historical Review* 95, 4 (October 1990): 985–6.

106 Margaret McCallum observes about pensions for Canadian First World War widows that 'Although not subject to a means test, soldiers' widows were not free of BPC [Board of Pension Commissioners] supervision.' See 'Assistance to Veterans,' 167.

107 This decreasing rate was also present in the Canadian Patriotic Fund allowances to soldiers' children during the First World War. Canada, Debates of the House of Commons, *Debates*, Fifth (Special War) Session – Eighteenth Parliament, 11 September 1939, p. 123.

108 NA, DAB, RG 36, Series 18, Vol. 28, File: Montreal Welfare Department, DAB 4-7, Conference on Working Relationships Between the Dependents' Allowance Board and Protestant Welfare Agencies of Montreal, 15 October 1941. James Snell has also found a reference to means-tested old age pensions and the investigations accompanying them as a 'Gestapo' system. James G. Snell, 'The First Grey Lobby: The Old Age Pensioners' Organization of British Columbia, 1932–1951,' *BC Studies* 102 (Summer 1994): 5. Cited in Struthers, 'Family Allowances, Old Age Security,' 191. American historians have argued that the years after the Second World War saw families attempting to reclaim the privacy they had lost during the war. See Duis, 'No Time for Privacy,' 39; William S. Graebner, *The Age of Doubt: American Thought and Culture in the 1940s* (Boston: Twayne Publishers, 1991), 1–2.

109 Stacey, *Arms, Men, and Government*, Appendix 'R,' 590. By 30 September 1944, 163,430 of 699,900 Quebec men aged 18–45 were enrolled in the armed forces. AUM, ACC, P 16/O4/52, Commission Canadienne de la Jeunesse, Comité provincial du Québec, Mémoire sur la famille. As of 31 March 1945,

171,007 men had enlisted. NA, DAB, RG 36, Series 18, Vol. 12, File: General Correspondence Re: Citizens' Committees, 'A' District – Montreal, Letter from H. Frechette, District Superintendent of Rehabilitation, DVA (Re-Establishment Division), Montreal, 7 August 1945. In 1951, approximately 15 per cent of households in the City of Montreal included at least one war veteran: *Ninth Census of Canada* 1951, Vol. 10, chap. 16, 427. This last statistic does not include those municipalities such as Verdun, Outremont, and Westmount, which were actually located *within* the greater city.

110 Béatrice Richard, *La mémoire de Dieppe: Radioscopie d'un mythe* (Montreal: VLB Éditeur, 2002), esp. chap. 6, 'Une mémoire en marge.'

111 On the lack of attention paid by francophone historians to Quebec's soldiers (and by extension, to its veterans), see Béatrice Richard, 'La participation des soldats canadiens-français à la Deuxième Guerre mondiale: une histoire de trous de mémoire' and Paul-André Comeau, 'L'oubli: thérapie collective ou exutoire traditionnel?' both in *Bulletin d'histoire politique* 3, 3–4 (Spring/Summer 1995): 383–96. Quebec veterans are barely alluded to in Peter Neary and J.L. Granatstein, eds., *The Veterans Charter and Post–World War II Canada* (Montreal and Kingston: McGill-Queen's UP, 1998). Neary's article about veterans in Canadian universities touches briefly upon this question: see his 'Canadian Universities and Canadian Veterans of World War II,' esp. 142–3.

112 NA, MSWL, MG 28 I 311, Vol. 1, File 91, Executive Meeting, 8 September 1944.

113 NA, DAB, RG 36, Series 18, Vol. 12, File: Committees Local – General Correspondence, 'Volunteer Citizens' Committees,' by Janet R. Keith.

114 *La Presse*: 23 May 1945, 9; 6 February 1946, 14; 25 April 1946, 21; 6 June 1946, 27.

115 ANQM, JOC, P 104, Container 170, File: Organisation, Service Jociste du Soldat, Circulaire spéciale 27/3/45; NA, DAB, RG 36 Series 18, Vol. 12, File: Committees Local-General Correspondence, Letter from Albert Valois, Diocesan Director of Catholic Action, Montreal, 3 August 1945.

116 'Les démobilisés ont besoin d'aide,' *La Presse*, 5 November 1945, 6.

117 NA, DVA, RG 38, Vol. 193, File 65-47-A, Monthly Report on Activities, Montreal, 3 September 1942.

118 In Quebec, 25.69 per cent of men aged 18 to 45 enlisted (voluntarily or through the NRMA). The percentage in other provinces ranged from 42.38 in Saskatchewan to 50.47 in British Columbia. Stacey, *Arms, Men, and Government*, Appendix 'R,' 590.

119 ANQM, JOC, P 104, Container 170, File: Organisation, Projet de Réhabilitation, 20 avril 1945.

120 ANQM, JOC, P 104: Container 58, File: Semaine de propagande – 1946, Semaine des vétérans. Pamplet: 'Donnons-leur notre Appui!'; Container 214, File: Service du Soldat, 1942–45, Directives concernant les retours d'outre-mer; *La Presse*, 30 September 1946, 7.

121 Richard, *La mémoire de Dieppe*, 143–46.

122 NA, MSWL, MG 28 I 311, Vol. 2, File 52, Letter from R.C.C.S. (Montreal) Women's Auxiliary, 17 October 1944. The opposite argument – that conscripts needed to be considered in rehabilitation efforts along with volunteers – is in ANQM, JOC, P 104, Container 216, File: Soldats (Service), Memorandum of the JOC To the Canadian Government in Favour of Demobilized Young Men [n.d. but after Oct. 1946].

123 NA, DVA, RG 38, Vol. 193, File 65-47-A, Monthly Report on Activities, Montreal, 4 October 1943.

124 NA, MSWL, MG 28 I 311, Vol. 3, File 64, Major-General G.B. Chisholm, Speech, 13 November 1944: 'Women's Responsibility for Mental Reestablishment of Soldiers.'

125 NA, DVA, RG 38, Vol. 193, File 65-47-A, Monthly Report, 3 September 1942.

126 NA, DVA, RG 38, Vol. 193, File 65-47-A, Monthly Report, 3 February 1944.

127 NA, DVA, RG 38, Vol. 197, File: Rehabilitation, Statistics: Women's Division, Proceedings: Training Conferences on Women's Rehabilitation, 88; Broadfoot, *The Veterans' Years*, 53. This sentiment was clearly gendered. On the 'surprisingly powerful male subculture produced by the war,' see Graebner, *The Age of Doubt*, 14–15.

128 Richard, *La mémoire de Dieppe*, 145–7.

129 NA, MSWL, MG 28 I 311, Vol. 3, File 64, Major-General G.B. Chisholm, Speech, 13 November 1944: 'Women's Responsibility for Mental Reestablishment of Soldiers.'

130 NA, DAB, RG 36, Series 18, Vol. 12, File: Local Committees – General Correspondence, Vol. 1, Article [no author, n.d. but probably December 1944], 7. On provisions for Canadian veterans after the First World War, see Desmond Morton and Glenn Wright, *Winning the Second Battle: Canadian Veterans and the Return to Civilian Life, 1915–1930* (Toronto: U of Toronto P, 1987). For the Second World War, see Neary and Granatstein, *The Veterans Charter*. Historians agree that veterans were far more generously treated after the Second World War than after the First. See, e.g., Desmond Morton, 'The Canadian Veterans' Heritage from the Great War,' and Jeff Keshen, 'Getting It Right the Second Time Around: The Reintegration of Canadian Veterans of World War II,' both in Neary and Granatstein, *The Veterans Charter*.

131 Rehabilitation, Montreal's Veterans' Welfare Bureau insisted, was '"a

family, as well as a social-economic problem, which all must assume."' NA, DVA, RG 38, Vol. 193, File: 65-4-A, Monthly Report on Activities – April, Montreal, 2 May 1944.

132 Theda Skocpol, *Protecting Soldiers and Mothers: The Political Origins of Social Policy in the United States* (Cambridge, MA: Belknap P of Harvard UP, 1992); Skocpol, 'Soldiers, Workers, and Mothers: Gendered Identities in Early U.S. Social Policy,' *Contention* 2, 3 (Spring 1993): 169.

133 For the argument that most welfare measures enacted from the 1930s on were designed to shore up the male breadwinner, see Christie, *Engendering the State.*

134 Morin, 'Women after the War,' 3.

135 AUM, Fonds Édouard-Montpetit, P 8/1, Comité de Reconstruction, 1941–43, Memorandum for the Committee on Reconstruction by F. Cyril James, 27 March 1941; also Memorandum regarding the activities of local committees in the field of Post-War Reconstruction, 17 August 1942.

136 NA, DVA, RG 38, Vol. 197, File: '"What Will I Do When the War Is Won" (Booklet),' Pamphlet entitled 'What Will I Do, When the War Is Won? Provisions already made and plans under way for the re-establishment of Canadian Service Personnel in civil life,' Issued for members of the Canadian Navy, Army and Air Force, Department of National Defence, Ottawa, 28 August 1943, 4.

137 Ottawa occasionally warned that provisions for veterans should not be viewed as an entitlement. In 1944, for instance, it claimed that educational training 'should not be regarded as a right, or as a reward for service to the state. It is more in the nature of compensation for loss of skills or opportunity resulting from a changed manner of living while in the armed services.' NA, DVA, RG 38, Vol. 184, File: Rehabilitation – Confidential Letters, Vol. 1, Office Manual on Resumption of Educational Training provided under the Post Discharge Re-Establishment Order, P.C. 7633, As amended by P.C. 775, March 1st 1944. It is clear, however, that veterans regarded such provisions as a right, and that this was due in no small part to Ottawa's marketing of the Veterans Charter.

138 Linda K. Kerber, *No Constitutional Right to Be Ladies: Women and the Obligations of Citizenship* (New York: Hill and Wang, 1998), esp. 223–4.

139 Stacey, *Arms, Men and Government,* Appendix 'O,' 587.

140 NA, DVA, RG 38, Vol. 193, File 65-47-A, Monthly Report on Activities, Montreal, 2 July 1943.

141 NA, MSWL, MG 28 I 311, Vol. 2: File 30, Annual Meeting 1945, Hospital Visiting Report; File 52, Letter from Mrs Wm. P. McFeat, Montreal, 18 October 1944.

142 NA, Montreal Council of Women (MCW), MG 28 I 164, Vol. 5, File 7, 54th Year Book and Annual Report 1947–48, Report of the Committee for the Welfare of Members of National Defense Services and Their Dependents 1947–48; NA, MSWL, MG 28 I 311, Vol. 2, File 30, Annual Meeting, 27 April 1949; Report on Hospital Visiting from April 1946 to end of April 1947.

143 See England, *Discharged*, chap. 16; Copp and McAndrew, *Battle Exhaustion*.

144 'N'oublions pas nos braves défenseurs!' *La Presse*, 5 March 1947, 18; McGill University Archives (MUA), Community Garden League, MG 2079, Container 7, File 248: Community Garden League Minute Book, 1941–1952, Minutes of Meeting of General Committee, 20 November 1952; President's Address, 1944 Annual Meeting.

145 NA, DVA, RG 38, Vol. 197, File: Rehabilitation, Special Casualties, Address by Walter S. Woods, 7 September 1942.

146 NA, DVA, RG 38, Vol. 193, File 65-47-A, Monthly Report, 2 November 1943. In July 1945, for instance, local Dominion Stores advertised the fact that they were holding jobs for returning soldiers. *La Presse*, 7 July 1945, 23.

147 *La Presse*, 5 November 1945, 14.

148 Broadfoot, *The Veterans' Years*, 47.

149 England, *Discharged*, 201–2.

150 Ibid., 156.

151 NA, DVA, RG 38, Vol. 193, File 65-47-A, Monthly Report, Montreal, 2 November 1943.

152 NA, DVA, RG 38: Vol. 193, File 65-47-A, Monthly Report, Montreal, 2 June 1943; Vol. 197, File: Rehabilitation, Reconstruction, Sub-Committee on Post-War Employment Opportunities, Committee on Reconstruction, Sub-Committee on Post-War Employment Opportunities, 4th meeting, 29 April 1942.

153 NA, DVA, RG 38, Vol. 193, File 65-47-A, Monthly Report, Montreal, 2 June 1944; *La Presse*, 30 September 1946, 8.

154 NA, DVA, RG 38 Vol. 184, File: News clippings on demobilization and rehabilitation, Transcript of article in the *Montreal Daily Star*, 'Rehabilitation,' 8 January 1941.

155 Michael D. Stevenson, 'National Selective Service and Employment and Seniority Rights for Veterans, 1943–1946,' in Neary and Granatstein, *The Veterans Charter*. Thinking along the same lines as Ford, Montreal's Veterans' Welfare Officer suggested, 'It should be the aim of employers to keep the ex-soldier as his inner guard against radicalism, not give him inspiration for it.' NA, DVA, RG 38, Vol. 193, File: 65-47-A, Monthly Report on Activities, Montreal, 3 February 1944.

156 AUM, Fonds Édouard-Montpetit, P 8/1, Committee on Reconstruction,

Sub-Committee on Post-War Employment Opportunities, 5th meeting, 12 May 1942; NA, DVA, RG 38, Vol. 184, File: Rehabilitation – Confidential Letters, Vol. 1, Office Manual on Resumption of Educational Training, 1 March 1944.

157 ANQM, JOC, P 104, Container 216, File: Aide à la Jeunesse, Pamphlet, Department of Social Welfare and Youth, Province of Quebec.

158 Peter Neary, 'Canadian Universities and Canadian Veterans of World War II,' in Neary and Granatstein, *The Veterans Charter*; Morton, *A Military History*, 226.

159 Peter Neary notes that McGill was the third-largest recipient of federal money for student-veterans, while Laval and l'Université de Montréal were in twenty-third and twenty-fifth place respectively. See 'Canadian Universities and Canadian Veterans of World War II,' in Neary and Granatstein, *The Veterans Charter*, 139, 142. Also NA, DVA, RG 38, Vol. 193, File 65-47-A, Monthly Report, Montreal, 3 October 1945; *La Presse*, 5 January 1946, 22.

160 ANQM, JOC, P 104, Container 239, File: Réhabilitation des militaires dans la vie civile, Service du Soldat, Notes en marge de l'entrevue avec monsieur Louis Charbonneau [n.d.]. Edgar Andrew Collard, in his history of McGill, writes: 'McGill and Sir George Williams had a very much larger proportion of veteran students than the Francophone universities. The reason for this was largely because admission to the Francophone universities was solely on the basis of the classical college baccalaureate. The Anglophone universities admitted on the basis of the matriculation or school-leaving certificate. Few veterans could make good the deficiencies in Latin, Greek and philosophy for admission to the French universities in the eighteen months from discharge allowed by DVA, but many could and did make good matriculation deficiencies.' Collard, ed., *The McGill You Knew: An Anthology of Memories, 1920–1960* (Don Mills, ON: Longman Canada, 1975), 41.

161 Neary, 'Canadian Universities,' 142. See also Neary, 'Introduction,' in Neary and Granatstein, *The Veterans Charter*, 8.

162 England, *Discharged*, 130; NA, DVA, RG 38, Vol. 184, File: Rehabilitation, Confidential Letters, Vol. 2, Counsellors' Reference Book, April 1945; Desmond Morton and J.L. Granatstein, *Victory 1945: Canadians from War to Peace* (Toronto: HarperCollins, 1995), 19, 150. On enlisted women and dependents' allowances: NA, RG 24, DND, Series E-1-b, Vol. 3371: File: HQ 428-1-1, Vol. 1, Memorandum to His Excellency, the Governor General-in-Council, from the Minister of National Defence for Air, Department of National Defence, Ottawa, 31 July 1941; File: HQ 428-1-1, Vol. 2, K.G. Nairn, A.M.A.F., Memorandum to Mr Ghewy, D.P.R., 18 June 1943; Memorandum

by K.G. Nairn, A/V/M, A.M.A.F., to A.M.O./A.H., 18 July 1944, Re: RCAF
Women's Division, Dependents' Allowance.

163 NA, DVA, RG 38, Vol. 184, File: Rehabilitation, Confidential Letters, Vol. 2,
Routine Letter No. 307, Ottawa, 18 June 1945, Re: Training of Ex-service
Women as Nurses' Aides or Practical Nurses.

164 NA, DVA, RG 38, Vol. 184, File: Rehabilitation, Confidential Letters, Vol. 2,
Confidential Letter No. 179, 3 January 1946.

165 *La Presse*, 23 February 1944, 3.

166 NA, DVA, RG 38, Vol. 197, File: Rehabilitation, Statistics – Women's Division, Proceedings: Training Conferences on Women's Rehabilitation
[1946], 50.

167 NA, MCW, MG 28 I 164, Vol. 2, Minutes of Adjourned meeting of sub-
executive, 16 May 1945; NA, Savage papers, MG 30 C 92, Vol. 3, Council of
Women – National – 1940–48. Minutes of Executive Meeting, 28 February–
1 March 1946. See also Ruth Roach Pierson, *'They're Still Women After All':
The Second World War and Canadian Womanhood* (Toronto: McClelland &
Stewart, 1986), esp. chap. 2.

168 NA, DVA, RG 38, Vol. 193, File 65-47-A, Monthly Report, Montreal,
2 February 1945; Monthly Report, Montreal, 9 March [April?] 1946.

169 NA, DVA, RG 38, Vol. 193, File 65-47-A, Monthly Report, 9 March [April?]
1946.

170 NA, DVA, RG 38, Vol. 197, File: Rehabilitation, Statistics – Women's Division, Proceedings: Training Conferences on Women's Rehabilitation, 86–8.

171 NA, DND, RG 24, Series E-1-b, Vol. 3371, File: HQ 428-3-1, Memorandum
from A.E. Walford, Major-General, Chairman, Personnel Members Committee, Department of National Defence (Army) to Defence Council
(Through Deputy Ministers), 31 July 1945.

172 Armed forces personnel had been surprised to discover, for instance, that
many enlisted women were important sources of financial support for their
mothers or for incapacitated husbands. Evidence of these women's financial obligations spurred calls for enlisted women to be permitted to allocate
dependents' allowances. NA, DND, RG 24, Series E-1-b, Vol. 3371: File: HQ
428-1-1, Vol. 1, Memorandum from J.A. Sully, Air Vice-Marshal, A.M.P., to
Minister (through C.A.S.), 10 November 1942; Minutes of a meeting of a
joint service committee of the personnel heads convened by air member
for personnel at the direction of defence council to consider and report
upon the question of *Rates of Pay for Women in the Forces* [29 December
1942]; File: HQ 428-1-3. W. Walker to Air Officer Commanding, No. 3
Training Command, Montreal, 15 December 1942; File: HQ 428-3-1, H.P.
Crabb to The Secretary, Department of National Defence for Air, Ottawa,
18 January 1943.

173 Certainly those unmarried service women discharged for pregnancy played little part in postwar reunion tales. NA, DVA, RG 38 Vol. 197, File: Rehabilitation, Statistics, Women's Division, Proceedings: Training Conferences on Women's Rehabilitation, 83–7. The fact that some women discharged for pregnancy had been pregnant at the time of enlistment suggests that joining the armed services may have been an effort to escape the censure of family and community. NA, DND, RG 24, Series E-1-b, Vol. 3371, File: HQ 428-1-1, Vol. 1, E.D. Martin to Air Officer Commanding, No. 3 Training Command, Montreal, 3 August 1942.

174 MUA, Montreal Council of Social Agencies (MCSA), MG 2076, C. 17, File 67, Jacob Tuckman, 'Vocational Guidance – A Community Responsibility,' 7 April 1949; NA, DAB, RG 36, Series 18, Vol. 12, File: General Correspondence Re: Citizens' Committees, 'A' District – Montreal, Letter from H.M. Hague, 25 July 1947.

175 American historian William Graebner notes, however, that some contemporary Hollywood films about returning veterans depicted 'the moment of homecoming ... as awkward, traumatic, or disappointing.' Graebner, *Age of Doubt*, 14.

176 Anne-Marie Sicotte, *Gratien Gélinas: La ferveur et le doute*, vol. 1, *1909–1956* (Montreal: Éditions Québec-Amérique, 1995), chaps. 13–20; Gratien Gélinas and Victor-Lévy Beaulieu, *Gratien, Tit-Coq, Fridolin, Bousille et les autres. Entretien* (Montreal: SRC et Stanké, 1993).

177 Gratien Gélinas, *Tit-Coq: Pièce en trois actes* (Montreal: Beauchemin, 1950); Tit-Coq: *Un film de Gratien Gélinas* (Productions Gratien Gélinas, 1953).

178 Gélinas and Beaulieu, *Gratien, Tit-Coq, Fridolin, Bousille et les autres*, 124–25.

179 Marcel Dubé, *Un simple soldat: Pièce en 5 actes et 15 tableaux* (Ottawa: Institut Littéraire du Québec, 1958). In her analysis of the 'myth' of Dieppe, Béatrice Richard argues that Joseph Latour is the 'incarnation du perdant canadien-français emprisonné dans sa révolte.' *La mémoire de Dieppe*, 96.

180 On American women's wartime sexual autonomy, see Elaine Tyler May, 'Rosie the Riveter Gets Married,' in Erenberg and Hirsch, *The War in American Culture*, 134.

Chapter 4

1 Archives nationales du Québec à Montréal (ANQM), Mouvement des Travailleurs Chrétiens (MTC), P257: Vol. 11, File: 5e anniversaire – Congrès – 1944 – Publicité et propagande, News clipping, 'Canadian Jocists Celebrate Mass Marriage Anniversary,' *Social Forum*, June 1944; Vol. 12, Scrapbook: Cent Mariés, 1939–, News clipping, 'First Anniversary of the Mass Marriage. All "Very Happy,"' *Montreal Standard*, [n.d. but July 1940].

2 The ACC claimed that its goal was 'influencer le temporel pour le rendre
conforme au plan de Dieu.' Archives de l'Université de Montréal (AUM),
Fonds de l'Action Catholique Canadienne (ACC), P16, File: P16/G5/8/4,
'Action Catholique Canadienne.'

3 The JOC operated on the principle of 'la non-mixité,' which meant that
young men and women organized separately in the Jeunesse Ouvrière
Catholique Masculine and the Jeunesse Ouvrière Catholique Féminine
(JOCF). For a good analysis of the opportunities provided to young working-
class women by the JOCF, see Lucie Piché, 'La Jeunesse Ouvrière Catholique
Féminine: Un lieu de formation sociale et d'action communautaire, 1931–
1966,' *Revue d'histoire de l'Amérique française* 52, 4 (Spring 1999): 481–506. See
also Lucie Piché, *Femmes et changement social au Québec: L'apport de la Jeunesse
ouvrière catholique féminine, 1931–1966* (Quebec: Presses de l'Université Laval,
2003); Louise Bienvenue, *Quand la jeunesse entre en scène: L'Action catholique
avant la Révolution tranquille* (Montreal: Boréal, 2003).

4 'Un avant-goût du congrès,' *Le Mouvement Ouvrier*, July–August 1944, 24;
ANQM, MTC, P257: Vol. 10, File: Statistiques – Cent Mariés, Les Cent Mariés
Reviennent sur la Scène, 1939–1944; Preuves vivantes; Les 105 mariages et
leurs développements [all n.d. but 1944]; Vol. 12, Scrapbook: Cent Mariés,
1939– , News clipping, 'First Anniversary of the Mass Marriage. All "Very
Happy," *Montreal Standard*, [n.d. but July 1940]. On the Service de préparation au mariage, see Gaston Desjardins, *L'Amour en patience: La sexualité
adolescente au Québec, 1940–1960* (Sainte-Foy: Presses de l'Université du
Québec, 1995); Michael Gauvreau, 'The Emergence of Personalist Feminism: Catholicism and the Marriage-Preparation Movement in Quebec,
1940–1966,' in Nancy Christie, ed., *Households of Faith: Family, Gender, and
Community in Canada, 1760–1969* (Montreal and Kingston: McGill-Queen's
UP, 2002), 319–47.

5 Suzanne Morton, 'The June Bride as the Working-Class Bride: Getting
Married in a Halifax Working-Class Neighbourhood in the 1920s,' in Bettina
Bradbury, ed., *Canadian Family History: Selected Readings* (Toronto: Copp
Clark Pitman, 1992), 373, 375; John R. Gillis, *For Better, For Worse: British
Marriages, 1600 to the Present* (New York: Oxford UP, 1985), 293–4. Denise
Girard has found that outside the bourgeoisie, very few brides wore white in
interwar Montreal; see her *Mariage et classes sociales: Les Montréalais
francophones entre les deux Guerres* (Sainte-Foy, QC: Presses de l'Université
Laval, 2000), 83–7, 100–3, 113–15. Few of the working-class women inter-
viewed by Denyse Baillargeon wore white to their interwar weddings. See
Ménagères au temps de la Crise (Montreal: Les Éditions du remue-ménage,
1991), 88–9.

6 Andrée Lévesque, *Making and Breaking the Rules: Women in Quebec, 1919–1939*, trans. Yvonne M. Klein (Toronto: McClelland & Stewart, 1994), 46; Gauvreau, 'Emergence of Personalist Feminism,' 319–20. The wedding is also briefly mentioned in Robert Rumilly, *Histoire de Montréal*, vol. 4 (Montreal: Fides, 1974), 293; Jean-Pierre Collin, *La Ligue ouvrière catholique canadienne, 1938– 1954* (Montreal: Boréal, 1996), 34; Marie-Paule Malouin, *Le mouvement familial au Québec. Les débuts: 1937–1965* (Montreal: Boréal, 1998), 47; William Weintraub, *City Unique: Montreal Days and Nights in the 1940s and '50s* (Toronto: McClelland & Stewart, 1996), 20.

7 See the *Journal of Canadian Studies* 29, 4 (Winter 1994–5), a special issue devoted to the Dionne quintuplets.

8 ANQM, MTC, P257, Vol. 10, File: Correspondance – Cent Mariés, Secrétariat Général, LOC, Montréal, to 'Chers amis,' 14 July 1945.

9 'Mark 5th Anniversary. Commemorate Mass Marriage of 106 Couples,' *Montreal Gazette*, 22 July 1944, 17; 'Mass Marriage Is Commemorated,' *Montreal Gazette*, 24 July 1944, 11; '115–Pound Cake, 200 Children 5 Years after Mass Marriage,' *Toronto Daily Star*, 22 July 1944, 25; 'Mass-Wedding Couples Mark 5th Anniversary,' *Globe and Mail*, 24 July 1944, 11; 'Mass Marriage of 1939 Recalled,' *Globe and Mail*, 25 July 1949, 12; '49 Couples Married at Stadium Observe 10th Anniversary at Mass,' *Montreal Gazette*, 25 July 1949, 15. Also ANQM, MTC, P257: Vol. 10, File: Statistiques – Cent Mariés, Preuves vivantes [1944]; Vol. 11, File: 5e anniversaire: Congrès – autorités réligieuses, News clipping, 'Quinze ans après: Que sont devenus les cent mariés de 1939?' *Le Petit Journal*, 22 April 1954; News clipping, 'Quinzième anniversaire des "105 mariages jocistes de 1939,"' *Action Populaire*, 19 April 1954. See also Malouin, *Le mouvement familial*, 39.

10 York University Archives (YUA), Maurice Duplessis Fonds, 1980-008/001, Reel 7, Léo-Paul Turcotte to Honorable M. Maurice Duplessis, 28 June 1944.

11 ANQM, MTC, P257, Vol. 11, File: Congrès du 5e anniversaire – organisations, Aimé Carbonneau and Pierre-Paul Asselin to 'Cher Monsieur,' 6 July 1944; 'La Charte de l'Oratoire,' *Le Mouvement Ouvrier*, September 1944, 20; Collin, *Ligue ouvrière catholique*, 45, 214n27. Robert Rumilly notes that Quebecers calling for the release of former Montreal mayor Camillien Houde from a federal internment camp also did so in the name of the Atlantic Charter and the Four Freedoms. See his *Histoire de Montréal*, Vol. 5, *1939– 1967* (Montreal: Fides, 1974), 109. For American commemorations of the Atlantic Charter, see John Bodnar, 'Public Memory in an American City: Commemoration in Cleveland,' in John R. Gillis, ed., *Commemorations: The Politics of National Identity* (Princeton, NJ: Princeton UP, 1994), 83–4. Bodnar suggests 'the principles enunciated in the Atlantic Charter, such as

the right to resist territorial aggrandizement by outsiders ... reinforced both American and ethnic interests during the war.' On Quebec families' new sense of entitlement in the 1940s, see Dominique Marshall, *Aux origines sociales de l'État-providence: Familles québécoises, obligation scolaire et allocations familiales 1940–1955* (Montreal: Presses de l'Université de Montréal, 1998), esp. chap. 6.

12 ANQM, MTC, P257, Vol. 11, File: 5e anniversaire: Congrès – autorités réligieuses, News clipping, 'Quinze ans après: Que sont devenus les cent mariés de 1939?' *Le Petit Journal,* 22 April 1954; News clipping, 'Quinzième anniversaire des "105 mariages jocistes de 1939,"' *Action Populaire,* 19 April 1954. On 1954 as an 'année mariale,' see Malouin, *Le mouvement familial,* 91; Jean Hamelin, *Histoire du catholicisme québécois: Le XXe siècle,* vol. 2, *De 1940 à nos jours* (Montreal: Boréal Express, 1984), 151.

13 *Le Mouvement Ouvrier,* July–August 1944 [n.p.]; ANQM, MTC, P257, Vol. 11, File: Discours du Congrès, 5e anniversaire 1944, André Laurendeau to Mr le Président Général, LOC, 23 July 1944; Discours de M. Winner. The LOC's invitation to Maurice Duplessis to attend the fifth anniversary celebrations, and its request for a message of congratulations, are in YUA, Maurice Duplessis Fonds, 1980–008/001, Reel 7, Aimé Carbonneau, président-général, LOC, to Honorable M. Maurice Duplessis, 28 June 1944; Léo-Paul Turcotte, propagandiste, LOC, to Honorable M. Maurice Duplessis, 28 June 1944.

14 *Le Mouvement Ouvrier,* July–August 1944, 10.

15 Bodnar, 'Public Memory in an American City,' 75, 76.

16 'De Churchill à St-Joseph,' *Le Mouvement Ouvrier,* July–August 1944, 8–9.

17 ANQM, MTC, P257: Vol. 10, File: Correspondance – Cent-Mariés, Jeanne Godbout to Bernadette St-Onge, 7 February 1945; Gracia Gaudet to Jeanne Godbout, 19 February 1945; Vol. 11, File: Discours du Congrès, 5e anniversaire 1944, Discours du Président, 5e anniversaire, 1944.

18 ANQM, MTC, P257: Vol. 12, Scrapbook: Cent Mariés, 1939– , News clipping, 'First Anniversary of the Mass Marriage. All "Very Happy,"' *Montreal Standard,* [n.d. but July 1940]; Vol. 10, File: Statistiques – Cent Mariés, Les 105 mariages et leurs développements [1944].

19 ANQM, MTC, P257: Vol. 10, File: Statistiques – Cent Mariés, Les Cent Mariés Reviennent sur la Scène, 1939–1944 [1944]; Preuves vivantes [1944]; Vol. 11, File: Discours du Congrès, 5e anniversaire, 1944, Discours de M. Winner; Vol. 12, Scrapbook: Cent Mariés, 1939– . News clipping, 'First Anniversary of the Mass Marriage. All "Very Happy,"' *Montreal Standard,* [n.d. but July 1940]. Examples of couples who appeared to agree that the Service de préparation au mariage had started them off on the right foot are in

ANQM, Service de préparation au mariage (SPM), P116, Boîte 60-0-002-13-06-001B-01, File: 1949 – Semaine des fiancés, Responses to questionnaire sent December 1948.

20 *Canadian Jewish Chronicle*: 2 January 1948, Congregational News, 11; '"Marriage and the Family" at the Y.W.H.A.,' 16 January 1948, 10; 6 February 1948, Congregational News, 11; Mona Gleason, *Normalizing the Ideal: Psychology, Schooling, and the Family in Postwar Canada* (Toronto: U of Toronto P, 1999), 58–9.

21 Katherine Arnup, *Education for Motherhood: Advice for Mothers in Twentieth-Century Canada* (Toronto: U of Toronto P, 1994); Veronica Strong-Boag, *The New Day Recalled: Lives of Girls and Women in English Canada, 1919–1939* (Toronto: Copp Clark Pitman, 1988); Cynthia Comacchio, *'Nations Are Built of Babies': Saving Ontario's Mothers and Children, 1900–1940* (Montreal and Kingston: McGill-Queen's UP, 1993); Elaine Tyler May, *Homeward Bound: American Families in the Cold War Era* (New York: Basic Books, 1988); Desjardins, *L'amour en patience*. On the enthusiasm for planning in the reconstruction years, see Peter S. McInnis, 'Planning Prosperity: Canadians Debate Postwar Reconstruction,' in Greg Donaghy, ed., *Uncertain Horizons: Canadians and Their World in 1945* (Ottawa: Canadian Committee for the History of the Second World War, 1997); Doug Owram, *The Government Generation: Canadian Intellectuals and the State, 1900–1945* (Toronto: U of Toronto P, 1986), chap. 11.

22 *Annuaire Statistique*, Quebec 1948, Table 78; *Annuaire Statistique*, Quebec 1950, Tables 64, 62. See also Hervé Gauthier, *Évolution démographique du Québec* (Quebec: Office de planification et de développement du Québec, 1977); Danielle Gauvreau and Peter Gossage, '"Empêcher la famille": Fécondité et contraception au Québec, 1920–1960,' *Canadian Historical Review* 78, 3 (September 1997): 478–510; John A. Dickinson and Brian Young, *A Short History of Quebec*, 2nd ed. (Toronto: Copp Clark Pitman, 1993), 263; Lévesque, *Making and Breaking the Rules*, 82–3.

23 ANQM, MTC, P257, Vol. 10, File: Statistiques – Cent Mariés, Les Cent Mariés Reviennent sur la Scène, 1939–1944 [1944]; Statistics in response to 1944 survey; Preuves vivantes [1944].

24 ANQM, MTC, P257, Vol. 10, File: Statistiques – Cent Mariés, Preuves vivantes [1944].

25 'Réflexions de 1999,' *Le Mouvement Ouvrier*, July–August 1944, 9–10.

26 ANQM, MTC, P257, Vol. 11, File: Discours du Congrès, 5e anniversaire 1944, Introductions to speakers: Introduction to Représentant du Premier Ministre (M. le Notaire Paul Gauthier).

27 ANQM, MTC, P257: Vol. 12, Scrapbook: Cent Mariés, 1939– , News clipping,

'First Anniversary of the Mass Marriage. All "Very Happy,"' *Montreal Standard*, [n.d. but July 1940]; Vol. 10, File: Statistiques – Cent Mariés, Les Cent Mariés Reviennent sur la Scène, 1939–1944 [1944].

28 ANQM, MTC, P257, Vol. 11, File: Discours du Congrès, 5e anniversaire 1944, Discours de Léo Turcotte, 1944 – 5e anniversaire.

29 ANQM, MTC, P257, Vol. 13: File: Campagne de Propagande – Travail féminin, Réunions, Réunion du 4 octobre 1943: conscription des femmes; File: Travail féminin – Mémoire, Mémoire sur la conscription du travail féminin, Par les comités généraux de la JOC et de la LOC, Montréal.

30 ANQM, MTC, P257, Vol. 11, File: Discours du Congrès, 5e anniversaire 1944, Discours de Mme Yvette Choquette, 1944 5e anniversaire.

31 ANQM, MTC, P257, Vol. 13, File: Campagne de Propagande – Allocation familiale, Leaflet: 'Quand la femme abandonne son foyer ... LE FOYER EN MEURT!' The Action catholique's Service de préparation au mariage also set out to convince participants that wives should not work outside the home. AUM, ACC, P16, File: P16/G5/9/13, 'Situation des jeunes en face du mariage.' Mémoire présenté par la JOC canadienne au Congrès Mondial de la Famille et de la Population tenue à Paris du 22 au 29 juin 1947. Lucie Piché notes that the JOCF espoused ideas of gender difference and the complementarity of masculine and feminine roles. See 'La Jeunesse Ouvrière Catholique Féminine,' 485–6, 505.

32 'À l'étranger aussi bien qu'au Canada, on a les yeux sur vous. D'après vous on jugera bien souvent les foyers ouvriers canadiens-français et catholiques.' ANQM, MTC, P257: Vol. 10, File: Statistiques – Cent Mariés, Preuves vivantes [1944]; Vol. 11, File: Discours du Congrès, 5e anniversaire 1944. Discours du Président, 5e anniversaire, 1944. Again, the Dionne quintuplets provide an interesting analogy here. As Kari Dehli argues, the quintuplets were portrayed as both special and ordinary; they were worth tracking, but were 'normal' enough to merit everyone's consideration. Kari Dehli, 'Fictions of the Scientific Imagination: Researching the Dionne Quintuplets,' *Journal of Canadian Studies* 29, 4 (Winter 1994–5): 94, 99.

33 ANQM, MTC, P257, Vol. 10, File: Statistiques – Cent Mariés, Preuves vivantes [1944].

34 ANQM, MTC, P257, Vol. 12, Scrapbook: 100 Mariés (5e anniversaire), News clipping, 'Happier, Say Couples Wed En Masse Five Years Ago,' *Toronto Daily Star*, [n.d. but July 1944].

35 'Leur vie ne contient rien de sensationnel à la manière des romans modernes,' *Le Mouvement Ouvrier*, June 1944, 16.

36 ANQM, MTC, P257, Vol. 10, File: Statistiques – Cent Mariés, Les Cent Mariés Reviennent sur la Scène, 1939–1944 [1944].

37 ANQM, MTC, P257, Vol. 11, File: Cent-Mariés – Couple 26, Husband and
wife to Mlle G. Filion, 22 July 1940. It is apparent from this letter that the
LOC correspondent had told the couple that almost all of the Cent-Mariés
were keeping in touch with the LOC. I have chosen not to use the couples'
real names, and instead refer to them by the order in which they are listed
in the Notre-Dame church registers. A compilation of the registers is located
in ANQM, MTC, P257, Vol. 10, File: Cent-Mariés de 1939 – Documentation,
Feuille de compilation des Registres de l'Église Notre-Dame de Montréal
(July 1954).

38 ANQM, MTC, P257: Vol. 11, File: Cent Mariés – Couple 8, Husband and wife
to M. and Mme G.E. Gince, n.d.; File: Cent Mariés – Couple 20, Husband
and wife to M. and Mme Nap. Chayer, 14 February 1946; File: Cent Mariés –
Couple 36, Husband and wife to M. and Mde Chayer, 14 July 1944; File:
Cent Mariés – Couple 37, Husband to Mrs Mad. Chayer, 30 December 1945;
Questionnaire [December 1945]; Vol. 10, File: Cent Mariés – Couple 7,
Husband to Monsieur Chayer, 8 February 1946.

39 On unemployment insurance, see Ruth Pierson, 'Gender and the Unem-
ployment Insurance Debates in Canada, 1934–1940,' *Labour/Le Travail* 25
(Spring 1990): 77–103; Ann Porter, 'Women and Income Security in the
Postwar Period: The Case of Unemployment Insurance, 1945–1962,' *Labour/
Le Travail* 31 (1993): 111–44.

40 ANQM, MTC, P257, Vol. 13, File: Campagne de Propagande – Allocation
familiale, Ernest Darsigny and Thérèse Guilbert to Marcel Charbonneau, 20
February 1943. Declared Darsigny and Guilbert, 'C'est bien beau de penser à
faire la guerre qui détruit mais il faut bien penser à reconstruire. Et c'est la
famille qui sera appelée à guérir les plaies béantes que laissera le présent
conflit.'

41 On nation-building, public forgetting, and public remembering, see John R.
Gillis, 'Memory and Identity: The History of a Relationship,' in Gillis, ed.,
Commemorations; Alan Gordon, *Making Public Pasts: The Contested Terrain of
Montréal's Public Memories, 1891–1930* (Montreal and Kingston: McGill-
Queen's UP, 2001).

42 On commemoration and wartime patriotism, see Gillis, 'Memory and
Identity: The History of a Relationship' and Bodnar, 'Public Memory in an
American City: Commemoration in Cleveland,' both in Gillis, ed., *Commemo-
rations*; also Jonathan Vance, *Death So Noble: Memory, Meaning, and the First
World War* (Vancouver: UBC P, 1997).

43 Rumilly, *Histoire de Montréal*, Vol. 5, 110, 114.

44 *Le Mouvement Ouvrier*, July–August 1944. Messages of congratulation from
André Laurendeau, M.L. Duplessis, Adélard Godbout [n.p.].

45 Marshall, *Aux origines sociales.*

46 ANQM, MTC, P257, Vol. 12, Scrapbook: 100 Mariés (5e anniversaire), News clipping, 'Mass-Wedding Couples Mark 5th Anniversary' *Globe and Mail,* 24 July 1944. News clipping, 'Happier, Say Couples Wed En Masse Five Years Ago,' *Toronto Daily Star,* [n.d. but July 1944]. See also 'The Happy Sequel to Quebec's Great Ball-park Wedding,' *Maclean's,* 6 December 1958.

47 May, *Homeward Bound*; Mary Louise Adams, *The Trouble with Normal: Postwar Youth and the Making of Heterosexuality* (Toronto: U of Toronto P, 1997).

48 Ian McKay, *The Quest of the Folk: Antimodernism and Cultural Selection in Twenti-eth-Century Nova Scotia* (Montreal and Kingston: McGill-Queen's UP, 1994). A fascinating response to *Life* magazine's assumptions about a quaint, pastoral Quebec is in YUA, Maurice Duplessis Fonds, 1980–008/001, Reel 7. P.H. Conway, o.p., *Life and French Canada,* Cahiers de l'École des Sciences Sociales, Politiques et Économiques de Laval, Vol. 2, no. 1 (Laval, QC: Éditions Cap Diamant, 1942).

49 V.C. Fowke, 'The National Policy – Old and New,' *Canadian Journal of Economics and Political Science* 18, 3 (August 1952): 271–86; Michael D. Behiels, *Prelude to Quebec's Quiet Revolution: Liberalism versus Neo-Nationalism, 1945–1960* (Montreal and Kingston: McGill-Queen's UP, 1985). The term 'revanche administrative' is used in Marshall, *Aux origines sociales,* 115.

50 That is, thirty-seven of the seventy files. ANQM, MTC, P257, Vol. 11, File: 5e anniversaire: Congrès – autorités réligieuses, News clipping, 'Quinze ans après. Que sont devenus les cent mariés de 1939?' *Le Petit Journal,* 22 April 1954.

51 Collin, *Ligue ouvrière catholique,* esp. chap. 4; Piché, *Femmes et changement social au Québec*; Hamelin, *Histoire du catholicisme,* 64, 68, 76; Malouin, *Le mouvement familial,* 39.

52 ANQM, MTC, P257, Vol. 21, File: Habitation, Forum sur l'habitation ouvrière [1948?]; Piché, 'La Jeunesse Ouvrière Catholique Féminine,' 489, 491.

53 ANQM, MTC, P257, Vol. 12, Scrapbook: 100 Mariés (5e anniversaire), News clipping, 'Happier, Say Couples Wed En Masse Five Years Ago,' *Toronto Daily Star,* [n.d. but July 1944]. The LOC's urban bias was noted by at least one of the couples married in the mass wedding: a couple living on a farm in Drummond County, for instance, responded to the LOC's questionnaires by noting that the questions regarding women's work didn't apply to them, as they were farmers and 'nous travaillons tous deux sur notre ferme.' ANQM, MTC, P257, Vol. 10, File: Cent Mariés – Couple 45, Questionnaire received 22 May 1940; Questionnaire [July/August 1942].

54 Maurice Lamontagne and J.-C. Falardeau, 'The Life-Cycle of French-

Canadian Urban Families,' *Canadian Journal of Economics and Political Science* 13, 2 (May 1947): 233–47; Jean-Charles Falardeau, 'Antécédents, débuts et croissance de la sociologie au Quebec,' *Recherches sociographiques* 15, 2–3 (May–August 1974): esp. 147–9; Philippe Garigue, 'French Canada: A Case-Study in Sociological Analysis,' *Canadian Review of Sociology and Anthropology* 1, 4 (November 1964): 186–92.

55 Piché, 'La Jeunesse Ouvrière Catholique Féminine,' 489n23.

56 Falardeau, 'Antécédents, débuts et croissance de la sociologie au Québec,' 144–5, 148–50; Garigue, 'French Canada: A Case-Study in Sociological Analysis'; Marlene Shore, *The Science of Social Redemption: McGill, the Chicago School, and the Origins of Social Research in Canada* (Toronto: U of Toronto P, 1987), 254–60, 269–70; Harry H. Hiller, *Society and Change: S.D. Clark and the Development of Canadian Sociology* (Toronto: U of Toronto P, 1982), chaps. 1–2.

57 May, *Homeward Bound*, 11–13, 227–46.

58 See Johannes C. Pols, 'The School as Laboratory: The Development of Psychology as a Discipline in Toronto, 1915–1955' (MA thesis, York University, 1991). My thanks to Marlene Shore for this reference.

59 On Gallup and the CIPO, see Daniel J. Robinson, *The Measure of Democracy: Polling, Market Research and Public Life, 1930–1945* (Toronto: U of Toronto P, 1999). On the Dionne quintuplets, see the special issue of the *Journal of Canadian Studies* 29, 4 (Winter 1994–95). Another Canadian example of social scientists and focus groups is the Crestwood Heights project, a study of Forest Hill families undertaken in the late 1940s and early 1950s. John R. Seeley et al., *Crestwood Heights* (Toronto: U of Toronto P, 1956).

60 On the church's attempts at modernization in postwar Quebec, see Desjardins, *L'amour en patience*, 19 and *passim*. He distinguishes between the discourse of 'orthodox' Catholicism and the discourse of 'reformist' Catholicism. See also Hamelin, *Histoire du catholicisme*, chap. 1; Collin, *Ligue ouvrière catholique*, 'Introduction,' chap. 1, and 176–7.

61 ANQM, MTC, P257: Vol. 10, File: Statistiques – Cent Mariés, Les Cent Mariés Reviennent sur la Scène, 1939–1944 [1944]; Vol. 12, Scrapbook: 100 Mariés (5e anniversaire), News clipping, 'Mass-Wedding Couples Mark 5th Anniversary,' *Globe and Mail*, 24 July 1944.

62 For example, ANQM, MTC, P257: Vol. 10, File: Cent Mariés – Couple 65; Vol. 11, File: Cent Mariés – Couple 25; File: Cent Mariés – Couple 26.

63 ANQM, MTC, P257: Vol. 10, File: Cent Mariés – Couple 89, Wife to LOC, 8 June 1940; Vol. 11, File: Cent Mariés – Couple 26, Wife to Mlle G. Filion, 22 July 1940.

64 For example, ANQM, MTC, P257, Vol. 11, File: Cent Mariés – Couple 18; File: Cent Mariés – Couple 103; File: Cent Mariés – Couple 25.

65 ANQM, MTC, P257, Vol. 10, File: Cent Mariés – Couple 82, Wife to Mme Napoléon Chayer [n.d. but April 1947?]. Also Vol. 11, File: Cent Mariés – Couple 28, Husband and wife to Mlle Filion, 27 May 1940; Husband and wife to Mr and Mme Chayer, 30 December 1946.

66 ANQM, MTC, P257, Vol. 10, File: Statistiques – Cent Mariés, Résultat de l'enquête sur les 105 mariages du Congrès jociste 1939 (Août 1942). On the power-knowledge complex and the normalizing power of 'the gaze,' see Michel Foucault, *Discipline and Punish: The Birth of the Prison,* trans. Alan Sheridan (New York: Vintage Books, 1977).

67 ANQM, MTC, P257, Vol. 10: File: Cent Mariés – Couple 97; File: Cent Mariés – Couple 65; File: Cent Mariés – Couple 24; Vol. 11: File: Cent Mariés – Couple 10. At least one couple had to withdraw from participating in the mass marriage because of poverty. Vol. 11, File: Cent Mariés – R.M., Y.R. (Annulé).

68 For example, ANQM, MTC, P257: Vol. 10: File: Cent Mariés – Couple 97; File: Cent Mariés – Couple 69; File: Cent Mariés – Couple 24; Vol. 11: File: Cent Mariés – Couple 28; File: Cent Mariés – Couple 48; File: Cent Mariés – Couple 10; File: Cent Mariés – Couple 33.

69 ANQM, MTC, P257, Vol. 10, File: Cent Mariés – Couple 65, Husband and wife to M. and Mme Nap. Chayer, 8 July 1945.

70 ANQM, MTC, P257, Vol. 11: File: Cent Mariés – Couple 39, Husband and wife to LOC, 8 February 1946; File: Cent Mariés – Couple 20, Husband and wife to M. and Mme Nap. Chayer, 14 February 1946.

71 ANQM, MTC, P257, Vol. 11, File: Cent Mariés – Couple 26, Husband and wife to Mlle G. Filion, 22 July 1940; Vol. 12, Scrapbook: 100 Mariés (5e Anniversaire), News clipping, 'Happier, Say Couples Wed En Masse Five Years Ago,' *Toronto Daily Star,* [n.d. but July 1944].

72 ANQM, MTC, P257: Vol. 10, File: Cent Mariés – Couple 65; Vol. 10, File: Cent Mariés – Couple 24; Vol. 11, File: Cent Mariés – Couple 10.

73 ANQM, MTC, P257, Vol. 16, File: Journée d'Étude Nationale, avril 1949. 'Programme de notre Journée d'Étude, printemps '49 – LOCF.' And see Simonne Monet-Chartrand, *Ma vie comme rivière: récit autobiographique 1939–1949,* vol. 2 (Montreal: Éditions du remue-ménage, 1982), 204–5, 223–5, 303–4.

74 ANQM, MTC, P257, Vol. 10, File: Cent-Mariés – Couple 35. Wife to LOC, 1 June 1947. Note the twenty-one-year-old French-Canadian, Catholic factory worker interviewed by the Canadian Youth Commission who wanted to 'put off having children for a few years,' and did not want to have 'too many children in a row.' Canadian Youth Commission, *Youth, Marriage, and the Family* (Toronto: Ryerson P, 1948), Appendix A, Case 6.

75 ANQM, MTC, P257, Vol. 13, File: Campagne de Propagande – Allocation familiale, Ernest Darsigny and Thérèse Guilbert to Marcel Charbonneau, 20 February 1943. On the LOC's community projects and lobbying efforts, see Collin, *Ligue ouvrière catholique*, esp. chaps. 4 and 5.

76 ANQM, MTC, P257: Vol. 17, File: Conseil National, Novembre 1946, Rapport des séances du Conseil Général de la L.O.C. tenues les 10 et 11 novembre 1946; Vol. 24, File: Divers: Faits, Document entitled F-A-I-T-S [n.d.]. On secularization, see Hamelin, *Histoire du catholicisme*, chap. 1.

77 All 105 couples married in the mass wedding chose to make marriage contracts. Marriage contracts were also discussed as part of the Action catholique's Service de préparation au mariage. ANQM, MTC, P257, Vol. 12, File: Scrapbook: Cent Mariés – 1939, 'All Very Happy,' *Standard* [July 1940]; ANQM, Jeunesse Ouvrière Catholique (JOC), P104, C. 213, File: Cours [1944]. Le Contrat de Mariage; ANQM, SPM, P116, Boîte: 60-0-002-13-06-003A-01, File: 1952 – Résumés de Cours, Sixième Cours, La préparation économique – Le contrat de mariage.

78 Unhappy couples could, however, seek a legal separation of bed-and-board, which to a certain extent freed them financially from their partners. National Archives of Canada (NA), Montreal Council of Women (MCW), MG28 I164, Vol. 8, File 1, Causerie donnée à Radio-Canada, CBF Montréal, octobre 1946 par Me [Maître] Elizabeth Monk, avocat, Montréal; James G. Snell, *In the Shadow of the Law: Divorce in Canada, 1900–1939* (Toronto: U of Toronto P, 1991), 14.

79 'Pourquoi sévit la crise du logement,' *La Presse*, 25 January 1945, 3; 'Mariages et naissances augmentent depuis 1939,' *La Presse*, 5 January 1946, 20; *Annuaire Statistique*, Quebec 1948, Table 74; *Annuaire Statistique*, Quebec 1950, Tables 60 and 58.

80 May, *Homeward Bound*; Doug Owram, *Born at the Right Time: A History of the Baby Boom Generation* (Toronto: U of Toronto P, 1996).

81 AUM, ACC, P16, File: P16/H3/18/84, 'Le Mariage Chrétien' (1946); ANQM, MTC, P257, Vol. 13, File: Campagne de propagande – Travail Féminin, Correspondance, Paul Guay to LOC, 17 October 1942; ANQM, MTC, P257, Vol. 24, File: Divers – Faits, 'Faits'; NA, Jewish Family Services of the Baron de Hirsch Institute (JFS), MG28 V86, Vol. 10, File: Minutes of Meetings of Case Committee, Family Welfare Dept., 1947, Presentation for Case Committee Meeting, 13 January 1948; NA, JFS, MG28 V86, Vol. 11, File: Minutes of Case Conferences: FWD and JCWB, 1944–46, Minutes of meeting between Family Welfare Dept and Jewish Child Welfare Bureau, 10 January 1945. On Montreal's Protestant Family Welfare Association and contraceptives, see Angus McLaren and Arlene Tigar McLaren, *The Bedroom and the*

State: The Changing Practices and Politics of Contraception and Abortion in Canada, 1880–1980 (Toronto: McClelland & Stewart, 1986), 124–5. On members of the armed services and condoms, see Collectif Clio, *L'histoire des femmes au Québec depuis quatre siècles*, 2nd ed. rev. (Montreal: Le Jour, 1992), 384; Earle Birney, *Turvey: A Military Picaresque* (Toronto: McClelland & Stewart, 1949), 136. Examples of newspaper reporting of illegal abortions include *La Presse*: 'Une garde-malade traduite en cour,' 8 July 1947, 17; 'La femme Odina Henri envoyée aux Assises,' 30 July 1947, 26; 'Mme Montpetit et le Dr Shear en correctionnelle,' 27 August 1947, 3; 'Marie Montpetit coupable d'homicide involontaire,' 26 February 1948, 3. On abortion in Montreal in an earlier period, see Lévesque, *Making and Breaking the Rules*, 84–94.

82 McGill University Archives (MUA), Montreal Council of Social Agencies (MCSA), MG 2076, C. 19, File 21, Report of the Committee on Unmarried Parenthood, March 1949.

83 As we saw in Chapter 1, however, the numbers of married women who worked for pay in Montreal were still relatively small. In 1951, 20.86 per cent of the city's female labour force was married; conversely, 11.79 per cent of Montreal wives worked for pay. *Ninth Census of Canada 1951*: Vol. 10, 286; Vol. 10, Table 8; Vol. 1, Table 29; Vol. 4, Table 8.

84 ANQM, JOC, P104: Container 28, File: Bulletin des Chefs de la JOCF, 1945–1946–1947, Bulletin mensuel JOCF, January 1946. 'Soyons femme! Votre futur royaume, Mesdemoiselles!'; Container 37, File: Bulletin des Chefs de la JOCF, 1948–1949. 'Enquête nationale: 'Pour être une femme de maison dépareillée': l'économie,' *Équipe Ouvrière*, November 1948; 'Nécessité familiale: Le budget familial ramènera l'harmonie et le bien-être au foyer,' *La Presse*, 5 January 1946, 20.

85 'La Charte de l'Oratoire,' *Le Mouvement Ouvrier*, September 1944, 20; Desjardins, *L'amour en patience*; Hamelin, *Histoire du catholicisme*; Collin, *Ligue ouvrière catholique*.

86 Collin, *Ligue ouvrière catholique*, 97, 99. In a similar vein, Michael Gauvreau argues that the AC's Service de préparation au mariage espoused a 'personalist feminism.' See his 'Emergence of Personalist Feminism.'

87 ANQM, MTC, P257, Vol. 11, File: Histoire de la LOC – documents, 'La LOC et la pénétration du milieu social ouvrier' (1950).

88 ANQM, MTC, P257: Vol. 7, File: Rapport M.T.C. et Fédés – Rapport d'action-comité – 1947, Rapport des Activités de la Ligue Ouvrière Catholique, Année 1944–45; Rapport de la Ligue Ouvrière Catholique 1944–45; Vol. 11, File: Discours du Congrès, 5e anniversaire 1944, Introductions to speakers: Introduction to Le Maire de Montréal. Jean-Pierre Collin estimates that at

the end of the 1940s, the LOC 'peut compter sur 3 800 militantes et près de 1 900 militants.' Collin, *Ligue ouvrière catholique*, 170. A complaint about the small number of participants attending the Action catholique's marriage preparation courses in 1946 is in AUM, ACC, P16, File: P16/H3/18/84, Rapport de la troisième réunion du comité diocésain du SPM, tenue au Secrétariat du Service, le 29 novembre 1946. It is thought that attendance at these courses increased dramatically in the 1950s, however. See Malouin, *Le mouvement familial*, 88.

89 Collin, *Ligue ouvrière catholique*, 14, 51, 64–70, 178–80; Hamelin, *Histoire du catholicisme*, 102 and chap. 2 more generally. And see Malouin, *Le mouvement familial*, 10, 84–6, 93–4, 126.

90 The opinion that the number of organizations prepared to assist Quebec families had multiplied dramatically in recent years is in AUM, ACC, P16, File: P16/R57, Institutions d'assistance aux familles.

91 Malouin, *Le mouvement familial*.

92 Ibid., 126, 128, 129.

93 Collin, *Ligue ouvrière catholique*, 15. Malouin, conversely, places the LOC squarely in the context of Quebec's *mouvement familial*. See *Le mouvement familial*, 37 and *passim*. I would argue that an organization that called itself 'le mouvement des papas et des mamans' and that subtitled its newspaper 'Le journal de la famille ouvrière' had much in common with the other groups that made up the *mouvement familial*.

94 AUM, ACC, P16, File: P16/R57, News clipping, André Laurendeau, 'Pour un mouvement des familles,' 22 November 1950.

95 AUM, ACC, P16, File: P16/O4/52, Commission Canadienne de la Jeunesse, Comité provincial du Québec, Mémoire sur la famille. The Quebec committee claimed that 'dans la majorité des foyers règne une compréhension lamentable du mariage et de ses obligations avec tout ce que cela comporte de mésententes et de négligence dans l'éducation des enfants,' 5.

96 AUM, ACC, P16, File: P16/O4/52, Commission Canadienne de la Jeunesse, Comité provincial du Québec, Mémoire sur la famille; File: P16/R57. Institutions d'assistance aux familles. And see Gleason, *Normalizing the Ideal*.

97 Quebec's submission on the family to the Canadian Youth Congress argued that broken homes were the result of a lack of preparation, a lack of religious principles, and poor economic conditions. AUM, ACC, P16, File: P16/O4/52, Commission Canadienne de la Jeunesse, Comité provincial du Québec, Mémoire sur la famille.

98 ANQM, SPM, P116; Desjardins, *L'Amour en patience*; Gauvreau, 'Emergence of Personalist Feminism'; Malouin, *Le mouvement familial*; Monet-Chartrand, *Ma vie comme rivière*.

99 The Service de préparation au mariage, for instance, explicitly criticized the parenting received by the generation that came of age in the 1940s. Gauvreau, 'Emergence of Personalist Feminism,' 327–30. For one parent's angry response to the teachings of the SPM, see Gauvreau, 'Emergence of Personalist Feminism,' 330–1.

100 AUM, ACC, P16, File: P16/G5/8/4. 'Action Catholique Canadienne'; Piché, 'La Jeunesse Ouvrière Catholique Féminine,' 488–9.

101 Malouin, *Le mouvement familial,* 34; Chartrand, *Ma vie comme rivière,* 250–1, 326–9; Denyse Baillargeon, '"We admire modern parents": The École des Parents du Québec and the Post-war Quebec Family, 1940–1959,' in Nancy Christie and Michael Gauvreau, eds., *Cultures of Citizenship in Post-war Canada, 1940–1955* (Montreal and Kingston: McGill-Queen's UP, 2003).

102 Collin, *Ligue ouvrière catholique,* 14, 16, and *passim.* In 1941, Simonne Monet Chartrand described Montreal's La Bonne Coupe cooperative as an exercise in democracy and popular participation. *Ma vie comme rivière,* 76–7.

103 Collin argues that the state's growing monopoly over political action was in fact the reason for the LOC's demise in the 1950s. See *Ligue ouvrière catholique,* 173–5, 179–80. On postwar citizenship and the cultivation of democracy, see Shirley Tillotson, *The Public at Play: Gender and the Politics of Recreation in Post-War Ontario* (Toronto: U of Toronto P, 2000).

104 One participant in a 1951 conference of the French section of the Canadian Welfare Council in Montreal summarized the conference by saying 'Le sens de cet inventaire c'est que nous sommes tous à la recherche de styles nouveaux de vie familiale dans tous les domaines.' AUM, ACC, P16, File: P16/R64, 'Vers l'Édification de la famille de demain,' Rapport des premières journées d'étude de la Commission française du Conseil canadien du Bien-être social, Hôpital de la Miséricorde, Montréal, les 9 et 10 mars 1951, Synthèse générale de la journée présentée par M. Roger Marier.

105 The Action catholique worried, for instance, that the French-Canadian family would become 'une assistée de l'État.' Yet it also criticized federal income tax policy and federal family allowances for not taking large families into account. AUM, ACC, P16, File: P16/R57, Institutions d'assistance aux familles; La famille nombreuse; Législation familiale.

106 One lesson in the Catholic Church's 1948 Cours d'Orientation dans la Vie denounced the 'false ideas' of marriage and the heathen influence propounded by newspapers, magazines, radio, and movies. AUM, ACC, P16, File: P16/G5/9/8, Cours d'Orientation dans la Vie, Le Centre Catholique, Université d'Ottawa, 1948, Neuvième leçon: 'Le Saint État du Mariage.' See also Adams, *The Trouble with Normal.* On advertisements in Quebec during

the Second World War, see Geneviève Auger and Raymonde Lamothe, *De la poêle à frire à la ligne de feu: La vie quotidienne des Québécoises pendant la guerre '39–'45* (Montreal: Boréal Express, 1981).

107 Mona Gleason, 'Psychology and the Construction of the "Normal" Family in Postwar Canada, 1945–60,' *Canadian Historical Review* 78 (September 1997): 477; Annalee Gölz, 'Family Matters: The Canadian Family and the State in the Postwar Period,' *Left History* 1 (Fall 1993): 9.

108 Gölz, 'Family Matters,' 15.

109 NA, Renée Vautelet papers, MG 30 C 196, Vol. 1, 'Quebec and Canada,' 3 January 1947.

110 'Égalité de préférence à autorité,' *La Presse*, 26 March 1949, 28; Dominique Marshall, 'The Language of Children's Rights, the Formation of the Welfare State, and the Democratic Experience of Poor Families in Quebec, 1940–55,' *Canadian Historical Review* 78, 3 (September 1997): 409–41.

111 AUM, ACC, P16, File: P16/O4/59, 'Jeunesse vs. Après-Guerre. Guide destiné aux jeunes pour l'étude des problèmes que leur posera l'après-guerre,' Publié par la Commission Canadienne de la Jeunesse; Canadian Youth Commission, *Youth, Marriage and the Family*, ix, 33–4.

112 ANQM, JOC, P104, C. 181, File: Commission Canadienne de la Jeunesse (Congrès – Janvier 1945). Comité de la famille, Résumé du rapport des délibérations, 27–8 January 1945.

113 Gleason, *Normalizing the Ideal*, 60.

114 Gleason, 'Psychology and the Construction of the "Normal" Family,' 446, 457–60, 464, 474.

115 For example, AUM, ACC, P16, File: P16/H3/18/84, 'Le Mariage Chrétien' (1946).

116 Piché, 'La Jeunesse Ouvrière Catholique Féminine,' 485–6, 505.

117 Robinson, *The Measure of Democracy*. As we have seen, the JOC and LOC relied on surveys to know their constituencies, and used survey results to educate participants about the realities of working-class life. AUM, ACC, P16, File: P16/G5/8/12, Surveys for 'Ceux qui n'ont pas plus que trois ans de mariage' and 'À ceux qui ne pensent pas sérieusement au mariage'; Enquête sur la situation religieuse. Canada – JOCF.

118 Desjardins, *L'Amour en patience*.

119 Colette, Fadette, Françoise, and Josette were advice columnists in *La Presse*, *Le Devoir*, *Le Petit Journal*, and *Photo-Journal* respectively.

120 See Magda Fahrni, 'Under Reconstruction: the Family and the Public in Postwar Montréal, 1944–1949' (PhD diss., York University, 2001), 237–40.

121 'Devoirs incombant aux Catholiques,' *La Presse*, 25 January 1945, 1–2.

122 Ruth Roach Pierson, *'They're Still Women After All': The Second World War and*

Canadian Womanhood (Toronto: McClelland & Stewart, 1986); May, *Homeward Bound*.

123 See Sherene Razack, 'Schools for Happiness: *Instituts familiaux* and the Education for Ideal Wives and Mothers,' in Veronica Strong-Boag and Anita Clair Fellman, eds., *Rethinking Canada: The Promise of Women's History*, 2nd ed. (Toronto: Copp Clark Pitman, 1991), 372, on the way in which Quebec's *instituts familiaux* of the 1950s were a manifestation of a long-standing clerical nationalism but also 'found an agreeable climate in the postwar world.'

124 The Action catholique's files include, for instance, a booklet entitled 'Your Marriage,' part of the New York State Department of Mental Hygiene's Guideposts to Mental Health series, published in 1949. AUM, ACC, P16, File: P16/R65. Clearly the AC was attuned to the thoughts of other 'experts' on family. And see Gleason, *Normalizing the Ideal*.

125 Gleason, *Normalizing the Ideal*; Adams, *The Trouble with Normal*; Franca Iacovetta, 'Making "New Canadians": Social Workers, Women, and the Reshaping of Immigrant Families,' in Franca Iacovetta and Mariana Valverde, eds., *Gender Conflicts: New Essays in Women's History* (Toronto: U of Toronto P, 1992).

126 'King, ET LA FAMILLE CANADIENNE,' *La Presse*, 1 June 1945, 14; ANQM, JOC, P104, C. 250, File: Service du B.E. Social, J.A. Bougie to Rév. Père V. Villeneuve, 18 February 1943.

127 ANQM, MTC, P257, Vol. 11, File: Discours du Congrès, 5e anniversaire 1944, Discours de Mme Yvette Choquette, 1944 5e anniversaire; Pierson, *'They're Still Women.'*

128 For the North American 'norm,' see May, *Homeward Bound*. For studies that question the pervasiveness of this norm, see Joanne Meyerowitz, ed., *Not June Cleaver: Women and Gender in Postwar America, 1945–1960* (Philadelphia: Temple UP, 1994); Franca Iacovetta, *Such Hardworking People: Italian Immigrants in Postwar Toronto* (Montreal and Kingston: McGill-Queen's UP, 1992); Susan Prentice, 'Workers, Mothers, Reds: Toronto's Postwar Daycare Fight,' *Studies in Political Economy* 30 (Fall 1989): 115–42; Line Chamberland, *Mémoires lesbiennes: Le lesbianisme à Montreal entre 1950 et 1972* (Montreal: Éditions du Remue-ménage, 1996).

129 Hamelin, *Histoire du catholicisme*; Collin, *Ligue ouvrière catholique*; Desjardins, *L'Amour en patience.*

130 Jürgen Habermas, 'The Public Sphere: An Encyclopedia Article (1964),' *New German Critique* 3 (Fall 1974): 49–55.

131 'ENFIN!' *Le Mouvement Ouvrier*, July–August 1944, 10; ANQM, MTC, P257, Vol. 11, File: Discours du Congrès, 5e anniversaire 1944, Discours du

Président, 5e anniversaire, 1944; Discours de Léo Turcotte, 1944 – 5e anniversaire. The 'taux décroissant' was abolished in 1949: see Marshall, *Aux origines sociales*, 291.

Chapter 5

1 National Archives of Canada (NA), Canadian Association of Consumers (CAC), MG 28 I 200, Vol. 1, File 1, Program Committee, 29 September 1947.

2 Royal Commission on Prices, *Minutes of Proceedings and Evidence*, No. 39 (Ottawa: King's Printer, 1948), Brief submitted by Kathleen M. Jackson, Secretary of the Family Division of the Canadian Welfare Council, 2076.

3 This appears to bear out the *first* part of Victoria de Grazia's triple-barrelled assertion: 'Some time in the mid-twentieth century, it also became axiomatic that access to consumer goods was a fundamental right of all peoples, that this right was best fulfilled by free enterprise, and that free enterprise operated optimally if guided by the profit motive unimpeded by state or other interference.' De Grazia, 'Introduction,' in *The Sex of Things: Gender and Consumption in Historical Perspective* (Berkeley: U of California P, 1996), 2. This chapter demonstrates that Canadians' opinions on free enterprise and the proper role of government in the 1940s were more varied than de Grazia suggests in the second and third parts of her statement. On American working-class scepticism about free enterprise during the Depression, see Alice Kessler-Harris, *A Woman's Wage: Historical Meanings and Social Consequences* (Lexington: U P of Kentucky, 1990), 74–80.

4 American historian Susan Strasser analyses the role of housewife as 'Mrs Consumer' in a capitalist economy in *Never Done: A History of American Housework* (New York: Pantheon, 1982), chap. 13. See also Victoria de Grazia, Introduction to 'Establishing the Modern Consumer Household,' in de Grazia, *The Sex of Things*, 152. The expression 'Purses on Legs' was used by Montreal liberal reformer Renée Vautelet to describe the public perception of female consumers. NA, Renée Vautelet papers, MG 30 C 196, Vol. 1, File: The High Cost of Living, Notes Lib. Womens Fed. [n.d.].

5 Susan Porter Benson, 'Living on the Margin: Working-Class Marriages and Family Survival Strategies in the United States, 1919–1941,' in de Grazia, *The Sex of Things*, 222. In Canada, the consumer activism of women on the left has been explored in: Joan Sangster, *Dreams of Equality: Women on the Canadian Left, 1920–1950* (Toronto: McClelland & Stewart, 1989); Ruth A. Frager, 'Politicized Housewives in the Jewish Communist Movement of Toronto, 1923–1933,' in Linda Kealey and Joan Sangster, eds., *Beyond the*

Vote: Canadian Women and Politics (Toronto: U of Toronto P, 1989); Linda Kealey, *Enlisting Women for the Cause: Women, Labour, and the Left in Canada, 1890–1920* (Toronto: U of Toronto P, 1998), chaps. 2, 5; Julie Guard, 'Women Worth Watching: Radical Housewives in Cold War Canada,' in Gary Kinsman, Dieter K. Buse, and Mercedes Steedman, eds., *Whose National Security? Canadian State Surveillance and the Creation of Enemies* (Toronto: Between the Lines, 2000).

6 Sylvie Murray, 'À la jonction du mouvement ouvrier et du mouvement des femmes: La Ligue auxiliaire de l'Association internationale des machinistes, Canada, 1903–1980' (MA thesis, Université du Québec à Montréal, 1988), 120. See also her more recent book on the postwar period, *The Progressive Housewife: Community Activism in Suburban Queens, 1945–1975* (Philadelphia: U of Pennsylvania P, 2003).

7 This argument is particularly common in the American literature: see William S. Graebner, *The Age of Doubt: American Thought and Culture in the 1940s* (Boston: Twayne Publishers, 1991), 1–2; Perry R. Duis, 'No Time for Privacy: World War II and Chicago's Families,' in Lewis A. Erenberg and Susan E. Hirsch, eds., *The War in American Culture: Society and Consciousness during World War II* (Chicago: U of Chicago P, 1996), 39. For Canada, see Doug Owram, *Born at the Right Time: A History of the Baby-Boom Generation* (Toronto: U of Toronto P, 1996), chaps. 1–3.

8 On the Depression and shame in the United States, see Duis, 'No Time for Privacy,' 19–20. For Canada, consider L.M. Grayson and Michael Bliss, eds., *The Wretched of Canada: Letters to R.B. Bennett, 1930–1935* (Toronto: U of Toronto P, 1971).

9 Jean-Pierre Charland and Mario Désautels, *Système technique et bonheur domestique: Rémunération, consommation et pauvreté au Québec, 1920–1960* (Quebec: Institut québécois de recherche sur la culture, 1992), esp. 79–80, 210.

10 *La Presse*: 'Le mot d'ordre des ménagères de l'ouest,' 26 May 1947, 4; 'Une manifestation des ménagères de Paris,' 22 September 1947, 1; 'La baisse des prix continue,' 20 February 1948, 1. On British women's postwar consumer activism, see James Hinton, 'Militant Housewives: The British Housewives' League and the Attlee Government,' *History Workshop Journal* 38 (1994): 128–56.

11 John Bohstedt, 'Gender, Household, and Community Politics: Women in English Riots, 1790–1810,' *Past and Present* 120 (1988): 265–84; Judith Smart, 'Feminists, Food and the Fair Price: The Cost-of-Living Demonstrations in Melbourne, August–September 1917,' in Joy Damousi and Marilyn Lake, eds., *Gender and War: Australians at War in the Twentieth Century* (Cambridge:

Cambridge UP, 1995); Susan Levine, 'Workers' Wives: Gender, Class and Consumerism in the 1920s United States,' *Gender and History* 3, 1 (1991): 45–64; Dana Frank, *Purchasing Power: Consumer Organizing, Gender, and the Seattle Labor Movement, 1919–1929* (Cambridge: Cambridge UP, 1994).

12 'Exception à la règle,' *La Presse*, 21 October 1944, 28; NA, Marion Creelman Savage papers, MG 30 C 92, Vol. 7, File: WPTB 1933–1944 [*sic*]. Poster: 'The Story of Inflation ... in one easy lesson.'

13 *La Presse*: 'L'ennemi se dresse, implacable,' 3 January 1944, 4; 'La récupération au programme de l'année nouvelle,' 3 January 1944, 4; 'Le marché noir est une plaie économique,' 7 July 1944, 6. And see Ruth Roach Pierson, *'They're Still Women After All': The Second World War and Canadian Womanhood* (Toronto: McClelland & Stewart, 1986), chap. 1; Geneviève Auger et Raymonde Lamothe, *De la poêle à frire à la ligne de feu: La vie quotidienne des Québécoises pendant la guerre '39–'45* (Montreal: Boréal Express, 1981); Amy Bentley, *Eating for Victory: Food Rationing and the Politics of Domesticity* (Urbana: U of Illinois P, 1998).

14 Joseph Schull, *The Great Scot: A Biography of Donald Gordon* (Montreal and Kingston: McGill-Queen's UP, 1979), 66–67; 'Exception à la règle,' *La Presse*, 21 October 1944, 28.

15 NA, Savage papers, MG 30 C 92, Vol. 7, File: WPTB – *Consumer News* 1944–1945, 'The Price of Freedom,' *Consumers' News* (May 1945), 1.

16 'L'inflation, le dernier ennemi,' *La Presse*, 7 May 1945, 4; NA, Savage papers, MG 30 C 92, Vol. 7: File: WPTB 1944–45, Directive No. 4 to Liaison Officers from Byrne Sanders, Director, Consumer Branch; File: WPTB – *Consumer News* 1944–45, 'Why It Could Happen Here,' *Consumers' News* (November/ December 1945), 4; File: WPTB 1933–1944 [*sic*]. Women's Regional Advisory Committee, Montreal, Minutes, 19 September 1944.

17 NA, Montreal Council of Women (MCW), MG 28 I 164: Vol. 2, Minutes, Local Council of Women, 20 February 1946; Vol. 5, File 6. Local Council of Women 52nd Year Book and Annual Report 1945–1946, Report of the Liaison Officer to the Women's Regional Advisory Committee (Consumer Branch) of the WPTB.

18 *La Presse*: 'Le Canada ne doit pas perdre patience,' 5 January 1946, 22; 'Le retour à l'état normal,' 3 January 1947, 6. Joy Parr argues that the production of household goods was deliberately given lower priority than the reconstruction of heavy industry. See *Domestic Goods: The Material, the Moral, and the Economic in the Postwar Years* (Toronto: U of Toronto P, 1999), chap. 3.

19 'La lutte à l'inflation,' *La Presse*, 27 December 1945, 12; NA, MCW, MG 28 I 164, Vol. 6, File 13, Letter from the LCW of Montreal [Food Conservation], 2 January 1948.

20 Jeff Keshen, 'One for All or All for One: Government Controls, Black Marketing and the Limits of Patriotism, 1939–47,' *Journal of Canadian Studies* 29, 4 (Winter 1994–95): 126. On the black market, see also Denyse Baillargeon, *Ménagères au temps de la crise* (Montreal: Éditions du remue-ménage, 1991), 141; *La Presse*: 'Un juge s'élève contre les responsables du marché noir,' 29 May 1946, 3; 'Violentes protestations contre le marché noir,' 30 September 1946, 11.

21 *La Bonne Parole*, May 1947, Témoignage, 8.

22 Archives nationales du Québec à Montréal (ANQM), P120, Fonds Fédération nationale Saint-Jean-Baptiste (FNSJB), P120/12–9, Minutes du Bureau de direction, octobre 1947–mai 1955, Bureau de Direction, 18 décembre 1948.

23 Jean-Marie Nadeau, *Horizons d'après-guerre: Essais de politique économique canadienne* (Montreal: Lucien Parizeau, 1944), 147–8, 219, 300–1.

24 York University Archives (YUA), Maurice Duplessis Fonds, 1980–008/001, Reel 7, 'Schéma – Discours' [n.d.], p. 2; Reel 3, Speech by Maurice Duplessis [n.d., no title], p. 14.

25 *La Presse*: 'Première victoire contre l'inflation,' 4 May 1946, 31; 'Le contrôle des prix reste nécessaire,' 26 July 1946, 6. See also Schull, *The Great Scot*, 59, 64.

26 F.R. Scott, 'Orderly Decontrol: 1947,' in *The Eye of the Needle: Satires, Sorties, Sundries* (Montreal: Contact Press, 1957), 61.

27 See, e.g., Nadeau, *Horizons d'après-guerre*, 'Avant-propos' and *passim*.

28 *La Presse*: 'Au Jour le Jour,' 27 March 1947, 13; 'Au Jour le Jour,' 4 November 1947, 15.

29 'Contrôle des prix,' *La Presse*, 15 December 1945, 30.

30 *La Presse*, 'Double moyen pour éviter l'inflation,' 3 January 1947, 6; 'La lutte à l'inflation,' 5 November 1947, 38; 'Subsides et contrôle des prix réclamés,' 11 November 1947, 4; 'Le contrôle des prix réclamé par deux organisations ouvrières,' *Le Devoir*, 16 December 1948, 3.

31 'Rétablissement du contrôle des prix,' *La Presse*, 20 December 1947, 30.

32 Gabrielle Roy, *The Cashier*, trans. Harry Binsse (Toronto: McClelland & Stewart, 1955), 160; *La Presse*: 'Va-t-on soulager le contribuable?', 28 January 1947, 1; 'Qui va bénéficier des dégrèvements prévus?' 5 March 1947, 1; 'Le fardeau restera assez lourd,' 4 February 1948, 6; NA, MCW, MG 28 I 164, Vol. 3, File 1A, Minutes, LCW, 19 November 1947.

33 'L'inflation est connue,' *La Presse*, 30 July 1947, 6. See also *La Presse*: 'Hausse accélérée du coût de la vie,' 6 August 1946, 1; 'Le coût de la vie monte légèrement,' 5 November 1948, 7; 'Le coût de la vie continue d'augmenter,' 5 July 1949, 17.

34 NA, MCW, MG 28 I 164, Vol. 3, File 1B, Minutes, Sub-Executive Committee
    of LCW, 1 December 1948; Baillargeon, *Ménagères*, 146; Parr, *Domestic Goods*,
    85–6. Belinda Davis notes that 'the feminization of the home front popula-
    tion' in Berlin during the First World War reinforced the popular percep-
    tion of consumers as female. 'Food Scarcity and the Empowerment of the
    Female Consumer in World War I Berlin,' in de Grazia, *The Sex of Things*,
    288.

35 NA, MCW, MG 28 I 164, Vol. 2, Minutes, Local Council of Women, 17 May
    1944. See also Marion V. Royce, *The Effect of the War on the Life of Women: A
    Study* (Geneva: World's YWCA, 1945), where Royce claims that Canadian
    women's voluntary cooperation with the Consumer Branch of the WPTB
    was responsible 'in large degree for the efficient enforcement of price
    control,' 62.

36 NA, MCW, MG 28 I 164, Vol. 2, Mrs E.C. Common to President, LCW,
    3 April 1946. Jeff Keshen argues that voluntary war-work in the realm of
    consumption may have led to 'enhanced recognition and self-confidence'
    for some women. See 'Revisiting Canada's Civilian Women during World
    War II,' *Histoire sociale/Social History* 30, 60 (November 1997): 245.

37 NA, MCW, MG 28 I 164, Vol. 12, 'Why Be Thrifty?' (Ottawa: National Coun-
    cil of Women, 1950); NA, Vautelet papers, MG 30 C 196, Vol. 1. 'L'associa-
    tion canadienne des consommateurs' [n.d. but after September 1947].

38 Magda Fahrni, 'Citizenship Under Reconstruction: Women's Public Claims
    in 1940s Canada,' paper presented to 'Paroles de femmes dans la guerre,'
    Université de Nantes, France, 8 June 2001. On cost-of-living protests by DA
    recipients, see also Nancy Christie, *Engendering the State: Family, Work, and
    Welfare in Canada* (Toronto: U of Toronto P, 2000), 263–4.

39 NA, CAC, MG 28 I 200, Vol. 1, File 1, The Canadian Association of Consum-
    ers [Constitution]; Program [29 September 1947]; 'Les femmes du Canada
    s'unissent,' *La Presse*, 20 November 1947, 4; Parr, *Domestic Goods*, chap. 4.

40 NA, MCW, MG 28 I 164, Vol. 11, File: MCW Scrapbook, 1942–1959, Part I,
    news clipping, 'Women Meet to Organize Program,' *Montreal Star*,
    29 September [1947].

41 'Première réunion de l'Association des Consommateurs,' *La Presse*, 3 Novem-
    ber 1947, 4.

42 NA, Vautelet papers, MG 30 C 196, Vol. 1. 'L'association canadienne des
    consommateurs' [n.d.]; NA, MCW, MG 28 I 164, Vol. 3, File 2, Minutes,
    Executive Committee of LCW, December 1949; 'Le devoir des Canadiennes,'
    La Presse, 28 November 1947, 4.

43 'Les femmes du Canada s'unissent,' *La Presse*, 20 November 1947, 4.

44 'Première réunion de l'Association des Consommateurs,' *La Presse*, 3 Novem-

ber 1947, 4; *La Bonne Parole*: Rapports des Comités, Rapport du Congrès du National Council of Women of Canada, July–August–September 1947, 13; 'Instrument d'action féminine collective,' October 1947, 1.

45 'La L.O.C. appuie une nouvelle organisation,' *La Presse*, 26 November 1947, 4. See also ANQM, Mouvement des Travailleurs Chrétiens (MTC), P257, Vol. 24, File: Divers – Rapport Comités LOCF, 9 October 1946–30 September 1950. Comité National de la LOCF tenu le 20 octobre 1947; '"Les femmes sont décidées,"' *Le Front Ouvrier*, 22 November 1947, 10–11; NA, CAC, MG 28 I 200, Vol. 1, File 3, News clipping, 'Consumers' Association Holds Annual Meeting,' *Canadian Unionist* (November 1949).

46 NA, CAC, MG 28 I 200, Vol. 1, File 2, CAC, Brief of Minutes of National Annual Meeting, 21–22 September 1948. At least one member of the CAC felt 'the labour people should have more representation in this group.' NA, CAC, MG 28 I 200, Vol. 1, File 1, Morning Session, September 30. On links between the CAC and women in the Ontario CCF, see Dan Azoulay, 'Winning Women for Socialism: The Ontario CCF and Women, 1947–1961,' *Labour/Le Travail* 36 (Fall 1995): 59–90.

47 See, e.g., Murray, 'À la jonction du mouvement ouvrier et du mouvement des femmes,' 97–8.

48 Archives de l'Université du Québec à Montréal (AUQAM), Fonds d'Archives du Conseil des Métiers et du Travail de Montréal (CMTM), 103P, File: 103P-102/6, Minutes: 23 January 1947; 13 February 1947; 27 February 1947; 10 April 1947; 12 June 1947; 27 November 1947; 11 March 1948. Quebec's Fédération provinciale du travail also urged supporters to 'Buy Union-Made Goods,' *Le Monde Ouvrier*, 14 February 1948, 8.

49 *Le Front Ouvrier*: 'M. Abbott dit NON! POURQUOI?' 1 November 1947, 10–11; 'Les unions ouvrières et le coût de la vie,' 6 December 1947, 3; 'Une expérience syndicale,' 28 February 1948, 2.

50 'Le régime alimentaire d'Ottawa,' *Le Monde Ouvrier*, 31 January 1948, 3. On the impact of large families on household budgets, see Charland et Désautels, *Système technique et bonheur domestique*, 29–30.

51 Quoted in 'Les ménagères n'en reviennent pas!' *Le Front Ouvrier*, 14 Febuary 1948, 3. See also 'Les prix qui montent!' *Le Front Ouvrier*, 17 January 1948, 17.

52 Denyse Baillargeon emphasizes the minimal levels of consumption among Montreal's working-class families in the 1930s, arguing that these families remained a site of production rather than consumption at least until the 1940s. See *Ménagères*, 160, 196. Susan Porter Benson makes a similar argument for American working-class families in the interwar period: see her article 'Gender, Generation, and Consumption in the United States:

Working-Class Families in the Interwar Period,' in Susan Strasser et al., eds., *Getting and Spending: European and American Consumer Societies in the Twentieth Century* (Washington, DC: Cambridge UP and the German Historical Institute, 1998), 223–40.

53 ANQM, MTC, P257: Vol. 5, File: Décisions du Conseil National, Décisions prises au conseil national de la LOC tenu à Montréal les 22–23 novembre 1947; Vol. 5, File: Comité National – oct. 48–septembre 1949. Rapport du comité national conjoint tenu le 28 juin 1949; Vol. 5, File: Comité National, octobre 1949–octobre 1950, Comité National Conjoint de la LOC tenu le 16 septembre 1949; Vol. 7, File: Rapport MTC et Fédés – Rapport d'action-comité – 1947, Aperçu des activités de la LOC pour l'année 1945–46, 26 juillet 1946; Vol. 18, File: Conseil National – février 1948, Rapport des Assemblées du Conseil National de la LOC tenues les 28–29 février 1948 à Montréal. See also *Le Front Ouvrier*, 31 January 1948, 4.

54 'Essor d'une coopérative de consommation,' *Le Front Ouvrier*, 16 July 1949, 8–9. Writing of the specialized movements of the Action catholique in the 1940s, Louise Bienvenue argues that 'leur ancienne méfiance à l'égard d'une ingérence étatique, qui ne pourrait qu'anémier le dynamisme de la société civile, est tenace.' Bienvenue, *Quand la jeunesse entre en scène: L'Action catholique avant la Révolution tranquille* (Montreal: Boréal, 2003), 246.

55 On Colette's true identity, see Andrée Lévesque, *Making and Breaking the Rules: Women in Quebec, 1919–1939*, trans. Yvonne M. Klein (Toronto: McClelland & Stewart, 1994), 24.

56 *La Presse*: 27 March 1948, 30; 29 November 1948, 19; 14 February 1949, 18. For a fuller discussion of these columns, see my doctoral dissertation 'Under Reconstruction: The Family and the Public in Postwar Montréal, 1944–1949' (PhD diss., York University, 2001), chap. 3.

57 *Report of the Royal Commission on Prices*, Vol. 1 (Ottawa: King's Printer, 1949), 31; *La Presse*: 'Spéculation injustifiée,' 25 November 1947, 3; 'Organisme prêt à agir,' 26 November 1947, 3; 'Réactions de la ménagère,' 2 December 1947, 4; *Montreal Gazette*: 'Fruit, Vegetable Prices Up as Imports Cut But Modification of Law Is Forecast,' 20 November 1947, 13; 'Grocers Scour Market for Vegetables as Price Trend Continues Upward Climb,' 21 November 1947, 15.

58 *La Presse*: 'Organisme prêt à agir,' 26 November 1947, 3; 'Spéculation injustifiée,' 25 November 1947, 3; *Montreal Gazette*: 'Enforcement Now Feared Impossible of New Ceilings Announced by Abbott as Grocers, Others Here Hail Action,' 25 November 1947, 1; 'Consumer Group to Fight Panic Buying in Montreal,' 28 November 1947, 4. On the lack of refrigerators and the daily shopping habits of Montreal's working-class families, see Baillargeon, *Ménagères*, 172; Sylvie Taschereau, 'Les petits commerçants de l'alimentation

et les milieux populaires montréalais, 1920–1940' (PhD diss., Université du Québec à Montréal, 1992), 202, 293, 317; Charland et Désautels, *Système technique et bonheur domestique,* 134–5. On the particular need for ice-boxes in Quebec, given the predominance of flats without cold-cellars, see Parr, *Domestic Goods,* 29.

59 '"N'achetez pas si c'est trop cher," dit Mme Marshall,' *La Presse,* 22 November 1947, 36.

60 'Increased Prices Laid to Producers,' *Montreal Gazette,* 29 November 1947, 7.

61 *La Presse*: 'Les fermiers se ravisent,' 25 November 1947, 3; 'Grèves de détaillants?,' 25 November 1947, 3; 'Le marché mort,' 26 November 1947, 3; 'Les acheteurs font la grève,' 27 November 1947, 3.

62 *La Presse*: 'Les fermiers se ravisent,' 25 November 1947, 3; 'Le contingent serait mince,' 28 November 1947, 3; 'Le commerce se stabilise,' 29 November 1947, 27; 'Les réductions sur les agrumes,' 20 February 1948, 29.

63 *La Presse*: 'Les prix se stabilisent,' 26 February 1948, 3; 'Les prix maxima de la viande tout prêts,' 21 February 1948, 17.

64 'Les prix qui montent!' *Le Front Ouvrier,* 17 January 1948, 17. Thérèse Casgrain noted to the Canadian Association of Consumers that less milk was delivered to the poorer sections of Montreal once prices went up. NA, CAC, MG 28 I 200, Vol. 1, File 1, Morning Session, September 30. On decreased purchases of milk in Canada more generally in 1948, see *Royal Commission on Prices, Minutes of Proceedings and Evidence,* No. 39 (Ottawa: King's Printer, 1948), Brief submitted by Kathleen M. Jackson, Secretary of the Family Division of the Canadian Welfare Council, 2079; *Royal Commission on Prices, Minutes of Proceedings and Evidence,* No. 41 (Ottawa: King's Printer, 1949), Brief submitted by Mrs Rae Luckock, National President, Housewives and Consumer Federation of Canada, 2194.

65 *Le Front Ouvrier*: 'Les dernières hausses de prix,' 6 December 1947, 3; 'Qu'on laisse la paix aux cultivateurs!' 6 December 1947, 3; 'Lettre d'un producteur de lait à des ouvriers,' 6 December 1947, 15; 'Qui est coupable?' 13 décembre 1947, 3; 'Beurre ou margarine?' 10 January 1948, 3; 'QUI fait monter les prix?' 7 February 1948, 1, 10, 11.

66 W.H. Heick, *A Propensity to Protect: Butter, Margarine and the Rise of Urban Culture in Canada* (Waterloo: Wilfrid Laurier UP, 1991). See also Ruth Dupré, '"If It's Yellow, It Must Be Butter": Margarine Regulation in North America since 1886,' *Journal of Economic History* 59, 2 (June 1999): 353–71.

67 Heick, *A Propensity to Protect,* 73.

68 'L'U.C.C. et la margarine,' *Le Devoir,* 15 December 1948, 3; NA, CAC, MG 28 I 100, Vol. 1, File 2. Minutes of the Board of Directors Meeting, 10–11 February 1948.

69 NA, Vautelet papers, MG 30 C 196, Vol. 2. 'The Community – Its Background and Development' (revised version, 1951).

70 'Lever l'interdiction sur l'oléomargarine,' *La Presse*, 21 February 1948, 49; AUQAM, CMTM, 103P, File: 103P-102/8. Minutes, Montreal Labour Council Meeting, 22 September 1949; NA, CAC, MG 28 I 200, Vol. 1, File 4. Canadian Association of Consumers, Executive Meeting, 9 March 1949. Renée Vautelet called Duplessis's treatment of the butter question 'a form of political bribe to rural voters.' NA, Vautelet papers, MG 30 C 196, Vol. 3, File: Allocution: Has butter a future? 'Has Butter a Future?' [n.d.].

71 Dupré, '"If It's Yellow,"' 353.

72 The Montreal LCW decided not to support a butter boycott proposed by the Lachine Community Council, for instance. NA, MCW, MG 28 I 164, Vol. 3, File 2, Minutes, LCW, 16 March 1949.

73 'Pas de changement au prix du beurre,' *La Presse*, 3 January 1947, 6; NA, MCW, MG 28 I 164, Vol. 3, File 1A, Report of the Recording Secretaries, 1946–47.

74 'Spéculation sur le beurre,' *Le Front Ouvrier*, 3 January 1948, 3.

75 'La vente de la margarine,' *La Presse*, 21 April 1948, 6.

76 ANQM, FNSJB, P120/12–9, Minutes du Bureau de direction, octobre 1947–mai 1955, Bureau de Direction, 18 septembre 1948, 16 octobre 1948.

77 *Le Devoir*: 'La Cour Suprême permet la vente de la margarine,' 14 December 1948, 1; 'Nous protégerons les droits de l'agriculture (M. Duplessis),' 15 December 1948, 10; 'La margarine,' 16 December 1948, 1; 'La vente de la margarine relève des provinces,' 16 October 1950, 1. See also Heick, *A Propensity to Protect*, chap. 7; Dupré, '"If It's Yellow,"' 356.

78 *La Presse*: 'Sort incertain de la margarine dans Québec,' 18 December 1948, 1; 'La couleur de la margarine,' 5 January 1949, 4; 'La vente de la margarine relève des provinces,' *Le Devoir*, 16 October 1950, 1; Heick, *A Propensity to Protect*, 98, 107; Dupré, '"If It's Yellow,"' 356.

79 NA, MCW, MG 28 I 164: Vol. 5, File 7, LCW 55th Year Book and Annual Report 1948–1949, Report of the Economics and Taxation Committee; Vol. 3, File 2, Minutes, LCW, 19 January 1949; Minutes, Sub-Executive Committee of LCW, 9 March 1949; Vol. 7, File 25, Telegram from Miss Esther W. Kerry, President, LCW of Montreal, to Maurice Duplessis, 13 January 1949; Vol. 7, File 25, LCW of Montreal, Third telegram to Mr. Duplessis re Margarine, 5 March 1949. Renée Vautelet also claimed that antimargarine legislation was illegitimate because it violated principles of democratic liberty. NA, Vautelet papers, MG 30 C 196, Vol. 1, File: Faits et chiffres, 'Le Soutien des prix favorise-t-il le consommateur?'

80 *Royal Commission on Prices, Minutes of Proceedings and Evidence*, No. 38 (Ottawa:

King's Printer, 1948), Brief submitted by Mrs R.J. Marshall, President, National Council of Women, and Mrs F.E. Wright, President, Canadian Association of Consumers, 2003. In the same brief, these two associations reiterated their request 'for the manufacture and sale of oleomargarine in Canada ...' 2005.

81 Quoted in William Weintraub, *City Unique: Montreal Days and Nights in the 1940s and '50s* (Toronto: McClelland & Stewart, 1996), 126.

82 Dominique Marshall, *Aux origines sociales de l'État-providence: Familles québécoises, obligation scolaire et allocations familiales 1940–1955* (Montreal: Presses de l'Université de Montréal, 1998), 264, 274, 291.

83 See, e.g., T.H. Marshall, 'Citizenship and Social Class,' in *Class, Citizenship, and Social Development* (New York: Anchor Books, 1965); Susan Pedersen, 'Gender, Welfare, and Citizenship in Britain during the Great War,' *American Historical Review* 95, 4 (1990): 983–1006.

84 My use of 'economic citizenship' differs from that of Alice Kessler-Harris, who defines the term as 'the freedom for women to compete in the labor market: the right to work' – a right accompanied by 'a set of political possibilities.' See Kessler-Harris, 'Gender Identity: Rights to Work and the Idea of Economic Citizenship,' *Schweizerische Zeitschrift fur Geschichte* 46, 3 (1996), esp. 412–15; Kessler-Harris, *In Pursuit of Equity: Women, Men and the Quest for Economic Citizenship in Twentieth-Century America* (New York: Oxford UP, 2001).

85 NA, Vautelet papers, MG 30 C 196, Vol. 1, File: Allocution – Why a Canadian Association of Consumers? 'Why a Canadian Association of Consumers?' [n.d.]. See also Charland et Désautels, *Système technique et bonheur domestique,* 86; Lizabeth Cohen, 'The New Deal State and the Making of Citizen Consumers,' in Strasser et al., eds., *Getting and Spending,* 111–25.

86 *Royal Commission on Prices, Minutes of Proceedings and Evidence,* No. 38 (Ottawa: King's Printer, 1948), Brief submitted by Mrs R.J. Marshall, President, National Council of Women, and Mrs F.E. Wright, President, Canadian Association of Consumers, 2011. Rae Luckock and Marjorie Ferguson of the Housewives and Consumer Federation of Canada likewise presented their brief to the Royal Commission on Prices in 1948 'in the belief that we are exercising our democratic right and responsibility as Canadian citizens to acquaint you with our views on these extremely serious problems and to ask for your earnest assistance in solving them.' *Royal Commission on Prices, Minutes of Proceedings and Evidence,* No. 41 (Ottawa: King's Printer, 1949), Brief submitted by Mrs Rae Luckock, National President, Housewives and Consumer Federation of Canada, 2195.

87 'Avantage qu'il nous faut conserver,' *La Presse,* 4 June 1948, 6; Advertisement for the Bank of Montreal, *Le Front Ouvrier,* 8 January 1949, 3.

88 'Le communisme est toujours dangereux,' *La Presse*, 5 May 1949, 13; Archives de l'Université de Montréal (AUM), Action catholique canadienne (ACC), P16, File: P16/R64, 'Vers l'Édification de la famille de demain.' Rapport des premières journées d'étude de la Commission française du Conseil canadien du bien-être social, Hôpital de la Miséricorde, Montréal, 9–10 mars 1951, Discours de Me Jean Lesage; NA, MCW, MG 28 I 164, Vol. 3, File 1B, Minutes, LCW, 19 May 1948; NA, Vautelet papers, MG 30 C 196, Vol. 1, File: L'Association Canadienne des Consommateurs, St-Vincent-de-Paul [n.d.].

89 NA, MCW, MG 28 I 164, Vol. 12, *Why Be Thrifty?* (Ottawa: National Council of Women, 1950). See also NA, CAC, MG 28 I 200, Vol. 1, File 3, Mrs F.E. Wright, President, Canadian Association of Consumers, to Presidents of National Women's Organizations, 29 November 1949; NA, Vautelet papers, MG 30 C 196, Vol. 3, File: Notes for talk to Canadian Association of Consumers Annual Meeting, 'Notes for talk to Canadian Association of Consumers Annual Meeting' [n.d.].

90 NA, Vautelet papers, MG 30 C 196, Vol. 1: File: L'Association canadienne des consommateurs, Article pour bulletin provincial [n.d.]; File: Social Reforms for Women, C.B.C. Xmas Eve 4.18 p.m.; File: Les droits de la femme, Untitled [n.d.].

91 NA, Vautelet papers, MG 30 C 196, Vol. 1: File: Brooke Claxton, candidat libéral, Text Radio Talk – June 24th; Radio Talk for Brooke Claxton, 1st of June; File: Assemblée Mackenzie King, élection 1945, Discours Assemblée Mackenzie King Élection 1945 (11 juin).

92 On the liberal nature of Canada's postwar political culture, see Shirley Tillotson, *The Public at Play: Gender and the Politics of Recreation in Post-War Ontario* (Toronto: U of Toronto P, 2000).

93 NA, Vautelet papers, MG 30 C 196, Vol. 1, File: The High Cost of Living, Notes Lib. Womens Fed. [n.d.]. See also Parr, *Domestic Goods*, 13.

94 Benson, 'Living on the Margin,' 236. On wages in Quebec, see Charland and Désautels, *Système technique et bonheur domestique*.

95 NA, Vautelet papers, MG 30 C 196, Vol. 1, 'L'industrie oubliée' (1949); 'L'association canadienne des consommateurs' [n.d].

96 Murray, *The Progressive Housewife*, esp. chap. 4. For other recent American work on this topic, see 'Dialogue: Reimagining the Family,' *Journal of Women's History* 13, 3 (Autumn 2001): 124–68. For a Canadian example, see Susan Prentice, 'Workers, Mothers, Reds: Toronto's Postwar Daycare Fight,' *Studies in Political Economy* 30 (Autumn 1989): 115–41.

97 McGill University Archives (MUA), Notre Dame de Grâce (NDG) Women's Club, MG 4023, Container 1: 14th Record Book, Minutes, 7 January 1944; 15th Record Book, Minutes of 23rd Charter Day Luncheon, 2 March 1945;

16th Record Book, Minutes, 18 October 1946; 17th Record Book, Minutes, 3 October 1947; 17th Record Book, Minutes, 17 October 1947; 19th Record Book, Minutes, 13 April 1949.

98 NA, MCW, MG 28 I 164, Vol. 3, File 1B, Minutes, Local Council of Women, 8 December 1948. See also 'Les femmes et l'élection municipale,' *La Bonne Parole*, November 1947, 2.

99 For a recent assessment of this literature, see Yves Bélanger et al. (ed.), *La Révolution tranquille: 40 ans plus tard: Un bilan* (Montreal: VLB Éditeur, 2000).

100 NA, CAC, MG 28 I 200, Vol. 1, File 3, President's Remarks, Annual Meeting of Canadian Association of Consumers, 28–29 September 1949; *Le Front Ouvrier*. 'La femme au foyer, une isolée?' 22 November 1947, 17; 'Éditorial féminin. "Gardons" le foyer,' 6 December 1947, 17.

101 NA, Vautelet papers, MG 30 C 196, Vol. 1, File: L'Association Canadienne des Consommateurs, St-Vincent de Paul [n.d.]. But, as Dana Frank notes, shopping's 'limited visibility' meant that 'the success of a boycott was always hard to prove and observance hard to police.' *Purchasing Power*, 248.

102 There are indications, for instance, that the CAC was initially slow to attract 'the women in the home'; as Thérèse Casgrain observed, it was the majority of women who did not belong to organized consumer groups who were probably most affected by the increased cost-of-living. NA, CAC, MG 28 I 200, Vol. 1: File 2, Minutes of the Board of Directors Meeting, 10–11 February 1948; File 1, Minutes, National Conference, 29 September 1947.

Chapter 6

1 I borrow the term from Alice Kessler-Harris, 'Gendered Interventions: Rediscovering the American Past,' in Mario Materassi and Maria Irene Ramalho de Sousa Santos, eds., *The American Columbiad: 'Discovering' America, Inventing the United States* (Amsterdam: VU UP, 1996).

2 Dominique Marshall, *Aux origines sociales de l'État-providence: Familles québécoises, obligation scolaire et allocations familiales 1940–1955* (Montreal: Presses de l'Université de Montréal, 1998); Dominique Marshall, 'Reconstruction Politics, the Canadian Welfare State and the Ambiguity of Children's Rights, 1940–1950,' in Greg Donaghy, ed., *Uncertain Horizons: Canadians and Their World in 1945* (Ottawa: Canadian Committee for the History of the Second World War, 1997); Susan Pedersen, *Family, Dependence, and the Origins of the Welfare State: Britain and France, 1914–1945* (Cambridge: Cambridge UP, 1993), 3–4.

3 Cynthia Comacchio, in her overview of 'modern' Canadian fatherhood, argues that by the 1940s, 'Material changes in getting a living, changing

ideas that made mothers the central force in home and family, and an increasing commitment to intervention in families by professionals and the state, had shoved fathers somewhat off-side in the domain that they allegedly continued to rule.' See 'Bringing Up Father: Defining a Modern Canadian Fatherhood, 1900–1940,' in *Family Matters: Papers in Post-Confederation Canadian Family History*, ed. Lori Chambers and Edgar-André Montigny (Toronto: Canadian Scholars' P, 1998), 304.

4 Most recent Canadian studies, in contrast, are concerned with fathers' place in postwar domesticity and consumer culture. See Robert Rutherdale, 'Fatherhood and Masculine Domesticity During the Baby Boom: Consumption and Leisure in Advertising and Life Stories,' in *Family Matters*, ed. Chambers and Montigny; Chris Dummitt, 'Finding a Place for Father: Selling the Barbecue in Postwar Canada,' *Journal of the Canadian Historical Association*, ns., 9 (1998): 209–23.

5 Historian Michel Brunet characterized pre–Quiet Revolution Quebec as 'anti-étatiste.' See B.L. Vigod, 'Ideology and Institutions in Quebec: The Public Charities Controversy 1921–1926,' *Histoire sociale / Social History* 11, 21 (May 1978): 168; Marshall, *Aux origines sociales*, 282.

6 On ambivalent attitudes toward state intervention in the field of housing in postwar Queens, see Sylvie Murray, *The Progressive Housewife: Community Activism in Suburban Queens, 1945–1965* (Philadelphia: U of Pennsylvania P, 2003). See esp. chap. 2, 'Housing and Access to Middle-Class Status.' According to Murray, among those who argued that housing was a 'right' and that the government ought to intervene to ensure that citizens were decently housed were workers' organizations and veterans' associations.

7 F.R. Scott, 'Orderly Decontrol: 1947,' in *The Eye of the Needle: Satires, Sorties, Sundries* (Montreal: Contact P, 1957), 61.

8 Archives nationales du Québec à Montréal (ANQM), Mouvement des Travailleurs Chrétiens (MTC), P257, Vol. 17, File: Conseil National, Novembre 1946, 'L'habitation ouvrière,' Conseil National de novembre 1946. On Montreal's postwar housing crisis, see Amélie Bourbeau, '"Tuer le taudis qui nous tuera." Crise du logement et discours sur la famille montréalaise d'après-guerre (1945–1960)' (MA thesis, Université de Montréal, 2002).

9 Archives de l'Université de Montréal (AUM), Action catholique canadienne (ACC), P16, File: P16/G5/8/4, Mémoire présenté par la JOC canadienne à l'Honorable Paul Martin [1948]; ANQM, Jeunesse Ouvrière Catholique (JOC), P106, C. 216, File: Soldats (Service), Memorandum of the JOC to the Canadian Government in Favour of Demobilized Young Men [n.d.].

10 'La famille, entreprise par excellence,' *Le Front Ouvrier*, 1 November 1947, 3.

11 The largely middle-class Canadian Association of Consumers, for instance, endorsed rent controls in 1948 because 'the housing crisis is still acute, particularly for the low-income groups ...' National Archives of Canada (NA), Canadian Association of Consumers (CAC), MG 28 I 200, Vol. 1, File 2, CAC, Brief of Minutes of National Annual Meeting, 21–22 September 1948. Likewise, the West End Consumers' League promised the Montreal Labour Council its cooperation in any protests the Council might undertake against rent increases. Archives de l'Université du Québec à Montréal (AUQAM), Conseil des métiers et du travail de Montréal (CMTM), 103P, File: 103P-102/6, Minutes, 10 April 1947.

12 NA, Montreal Council of Women (MCW), MG 28 I 164, Vol. 2, Resolution on Rental Control, endorsing those drawn up by the Canadian Legion, 15 November 1944.

13 AUQAM, CMTM, 103P, File: 103P-102/6, Minutes, 11 March 1948; File: 103P-102/8. Minutes, 10 November 1949; Minutes, 29 November 1949.

14 NA, MCW, MG 28 I 164, Vol. 3, File 1B, Minutes, Sub-Executive Committee of LCW, 13 October 1948; AUQAM, Fonds Henri-Gagnon, 54P, File: 54P 3g/2. Brochure: 'Eviction! Qui sera le suivant?' [n.d.]; ANQM, MTC, P257, Vol. 5, File: Comité National, octobre 1947–septembre 1948. Comité national conjoint, 17 septembre 1948; *La Presse* (Montreal): 'Pour enquêter sur le revenu de l'immeuble,' 5 December 1946, 37; 'Subsides et contrôle des prix réclamés,' 11 November 1947, 4; 'Revendications de locataires,' 26 March 1949, 28; 'Les locataires vont préparer leur lutte,' 28 November 1949, 35; 'Deux réunions de locataires,' 6 December 1949, 25.

15 AUQAM, CMTM, 103P, File: 103P-102/8, Minutes, Montreal Labour Council, 10 November 1949.

16 Jean-Pierre Collin, 'Crise du logement et Action catholique à Montreal, 1940–1960,' *Revue d'histoire de l'Amérique française* 41, 2 (Fall 1987): 183.

17 AUQAM, Fédération provinciale du travail du Québec (FPTQ), 84P, File: 84P, 6/3, Mémoires de la FPTQ et du CMTC, 1945–1952, Mémoire Législatif présenté au Premier Ministre et aux Membres du Gouvernement de la Province de Québec par la Fédération provinciale du travail du Québec au nom du Congrès des métiers et du travail du Canada le 4 décembre 1946.

18 ANQM, MTC, P257: Vol. 5, File: Comité National, octobre 1949–octobre 1950, Comité national conjoint, 4 novembre 1949; Vol. 5, File: Décisions du Conseil National, Décisions prises au conseil national de la LOC tenu à Montréal les 22–23 novembre 1947; Décisions du Conseil National de la LOC tenu au Centre National, les 19–20 novembre 1949; Vol. 7, File: Rapport MTC et Fédés – Rapport d'action-comité, 1947, La LOC, Rapport, 1946–1947. For a thorough discussion of the Action catholique's cooperative

movement and campaign for a 'crédit ouvrier,' see Collin, 'Crise du logement.'

19 ANQM, MTC, P257, Vol. 21, File: Habitation – Habitation ouvrière, Dollard Pépin to LOC, 18 March 1948; Rolland Rivard to LOC, 30 September 1948; also ANQM, MTC, P257, Vol. 11, File: Cent Mariés – Couple 39.

20 ANQM, MTC, P257: Vol. 21, File: Habitation, Mémoire de la L.O.C. sur l'Habitation Ouvrière, preparé pour le Comité d'habitation de la Chambre de Commerce Senior de Montréal [1947?]; Mémoire sur le crédit ouvrier, présenté par la Ligue Ouvrière Catholique à l'Honorable Premier Ministre de la Province de Québec, Monsieur Maurice Duplessis; Programme souvenir: Bénédiction solennelle des premières maisons de l'habitation ouvrière, 6 août 1944, Les Saules, Québec; Vol. 23, File: Habitation – À chaque famille sa maison. Census figures demonstrate that Montreal was a city of tenants and a city of apartments and flats. In 1951, nearly 83 per cent of the city's 'occupied dwellings' were rented, rather than owned, by their inhabitants: 97 per cent of these rented dwellings were apartments or flats; 92 per cent of the city's total occupied dwellings were apartments or flats. *Ninth Census of Canada 1951*, Vol. 3, Table 10. On housing in postwar North America, see Veronica Strong-Boag, 'Home Dreams: Women and the Suburban Experiment in Canada, 1945–60,' *Canadian Historical Review* 72, 4 (1991): 471–504; Kenneth T. Jackson, *Crabgrass Frontier: The Suburbanization of the United States* (New York: Oxford UP, 1985). On American families' desires for privacy in the wake of the war, see William S. Graebner, *The Age of Doubt: American Thought and Culture in the 1940s* (Boston: Twayne Publishers, 1991), 1–2; Perry R. Duis, 'No Time for Privacy: World War II and Chicago's Families,' in Lewis A. Erenberg and Susan E. Hirsch, eds., *The War in American Culture: Society and Consciousness during World War II* (Chicago: U of Chicago P, 1996), 39.

21 *La Presse*, 'Articles de ménage': 6 August 1946, 17; 8 April 1947, 19. See also Jeff Keshen, 'One for All or All for One: Government Controls, Black Marketing and the Limits of Patriotism, 1939–47,' *Journal of Canadian Studies* 29, 4 (Winter 1994–5): 133.

22 NA, MCW, MG 28 I 164, Vol. 5, File 6, 51st Year Book and Annual Report 1944–45, Report of the Committee on Housing and Town Planning. For similar debates between municipal authorities in Vancouver and the federal government, see Canada, House of Commons, *Debates*, 28 April 1947, 2484.

23 NA, MCW, MG 28 I 164: Vol. 6, File 5, Digest of Address given by J.S. Hodgson, CMHC, 17 Nov. 1948; Vol. 7, File 27, 'Housing – Their Problem: A Study of the Dwellings of 298 Montreal Families,' March 1947; Vol. 6, File 5. News clipping, 'New Homes for War Veterans Well Planned,' *Montreal Daily Star* [n.d. but 1946?].

24 NA, MCW, MG 28 I 164, Vol. 5, File 7, 53rd Year Book and Annual Report 1946–47, Report of the Committee on Housing and Town Planning; 54th Year Book and Annual Report 1947–48, Report of the Housing and Town Planning Committee.

25 *La Presse*: 15 August 1945, 5; 26 October 1945, 8; 28 November 1945, 3.

26 NA, Montreal Soldiers' Wives League (MSWL), MG 28 I 311, Vol. 5, File 25, Report of Mrs Basil Hingston – Visiting of Next-of-kin [n.d.]; ANQM, MTC, P 257, Vol. 21, File: Habitation – Enquête de l'habitation ouvrière et logement, 'La situation du logement à Montreal' [n.d.]; ANQM, JOC, P 104, Container 216, File: Soldats (Service), Memorandum of the JOC to the Canadian Government in Favour of Demobilized Young Men [n.d. but after October 1946].

27 NA, MCW, MG 28 I 164, Vol. 3, File 1A, Minutes of Meeting of Sub-Executive Committee, 9 April 1947.

28 *La Presse*: 5 January 1946, 11; 28 November 1945, 27.

29 See also Marc H. Choko, 'Le mouvement des squatters à Montréal 1946–1947,' *Cahiers d'histoire* 2, 2 (Spring 1982): 26–39.

30 AUQAM, Fonds Henri-Gagnon, 54P, File: 54P 3g/2, Telegraph from Henri Gagnon, President, Quebec Veterans' League, to J.S. Hodgson, Central Mortgage and Housing Corporation, Montreal, Hon. C.D. Howe, Ottawa, Hon. Ian Mackenzie, Ottawa, 18 July 1947; Brochure: 'Éviction! Qui sera le suivant?' [n.d.].

31 'Le mouvement des squatters,' *La Presse*, 30 September 1946, 3; 'L'ordre et la justice. Le cas des "squatters,"' *La Patrie* (Montreal), 25 October 1946, 8; 'Aux prises avec les "squatters,"' *La Patrie*, 6 November 1946, 3; 'Quatre squatters s'installent rue Rideau à Ottawa,' *La Patrie*, 9 December 1946, 24. On Vancouver, see Jill Wade, '"A Palace for the Public": Housing Reform and the 1946 Occupation of the Old Hotel Vancouver,' *BC Studies* 69–70 (Spring–Summer 1986): 288–310.

32 'L'ordre et la justice. Le cas des "squatters,"' *La Patrie*, 25 October 1946, 8.

33 'Les "squatters" de la rue McGill College disposés à payer un loyer raisonnable,' *La Patrie*, 24 October 1946, 3, 23.

34 'La situation tendue sur le front des "squatters,"' *La Patrie*, 4 November 1946, 23.

35 AUQAM, Fonds Henri-Gagnon, 54P, File: 54P 3g/3, News clipping, 'Former Residences of Squatters Rife with Disease, Survey Shows,' *Montreal Gazette*, 1 November 1946.

36 'La situation tendue sur le front des "squatters,"' *La Patrie*, 4 November 1946, 3.

37 '"Squatters" vs "Barbottes,"' *La Patrie*, 30 October 1946, 3, 23. 'Barbotte' was the slang word used to describe illegal places of gambling.

38 AUQAM, Fonds Henri-Gagnon, 54P, File: 54P 3g/2, Brochure, 'Vous êtes un vétéran?'

39 AUQAM, Fonds Henri-Gagnon, 54P, File: 54P 3g/3, News clipping, 'L'invasion des "squatters,"' *Le Canada*, (n.d.).

40 'Red-Led Vets Invade N.D.G. Seize Decarie Blvd. House,' *Montreal Herald*, 5 November 1946, 24.

41 'La 3e invasion des squatters,' *La Presse*, 5 November 1946, 3, 26;, 'Les "squatters" s'installent par surprise dans un logis de Snowdon,' *La Patrie*, 5 November 1946, 3, 23.

42 'Pour les vétérans,' *La Presse*, 2 November 1946, 30.

43 *La Patrie*:'Les vétérans ne tolèrent pas qu'on leur coupe l'eau,' 25 October 1946, 6; '"Squatters" vs "Barbottes,"' 30 October 1946, 3. The Snowdon section was subsequently suspended by the Canadian Legion for supporting the squatters. 'Menées communistes à la Légion canadienne,' *Le Devoir* (Montreal), 4 November 1946, 10.

44 'L'ordre et la justice. Le cas des "squatters,"' *La Patrie*, 25 October 1946, 8.

45 AUQAM, Fonds Henri-Gagnon, 54P, File: 54P 3g/3, News clipping, 'L'invasion des "squatters,"' *Le Canada* (n.d.).

46 In mid-December, an attempt was made by Gagnon et al. to take over a fourth house, on Côte Ste-Catherine, but they were prevented from doing so by the municipal police. 'Cette maison n'appartient pas à la ville,' *Le Devoir*, 12 December 1946, 3.

47 'Les ennuis de l'éviction,' *La Patrie*, 16 July 1947, 2; 'Avis servis à quatre familles de squatters,' *La Presse*, 30 July 1947, 3; 'Les squatters n'ont pas reçu leur avis,' *La Patrie*, 31 July 1947, 7.

48 'Manifestation de squatters interrompue par la police,' *La Patrie*, 18 July 1947, 5.

49 'Les squatters délogés sous la pluie,' *La Presse*, 16 July 1947, 1, 19; '7 familles seront logées à Longueuil,' *La Patrie*, 19 July 1947, 19; '35 personnes vivent sous la tente et la pluie, à l'île Sainte-Hélène,' *La Patrie*, 22 July 1947, 5.

50 *La Presse*, 16 July 1947, 3; *Montreal Herald*, 16 July 1947, 3. For other photographs of squatters' children, see, e.g., *La Presse*, 5 November 1946, 3; *La Patrie*, 5 November 1946, 3; *Montreal Herald*, 5 November 1946, 24; and the news clipping headlined 'Ils ont enfin un toît [*sic*] sur leurs têtes,' located in AUQAM, Fonds Henri-Gagnon, 54P, File: 54P 3g/3 [unidentified source, n.d.].

51 See, e.g., 'Les "squatters" logent à l'hôtel,' *La Patrie*, 15 November 1946, 3; 'Red-Led Vets Invade N.D.G. Seize Decarie Blvd. House,' *Montreal Herald*, 5 November 1946, 1.

52 'Les vétérans ne tolèrent pas qu'on leur coupe l'eau,' *La Patrie*, 25 October 1946, 3, 6.

53 'Les "squatters" veulent "défendre" leur abri,' *La Patrie*, 29 October 1946, 3.

54 'Un nouveau "squatter" à 2054 rue McGill College,' *La Patrie*, 8 November 1946, 6.

55 AUQAM, Fonds Henri-Gagnon, 54P, File: 54P 3g/2, Brochure, 'Éviction! Qui sera le suivant?' [n.d.].

56 Letter to the editor from 'P.L.,' *Montreal Herald*, 21 July 1947, 10.

57 Jill Wade, '"A Palace for the Public."' A Gallup poll taken in late 1946 reported that a majority of Canadians and Quebecers thought homeless veterans' illegal occupation of government buildings to be justified. 'Une illégalité reçue comme moindre mal,' *La Presse*, 2 November 1946, 30.

58 *La Presse*, 5 November 1946: 'Des vétérans devenus squatters malgré eux,' 3, 26; 'La 3e invasion des squatters,' 3, 26. See also 'Déménagement des "squatters,"' *La Patrie*, 7 November 1946, 7.

59 'La situation tendue sur le front des "squatters,"' *La Patrie*, 4 November 1946, 3.

60 AUQAM, Fonds Henri-Gagnon, 54P, File: 54P 3g/3, Ligue des vétérans sans logis, 1946–48, News clipping: 'L'accusation de communisme inquiète les "squatters"' [unidentified source, n.d.].

61 AUQAM, Fonds Henri-Gagnon, 54P, File: 54P 3g/3. News clipping, 'L'invasion des "squatters,"' *Le Canada* [n.d.].

62 'Le contrôle des loyers resterait,' *La Presse*, 3 November 1949, 25; 'Les locataires vont préparer leur lutte,' 28 November 1949, 35.

63 '"L'autorité défaillante est le premier coupable,"' *Le Devoir*, 5 November 1946, 9.

64 'Les squatters délogés sous la pluie,' *La Presse*, 16 July 1947, 19. There was little mention of the provincial arm of the state in the coverage of the squatters' campaign, although Premier Duplessis did go on record as calling the Montreal Squatters' Movement a 'campagne communiste dirigée par Moscou.' 'Une campagne communiste dirigée par Moscou,' *Le Devoir*, 31 October 1946, 8.

65 AUQAM, Fonds Henri-Gagnon, 54P, File 54P, 3g/2, Ligue des vétérans sans logis, 1946–48, Telegraph sent 18 July 1947 from Henri Gagnon, President, Quebec Veterans' League, to J.S. Hodgson, C.D. Howe, and Ian Mackenzie.

66 'Nous logerons les vétérans,' *La Patrie*, 14 July 1947, 21.

67 The Ligue des Vétérans sans logis, for instance, blamed 'les autorités municipales,' among others, for the lack of decent family housing in Montreal. AUQAM, Fonds Henri-Gagnon, 54P, File 54P 3g/2, Brochure: 'Éviction! Qui sera le suivant?' See also 'La police et les "squatters,"' *Le Devoir*, 29 October 1946, 3.

68 'Les squatters délogés sous la pluie,' *La Presse*, 16 July 1947, 19.

69 'Une plainte de conspiration réclamée contre H. Gagnon D. Durocher et Nap. Auger,' *La Presse*, 6 November 1946, 3, 21; 'Henri Gagnon écroué et accusé de conspiration, *La Presse*, 8 November 1946, 3, 30; 'Les "squatters" devront subir leur enquête lundi,' *La Patrie*, 4 November 1946, 3.

70 'Trois familles de sans-logis aux cellules,' *Le Devoir*, 14 November 1946, 3.

71 'Les squatters en cour menottes aux mains,' *La Patrie*, 14 November 1946, 9.

72 'Les squatters d'Ottawa condamnés à l'amende,' *La Patrie*, 11 December 1946, 6.

73 Choko, 'Le mouvement des squatters,' 35.

74 'Le Viger abritera des familles de vétérans,' *La Presse*, 3 October 1946, 8; 'Déménagement des "squatters,"' *La Patrie*, 7 November 1946, 7.

75 'Island Tent Colony to Close This Week,' *Montreal Herald*, 21 July 1947, 5.

76 For the union's statistics on the percentage of teachers who struck, see Archives de l'Université Laval (AUL), Fonds de l'Alliance des Professeurs de Montréal (APM), 250, File 250/5/3, Livre VI, Assemblées générales tenues par l'APCM du 12 janvier 1949 au 7 novembre 1951, Assemblée générale de l'APCM tenue le 18 février 1949.

77 On Catholic lay teachers' earlier attempts at organizing, see Geoffrey Ewen, 'Montreal Catholic School Teachers, International Unions, and Archbishop Bruchési: The Association de bien-être des instituteurs et institutrices de Montréal, 1919–20,' *Historical Studies in Education / Revue d'histoire de l'éducation* 12, 1–2 (2000): 54–72.

78 'Déclaration du ministère du travail,' *Le Devoir* (Montreal), 18 January 1949, 3.

79 'Le statut des instituteurs,' *La Presse*, 24 January 1949, 1; 'Striking Teachers' Return Urged by Local Parents' Associations,' *Montreal Gazette*, 24 January 1949, 3; Robert Gagnon, *Histoire de la Commission des écoles catholiques de Montréal* (Montreal: Boréal, 1996), 223.

80 James D. Thwaites and Nadine L.C. Perron-Thwaites, 'Une petite grève d'envergure: L'Alliance contre la C.É.C.M. en 1949 et ses suites,' *McGill Law Journal* 40 (1995): 780–801. See also the brief summaries of the strike in Jacques Rouillard, *Histoire du syndicalisme québécois* (Montreal: Boréal, 1989), 275–278; Gagnon, *Histoire de la Commission*, 219–24.

81 This was by no means a new situation: on the post–First World War period, see Ewen, 'Montreal Catholic School Teachers,' 57.

82 AUL, APM (250), File 250/15/2, Handwritten list on letterhead of La Fédération des Instituteurs et des Institutrices catholiques des Cités et Villes de la Province de Québec: 'Ceux qui ont offert aide et secours financier à L'Alliance.'

83 *Le Devoir*: '1,500 instituteurs en grève ce matin,' 17 January 1949, 1, 3; 'Me Simard empêche le règlement de la grève,' 19 January 1949, 1; 'Les

instituteurs retournent en classe,' 24 January 1949, 1, 3. *Montreal Gazette*: 'Catholic Schools Strike Is On; English Teachers Join French,' 17 January 1949, 3; 'Striking Teachers' Return Urged by Local Parents' Associations,' 24 January 1949, 3.

84 Caption to photographs, *Le Front Ouvrier*, 22 January 1949, 10; *Le Devoir*: '1,500 instituteurs en grève ce matin,' 17 January 1949, 1, 3; 'Ce que femme veut ...' 22 January 1949, 9.

85 'Les parents et la grève des professeurs,' *Le Front Ouvrier*, 22 January 1949, 10.

86 'Ce que femme veut ... ,' *Le Devoir*, 22 January 1949, 9. On the high proportion of lay teachers in the public system who were women, see Nadia Fahmy-Eid, 'Un univers articulé à l'ensemble du système scolaire québécois,' 36, 43–44, in *Les couventines: L'éducation des filles au Québec dans les congrégations religieuses enseignantes 1840–1960*, ed. Micheline Dumont and Nadia Fahmy-Eid (Montreal: Boréal Express, 1986); Micheline Dumont, 'Les congrégations religieuses enseignantes,' in *Les couventines*, 263–4; Gagnon, *Histoire de la Commission*, 225.

87 Caption to photographs, *Le Front Ouvrier*, 22 January 1949, 10.

88 Archives de la Commission des écoles catholiques de Montréal (ACECM), Dossier: Alliance – Convention collective – Généralités – Grève – 1949 – III. Sœur Marie-Anne-Françoise to Eugène Doucet, 9 July 1949.

89 On the importance of clerics to the teaching staff of both the private and public systems in Quebec, see Micheline Dumont, *Girls' Schooling in Quebec, 1639–1960* (Ottawa: Canadian Historical Association, 1990); Dumont and Fahmy-Eid, *Les couventines*.

90 ACECM, Dossier: Alliance – Convention collective – Généralités – Grève – 1949 – I, Sœur Sainte-Anne-des-Miracles to Eugène Simard, 1 February 1949.

91 ACECM, Dossier: Alliance – Convention collective – Généralités – Grève – 1949 – I, La Commission des écoles catholiques de Montréal, Service des études, District numéro 4, Énumération des actes posés. The teaching brothers of l'École Christophe-Colomb likewise claimed not to have noticed whether a particular lay teacher was picketing. ACECM, Dossier: Alliance – Convention collective – Généralités – Grève – 1949 – I, La Commission des écoles catholiques de Montréal, Service des études, District numéro 5, Énumération des actes posés. See also AUM, ACC, P16/N6, 1, 2, News clipping, 'Blocs-Notes,' *Le Devoir*, 22 January 1949.

92 'Teachers' Strike Ended, Classes Resume Today; Walk-Out Now Week Old,' *Montreal Gazette*, 24 January 1949, 1.

93 AUL, APM (250), File 250/5/3, Livre VI, Assemblées générales tenues par l'A.P.C.M. du 12 janvier 1949 au 7 novembre 1951. Dimanche le 23 janvier 1949; 'L'aide des parents est bien reçue,' *La Presse*, 24 January 1949, 1; 'Les

parents et la grève des professeurs,' *Le Front Ouvrier*, 22 January 1949, 10; 'Striking Teachers' Return Urged by Local Parents' Associations,' *Montreal Gazette*, 24 January 1949, 3; 'Les instituteurs retournent en classe,' *Le Devoir*, 24 January 1949: 1, 3; 'Les instituteurs ont entendu l'appel des parents,' *Le Devoir*, 24 January 1949, 1.

94 AUL, APM (250), File 250/5/3, Livre VI, Assemblées générales tenues par l'A.P.C.M. du 12 janvier 1949 au 7 novembre 1951. Cessation de travail, lundi le 17 janvier 1944. See also *Le Front Ouvrier*, 29 January 1949, 20; '1,500 instituteurs en grève ce matin,' *Le Devoir*, 17 January 1949, 1, 3. Note the photograph of an empty classroom published in *Le Front Ouvrier*, 22 January 1949, 10.

95 AUL, APM (250), File 250/5/3, Livre VI, Assemblées générales tenues par l'A.P.C.M. du 12 janvier 1949 au 7 novembre 1951. Cessation de travail, lundi le 17 janvier 1944.

96 '1,500 instituteurs en grève ce matin,' *Le Devoir*, 17 January 1949, 1.

97 ACECM, Dossier: Alliance – Convention collective – Généralités – Grève – 1949 – I, La Commission des écoles catholiques de Montréal, Service des études, District numéro 4, Énumération des actes posés; La Commission des écoles catholiques de Montréal, Service des études, District numéro 1, Énumération des actes posés; Eugène Simard to Joseph Dansereau, 19 January 1949; Joseph Dansereau to Messieurs les Commissaires, 17 February 1949.

98 AUL, APM (250), File 250/15/2, 'Tous ceux qui nous ont accordé généreusement leur appui pendant la cessation du travail du 17 janvier 1949'; Telegram from Les élèves de St-Louis de Gonzague to APCM, 17 January 1949; Telegram from Marcel Patenaude to Mlle Lafrance, Institutrice, École St-Louis de Gonzague, 21 January 1949; Telegram from Bernard Binette to Marcel Pelletier, 21 January 1949.

99 AUL, APM (250), File 250/15/2, Henri Véronneau to APCM, 17 January 1949; Roland Barrette to Léo Guindon, 17 January 1949. See also Mr and Mde Rodolphe Nadeau to Mlle Marie Lessard and Mlle Marguerite Dubois, 18 January 1949.

100 AUL, APM (250), File 250/15/2, Letter from Joseph P. Moncel to Révérend Frère Amédée-Stanislas, Directeur, École Saint-Charles-Garnier, 19 January 1949. For a similar letter from a parent to a school principal (also a teaching brother), see Adrien Séguin, Rep. Congrès canadien du travail; Trésorier Conseil du Travail de Montréal; Directeur FCEM, to Monsieur le Directeur, École St-Charles, rue Island, Pte St-Charles, Montréal, 24 January 1949.

101 AUL, APM (250), Dossier 250/15/2, André Plante and L. Perreault to APCM, 14 January 1949. For similar letters see, in the same file: Telegram

from Local 102, Ouvriers unis des textiles d'Amérique, to APCM, 17 January 1949; Telegram from United Brewery Workers, CIO-CCL, to APCM, 17 January 1949; Telegram from J. Eucher Corbeil, président-général, Fraternité canadienne des employés de chemin de fer et autres transports, to APCM, 18 January 1949.

102 ACECM, Dossier: Alliance – Convention collective – Généralités – Grève – 1949 – I, M and Mme M. Deniger to CECM, 15 January 1949.

103 Ewen, 'Montreal Catholic School Teachers,' 57; Gagnon, *Histoire de la Commission*, 13–14.

104 ACECM, Dossier: Alliance – Convention collective – Généralités – Grève – 1949 – I, La Commission des écoles catholiques de Montréal, Service des études, District numéro 6, Cas des écoles où le principal et plusieurs professeurs étaient présents mais les élèves absents.

105 I have found six letters in school board files opposing the strike. At least two of these came from parents; the authors of the other four letters did not indicate whether they had children in the school system.

106 ACECM, Dossier: Alliance – Convention collective – Généralités – Grève – 1949 – I, Albert Cesari Jessery to Eugène Simard, 18 January 1949. Emphases in the original.

107 ACECM, Dossier: Alliance – Convention collective – Généralités – Grève – 1949 – I, R. Messier to Eugène Simard, 17 January 1949.

108 '1,500 instituteurs en grève ce matin,' *Le Devoir*, 17 January 1949, 3; 'Duplessis Scores Teachers' Strike,' *Montreal Gazette*, 17 January 1949, 3.

109 AUL, APM (250), Dossier 250/13/4/3, 'Radio, conférences. Mardi, 18 janvier 1949, Programme: CCF. Poste: CHLP.'

110 ACECM, Boîte 216, École St-Stanislas, Département de l'Instruction Publique, Journal de l'École pour l'année scolaire 1948–1949. Many younger brothers and sisters of teachers also stayed home from school. ACECM, Dossier: Alliance – Convention collective – Généralités – Grève – 1949 – I, Joseph Dansereau to Messieurs les Commissaires, 17 February 1949.

111 On the federal government sidestepping the thorny question of workers' rights to promote instead the innocuous rights of children, see Marshall, 'Reconstruction Politics,' 265–6.

112 On the policy of the Commission des écoles catholiques de Montréal (CECM) not to hire married women, see Gagnon, *Histoire de la Commission*, 225–6. The CECM appears to have suspended this policy for the duration of the 1949 strike. ACECM, Dossier: Alliance – Convention collective – Généralités – Grève – 1949 – I, Copie de résolution adoptée par la Commis-

sion des écoles catholiques de Montréal, Séance du 14 janvier 1949 suite de la session régulière du 13 janvier, 15ième.

113 '1,500 instituteurs en grève ce matin,' *Le Devoir*, 17 January 1949, 1, 3.

114 'Fin de la grève; retour en classe,' *La Presse*, 24 January 1949, 1; 'Les instituteurs ont entendu l'appel des parents,' *Le Devoir*, 24 January 1949, 1; AUM, Collection Gisèle Morin-Lortie, P 272, École des Parents du Québec, Coupures de presse, Vol. 2; 'Parents et instituteurs s'entendent. Le geste de l'École des Parents fait retourner les petits à l'école,' *La Presse*, 24 January 1949.

115 ACECM, Dossier: Alliance – Convention collective – Généralités – Grève – 1949 – I, Odile P. Panet-Raymond, Présidente, L'École des Parents du Québec, to Eugène Simard, Président, CECM, 21 January 1949; 'L'École des Parents,' *Le Devoir*, 24 January 1949, 1.

116 AUL, APM (250), File 250/17/2. *École des Parents, section Longueuil.* See also Denyse Baillargeon, '"We admire modern parents." The École des Parents du Québec and the Post-war Quebec Family, 1940–1959,' in Nancy Christie and Michael Gauvreau, eds., *Cultures of Citizenship in Post-war Canada, 1940–1955* (Montreal and Kingston: McGill-Queen's UP, 2003).

117 For instance, André Laurendeau, Gérard and Alexandrine Pelletier, Claude Ryan, and Simonne Monet-Chartrand all participated in the École's activities. Simonne Monet-Chartrand, *Ma vie comme rivière: Récit autobiographique*, vol. 2, *1939–1949* (Montreal: Éditions du remue-ménage, 1982), 251.

118 Ibid., 174, 327–28; AUM, ACC, P16, File: P16/O5/45, Programme des cours de l'École des Parents de Québec, 1949–50.

119 AUL, APM (250), File 250/17/2, *École des Parents du Québec;* AUM, ACC, P16, File: P16/O5/45, Programme des cours de l'École des Parents de Québec, 1949–50; Marie-Paule Malouin, *Le mouvement familial au Québec. Les débuts: 1937–1965* (Montreal: Boréal, 1998), 46. English-language CBC Radio also broadcast a show entitled *School for Parents* between 1954 and 1962: see Mona Gleason, *Normalizing the Ideal: Psychology, Schooling, and the Family in Postwar Canada* (Toronto: U Toronto P, 1999), 50.

120 AUM, Collection Gisèle Morin-Lortie, P 272, École des Parents du Québec, Coupures de presse, Vol. 2. 'Parents et instituteurs s'entendent. La geste de l'École des Parents fait retourner les petits à l'école,' *La Presse*, 24 January 1949. See also AUM, ACC, P16/O5, 45, École des Parents du Québec, News clipping, 'Clinique de l'École des Parents du Québec,' *Le Devoir*. Mona Gleason notes that psychologists in English Canada also argued 'that parents and teachers should forge a powerful alliance in the battle to ensure well-adjusted, democracy-loving children.' *Normalizing the Ideal*, 123.

121 'Striking Teachers' Return Urged by Local Parents' Associations,' *Montreal Gazette*, 24 January 1949, 3.

122 In a slightly different context, Dominique Marshall argues that the rights of families often superseded those of workers in the postwar period. Family allowances, for instance, were Ottawa's answer to unionized workers' demands for higher wages. *Aux origines sociales*, 144.

123 AUL, APM (250), Dossier 250/13/4/3, 'Causerie de M. Léo Guindon, président de L'Alliance des Professeurs catholiques de Montréal. Poste C.K.A.C., 7.30 heures p.m., Montréal, le 26 janvier 1949.'

124 Letter to the editor from Marguerite Roux, *Le Devoir*, 24 January 1949, 2.

125 *Le Devoir*: 'Et les parents?' 18 January 1949, 1; 'Les instituteurs ont entendu l'appel des parents,' 24 January 1949, 1. See also AUM, ACC, P16: File: P16/N6, 1, 2, News clipping, 'Bloc-Notes,' *Le Devoir*, 22 January 1949; File: P16/R57, News clipping, 'Pour un mouvement des familles,' *Le Devoir*, 22 November 1950.

126 AUL, APM (250), Dossier 250/13/4/3, Transcript of article by Gérard Filion, 'De rouge en bleu, de bleu en rouge,' *Le Devoir*, 23 November 1949. For similar arguments, see Adrien Bluteau, ptre, 'L'école bâtit la nation,' in *L'Enseignement secondaire au Canada*, 28, 5 (May 1949); AUM, ACC, P16/N6, 1, 2, News clipping, 'Le seul sens d'une collaboration entre l'école et la famille,' *Notre Temps*, 19 November 1949.

127 'Éducation et grève,' *Relations* 98 (February 1949): 30–31. This division of the school board commissioners had been established by Duplessis's provincial government in 1947. Previously, there had been nine commissioners: three appointed by the municipality; three by the provincial government; and three by the Archbishop's palace. Thwaites and Perron-Thwaites, 'Une petite grève,' 784.

128 Fahmy-Eid, 'Un univers articulé à l'ensemble du système scolaire québécois,' 41.

129 York University Archives (YUA), Maurice Duplessis Fonds, 1980–008/001, Reel 7. 'Schéma – Discours' [1944], p. 3. He did not, however, revoke the legislation once he returned to power in 1944.

130 Dominique Marshall also argues, 'By the 1940s, there was a widespread belief in education, and cases where parents opposed the fourteen-year-old leaving age were exceptional.' See 'The Language of Children's Rights, the Formation of the Welfare State, and the Democratic Experience of Poor Families in Quebec, 1940–55,' *Canadian Historical Review* 78, 3 (September 1997): 414.

131 AUM, Collection Gisèle Morin-Lortie, P 272, École des Parents du Québec, Coupures de presse, Volume 2. 'Droits des parents en éducation revendiqués,' *La Presse*, 25 February 1949.

132 Marshall, *Aux origines sociales*, chap. 5.

133 On the new rights of children, see 'Égalité de préférence à autorité,' *La Presse*, 26 March 1949, 28; Marshall, 'Reconstruction Politics'; Marshall, 'The Language of Children's Rights.'

134 YUA, Maurice Duplessis Fonds, 1980-008/001: Reel 1, 'Empiètements et centralisation du pouvoir fédéral'; Reel 3, Speech by Maurice Duplessis, no title, n.d., pp. 13–14 ('Raison et Ration'); Reel 7, 'Schéma – Discours' [1944?], 2–3.

135 'Le contrôle des prix réclamé par deux organisations ouvrières,' *Le Devoir*, 16 December 1948, 3; 'La lutte à l'inflation,' *La Presse*, 5 November 1947, 38; 'Campagne en faveur d'une baisse des prix,' *La Presse*, 22 November 1947, 62; 'Revendications de locataires,' *La Presse*, 26 March 1949, 28; 'Le contrôle des prix,' *Le Travail*, September 1945, 2; 'Commision [*sic*] Royale d'enquête sur la hausse continuelle des prix,' *Le Travail*, February 1948, 10.

136 *Le Front Ouvrier* called for an end to wartime restrictions in an article published 29 September 1945, 'Le rationnement de la viande,' 4. For its support for price controls, see 29 November 1947, 'Pompez, mes vieux,' 3.

Conclusion

1 Gwethalyn Graham, *Earth and High Heaven* (Philadelphia: J.B. Lippincott Company, 1944), 15.

2 Hugh MacLennan, *The Watch That Ends the Night* (New York: Scribner, 1959), 255.

3 William Weintraub, *City Unique: Montreal Days and Nights in the 1940s and '50s* (Toronto: McClelland & Stewart, 1996).

4 Natalie Zemon Davis, 'The Shapes of Social History,' *Storia della Storiografia* 17 (1990): 31.

5 Jean-Pierre Collin, *La Ligue ouvrière catholique canadienne, 1938–1954* (Montreal: Boréal, 1996); see also Louise Bienvenue, *Quand la jeunesse entre en scène: L'Action catholique avant la Révolution tranquille* (Montreal: Boréal, 2003).

6 Dominique Marshall, *Aux origines sociales de l'État-providence* (Montreal: Presses de l'Université de Montréal, 1998), especially 286–7.

7 Paul-André Linteau, 'Un débat historiographique: L'entrée du Québec dans la modernité et la signification de la Révolution tranquille,' in Yves Bélanger et al., eds., *La Révolution tranquille: 40 ans plus tard: un bilan* (Montreal: VLB Éditeur, 2000), 34. Nationalism and interventionist liberalism had, however, merged to some degree in the Bloc populaire canadien, the political party that had emerged out of the Second World War conscription crisis. See Paul-André Comeau, *Le Bloc populaire 1942–1948* (Montreal: Québec-Amérique, 1982).

Bibliography

Primary Sources

Archival Collections

Archives de la Commission des écoles catholiques de Montréal (ACECM)
  École St-Stanislas. Département de l'Instruction Publique. Boîte 216
  Alliance – Convention collective – Généralités – Grève – 1949. Dossiers
Archives nationales du Québec à Montréal (ANQM)
  Église Catholique, Diocèse de Montréal, Service de préparation au mariage.
    P116
  Fonds de la Fédération nationale Saint-Jean-Baptiste. P120
  Fonds de la Jeunesse Ouvrière Catholique. P104
  Fonds du Mouvement des Travailleurs Chrétiens. P257
  Fonds de la Société Saint-Vincent-de-Paul de Montréal. P61
Archives de l'Université Laval (AUL)
  Fonds de l'Alliance des Professeurs de Montréal. 250
Archives de l'Université de Montréal (AUM)
  Fonds de l'Action catholique canadienne. P16
  Fonds Gisèle Morin-Lortie. P272
  Fonds Édouard-Montpetit. Comité de Reconstruction, 1941–1943. P8/1
Archives de l'Université du Québec à Montréal (AUQAM)
  Fonds d'Archives du Conseil des Métiers et du Travail de
    Montréal. 103P
  Fonds d'Archives de la Fédération Provinciale du Travail du Québec. 84P
  Fonds Henri-Gagnon. 54P
McGill University Archives, Montreal (MUA)
  Montreal Council of Social Agencies. MG 2076

Montreal Parks and Playgrounds Association/Community Gardens League.
MG 2079
Notre Dame de Grâce Women's Club. MG 4023
National Archives of Canada, Ottawa (NA)
Canadian Association of Consumers. MG 28 I 200
Canadian Council on Social Development. MG 28 I 10
Thérèse Casgrain Papers. MG 32 C 25
Department of Finance. RG 19
Department of Labour. RG 27
Department of National Defence. RG 24
Department of National Health and Welfare. RG 29
Department of Veterans Affairs. RG 38
Dependents' Allowance Board. RG 36, Series 18
Jewish Family Services of the Baron de Hirsch
Institute. MG 28 V 86
Montreal Council of Women. MG 28 I 164
Montreal Soldiers Wives League. MG 28 I 311
Marion Creelman Savage Papers. MG 30 C 92
Society for the Protection of Women and Children
(Montreal). MG 28 I 129
Summerhill Homes. MG 28 I 388
Renée Vautelet Papers. MG 30 C 196
Wartime Prices and Trade Board, Consumer Branch. RG 64-A-24
York University Archives (YUA)
Maurice Duplessis Fonds 1980–008/001

Government Documents

Canada. Department of Labour. *The Labour Gazette.* Ottawa: Department of
Labour, 1945–1949.
Canada. Department of Trade and Commerce. Dominion Bureau of Statistics.
The Future Population of Canada. Bulletin no. F-4. Ottawa: 1946.
Canada. *Eighth Census of Canada.* Ottawa: Dominion Bureau of Statistics, 1941.
Canada. *Ninth Census of Canada.* Ottawa: Dominion Bureau of Statistics, 1951.
Canada. Parliament. House of Commons. *Debates.* 1939–42, 1944–5, 1949.
Canada. *Report of the Royal Commission on Prices.* Vol. 1. Ottawa: King's Printer,
1949.
Canada. Royal Commission on Prices. *Minutes of Proceedings and Evidence,* Nos.
38, 39, 41. Ottawa: King's Printer, 1948–49.
Canada. *Statutes of Canada.* Ottawa: King's Printer, 1944–49.

Charles, Enid. *The Changing Size of the Family in Canada.* Census Monograph No. 1. Ottawa: King's Printer, 1948.

Leacy, F.H., ed. *Historical Statistics of Canada.* 2nd ed. Ottawa: Statistics Canada in joint sponsorship with the Social Science Federation of Canada, 1983.

Quebec. Bureau of Statistics. *Annuaire Statistique.* Quebec: King's Printer, 1945–46, 1948, 1950.

Newspapers and Periodicals

La Bonne Parole (Montreal)
Canadian Jewish Chronicle (Montreal)
Canadian Unionist (Ottawa)
Le Devoir (Montreal)
L'Enseignement secondaire au Canada (Sainte-Foy)
Le Front Ouvrier (Montreal)
Globe and Mail (Toronto)
Maclean's
Le Monde Ouvrier (Montreal)
Montreal Gazette
Montreal Herald
Le Mouvement Ouvrier (Montreal)
La Patrie (Montreal)
La Presse (Montreal)
Relations (Montreal)
Toronto Daily Star
Le Travail (Montreal)

Other Printed Primary Sources

Birney, Earle. *Turvey: A Military Picaresque.* Toronto: McClelland & Stewart, 1949.

Callaghan, Morley. *The Loved and the Lost.* Toronto: Macmillan, 1977 [1951].

Canadian Youth Commission. *Youth, Marriage and the Family.* Toronto: Ryerson P, 1948.

Carrière, Gabrielle. *Comment gagner sa vie: Carrières féminines.* Montreal: Éditions Beauchemin, 1942.

Cassidy, Harry M. *Public Health and Welfare Reorganization.* Toronto: Ryerson P, 1945.

– *Social Security and Reconstruction in Canada.* Toronto: Ryerson P, 1943.

Dubé, Marcel. *Un simple soldat: Pièce en 5 actes et 15 tableaux.* Ottawa: Institut littéraire du Québec, 1958.

England, Robert. *Discharged: A Commentary on Civil Re-establishment of Veterans in Canada.* Toronto: Macmillan, 1943.

Gélinas, Gratien. *Tit-Coq: Pièce en trois actes.* Montreal: Beauchemin, 1950.

Graham, Gwethalyn. *Earth and High Heaven.* Philadelphia: J.B. Lippincott Company, 1944.

Hughes, Everett C. *French Canada in Transition.* Chicago: U of Chicago P, 1963 [1943].

Jamieson, Stuart M. 'French and English in the Institutional Structure of Montreal: A Study of the Social and Economic Division of Labour.' MA thesis, McGill University, 1938.

Lamontagne, Maurice, and J.-C. Falardeau. 'The Life Cycle of French-Canadian Urban Families.' *Canadian Journal of Economics and Political Science* 13, 2 (May 1947): 233–47.

MacLennan, Hugh. *Two Solitudes.* Toronto: Macmillan, 1945.

– *The Watch That Ends the Night.* New York: Scribner, 1959.

Marsh, Leonard. *Report on Social Security for Canada.* Toronto: U of Toronto P, 1975 [1943].

Miner, Horace. *St. Denis: A French-Canadian Parish.* Chicago: U of Chicago P, 1963 [1939].

Morin, Renée. 'Women after the War.' *Canadian Affairs* 2, 4 (1 March 1945).

Nadeau, Jean-Marie. *Horizons d'après-guerre. Essais de politique économique canadienne.* Montreal: Lucien Parizeau, 1944.

Richler, Mordecai. *The Apprenticeship of Duddy Kravitz.* Harmondsworth, UK: Penguin, 1959.

Roy, Gabrielle. *The Cashier.* Trans. Harry Binsse. Toronto: McClelland & Stewart, 1955.

– *The Tin Flute.* Trans. Hannah Josephson. Toronto: McClelland & Stewart, 1969 [1947].

Royce, Marion V. *The Effect of the War on the Life of Women: A Study.* Geneva: World's YWCA, 1945.

Scott, F.R. *The Eye of the Needle: Satires, Sorties, Sundries.* Montreal: Contact P, 1957.

Seeley, John R. et al. *Crestwood Heights.* Toronto: U of Toronto P, 1956.

Tit-Coq. Un film de Gratien Gélinas. Productions Gratien Gélinas, 1953.

Secondary Sources

Books

Adams, Mary Louise. *The Trouble with Normal: Postwar Youth and the Making of Heterosexuality.* Toronto: U of Toronto P, 1997.

Anctil, Pierre. *Tur Malka: Flâneries sur les cimes de l'histoire juive montréalaise.* Sillery, QC: Septentrion, 1997.

Arnup, Katherine. *Education for Motherhood: Advice for Mothers in Twentieth-Century Canada.* Toronto: U of Toronto P, 1994.

Auger, Geneviève, and Raymonde Lamothe. *De la poêle à frire à la ligne de feu: La vie quotidienne des Québécoises pendant la guerre '39–'45.* Montreal: Boréal Express, 1981.

Baillargeon, Denyse. *Ménagères au temps de la Crise.* Montreal: Éditions du remue-ménage, 1991.

Banting, Keith G. *The Welfare State and Canadian Federalism.* 2nd ed. Montreal and Kingston: McGill-Queen's UP, 1987.

Barry, Francine. *Le travail de la femme au Québec: L'évolution de 1940 à 1970.* Montreal: Presses de l'Université du Québec, 1977.

Behiels, Michael D. *Prelude to Quebec's Quiet Revolution: Liberalism versus Neo-Nationalism, 1945–1960.* Montreal and Kingston: McGill-Queen's UP, 1985.

Bélanger, Yves, Robert Comeau, and Céline Métivier, eds. *La Révolution tranquille: 40 ans plus tard: un bilan.* Montreal : VLB Éditeur, 2000.

Bentley, Amy. *Eating for Victory: Food Rationing and the Politics of Domesticity.* Urbana: U of Illinois P, 1998.

Bérubé, Allan. *Coming Out Under Fire: The History of Gay Men and Women in World War Two.* New York: Free P, 1990.

Bienvenue, Louise. *Quand la jeunesse entre en scène: L'Action catholique avant la Révolution tranquille.* Montreal: Boréal, 2003.

Bothwell, Robert, Ian Drummond, and John English. *Canada 1900–1945.* Toronto: U of Toronto P, 1987.

– *Canada since 1945: Power, Politics, and Provincialism.* Rev. ed. Toronto: U of Toronto P, 1989.

Bradbury, Bettina. *Working Families: Age, Gender, and Daily Survival in Industrializing Montreal.* Toronto: McClelland & Stewart, 1993.

– ed. *Canadian Family History: Selected Readings.* Toronto: Copp Clark Pitman, 1992.

Broadfoot, Barry. *The Veterans' Years: Coming Home from the War.* Vancouver: Douglas & McIntyre, 1985.

Brooke, Stephen, ed. *Reform and Reconstruction: Britain after the War, 1945–51.* Manchester: Manchester UP, 1995.

Bruce, Jean. *After the War.* Don Mills, ON: Fitzhenry & Whiteside, 1982.

Casgrain, Thérèse F. *A Woman in a Man's World.* Trans. Joyce Marshall. Toronto: McClelland & Stewart, 1972.

Chamberland, Line. *Mémoires lesbiennes: Le lesbianisme à Montréal entre 1950 et 1972.* Montreal: Éditions du Remue-ménage, 1996.

Chambers, Lori, and Edgar-André Montigny, eds. *Family Matters: Papers in Post-Confederation Canadian Family History.* Toronto: Canadian Scholars' P, 1998.

Charland, Jean-Pierre, and Mario Désautels. *Système technique et bonheur domestique: Rémunération, consommation et pauvreté au Québec, 1920–1960.* Quebec: Institut québécois de recherche sur la culture, 1992.

Childs, David. *Britain since 1945: A Political History.* 3rd ed. London: Routledge, 1992.

Choko, Marc H. *Canadian War Posters, 1914–1918, 1939–1945.* Laval, QC: Éditions du Méridien, 1994.

Christie, Nancy. *Engendering the State: Family, Work, and Welfare in Canada.* Toronto: U of Toronto P, 2000.

Christie, Nancy, and Michael Gauvreau, eds. *Cultures of Citizenship in Post-war Canada, 1940–1955.* Montreal and Kingston: McGill-Queen's UP, 2003.

Collard, Edgar Andrew, ed. *The McGill You Knew: An Anthology of Memories 1920–1960.* Don Mills, ON: Longman Canada, 1975.

Collectif Clio. *L'histoire des femmes au Québec depuis quatre siècles.* 2nd rev. ed. Montreal: Le Jour, 1992.

Collin, Jean-Pierre. *La Ligue ouvrière catholique canadienne, 1938–1954.* Montreal: Boréal, 1996.

Comacchio, Cynthia R. *Nations Are Built of Babies: Saving Ontario's Mothers and Children, 1900–1940.* Montreal and Kingston: McGill-Queen's UP, 1993.

Cook, Ramsay. *Canada, Quebec, and the Uses of Nationalism.* 2nd ed. Toronto: McClelland & Stewart, 1986.

Copp, Terry. *The Anatomy of Poverty: The Condition of the Working Class in Montreal, 1897–1929.* Toronto: McClelland & Stewart, 1974.

Copp, Terry, and Bill McAndrew. *Battle Exhaustion: Soldiers and Psychiatrists in the Canadian Army, 1939–1945.* Montreal and Kingston: McGill-Queen's UP, 1990.

Cott, Nancy F. *The Bonds of Womanhood: 'Woman's Sphere' in New England, 1780–1835.* New Haven: Yale UP, 1977.

Creighton, Donald. *The Forked Road: Canada, 1939–1957.* Toronto: McClelland & Stewart, 1976.

Dagenais, Michèle. *Des pouvoirs et des hommes: L'administration municipale de Montréal, 1900–1950.* Montreal and Kingston: McGill-Queen's UP and the Institute of Public Administration of Canada, 2000.

Damousi, Joy, and Marilyn Lake, eds. *Gender and War: Australians at War in the Twentieth Century.* Cambridge: Cambridge UP, 1995.

Davidoff, Leonore, and Catherine Hall. *Family Fortunes: Men and Women of the English Middle Class, 1780–1850.* London: Hutchinson, 1987.

De Grazia, Victoria, with Ellen Furlough, eds. *The Sex of Things: Gender and Consumption in Historical Perspective.* Berkeley: U of California, 1996.

Desjardins, Gaston. *L'amour en patience: La sexualité adolescente au Québec, 1940–1960.* Sainte-Foy, QC: Presses de l'Université du Québec, 1995.

Deutsch, Sarah. *Women and the City: Gender, Space and Power in Boston, 1870–1940.* New York: Oxford UP, 2000.

Dickinson, John A., and Brian Young. *A Short History of Quebec.* 2nd ed. Toronto: Copp Clark Pitman, 1993.

Donaghy, Greg, ed. *Uncertain Horizons: Canadians and Their World in 1945.* Ottawa: Canadian Committee for the History of the Second World War, 1997.

Dumont, Micheline. *Girls' Schooling in Quebec, 1639–1960.* Ottawa: Canadian Historical Association, 1990.

Dumont, Micheline, and Nadia Fahmy-Eid. *Les Couventines: L'éducation des filles au Québec dans les congrégations religieuses enseignantes 1840–1960.* Montreal: Boréal Express, 1986.

Erenberg, Lewis A., and Susan E. Hirsch, eds. *The War in American Culture: Society and Consciousness during World War II.* Chicago: U of Chicago P, 1996.

Fahmy-Eid, Nadia, and Micheline Dumont. *Maîtresses de maison, maîtresses d'école: Femmes, familles et éducation dans l'histoire du Québec.* Montreal: Boréal Express, 1983.

Fee, Margery, and Janice McAlpine. *Guide to Canadian English Usage.* Toronto: Oxford UP, 1997.

Ferretti, Lucia. *Brève histoire de l'Église catholique au Québec.* Montreal: Boréal, 1999.

Foucault, Michel. *Discipline and Punish: The Birth of the Prison.* Trans. Alan Sheridan. New York: Vintage Books, 1977.

Frank, Dana. *Purchasing Power: Consumer Organizing, Gender, and the Seattle Labor Movement, 1919–1929.* Cambridge: Cambridge UP, 1994.

Friedan, Betty. *The Feminine Mystique.* New York: W.W. Norton & Co., 1963.

Frye, Northrop. *The Secular Scripture: A Study of the Structure of Romance.* Cambridge, MA: Harvard UP, 1976.

Gagnon, Robert. *Histoire de la Commission des écoles catholiques de Montréal.* Montreal: Boréal, 1996.

Garigue, Philippe. *La vie familiale des canadiens français.* Montreal: Presses de l'Université de Montréal, 1970 [1962].

Gauthier, Hervé. *Évolution démographique du Québec.* Quebec: Office de planification et de développement du Québec, 1977.

Gélinas, Gratien, and Victor-Lévy Beaulieu. *Gratien, Tit-Coq, Fridolin, Bousille et les autres. Entretien.* Montreal: SRC et Stanké, 1993.

Gillis, John R., ed. *Commemorations: The Politics of National Identity.* Princeton, NJ: Princeton UP, 1994.

Gillis, John R. *For Better, For Worse: British Marriages, 1600 to the Present.* New York: Oxford UP, 1985.

Girard, Denise. *Mariage et classes sociales: Les Montréalais francophones entre les deux Guerres.* Sainte-Foy, QC: Presses de l'Université Laval, 2000.

Gleason, Mona. *Normalizing the Ideal: Psychology, Schooling, and the Family in Postwar Canada.* Toronto: U of Toronto P, 1999.

Gledhill, Christine, and Gillian Swanson, eds. *Nationalising Femininity: Culture, Sexuality and British Cinema in the Second World War.* Manchester: Manchester UP, 1996.

Gordon, Alan. *Making Public Pasts: The Contested Terrain of Montréal's Public Memories, 1891–1930.* Montreal and Kingston: McGill-Queen's UP, 2001.

Gossage, Carolyn. *Greatcoats and Glamour Boots: Canadian Women at War, 1939–1945.* Toronto: Dundurn P, 1991.

Graebner, William S. *The Age of Doubt: American Thought and Culture in the 1940s.* Boston: Twayne Publishers, 1991.

Granatstein, J.L. *The Ottawa Men: The Civil Service Mandarins, 1935–1957.* Toronto: Oxford UP, 1982.

Grayson, L.M., and Michael Bliss, eds. *The Wretched of Canada: Letters to R.B. Bennett, 1930–1935.* Toronto: U of Toronto P, 1971.

Groulx, Lionel-Henri. *Le travail social. Analyse et évolution: Débats et enjeux.* Laval, QC: Éditions agence d'Arc, 1993.

Guest, Dennis. *The Emergence of Social Security in Canada.* 3rd ed. Vancouver: UBC P, 1997.

Habermas, Jürgen. *The Structural Transformation of the Public Sphere: An Inquiry into a Category of Bourgeois Society.* Trans. Thomas Burger with the assistance of Frederick Lawrence. Cambridge, MA: MIT Press, 1989 [original German publication 1962].

Hamelin, Jean. *Histoire du catholicisme québécois. Le XXe siècle.* Vol. 2. *De 1940 à nos jours.* Dir. Nive Voisine. Montreal: Boréal Express, 1984.

Hareven, Tamara K. *Family Time and Industrial Time: The Relationship between the Family and Work in a New England Industrial Community.* Cambridge: Cambridge UP, 1982.

Hartley, Jenny. *Millions Like Us: British Women's Fiction of the Second World War.* London: Virago, 1997.

Hartmann, Susan M. *The Home Front and Beyond: American Women in the 1940s.* Boston: Twayne Publishers, 1982.

Heick, W.H. *A Propensity to Protect: Butter, Margarine and the Rise of Urban Culture in Canada.* Waterloo: Wilfrid Laurier UP, 1991.

Heron, Craig, ed. *The Workers' Revolt in Canada, 1917–1925.* Toronto: U of Toronto P, 1998.

Heron, Liz, ed. *Truth, Dare, or Promise: Girls Growing Up in the Fifties.* London: Virago, 1985.

Hibbert, Joyce, ed. *The War Brides.* Toronto: Peter Martin, 1978.

Higonnet, Margaret Randolph, et al., eds. *Behind the Lines: Gender and the Two World Wars.* New Haven: Yale UP, 1987.

Hiller, Harry H. *Society and Change: S.D. Clark and the Development of Canadian Sociology*. Toronto: U of Toronto P, 1982.

Iacovetta, Franca. *Such Hardworking People: Italian Immigrants in Postwar Toronto*. Montreal and Kingston: McGill-Queen's UP, 1992.

Iacovetta, Franca, and Wendy Mitchinson, eds. *On the Case: Explorations in Social History*. Toronto: U of Toronto P, 1998.

Iacovetta, Franca, and Mariana Valverde, eds. *Gender Conflicts: New Essays in Women's History*. Toronto: U of Toronto P, 1992.

Jackson, Kenneth T. *Crabgrass Frontier: The Suburbanization of the United States*. New York: Oxford UP, 1985.

Jeffords, Susan. *The Remasculinization of America: Gender and the Vietnam War*. Bloomington: Indiana UP, 1989.

Kealey, Linda. *Enlisting Women for the Cause: Women, Labour, and the Left in Canada, 1890–1920*. Toronto: U of Toronto P, 1998.

Kerber, Linda K. *No Constitutional Right to Be Ladies: Women and the Obligations of Citizenship*. New York: Hill and Wang, 1998.

Kerr, Donald, and Deryck W. Holdsworth, eds. *Historical Atlas of Canada*. Vol. 3: *Addressing the Twentieth Century, 1891–1961*. Toronto: U of Toronto P, 1990.

Kessler-Harris, Alice. *In Pursuit of Equity: Women, Men and the Quest for Economic Citizenship in Twentieth-Century America*. New York: Oxford UP, 2001.

– *A Woman's Wage: Historical Meanings and Social Consequences*. Lexington: UP of Kentucky, 1990.

Korinek, Valerie J. *Roughing it in the Suburbs: Reading* Chatelaine *Magazine in the Fifties and Sixties*. Toronto: U of Toronto P, 2000.

Koven, Seth, and Sonya Michel, eds. *Mothers of a New World: Maternalist Politics and the Origins of Welfare States*. New York: Routledge, 1993.

Kuffert, L.B. *A Great Duty: Canadian Responses to Modern Life and Mass Culture, 1939–1967*. Montreal and Kingston: McGill-Queen's UP, 2003.

LaMarsh, Judy. *Memoirs of a Bird in a Gilded Cage*. Toronto: McClelland & Stewart, 1968.

Landes, Joan B., ed. *Feminism, the Public and the Private*. Oxford: Oxford UP, 1998.

Landes, Joan B. *Women and the Public Sphere in the Age of the French Revolution*. Ithaca, NY: Cornell UP, 1988.

Laurin, Nicole, et al. *À la recherche d'un monde oublié: Les communautés religieuses de femmes au Québec de 1900 à 1970*. Montreal: Le Jour, 1991.

Lebsock, Suzanne. *The Free Women of Petersburg: Status and Culture in a Southern Town, 1784–1860*. New York: Norton, 1984.

Lévesque, Andrée. *Making and Breaking the Rules: Women in Quebec, 1919–1939*. Trans. Yvonne M. Klein. Toronto: McClelland & Stewart, 1994.

– *Résistance et transgression: Études en histoire des femmes au Québec*. Montreal: Éditions du remue-ménage, 1995.
– *Virage à gauche interdit: Les communistes, les socialistes et leurs ennemis au Québec 1929–1939*. Montreal: Boréal Express, 1984.
Light, Beth, and Ruth Roach Pierson, eds. *No Easy Road: Women in Canada 1920s to 1960s*. Toronto: New Hogtown Press, 1990.
Linteau, Paul-André. *Brève histoire de Montréal*. Montreal: Boréal, 1992.
– *Histoire de Montréal depuis la Confédération*. Montreal: Boréal, 1992.
Linteau, Paul-André, René Durocher, and Jean-Claude Robert. *Histoire du Québec contemporain*. Vol. 1. *De la Confédération à la crise (1867–1929)*. Montreal: Boréal Compact, 1989.
Linteau, Paul-André, René Durocher, Jean-Claude Robert, and François Ricard. *Histoire du Québec contemporain*. Vol. 2. *Le Québec depuis 1930*. Rev. ed. Montreal: Boréal Compact, 1989.
Little, Margaret. *No Car, No Radio, No Liquor Permit: The Moral Regulation of Single Mothers in Ontario, 1920–1997*. Toronto: Oxford UP, 1998.
McKay, Ian. *The Quest of the Folk: Antimodernism and Cultural Selection in Twentieth-Century Nova Scotia*. Montreal and Kingston: McGill-Queen's UP, 1994.
McLaren, Angus, and Arlene Tigar McLaren. *The Bedroom and the State: The Changing Practices and Politics of Contraception and Abortion in Canada, 1880–1980*. Toronto: McClelland & Stewart, 1986.
Malouin, Marie-Paule. *Le mouvement familial au Québec. Les débuts: 1937–1965*. Montreal: Boréal, 1998.
– ed. *L'univers des enfants en difficulté au Québec entre 1940 et 1960*. Montreal: Bellarmin, 1996.
Marshall, Dominique. *Aux origines sociales de l'État-providence: Familles québécoises, obligation scolaire et allocations familiales 1940–1955*. Montreal: Presses de l'Université de Montréal, 1998.
Marshall, T.H. *Class, Citizenship, and Social Development*. New York: Anchor Books, 1965.
May, Elaine Tyler. *Homeward Bound: American Families in the Cold War Era*. New York: Basic Books, 1988.
Meyerowitz, Joanne, ed. *Not June Cleaver: Women and Gender in Postwar America, 1945–1960*. Philadelphia: Temple UP, 1994.
Minns, Raynes. *Bombers and Mash: The Domestic Front, 1939–45*. London: Virago, 1980.
Miron, John R. *Housing in Postwar Canada: Demographic Change, Household Formation, and Housing Demand*. Montreal and Kingston: McGill-Queen's UP, 1988.
Monet-Chartrand, Simonne. *Ma vie comme rivière: récit autobiographique 1939–1949*. Vol. 2. Montreal: Éditions du remue-ménage, 1982.

Morgan, Cecilia. *Public Men and Virtuous Women: The Gendered Languages of Religion and Politics in Upper Canada, 1791–1850*. Toronto: U of Toronto P, 1996.

Morton, Desmond. *A Military History of Canada: From Champlain to the Gulf War*. 3rd ed. Toronto: McClelland & Stewart, 1992.

– *1945: When Canada Won the War*. Ottawa: Canadian Historical Association, 1995.

– *Working People: An Illustrated History of the Canadian Labour Movement*. 3rd ed. Toronto: Summerhill P, 1990.

Morton, Desmond, and J.L. Granatstein. *Victory 1945: Canadians from War to Peace*. Toronto: HarperCollins, 1995.

Morton, Desmond, and Glenn Wright. *Winning the Second Battle: Canadian Veterans and the Return to Civilian Life, 1915–1930*. Toronto: U of Toronto P, 1987.

Moscovitch, Allan, and Jim Albert, eds. *The 'Benevolent' State: The Growth of Welfare in Canada*. Toronto: Garamond, 1987.

Murray, Sylvie. *The Progressive Housewife: Community Activism in Suburban Queens, 1945–1965*. Philadelphia: U of Pennsylvania P, 2003.

Neary, Peter, and J.L. Granatstein, eds. *The Veterans Charter and Post–World War II Canada*. Montreal and Kingston: McGill-Queen's UP, 1998.

Neatby, Nicole. *Carabins ou activistes? L'idéalisme et la radicalisation de la pensée étudiante à l'Université de Montréal au temps du Duplessisme*. Montreal and Kingston: McGill-Queen's UP, 1999.

O'Neill, William L. *American High: The Years of Confidence, 1945–1960*. New York: Free P, 1986.

Owram, Doug. *Born at the Right Time: A History of the Baby Boom Generation*. Toronto: U of Toronto P, 1996.

– *The Government Generation: Canadian Intellectuals and the State, 1900–1945*. Toronto: U of Toronto P, 1986.

Palmer, Bryan D. *Descent into Discourse: The Reification of Language and the Writing of Social History*. Philadelphia: Temple UP, 1990.

– *Working-Class Experience: Rethinking the History of Canadian Labour, 1800–1991*. 2nd ed. Toronto: McClelland & Stewart, 1991.

Parr, Joy. *Domestic Goods: The Material, the Moral, and the Economic in the Postwar Years*. Toronto: U of Toronto P, 1999.

– *The Gender of Breadwinners: Women, Men, and Change in Two Industrial Towns, 1880–1950*. Toronto: U of Toronto P, 1990.

– ed. *A Diversity of Women: Ontario, 1945–1980*. Toronto: U of Toronto P, 1995.

Peate, Mary. *Girl in a Sloppy Joe Sweater: Life on the Canadian Home Front during World War Two*. Montreal: Optimum Publishing International, 1988.

Pedersen, Susan. *Family, Dependence, and the Origins of the Welfare State: Britain and France, 1914–1945*. Cambridge: Cambridge UP, 1993.

Pelletier, Gérard. *Years of Impatience 1950–1960*. Trans. Alan Brown. Toronto: Methuen, 1984 [1983].

Piché, Lucie. *Femmes et changement social au Québec: L'apport de la Jeunesse ouvrière catholique féminine, 1931–1966*. Quebec: Presses de l'Université Laval, 2003.

Pierson, Ruth Roach. *'They're Still Women After All': The Second World War and Canadian Womanhood*. Toronto: McClelland & Stewart, 1986.

Prentice, Alison, Paula Bourne, Gail Cuthbert Brandt, Beth Light, Wendy Mitchinson, and Naomi Black. *Canadian Women: A History*. Toronto: Harcourt Brace Jovanovich, 1988.

Ramirez, Bruno. *Les premiers Italiens de Montréal: L'origine de la Petite Italie du Québec*. Montreal: Boréal Express, 1984.

Ricard, François. *The Lyric Generation: The Life and Times of the Baby Boomers*. Trans. Donald Winkler. Toronto: Stoddart, 1994.

Richard, Béatrice. *La mémoire de Dieppe: Radioscopie d'un mythe*. Montreal: VLB Éditeur, 2002.

Riley, Denise. *'Am I That Name?' Feminism and the Category of 'Women' in History*. Minneapolis: U of Minnesota P, 1988.

Robert, Jean-Claude. *Atlas historique de Montréal*. Montreal: Art Global & Libre Expression, 1994.

Robinson, Daniel J. *The Measure of Democracy: Polling, Market Research, and Public Life, 1930–1945*. Toronto: U of Toronto P, 1999.

Rouillard, Jacques. *Histoire de la CSN (1921–1981)*. Montreal: Confédération des syndicats nationaux et Éditions du Boréal Express, 1981.

– *Histoire du syndicalisme québécois*. Montreal: Boréal, 1989.

Roy, Fernande. *Progrès, harmonie, liberté: Le libéralisme des milieux d'affaires francophones à Montréal au tournant du siècle*. Montreal: Boréal, 1988.

Rumilly, Robert. *Histoire de Montréal*. Vol. 4. Montreal: Fides, 1974.

– *Histoire de Montréal*. Vol. 5. Montreal: Fides, 1974.

Ryan, Mary P. *Women in Public: Between Banners and Ballots, 1825–1880*. Baltimore: Johns Hopkins UP, 1990.

Rybczynski, Witold. *A Clearing in the Distance: Frederick Law Olmsted and North America in the Nineteenth Century*. Toronto: HarperFlamingo, 1999.

Sanders, Wilfrid. *Jack et Jacques: L'opinion publique au Canada pendant la Deuxième Guerre mondiale*. Montreal: Comeau & Nadeau, Éditeurs, 1996.

Sangster, Joan. *Dreams of Equality: Women on the Canadian Left, 1920–1950*. Toronto: McClelland & Stewart, 1989.

– *Earning Respect: The Lives of Working Women in Small-Town Ontario, 1920–1960*. Toronto: U of Toronto P, 1995.

Schull, Joseph. *The Great Scot: A Biography of Donald Gordon*. Montreal and Kingston: McGill-Queen's UP, 1979.

Scott, Joan Wallach. *Gender and the Politics of History*. New York: Columbia UP, 1988.

Shore, Marlene. *The Science of Social Redemption: McGill, the Chicago School, and the Origins of Social Research in Canada*. Toronto: U of Toronto P, 1987.

Sicotte, Anne-Marie. *Gratien Gélinas: La ferveur et le doute*. Vol. 1, *1909–1956*. Montreal: Éditions Québec-Amérique, 1995.

Sissons, Michael, and Philip French, eds. *Age of Austerity, 1945–51*. London: Hodder and Stoughton, 1963.

Skocpol, Theda. *Protecting Soldiers and Mothers: The Political Origins of Social Policy in the United States*. Cambridge, MA: Belknap P of Harvard UP, 1992.

Smart, Patricia. *Les femmes du Refus global*. Montreal: Boréal, 1998.

Snell, James G. *In the Shadow of the Law: Divorce in Canada, 1900–1939*. Toronto: U of Toronto P, 1991.

Stacey, C.P. *Arms, Men and Governments: The War Policies of Canada, 1939–1945*. Ottawa: Queen's Printer, 1970.

Stansell, Christine. *City of Women: Sex and Class in New York 1789–1860*. Urbana: U of Illinois P, 1986.

Steedman, Carolyn. *Landscape for a Good Woman: A Story of Two Lives*. London: Virago, 1986.

Strasser, Susan. *Getting and Spending: European and American Consumer Societies in the Twentieth Century*. Washington, DC: Cambridge UP and the German Historical Institute, 1998.

– *Never Done: A History of American Housework*. New York: Pantheon Books, 1982.

Strong-Boag, Veronica. *The New Day Recalled: Lives of Girls and Women in English Canada, 1919–1939*. Toronto: Copp Clark Pitman, 1988.

Struthers, James. *The Limits of Affluence: Welfare in Ontario, 1920–1970*. Toronto: U of Toronto P, 1994.

– *No Fault of Their Own: Unemployment and the Canadian Welfare State 1914–1941*. Toronto: U of Toronto P, 1983.

Summerfield, Penny. *Women Workers in the Second World War: Production and Patriarchy in Conflict*. London: Croom Helm, 1984.

Sutherland, Neil. *Growing Up: Childhood in English Canada from the Great War to the Age of Television*. Toronto: U of Toronto P, 1997.

Tillotson, Shirley. *The Public at Play: Gender and the Politics of Recreation in Post-War Ontario*. Toronto: U of Toronto P, 2000.

Trudeau, Pierre Elliott, ed. *The Asbestos Strike*. Trans. James Boake. Toronto: James Lewis & Samuel, 1974 [1956].

Tuttle, William M., Jr. *'Daddy's Gone to War': The Second World War in the Lives of America's Children*. New York: Oxford UP, 1993.

Ursel, Jane. *Private Lives, Public Policy: 100 Years of State Intervention in the Family.* Toronto: Women's P, 1992.

Vaillancourt, Yves. *L'évolution des politiques sociales au Québec 1940–1960.* Montreal: Presses de l'Université de Montréal, 1988.

Vallières, Pierre. *White Niggers of America.* Trans. Joan Pinkham. Toronto: McClelland & Stewart, 1971 [1968].

Vance, Jonathan. *Death So Noble: Memory, Meaning, and the First World War.* Vancouver: UBC P, 1997.

Walkowitz, Daniel J. *Working with Class: Social Workers and the Politics of Middle-Class Identity.* Chapel Hill: U of North Carolina P, 1999.

Weintraub, William. *City Unique: Montreal Days and Nights in the 1940s and '50s.* Toronto: McClelland & Stewart, 1996.

Weisbord, Merrily. *The Strangest Dream: Canadian Communists, the Spy Trials, and the Cold War.* 2nd ed. Montreal: Véhicule, 1994.

Whitaker, Reg, and Gary Marcuse. *Cold War Canada: The Making of a National Insecurity State, 1945–57.* Toronto: U of Toronto P, 1994.

Articles

Azoulay, Dan. 'Winning Women for Socialism: The Ontario CCF and Women, 1947–1961.' *Labour/Le Travail* 36 (Fall 1995): 59–90.

Baillargeon, Denyse. 'L'encadrement de la maternité au Québec entre les deux guerres: les gardes de La Métropolitaine, les Gouttes de lait et l'Assistance maternelle.' *Bulletin du Regroupement des chercheurs-chercheures en histoire des travailleurs et travailleuses du Québec* 16, 2–3 (Summer/Fall 1990): 19–45.

– 'Les infirmières de la Métropolitaine au service des Montréalaises.' In Évelyne Tardy et al., eds., *Les Bâtisseuses de la Cité.* Montreal: ACFAS, 1993.

Baker, Paula. 'The Domestication of Politics: Women and American Political Society, 1780–1920.' *American Historical Review* 89, 3 (June 1984): 620–47.

Behiels, Michael D. '"Normalizing" the Writing of Quebec History.' *Left History* 6, 1 (Spring 1999): 91–9.

Bohstedt, John. 'Gender, Household, and Community Politics: Women in English Riots, 1790–1810.' *Past and Present* 120 (1988): 265–84.

Bradbury, Bettina. 'Women's History and Working-Class History.' *Labour/Le Travail* 19 (Spring 1987): 23–43.

Brandt, Gail Cuthbert. '"Pigeon-Holed and Forgotten": The Work of the Sub-committee on the Post-War Problems of Women, 1943.' *Histoire sociale/Social History* 15, 29 (May 1982): 239–59.

– '"Weaving It Together": Life Cycle and the Industrial Experience of Female Cotton Workers in Quebec, 1910–1950.' *Labour / Le Travail* 7 (Spring 1981): 113–25.

Brooke, John L. 'Reason and Passion in the Public Sphere: Habermas and the Cultural Historians.' *Journal of Interdisciplinary History* 29, 1 (Summer 1998): 43–67.

Brushett, Kevin. '"People and Government Travelling Together": Community Organization, Urban Planning and the Politics of Post-War Reconstruction in Toronto 1943–1953.' *Urban History Review* 27, 2 (March 1999): 44–58.

Calliste, Agnes. 'Canada's Immigration Policy and Domestics from the Caribbean: The Second Domestic Scheme.' In Jesse Vorst et al., eds., *Race, Class, Gender: Bonds and Barriers.* Toronto: Garamond and Society for Socialist Studies, 1989.

Campbell, Lara. '"A Barren Cupboard at Home": Ontario Families Confront the Premiers during the Great Depression.' In Edgar-André Montigny and Lori Chambers, eds., *Ontario since Confederation: A Reader.* Toronto: U of Toronto P, 2000.

Choko, Marc H. 'Le mouvement des squatters à Montréal 1946–1947.' *Cahiers d'histoire* 2, 2 (Spring 1982): 26–39.

Cliche, Marie-Aimée. '"Est-ce une bonne méthode pour élever les enfants?" Le débat sur les punitions corporelles dans les courriers du cœur au Québec de 1925 à 1969.' *Canadian Historical Review* 82, 4 (December 2001) : 662–89.

Collin, Jean-Pierre. 'Crise du logement et Action catholique à Montréal, 1940–1960.' *Revue d'histoire de l'Amérique française* 41, 2 (Fall 1987): 179–203.

Comacchio, Cynthia R. 'Beneath the "Sentimental Veil": Families and Family History in Canada.' *Labour / Le Travail* 33 (Spring 1994): 279–302.

– '"A Postscript for Father": Defining a New Fatherhood in Interwar Canada.' *Canadian Historical Review* 78, 3 (September 1997): 385–408.

Comeau, Paul-André. 'L'oubli: Thérapie collective ou exutoire traditionnel?' *Bulletin d'histoire politique* 3, 3–4 (Spring / Summer 1995): 393–6.

Davis, Donald F., and Barbara Lorenzkowski. 'A Platform for Gender Tensions: Women Working and Riding on Canadian Urban Public Transit in the 1940s.' *Canadian Historical Review* 79, 3 (September 1998): 431–65.

Davis, Natalie Zemon. 'The Shapes of Social History.' *Storia della Storiografia* 17 (1990): 28–34.

Dehli, Kari. 'Fictions of the Scientific Imagination: Researching the Dionne Quintuplets.' *Journal of Canadian Studies* 29, 4 (Winter 1994–95): 86–110.

Delano, Page Dougherty. 'Making Up for War: Sexuality and Citizenship in Wartime Culture.' *Feminist Studies* 26, 1 (Spring 2000): 33–68.

'Dialogue: Reimagining the Family.' *Journal of Women's History* 13, 3 (Autumn 2001): 124–68.

Dummitt, Chris. 'Finding a Place for Father: Selling the Barbecue in Postwar Canada.' *Journal of the Canadian Historical Association* 9 (1998): 209–23.

Dupré, Ruth. '"If It's Yellow, It Must Be Butter": Margarine Regulation in North America since 1886.' *Journal of Economic History* 59, 2 (June 1999): 353–71.

Ewen, Geoffrey. 'Montreal Catholic School Teachers, International Unions, and Archbishop Bruchési: The Association de bien-être des instituteurs et institutrices de Montréal, 1919–20.' *Historical Studies in Education / Revue d'histoire de l'éducation* 12, 1–2 (2000): 54–72.

Falardeau, Jean-Charles. 'Antécédents, débuts et croissance de la sociologie au Québec.' *Recherches sociographiques* 15, 2–3 (May–August 1974): 135–65.

Finkel, Alvin. 'Competing Master Narratives on Post-War Canada.' *Acadiensis* 29, 2 (Spring 2000): 188–204.

– 'Paradise Postponed: A Re-examination of the Green Book Proposals of 1945.' *Journal of the Canadian Historical Association* 4 (1993): 120–42.

– 'The State of Writing on the Canadian Welfare State: What's Class Got to Do With It?' *Labour/Le Travail* 54 (Fall 2004): 151–74.

Fowke, V.C. 'The National Policy – Old and New.' *Canadian Journal of Economics and Political Science* 18, 3 (August 1952): 271–86.

Frager, Ruth A. 'Politicized Housewives in the Jewish Communist Movement of Toronto, 1923–1933.' In Linda Kealey and Joan Sangster, eds., *Beyond the Vote: Canadian Women and Politics.* Toronto: U of Toronto P, 1989.

Fraser, Nancy, and Linda Gordon. 'Contract versus Charity: Why Is There No Social Citizenship in the United States?' *Socialist Review* 22, 3 (1992): 45–67.

Garigue, Philippe. 'French Canada: A Case-Study in Sociological Analysis.' *Canadian Review of Sociology and Anthropology* 1, 4 (November 1964): 186–92.

Garton, Stephen, and Margaret E. McCallum. 'Workers' Welfare: Labour and the Welfare State in 20th-Century Australia and Canada.' *Labour / Le Travail* 38 (Fall 1996): 116–41.

Gauvreau, Danielle, and Peter Gossage. '"Empêcher la famille": Fécondité et contraception au Québec, 1920–60.' *Canadian Historical Review* 78, 3 (September 1997): 478–510.

Gauvreau, Michael. 'The Emergence of Personalist Feminism: Catholicism and the Marriage-Preparation Movement in Quebec, 1940–1966.' In Nancy Christie, ed., *Households of Faith: Family, Gender, and Community in Canada, 1760–1969.* Montreal and Kingston: McGill-Queen's UP, 2002.

Gilliland, Jason. 'Visions and Revisions of House and Home: A Half-Century of Change in Montreal's "Cité-jardin."' In H. Nicol and G. Halseth, eds., *(Re)Development at the Urban Edges: Reflections on the Canadian Experience.* Waterloo: Department of Geography, University of Waterloo, 2000.

Gleason, Mona. 'Psychology and the Construction of the "Normal" Family in Postwar Canada, 1945–60.' *Canadian Historical Review* 78, 3 (September 1997): 442–77.

Gölz, Annalee. 'Family Matters: The Canadian Family and the State in the Postwar Period.' *Left History* 1 (Fall 1993): 9–50.

Guard, Julie. 'Fair Play or Fair Pay? Gender Relations, Class Consciousness, and Union Solidarity in the Canadian UE.' *Labour / Le Travail* 37 (Spring 1997): 149–77.

– 'Women Worth Watching: Radical Housewives in Cold War Canada.' In G. Kinsman, D. Buse, and M. Steedman, eds., *Whose National Security? Canadian State Surveillance and the Creation of Enemies.* Toronto: Between the Lines, 2000.

Habermas, Jürgen. 'The Public Sphere: An Encyclopedia Article (1964).' *New German Critique* 3 (Fall 1974): 49–55.

Hamel, Thérèse. 'Obligation scolaire et travail des enfants au Québec: 1900–1950.' *Revue d'histoire de l'Amérique française* 38, 1 (Summer 1984): 39–58.

Hareven, Tamara K. 'Family History at the Crossroads.' *Journal of Family History* 12, 1–3 (1987): lx–xxiii.

Hartmann, Susan M. 'Prescriptions for Penelope: Literature on Women's Obligations to Returning World War II Veterans.' *Women's Studies* 5 (1978): 223–39.

Harvey, Fernand, and Paul-André Linteau. 'Les étranges lunettes de Ronald Rudin.' *Revue d'histoire de l'Amérique française* 51, 3 (Winter 1998): 425–8.

Hewitt, Nancy A. 'Did Women Have a Reconstruction? Gender in the Rewriting of Southern History.' *Proceedings and Papers of the Georgia Association of Historians* 14 (1993): 1–11.

Hinton, James. 'Militant Housewives: The British Housewives' League and the Attlee Government.' *History Workshop Journal* 38 (1994): 128–56.

Hohendahl, Peter. 'Jürgen Habermas: "The Public Sphere" (1964).' *New German Critique* 3 (Fall 1974): 45–8.

Jamieson, Ruth. 'The Man of Hobbes: Masculinity and Wartime Necessity.' *Journal of Historical Sociology* 9, 1 (March 1996): 19–42.

Kealey, Gregory. '1919: The Canadian Labour Revolt.' *Labour / Le Travail* 13 (Spring 1984): 11–44.

Kent, David A. '"Gone for a Soldier": Family Breakdown and the Demography of Desertion in a London Parish, 1750–91.' *Local Population Studies* 45 (1990): 27–42.

Kerber, Linda K. '"I Hav Don ... much to Carrey on the Warr": Women and the Shaping of Republican Ideology after the American Revolution.' In Harriet B. Applewhite and Darline G. Levy, eds., *Women and Politics in the Age of the Democratic Revolution.* Ann Arbor: U of Michigan P, 1990.

– 'Separate Spheres, Female Worlds, Woman's Place: The Rhetoric of Women's History.' *Journal of American History* 75 (June 1988): 9–39.

Keshen, Jeff. 'One For All or All For One: Government Controls, Black Marketing and the Limits of Patriotism, 1939–47.' *Journal of Canadian Studies* 29, 4 (Winter 1994–5): 111–43.

– 'Revisiting Canada's Civilian Women during World War II.' *Histoire sociale/ Social History*, 30, 60 (November 1997): 234–66.

– 'Wartime Jitters over Juveniles: Canada's Delinquency Scare and Its Consequences, 1939–1945.' In Jeffrey Keshen, ed., *Age of Contention: Readings in Canadian Social History, 1900–1945*. Toronto: Harcourt Brace, 1997.

Kessler-Harris, Alice. 'Gender Identity: Rights to Work and the Idea of Economic Citizenship.' *Schweizerische Zeitschrift fur Geschichte* 46, 3 (1996): 411–26.

– 'Gendered Interventions: Rediscovering the American Past.' In Mario Materassi and Maria Irene Ramalho de Sousa Santos, eds. *The American Columbiad: 'Discovering' America, Inventing the United States*. Amsterdam: VU UP, 1996.

Klausen, Susanne. 'The Plywood Girls: Women and Gender Ideology at the Port Alberni Plywood Plant, 1942–1991.' *Labour / Le Travail* 41 (Spring 1998): 199–235.

Lévesque, Andrée. 'Les Québécoises et les débuts de l'État providence.' In Brigitte Studer et al., eds., *Frauen und Staat / Les Femmes et l'État*. Basel: Schwabe & Co., 1998.

Levine, Susan. 'Workers' Wives: Gender, Class and Consumerism in the 1920s United States.' *Gender and History* 3, 1 (1991): 45–64.

Lewis, Jane. 'Gender, the Family and Women's Agency in the Building of "Welfare States": The British Case.' *Social History* 19, 1 (January 1994): 37–55.

Lewis, Norah. '"Isn't this a terrible war?" The Attitudes of Children to Two World Wars.' *Historical Studies in Education* 7, 2 (1995): 193–215.

Little, Margaret. 'The Blurring of Boundaries: Private and Public Welfare for Single Mothers in Ontario.' *Studies in Political Economy* 47 (Summer 1995): 89–109.

McCallum, Margaret E. 'Assistance to Veterans and their Dependants: Steps on the Way to the Administrative State, 1914–1929.' In W.W. Pue and B. Wright, eds., *Canadian Perspectives on Law and Society: Issues in Legal History*. Ottawa: Carleton UP, 1988.

McClintock, Megan J. 'Civil War Pensions and the Reconstruction of Union Families.' *Journal of American History* 83, 2 (September 1996): 456–80.

McInnis, Peter S. 'Teamwork for Harmony: Labour-Management Production Committees and the Postwar Settlement in Canada.' *Canadian Historical Review* 77, 3 (September 1996): 317–52.

Marks, Lynne. 'Indigent Committees and Ladies Benevolent Societies: Intersections of Public and Private Poor Relief in Late Nineteenth Century Small Town Ontario.' *Studies in Political Economy* 47 (Summer 1995): 61–87.

Marshall, Dominique. 'The Language of Children's Rights, the Formation of the Welfare State, and the Democratic Experience of Poor Families in Quebec, 1940–55.' *Canadian Historical Review* 78, 3 (September 1997): 409–41.

Mettler, Suzanne. 'Dividing Social Citizenship by Gender: The Implementation of Unemployment Insurance and Aid to Dependent Children, 1935–1950.' *Studies in American Political Development* 12 (Fall 1998): 303–42.

Michel, Sonya. 'Danger on the Home Front: Motherhood, Sexuality, and Disabled Veterans in American Postwar Films.' *Journal of the History of Sexuality* 3, 1 (July 1992): 109–28.

'Michelle Perrot: Histoire du privé.' *Les Cahiers du GRIF* 37/38 (Spring 1988): 155–63.

Montgomerie, Deborah. 'Reassessing Rosie: World War II, New Zealand Women and the Iconography of Femininity.' *Gender and History* 8, 1 (April 1996): 108–32.

Orloff, Ann Shola. 'Gender and the Social Rights of Citizenship: The Comparative Analysis of Gender Relations and Welfare States.' *American Sociological Review* 58 (June 1993): 303–28.

– 'Reply: Citizenship, Policy, and the Political Construction of Gender Interests.' *International Labor and Working-Class History* 52 (Fall 1997): 35–50.

Pedersen, Susan. 'Gender, Welfare, and Citizenship in Britain during the Great War.' *American Historical Review* 95, 4 (1990): 983–1006.

Piché, Lucie. 'La Jeunesse Ouvrière Catholique Féminine: Un lieu de formation sociale et d'action communautaire, 1931–1966.' *Revue d'histoire de l'Amérique française* 52, 4 (Spring 1999): 481–506.

Pierson, Ruth Roach. 'Gender and the Unemployment Insurance Debates in Canada, 1934–1940.' *Labour / Le Travail* 25 (Spring 1990): 77–103.

Porter, Ann. 'Women and Income Security in the Postwar Period: The Case of Unemployment Insurance, 1945–1962.' *Labour / Le Travail* 31 (1993): 111–44.

Prentice, Susan. 'Workers, Mothers, Reds: Toronto's Postwar Daycare Fight.' *Studies in Political Economy* 30 (Autumn 1989): 115–41.

Razack, Sherene. 'Schools for Happiness: Instituts familiaux and the Education for Ideal Wives and Mothers.' In Veronica Strong-Boag and Anita Clair Fellman, eds., *Rethinking Canada: The Promise of Women's History.* 2nd ed. Toronto: Copp Clark Pitman, 1991.

Richard, Béatrice. 'La participation des soldats canadiens-français à la Deuxième Guerre mondiale: Une histoire de trous de mémoire.' *Bulletin d'histoire politique* 3, 3–4 (Spring/Summer 1995): 383–92.

Riley, Denise. 'The Free Mothers: Pronatalism and Working Mothers in Industry at the End of the Last War in Britain.' *History Workshop* 11 (Spring 1981): 59–118.

Rosaldo, Michelle Zimbalist. 'Women, Culture, and Society: A Theoretical

Overview.' In Michelle Rosaldo and Louise Lamphere, eds., *Women, Culture and Society*. Stanford: Stanford UP, 1974.

Rose, Sonya O. 'Sex, Citizenship, and the Nation in World War II Britain.' *American Historical Review* 103, 4 (October 1998): 1147–76.

Rudin, Ronald. 'Revisionism and the Search for a Normal Society: A Critique of Recent Quebec Historical Writing.' *Canadian Historical Review* 73, 1 (1992): 30–61.

Rutherdale, Robert. 'Fatherhood and the Social Construction of Memory: Breadwinning and Male Parenting on a Job Frontier, 1945–1966.' In Joy Parr and Mark Rosenfeld, eds., *Gender and History in Canada*. Toronto: Copp Clark, 1996.

Saraceno, Chiara. 'Reply: Citizenship Is Context-Specific.' *International Labor and Working-Class History* 52 (Fall 1997): 27–34.

Skocpol, Theda. 'Soldiers, Workers, and Mothers: Gendered Identities in Early U.S. Social Policy.' *Contention* 2, 3 (Spring 1993): 157–83.

Smith, Helen, and Pamela Wakewich. '"Beauty and the Helldivers": Representing Women's Work and Identities in a Warplant Newspaper.' *Labour / Le Travail* 44 (Fall 1999): 71–107.

Smith-Rosenberg, Carroll. 'The Female World of Love and Ritual: Relations between Women in Nineteenth-Century America.' *Signs* 1 (Autumn 1975): 1–29.

Sonnen, John S. 'Out of the Attic, or What Price Memorabilia? A Minnesota Couple's World War II Letters.' *Minnesota History* 53, 2 (Summer 1992): 56–67.

Stansell, Christine. Response to Joan Scott. *International Labor and Working-Class History* 31 (Spring 1987).

Strong-Boag, Veronica. 'Canada's Wage-Earning Wives and the Construction of the Middle Class, 1945–60.' *Journal of Canadian Studies* 29, 3 (Fall 1994): 5–25.

– 'Home Dreams: Women and the Suburban Experiment in Canada, 1945–60.' *Canadian Historical Review* 72, 4 (1991): 471–504.

– 'Wages for Housework: Mothers' Allowances and the Beginnings of Social Security in Canada.' *Journal of Canadian Studies* 14 (1979): 21–34.

Taschereau, Sylvie. 'L'arme favorite de l'épicier indépendant: éléments d'une histoire sociale du crédit (Montréal, 1920–1940).' *Journal of the Canadian Historical Association* 4 (1993): 265–92.

Thwaites, James D., and Nadine L.C. Perron-Thwaites. 'Une petite grève d'envergure: L'Alliance contre la C.É.C.M. en 1949 et ses suites.' *McGill Law Journal* 40 (1995): 780–801.

Tilly, Louise A. 'Women, Work, and Citizenship.' *International Labor and Working-Class History* 52 (Fall 1997): 1–26.

– 'Women's History and Family History: Fruitful Collaboration or Missed Connection?' *Journal of Family History* 12, 1–3 (1987): 303–15.

Valverde, Mariana. 'The Mixed Social Economy as a Canadian Tradition.'
   Studies in Political Economy 47 (Summer 1995): 33–60.
Vigod, B.L. 'Ideology and Institutions in Quebec: The Public Charities Contro-
   versy 1921–1926.' *Histoire sociale / Social History* 11, 21 (May 1978): 167–82.
Wade, Jill. '"A Palace for the Public": Housing Reform and the 1946 Occupation
   of the Old Hotel Vancouver.' *BC Studies* 69–70 (Spring 1986): 288–310.
– 'Wartime Housing Limited, 1941–1947: Canadian Housing Policy at the
   Crossroads.' *Urban History Review* 15, 1 (1986): 41–59.
Webber, Jeremy. 'The Malaise of Compulsory Conciliation: Strike Prevention in
   Canada during World War II.' In Bryan D. Palmer, ed., *The Character of Class
   Struggle: Essays in Canadian Working-Class History, 1850–1985.* Toronto:
   McClelland & Stewart, 1986.
Wells, Don. 'The Impact of the Postwar Compromise on Canadian Unionism:
   The Formation of an Auto Worker Local in the 1950s.' *Labour / Le Travail* 36
   (Fall 1995): 147–73.
Wells, Donald M. 'Origins of Canada's Wagner Model of Industrial Relations:
   The United Auto Workers in Canada and the Suppression of "Rank and File"
   Unionism, 1936–1953.' *Canadian Journal of Sociology* 20 (Spring 1995): 193–225.
Wilkinson, Patrick. 'The Selfless and the Helpless: Maternalist Origins of the
   U.S. Welfare State.' *Feminist Studies* 25, 3 (Fall 1999): 571–97.
Wolfe, Jeanne M., and Grace Strachan. 'Practical Idealism: Women in Urban
   Reform, Julia Drummond, and the Montreal Parks and Playgrounds Associa-
   tion.' In Caroline Andrew and Beth Moore Milroy, eds., *Life Spaces: Gender,
   Household, Employment.* Vancouver: UBC P, 1988.

Theses and Unpublished Papers

Bourbeau, Amélie. '"Tuer le taudis qui nous tuera." Crise du logement et
   discours sur la famille montréalaise d'après-guerre (1945–1960).' MA thesis,
   Université de Montréal, 2002.
Brown, Deidre Rowe. 'Public Attitudes towards Canadian Women During and
   Immediately after World War Two.' MA thesis, University of Toronto, 1992.
Cohen, Lizabeth. 'A Consumers' Republic: The Politics of Mass Consumption in
   America.' Paper presented at York University, Toronto, 2 March 2000.
Durflinger, Serge. 'The Patriotism of Local Identity: Verdun, Québec Responds
   to the Second World War.' Paper presented to the CHA meetings, Brock
   University, 1996.
Endicott, Valerie. '"Woman's Place [Was] Everywhere": A Study of Women Who
   Worked in Aircraft Production in Toronto during the Second World War.'
   MA thesis, University of Toronto, 1991.

Fahrni, Magda. 'Citizenship under Reconstruction: Women's Public Claims in
    1940s Canada.' Paper presented to the 'Paroles de femmes dans la guerre'
    conference, Université de Nantes, France, 8 June 2001.
– 'Under Reconstruction: The Family and the Public in Postwar Montréal,
    1944–1949.' PhD diss., York University, 2001.
Jackson, Paul. 'The Prejudice of Good Order: Homosexuality and the Canadian
    Military, 1939–1945.' PhD diss., Queen's University, 2002.
Murray, Sylvie. 'A la jonction du mouvement ouvrier et du mouvement des
    femmes: La Ligue auxiliaire de l'Association internationale des machinistes,
    Canada, 1903–1980.' MA thesis, UQAM, 1988.
Oliver, Dean. 'When the Battle's Won: Military Demobilization in Canada,
    1939–1946.' PhD diss. York University, 1996.
Pols, Johannes C. 'The School as Laboratory: The Development of Psychology
    as a Discipline in Toronto, 1915–1955.' MA thesis, York University, 1991.
Taschereau, Sylvie. 'Les petits commerçants de l'alimentation et les milieux
    populaires montréalais, 1920–1940.' PhD diss., UQAM, 1992.

Photo Credits

Archives nationales du Québec à Montréal, Fonds Conrad-Poirier: Mass marriage (P48, S1, P3704); 'New Babies Everywhere' (P48, S1, P10432); children in wartime housing complex (P48, S1, P10491); liquor store line-up (P48, S1, P11906); mothers and children to meet with Duplessis (P48, S1, P12292); rehabilitation at Ste Anne's Military Hospital (P48, S1, P13783); Saint-Henri restaurant (P48, S1, P11918); mother and child at Hôpital Sainte-Justine (P48, S1, P12196).

Library and Archives Canada: couple in train station (Department of National Defence, PA-128213); VE-Day celebrations (Montreal Star, PA-152316)

Ville de Montréal, Gestion de documents et archives: Bonsecours Market (VM 94/Y1, 17, 1206 [planche contact Z-1216]); 'City of Skyscrapers' (VM 94/Y1, 17, 1546 [planche contact Z-1571]).

Index

STUDIES IN GENDER AND HISTORY

General editors: Franca Iacovetta and Karen Dubinsky